# THE VIEW
# FROM RINGSIDE

## INSIDE THE TUMULTUOUS WORLD OF BOXING

# BOOKS BY THOMAS HAUSER

### General Non-Fiction
*Missing*
*The Trial of Patrolman Thomas Shea*
*For Our Children (with Frank Macchiarola)*
*The Family Legal Companion*
*Final Warning: The Legacy of Chernobyl (with Dr. Robert Gale)*
*Arnold Palmer: A Personal Journey*
*Confronting America's Moral Crisis (with Frank Macchiarola)*
*Healing: A Journal of Tolerance and Understanding*
*Miscellaneous*
*With This Ring (with Frank Macchiarola)*
*A God To Hope For*

### About Boxing
*The Black Lights: Inside the World of Professional Boxing*
*Muhammad Ali: His Life and Times*
*Muhammad Ali: Memories*
*Muhammad Ali: In Perspective*
*Muhammad Ali & Company*
*A Beautiful Sickness*
*A Year At The Fights*
*Brutal Artistry*
*The View From Ringside*

### Fiction
*Ashworth & Palmer*
*Agatha's Friends*
*The Beethoven Conspiracy*
*Hanneman's War*
*The Fantasy*
*Dear Hannah*
*The Hawthorne Group*
*Martin Bear & Friends*
*Mark Twain Remembers*
*Finding The Princess*

# THE VIEW
# FROM RINGSIDE

## INSIDE THE TUMULTUOUS WORLD OF BOXING

### BY THOMAS HAUSER

www.sportclassicbooks.com

Published in the United States of America by Sport Media Publishing Inc., Wilmington, Delaware, and simultaneously in Canada.

For information about permission to reproduce selections from this book, please write to:
Permissions
Sport Media Publishing, Inc.,
21 Carlaw Ave.,
Toronto, Ontario, Canada, M4M 2R6
www.sportclassicbooks.com


Cover design: Paul Hodgson / pHd
Cover photo: E. H. Wallop
Author photo: Holger Keifel
Interior design: Greg Oliver

ISBN: 1-894963-25-3

Library of Congress Control Number: 2003023437


Printed in Canada

*For Frank Macchiarola,
mentor and friend*

# AUTHOR'S NOTE

*The View From Ringside* contains the articles about professional boxing that I authored in 2002 and the first half of 2003. The articles I wrote about the sweet science prior to that date have been published in *Muhammad Ali & Company*, *A Beautiful Sickness*, and *A Year at the Fights*. Special thanks are due to Secondsout.com, Showtime Boxing and *Boxing Digest*, under whose aegis the articles in this book first appeared.

# TABLE OF CONTENTS

# ROUND 4
# CURIOSITIES     235

# ROUND 1

# FIGHTS AND FIGHTERS

*Lewis-Tyson was a great "writers' fight." This was the first of three articles that I wrote about it for Secondsout.com once it became clear that the fight was going to happen.*

# LEWIS-TYSON: THE GATHERING STORM

In mid-January of this year, Mike Tyson visited Jose Torres in New York. Tyson and Torres share a unique bond. In the 1960s, Torres was trained and managed by Cus D'Amato, who guided him to the world light-heavyweight championship. Twenty years later, D'Amato began the process of shaping Tyson's ring destiny.

The Tyson-Torres relationship, like many of Mike's personal interactions, has been inconsistent. But Torres is one of the few men who Tyson feels he can open up to and receive an understanding ear in return. As the two men talked, Tyson seemed on edge.

"Are you in trouble?" Torres asked.

"Yes."

"What's the problem?"

"I have rage," Tyson told him. "And I can't control it."

"If you know that, you can make it better," Torres said. "But you'll need help."

One week later, Tyson's rage led to a cataclysmic explosion at the kick-off press conference for his proposed bout against Lennox Lewis. That meant, for a while, Lewis-Tyson was Lewis-Tysoff. In the weeks that followed, the charts of fight organizers began to resemble a map of the electoral college. Nevada, California, New York, Texas, Georgia, and Colorado all turned their back on the contest. Washington DC, Michigan, and Tennessee pursued it. Finally, the bout landed in Memphis, where Lewis and Tyson are expected to do battle on June 8. But in deference to Tyson's peculiarities and Lewis' demands re same, the promotion has taken on a surreal quality with bizarre overtones and unprecedented contract clauses.

Let's start with some numbers.

Mike Tyson's name has become synonymous with money, and the bout's finances reflect that reality. There are 19,185 tickets priced from $250 to $2,400. The pay-per-view price has been set at $54.95, which makes it the most expensive PPV event ever. The goal of event organizers is to surpass the all-time record of 1,990,000 buys set by Holyfield-Tyson II in 1997. However, those ubiquitous "black boxes" are more in evidence now than five years ago, and two million buys seems like an unrealistic target.

A tangled web of contracts dictates how the fight will be financed and conducted. There are contracts between HBO and Showtime; HBO and Lewis; Showtime and Tyson; HBO, Showtime, and the promotional triad of Main Events, Lion Promotions, and Fight Night; the three primary promoters and Prize Fight Boxing (the local promoter); and the promotional triad and The Pyramid.

There is financial parity between HBO and Showtime on the fight. The two cable giants will split all production, travel, and marketing costs equally and share equally in the various revenue streams that flow from the bout. Main Events and the other promoters will be paid largely out of the promotion budget. But internally, there are differences. Lewis and Tyson are each guaranteed $17.5-million by their respective networks. After HBO makes a profit of $5-million, Lewis will receive virtually all of the remaining profit from HBO's end. Tyson is believed to have a slightly less advantageous profit split with Showtime. Even if pay-per-view sales disappoint, this will be Lewis' biggest payday ever.

The live pay-per-view telecast of the bout will be handled by a neutral announcing team. HBO and Showtime will also have separate announcing teams on site. If Lewis wins, HBO will televise its version of the fight on a tape-delay basis and pay Showtime $3-million. If Tyson wins, Showtime will air the tape delay with its announcing team and pay HBO $3-million.

If that sounds simple, it's not. As one HBO insider acknowledged, "Virtually every negotiating point has been a hassle."

Take, for example, the issue of who will be the ring announcer. Jimmy Lennon has long been identified with Showtime. Michael Buffer is thought of in conjunction with HBO. The HBO-Showtime contract says that Lennon and Buffer will have financial parity in the production budget as well as airtime parity. But Buffer usually gets more money than Lennon and is being asked by the joint promotion to take a pay cut. Then there's the matter of which ring announcer will say what. The current script reads like the lead-in to a stilted Academy Award presentation:

Lennon: Ladies and gentlemen around the world, welcome to Memphis, Tennessee.

Buffer: This bout is sanctioned by the World Boxing Council and International Boxing Federation.

Lennon: The officials at ringside are . . .

Buffer: The referee is Bozo the Clown, and the three judges . . .

Lennon will then introduce Tyson. Buffer will introduce Lewis. It has been agreed that, somewhere in the mix, Buffer will intone, "Let's get ready to rumble." And the bell will ring.

Should Lewis win by knockout or disqualification, Buffer will announce the result. Should Tyson win by knockout or disqualification, Lennon will announce the result. If the fight goes the distance, rather than rob the moment of it's suspense, the two men will alternate the reading of the scorecards or flip a coin to determine who says what. Except—and this is a big "except"—Buffer wasn't consulted when the HBO-Showtime contract was entered into and hasn't agreed to its terms yet.

For those who are superstitious, Lewis' record in recent title fights when Buffer is not the ring announcer is 1-2-1. That includes one-punch knockout losses to Oliver McCall and Hasim Rahman and the draw in Lewis-Holyfield I. By contrast, Lennox has never lost with Buffer at ringside; but neither has Tyson, dating back to the early days for both men on ESPN.

As for Jimmy Lennon, all of Tyson's losses (Buster Douglas and both Holyfield fights) as well as his two no-contests (Orlin Norris and Andrew Golota) have come with Showtime's favorite announcer at ringside. Overall, Tyson is 10-3-2 with Lennon on hand, and Lewis is 3-0-1 (Holyfield I and II plus Rahman II and Tony Tucker).

This is the sort of minutiae that the greatest minds in the sports and communications industries are now pondering. But there remains a more troubling issue—Mike Tyson's conduct.

In some respects, Lewis-Tyson is being packaged as a real-life version of professional wrestling. But the sad truth is, the heavyweight championship is up for grabs, and virtually everyone involved with the promotion is saying, "We can't do this because it might make Mike angry," or "We can't do that because everyone will find out how out of control Mike really is."

Tyson, in essence, is saying to the world, "I'm going to do what I want to do. Like it or leave it, and leave me the fuck alone." He has surrounded himself with enablers and, whatever he does, there are always people who tell him, "Yeah, Mike; you're right."

The licensing deliberations that led to Lewis-Tyson might have addressed what Tyson does. They did not address why he does it. The man has problems and everyone associated with him, including Tyson himself, knows it.

On April 30, Tyson met with a carefully chosen group of reporters in Maui, where he is training for the fight. Tim Smith of the *New York Daily News* was among them. "It was bizarre," Smith said later. "Mike had a towel that he kept chewing on. He was very obscene, and his thoughts weren't really connected. He threw out the N-word like he was seeding a flower garden and talked about everything from Buddha to how Jesus smoked marijuana."

The press session began with Tyson responding to a female reporter who asked about the upcoming fight: "It's no doubt I'm going to win this fight, and I feel confident about winning this fight." Then he added, "I normally don't do interviews with women unless I fornicate with them. So you shouldn't talk anymore unless you want to, you know." Thereafter, reporters were treated to a bizarre stream of consciousness:

● "I could play the game and say I'm somebody I'm not, but I'm not that kind of person. I'm uninhibited. If I'm being interviewed by a lady, I have to say, 'Hey, you're looking good.' I just have to be Mike."

● "The people want to be lied to. That's the deal. The people don't want to believe their idol is a freak; that he likes to get fellatio. They don't want to believe that he might want somebody to stick their finger up his butt. But the truth is, he might like that."

● "I think it's un-American not to go out with a woman, not to be with a beautiful woman, not to get my cock sucked. You know what I mean? I may like to fornicate more than other people. It's just who I am. I sacrifice so much of my life; can I at least get laid? I mean, I've been robbed of most of my money; can I at least get a blow job without people wanting to harass me and wanting to throw me in jail?"

● "We all cheat on our fucking wives one way or another. Please forgive me for talking the way I am. I'm into forbidden fruits like everyone else. I want my dick sucked too. I want to love a woman too. Sometimes I want to love more than one woman. Don't crucify me because of who I am and I tell the world who I am. That's just who I am. You guys wrote so much bad about me; I don't know when the last time was that I fucked a decent woman. You said I was a fucked up nigger. I don't know nothing but strippers and whores and bitches and all that shit because you guys put that shit on me."

On several occasions, Tyson's adviser Shelly Finkel was heard to whisper, "Let's get everyone out of here before he explodes." But the session continued. There were moments of self-pity:

● "I wake up every morning and hate myself. I don't have any dignity left. I lost my dignity in prison."

● "I could be a decent guy. I could be a literate guy. I could have been a lot of things in life. But Cus got me first and I became a fighter. There are a lot of things I could have been. I could have been smart and intelligent. My family are educated people. I'm a numbskull."

● "My brother is a different kind of animal. He wanted to be something. My sister was so bright. My brother is so bright. I wasn't born with their intelligence. That's my problem. I was always envious of my brother. I hated my brother. Me and my brother are so different. I look at him. He's a beautiful, brilliant, strange guy. We're not close. If he wasn't my brother, I wouldn't even like him. He wouldn't even be my type of person. Everybody loved my brother and my sister. I went to my sister's funeral. She never wanted a nickel from me. They always had more dignity and pride than me. I was heavyweight champion of the world, but they never wanted anything. I always respected them. My sister was obese. She was five hundred pounds. Her heart stopped. She was 25. I was always jealous of them because they had nothing but everybody loved them. I was always nothing. Compared to them, I'm nothing. Everybody in the neighborhood loved them. But me; I was shit. They always told me I was going to die. You ain't shit. Who the hell am I? I don't know what happened to me. I don't even know if I came from the same father."

Then the self-pity gave way to anger:

● "I'm the most irresponsible person in the world. The reason I'm like that is because, at 21, you all gave me fifty or a hundred million dollars and I didn't know what to do. I'm from the ghetto. I don't know how to act. One day I'm in a dope house robbing somebody. The next thing I know, 'You're the heavyweight champion of the world.' I'm 20 years old. I'm the heavyweight champion of the world. Most of my girlfriends are 15, 16 years old. I'm 20 years old with a lot of money. Who am I? What am I? I don't even know who I am. I'm just a dumb child. I'm being abused. I'm being robbed by lawyers. I think I have more money than I do. I'm just a dumb pugnacious fool. I'm just a fool who thinks I'm someone. And you tell me I should be responsible? I'm angry at the world."

● "I offend people. I ask this lady a lewd question because I'm in a lot of pain. I have some pain I'm gonna have for the rest of my life. So every now and then, I kick your fucking ass and stomp on you and put some kind of pain and inflict some of the pain on you because you deserve to feel the pain that I feel. I wish that you guys had children so I could kick them in the fucking head or stomp on their testicles so you could feel my pain because that's the pain I have waking up every day."

● "At times, I come across as crude or crass. That irritates you when I come across like a Neanderthal or a babbling idiot, but I like to be that person. I like to show you all that person, because that's who you come to see. I'm not in a mood right now to do a tirade. But if you said something disrespectful about my kids or my mother, I'd come out and kill you."

● "If I take this camera and put it in your face for 20 years, I don't know what you might be. You might be a homosexual if I put that camera on you since you were 13 years old. I've been on that camera since I was 13 years old."

● "You guys don't like the way I carry myself and you make names about me. Then I become insecure about that. My fuse is so short right now that, if anyone disrespects me, I might kill them."

The following day, Tyson sat for a session with Rita Cosby of the Fox News Channel. And his thoughts were a chilling portrait of a man in pain:

● "I don't know if I'm mentally sick, but I have episodes sometimes.

I'm a depressant kind of dude. I have episodes and I'm human, but no one cares about my health as a human; you know what I mean? I probably need to talk to somebody. But how could I talk to somebody that just looks at me when I'm really getting ready to feel this guy and put my heart out and says, 'Well, time's up. Hold it, Mike; I'm sorry. Drop the $250 off at the desk with my secretary and make an appointment to come back next week.' I'm ready to pull out my heart with this white motherfucker. He just got me comfortable, and I'm thinking he's real and I'm getting ready to—'I'm sorry; hold that thought. Go to Mary, pay the $250, and make an appointment for next week. We're going to make some leeways, Mike. I can see that coming.' Right then, I leave that place that was supposed to help me, and I leave more fucked up than I am when I first went in there. Is this a fucking game? So I stopped going; you know what I mean? I stopped going, so now they put me on this Zoloft stuff, right, and I'm so—I'm really; I'm pathetic sometimes and real shallow. I'm so dick conscious where, you know, I'm taking Zoloft and I don't get an erection. I'm just gone then, man; I'm just gone. I mean, it's ruined and rot and I'm an extreme sexual type person. I got to start taking this stuff, and it probably is making me feel a little better. But you know, it makes me feel bad because I like, you know, like I'm saying, I'm penis centered and it's just; I don't know. Now that's a big fight within itself right there, and that's not even talking about what I really have to deal with. That's not the real problem, but that turns into it. But now I got another problem to deal with; and the real problem, it just hasn't been dealt with at all. It hasn't been addressed so to speak, and I say what the fuck do I do? You don't understand the severity of what I'm dealing with. So let me just have a couple of my episodes. Let me take care of my children. Let me screw as many women as I want. Let me smoke what I want. Let me do what I want. Let me live my life because I'm not going to let these people just tear me apart and the guys try to label me; label me a schizoid, label me a manic depressive, label me a crazy mother-fucker. I'm probably more schizoid than I am anything. But if you label me so many things, you drive a motherfucker insane. I'm surprised I'm not suicidal. I haven't killed myself, but I wouldn't do that. I prefer to kill someone else than to kill myself."

What does Mike Tyson want?

"Are you kidding?" Roy Jones, Jr. responds when asked that question. "He wants to go back to jail. That's the only place Mike is comfortable. It's the only place where he feels he fits in."

"Mike Tyson talks a lot about doing bad things," says George Foreman. "But all you have to do is go into prisons and you'll hear that stuff all the time. And unfortunately, if Mike keeps doing the things he's doing now, he'll wind up in prison again."

There's no doubt that Tyson is inclined toward antisocial behavior. There's a frightening mix of sex and violence in his thoughts, and often the two converge. The world is familiar with some of the comments he has made about ripping Lennox Lewis' heart out and eating Lewis' children. In Maui, Tyson continued in that vein: "I'll smear his pompous brains all over the ring when I hit him . . . I want to implant my fist in his mind. I want to reach in and touch his brain."

But there was something more, and it was scary. Recounting an incident that occurred in Los Angeles, Tyson recalled, "Every time I try to do something to satisfy somebody else, I wind up getting fucked. Forgive my language because, if I don't curse or say nigger, fuck, or shit, you won't understand what I'm saying. I'm with my wife, and we're at this place in Los Angeles. Monica says, 'There goes Lennox Lewis. Go say hi to him.' I say hi, and he looks at me like, 'Motherfucker! What you looking at me for?' I wanted to punch my wife in the face. She made me look like a punk. This guy just stared me down like a mad dog. I felt like my wife took my balls right from under me for this guy. She gave this punk-ass motherfucker my nuts. It made me a punk right in front of her because I wanted to be a nice guy for my wife. I wanted to show her I could change and I'm not like people say I am. I don't need a woman that says, 'Go say hi to him.' I need a woman that says, 'That punk motherfucker wants to hurt you, baby,' and starts going right at him. I need a woman to jump in there and punch him, and then I'll jump in."

Lennox Lewis has responded to Tyson's comments with disdain. After calling Tyson "ignorant, arrogant, and an imbecile," the champion observed, "Some of the things he's been saying make him sound like a cartoon character. When he was incarcerated, he said he was reading books. It must have been comic books."

Still, as the object of Tyson's hatred, Lewis is understandably concerned. He is well aware that Tyson bit off a piece of Evander Holyfield's ear in the ring. And Tyson bit Lewis on the thigh during their press conference brawl in New York. Regarding the latter incident, Tyson has said, "He [Lewis] should have died that night; those guys putting their hands on me. But I wasn't with the right crew. That's the whole thing. I was with guys who just wanted to be seen on television. If I was with the right crew, all of them guys would have been finished right there."

Is Tyson bringing the "right crew" to Memphis? Both the Lewis camp and event organizers have expressed concern regarding the "element" that Iron Mike attracts to fights. There's also the risk that a high-profile event of this nature could become a terrorist target. Thus, security has been an overriding theme throughout the negotiations. Federal, state, and local authorities have all become involved. Metal detectors will be employed at fight-related events. And the contracts contemplate a number of bizarre scenarios.

For example, if either fighter is disqualified on an "extraordinary" foul—that is, a foul outside the normal realm of competition such as biting an opponent or assaulting the referee—$3-million will be deducted from that fighter's purse and paid to his opponent. Moreover, under those circumstances, the victorious fighter's television network [HBO for Lewis and Showtime for Tyson] can decline to televise the bout on a tape-delay basis and refuse to pay its opposite number the previously-agreed-upon license fee.

Larry Hazzard (commissioner of the New Jersey Board of Athletic Control) will be the court of last resort regarding the determination of what constitutes an extraordinary foul. Other than that, Hazzard will not have an official role in administering the fight.

There will be no joint pre-fight activities for the fighters. They will hold separate press conferences and weigh-in separately. The role of both entourages will be minimized at press events. On fight night, only a select few will be allowed to escort the fighters to the ring, and fewer still will be allowed into the ring before and after the fight. As the champion, Lewis will enter the ring last and be introduced after Tyson. The present plan is for each fighter to be escorted to the ring by a police guard. As the cops enter the ring, they will form a line bisecting the enclosure from neutral corner to neutral corner. There will be no ritual touching of gloves. After the fighters are introduced, the police will leave and the bell for round one will sound.

In sum, we are about to witness a fight for the heavyweight championship of the world in which one of the participants is considered so unstable and so given to criminal assaults that normal procedures aren't being followed and public appearances have to be curtailed. "Usually," notes one member of the Lewis camp, "security is on hand to protect the fighter from the crowd. Here, security will be in place to protect everyone else from the fighter."

Tyson's advocates, in turn, complain that Lewis has had his way on almost every negotiating point, including reimbursement for a $35,000 bracelet that was lost in the press conference scuffle and a six-figure sub rosa pay-out for the bite to his thigh. "If Lennox could have his own ring, he'd demand it," grumbles one Tyson supporter.

Sadly, all of this is obscuring the fact that Lewis-Tyson could turn out to be a great fight. "We want this to be a major sporting event, not a circus," HBO Sports president Ross Greenburg says. But the more Lewis-Tyson is hyped as a media happening, the less attention is focused on its fistic merits.

At the moment, Lewis is listed as a 2-to-1 favorite. Those odds are expected to drop by fight time. But most likely, this will be the first time in his career that Iron Mike has entered the ring as an underdog. That's because Tyson isn't the fighter he once was. To prepare for the young Mike Tyson, opponents were well advised to spar with a tank that was firing live ammunition. In the ring, Tyson hasn't been "Tyson" for a decade.

Still, Tyson appears to be getting himself into better shape for this fight than he's been in for years. Would he be better off if he'd started that process six months ago instead of last month? Absolutely. But he's still the most dangerous opponent that Lewis has ever faced.

Some observers liken Tyson to David Tua in terms of size and power. By that standard, Lennox should be able to control the bout by keeping Mike at the end of his jab all night. But Lewis' trainer, Emanuel Steward, puts that notion to rest when he says, "Mike is a much more dangerous opponent than Tua. He punches harder. He punches well with both hands. He's faster. He fights with more intensity and puts a lot more pressure on his opponents. He's been in more big fights. There's no comparison, really."

Meanwhile, Lewis is an interesting blend of power and fragility. He's a professional fighter, who acts like a professional and takes all of his skills into the ring with him when he fights. But Lennox has never fought anyone with the blend of Tyson's handspeed and power. And while no one questions Lewis' heart, his chin is suspect. He isn't known for getting off the canvas to win. In fact, he isn't known for getting off the canvas. Great fighters in their prime don't lose to opponents like Oliver McCall and Hasim Rahman. And Lewis will be carrying an extra burden into the ring with him. Somewhere in his mind, he'll be worrying about Tyson's extra-legal behavior. It won't just be a question of "protect yourself at all times." It will be "protect yourself against all tactics." Also, bear in mind that, in the rematch against McCall, Lennox seemed a bit intimidated by McCall's craziness. And that was a night when he had dead meat in front of him.

Neither Lewis nor Tyson makes adjustments particularly well during a fight. To beat Tyson, an opponent has to take control of the bout, stand his ground, and keep Tyson busy. When that happens, as rounds progress, Mike's spirit tends to wane. But everyone knows that, at some point during the fight, Tyson will hit Lewis. The relevant questions are, "Where, how hard, and how often?" One punch on the jaw from Tyson can short-circuit a lot of fine-tuning.

Every moment of Lewis-Tyson will be marked by high drama. People who pay their money to see a circus might get their wish; or they could end up watching a great fight. ❑

*As Lewis-Tyson approached, there was an almost insatiable demand for media coverage.*

# LEWIS-TYSON DRAWS CLOSER

Two months ago, Mike Tyson came back to New York to visit with Zab Judah. Over the years, the two men have developed a close relationship. And while some observers question whether Iron Mike has been the catalyst for changes in Judah's conduct, Zab notes that Tyson has changed too. "When Mike got out of jail," says Judah, "it was like, he was different from when he went in."

Generally, when the two men are together, Tyson leads and Zab follows. This past March, Tyson led Judah to a cemetery in Queens to pay homage to Abe Attell (the legendary featherweight who reigned as world champion for nine years in the early 1900s). Attell lost only nine times in a 171-bout career. He is also widely believed to have been the bagman who carried cash from gambler Arnold Rothstein to the Chicago White Sox baseball players who participated in the fix of the 1919 World Series.

"It was weird," Judah recalled later. "Mike sat at the grave and talked to a dead man for six hours. He just sat there and talked. Sometimes he got up and walked around, but mostly he just sat and talked. Six hours!"

The upcoming heavyweight championship bout between Lennox Lewis and Mike Tyson has engendered a lot of ugliness, a lot of anxiety, and a lot of passion. Most of that emotion is about Tyson. The whole world is familiar with the story of how Mike went from custody to Cus back to custody again. It has grown accustomed to his bizarre behavior. And it has learned that, when Mike Tyson speaks, words of wisdom don't necessarily reverberate throughout the room. Indeed, given Tyson's past declarations [e.g. "I can sell out Madison Square Garden masturbating"], it has been suggested that the traditional "tale of the tape" for Lewis-Tyson include the size of each fighter's male organ. One half expects Tyson to enter the ring on June 8 with "suckmycock.com" painted on his back.

Everyone has an opinion about Tyson. Various scribes have suggested that he's "the ultimate celebrity psycho in the midst of a public breakdown . . . a behavioral retard . . . [and] unfit for any public appearance at all, whether in the ring or out of it." Oscar De La Hoya calls Tyson "the worst role model in the world," and adds, "I think he's seriously sick." Tim Graham of ESPN opines, "Good old Mike; never disappoints. He's often a boor, but never a bore.

That's because he's insane."

Dr. Robert Butterworth (a Los Angeles-based clinical psychologist) recently put his two cents into the mix with the critique, "We all have impulses. The brain is the mediating factor. It puts the brakes on. For Tyson, it's like an old Western. Someone shot the driver off the stage coach and no one is holding the reins."

Olympic super-heavyweight gold medallist Audley Harrison (who had his own problems with the law and spent 18 months in prison when he was young) observes, "Mike's problem is, you get to a certain age in life and you should know what you want. Then you stay away from the things that make you unhappy and go to the things that make you happy. But Mike doesn't know that yet."

Tyson's defenders claim that he's endlessly provoked by a "poke the beast, get him to growl" mentality that pervades the media and general public. They also suggest that much of his conduct is clever marketing designed to hype his fights. But that view is credible only if one believes that Tyson spent three years in prison for raping Desiree Washington, went back to prison for assaulting two motorists after a traffic accident, and bit off a piece of Evander Holyfield's ear as part of a long-term marketing plan. HBO has a slogan, "It's not TV; it's HBO." Showtime could adopt the slogan, "It's not an act; it's Tyson."

Tyson is in remission at the moment, but could erupt at any time. Meanwhile, his conduct is reinforced by Team Tyson; a group of enablers ranging from advisor Shelly Finkel to co-trainer Stacey McKinley. Finkel isn't stupid, although there are times when his loyalty to Tyson compels him to act as though he is. Shelly is one of the most knowledgeable people in boxing, and it's sad to see the contortions he goes through in seeking to justify, defend, and explain away his fighter's misconduct.

McKinley takes things a step further. "I respect Mike's views on life and everything he does," he told reporters recently. Then McKinley added, "The boxing ring is what we call a killing floor. I won't be satisfied unless Lewis gets some broken ribs or a broken jaw. That's what I'm looking for; I want to see something broken. We practice on how to cave in all his ribs, break his jaw, crack his skull. I've told Mike, 'You've got to break something.' "

Properly admonished, Tyson told Sky Television, "I wish Lewis was dead. I wish I could kill him now."

Lewis, in return, has labeled Tyson "a puppy with some problems." Meeting with the media earlier this month at his training camp in the Poconos, the champion opined, "I think, a lot of times, Tyson is talking for his own benefit. He's trying to make himself out to be some kind of bad man, that he can say and do whatever he wants. But he's going to learn that there are repercussions."

Then Lewis turned his attention to the brawl that occurred at the now-infamous January 22nd kick-off press conference in New York. "I was punching him, and he was biting me. I'm a fighter; he's a biter. Everybody knows Mike Tyson is a dirty fighter. I'm going to insist that he have a big lunch and dinner. I'm going to have my hair pinned up, so he can't pull my hair."

But after that, Lewis turned serious. "Bite on the leg; bite on the leg. That changed everything. Up until that, Mike Tyson was just another guy I was going to fight. Now I feel like anyone beating him would be a victory for decency in boxing. Tyson talks about being a victim, but anyone could say that. I could say that. I never grew up in a nice place, a nice world, but look how I turned out. Tyson can choose how he turns out. He's got to stop using his background as an excuse. It's such a silly excuse because, when you look at it, it doesn't mean anything; especially to me. I'm tired of Tyson's talk, of the attention he gets for simply being someone who can't take any control of his life. I'll be glad to see him coming into the ring because that's where it gets hard, where whatever you say doesn't mean a thing and you have to be honest and just fight."

The architect of Lewis' fight plan will be trainer Emanuel Steward, who has been with the champion for 16 fights. Steward projects an aura of confidence when talking about Lewis-Tyson.

"When you fight Tyson," says Steward, "you have to be assertive. You cannot fight a cautious fight. Tyson is used to fighting people who run from him. This time, he'll be fighting someone who wants to knock him out; who is going to be aggressive in a certain way. It could be a very exciting fight early because, even though Lennox has a great advantage technically and physically, he's liable to get excited and end up going toe-to-toe to try to knock Tyson out. It could end up being a slugfest. Tyson might land a few blows, but it won't be enough to hold Lennox off."

"Lennox isn't afraid of Mike, and Mike knows it," Steward continues. "I've watched Tyson. He's always had this thing about Lennox where Lennox intimidates him a lot. Mike has admitted that. In fact, he's continually making comments about Lennox intimidating him and picking on him. That's a role that Mike isn't used to. That, plus the fact that Mike doesn't want to fight Lennox, has him in a terrible state of mind. Tyson doesn't want to be at this fight. You can see that in the man' s face when he speaks. And Lennox has no fear of Tyson. Lennox almost laughs at Mike Tyson. He's going to knock Tyson out. I don't think the fight will go four rounds. It will be a total mismatch after the first 45 seconds or so."

But at times, the river of Steward's confidence seems more wide than deep. "Tyson will be the best pure puncher Lennox has fought," he acknowledges. "I have a lot of respect and, to some degree, a little fear of Tyson's punching power. When Mike was young, he was the most devastating heavyweight I've ever seen in my life. And he still brings a certain rage, intensity, and punching power that no other heavyweight brings into the ring. Tyson is very dangerous when he gets inside. And he's particularly dangerous with short punches. He does a great job with those little short arms once he gets in close. And Tyson is a smart fighter. He doesn't just go in there and throw wild punches. He knows where his punches are going and gets in good position. He does something that's really beautiful. He doesn't just take one step to throw a punch. Sometimes, he'll take two steps to get into position to throw a punch. He waits until he gets right under you and then, when you hold your hands out, he knows how to go up in between them. I think Tyson is going to come out and attack Lennox with more intensity and viciousness than anyone Lennox has ever fought," Steward says in closing. "And trying to get sparring partners to prepare for Tyson is very difficult because no one bobs and moves his head or has the speed and intensity that Tyson has when he's right."

"I respect one thing about Tyson," Lewis acknowledges. "I know he has power in his punch. And Tyson is a desperate man, which can make him dangerous but it also makes him very vulnerable. I'm going to turn it on. I'm going to say to the Americans who have not shown me much respect over the years, 'Hey, I'm really the very best.' I'm going to ask, 'Why haven't you people given me my acclaim?' And then I'm just going to take it. Tyson was a good champion once, no doubt. He matured very early, while I matured late. But when they talk about him now, they're really talking about the past. I'm operating in the present. I've answered a lot of questions about myself, fighting people like Morrison, Golota, Mercer, and Holyfield. There were all kinds of questions about me; my chin, my stamina, my heart, whether I could take it when the going gets tough. Throughout my career I've answered all those questions. Mike Tyson is the last question. This is about the history of boxing in my time."

That, of course, leads to another question: "Is Lewis-Tyson good or bad for boxing?"

It has been 15-1/2 years since Mike Tyson first won the WBC heavyweight crown. And rather than be elevated by the sport, there are times when he seems determined to drag boxing into the gutter with him. Thus, Lewis says, "For a long time, there has been a need to put an end to the Mike Tyson story. It has become increasingly bad for boxing. People look at the sport, they see Tyson, and they wonder how could this man, who doesn't respect women, doesn't really respect anything, become some kind of icon? The sooner the Mike Tyson story is over, the better. And the end is coming on June 8 in Memphis, Tennessee, at the end of my fist."

But the truth is, Tyson could win. And if he does, Lewis-Tyson will send a message that contradicts a lot of what society hopes to teach about standards and accountability. It will be one of those rare sports events that has a trickle-down effect. Thus, a lot of people don't want Lewis-Tyson to happen. Bob Arum expresses their view when he says, "Mike Tyson is the biggest disgrace in the history of boxing. It's everything that's wrong about the sport and society. He should be locked up in an insane asylum instead of having people pay to see him. Everyone is catering to an insane man."

Arum, of course, doesn't have a stake in the promotion. But HBO does. And at times, even HBO Sports president Ross Greenburg seems ambivalent about the event. "There was tremendous pressure put on us by the Lewis camp to make the fight," Greenburg acknowledges. "We would have had one very unhappy heavyweight champion if we hadn't allowed Lennox to fight Mike Tyson."

So to repeat the question: Is Lewis-Tyson good or bad for boxing?

"We'll know the answer to that on June 8," Greenburg answers. "It could energize the sport. But if it's not a sporting event, if it becomes a circus, if something miserable happens . . ." His voice trails off; then picks up again. "But I'm hopeful. That's why we made the deal."

Life will be simpler for a lot of people if Lewis wins.

Meanwhile, what should boxing fans look for in the days ahead?

With Mike Tyson, one should expect the unexpected. Anything can happen. And once the bell rings, there's no script. But one final point is worthy of mention.

There has been a lot of talk lately about how Lewis-Tyson is Tyson's "last chance." That's nonsense. The public fascination with Tyson is such that people will always pay to see him fight. Even if Tyson is decimated by Lewis, he'll be able to fight three punching bags in a row, pronounce himself "rededicated" to boxing, and get an infinite number of title shots. The winner of Ruiz-Johnson would fight him in a heartbeat. There's big money in a Tyson-Holyfield rematch. And if Tyson falls to the level of an aging Leon Spinks, people will pay just to see him get beaten up. Mike Tyson will fight for big money as long as he stays out of jail and wants to. ❏

*Mike Tyson took a lot of punches in Lewis-Tyson. And some people thought that he deserved every one of them.*

# REFLECTIONS ON LEWIS-TYSON

Boxing, more than any other sport, is dependent upon a single great athlete at any given time to enter the public consciousness.

On June 8, Lennox Lewis and Mike Tyson did battle at The Pyramid in Memphis. Each man hoped to establish his greatness. But their encounter was also viewed as a confrontation between good and evil.

There's a debate as to whether Tyson has suffered more at the hands of society than society has suffered at the hands of Tyson. However, it's clear that the bar has been set so low as a standard for his behavior that he draws praise for simply being surly and not breaking any law. Alan Hubbard of *The Independent* has called him "a deranged parody" and noted, "The last time anything of substance came out of Tyson's mouth, it was Evander Holyfield's ear." Jerry Izenberg of the *Newark Star-Ledger* referred to Lewis-Tyson as "a fight between a guy in a white hat and a guy in a ski mask."

In the weeks leading up to the bout, a dark cloud hovered over the Tyson camp. At times, it seemed as though people were ducking just to get out of the way of his words. Tyson's conduct decimated the pageantry that normally accompanies a heavyweight championship fight, stripped the occasion of its niceties, and reduced the event to its brutal essence; two men trying to inflict maximum physical damage upon one another.

Much of what leads up to a major fight is a dominance ritual. Purses, the color of trunks, who enters the ring first. Here, in many respects, the entire promotion deferred to Tyson's peculiarities. It was more than a matter of keeping the fighters apart to avoid a pre-fight brawl like the one that occurred at their January 22 press conference. It was keeping Tyson away from everyone. During fight week, Showtime and HBO couldn't even get him to sit down and talk civilly with the media for 10 minutes despite the fact that this was a $150-million promotion.

Tyson's conduct engendered a near-unanimous rooting interest within the media against him. But the same reasons that led many people to feel that the fight shouldn't take place made it even more compelling drama. And underlying it all was the fear that Tyson would win.

Tyson has never gone to jail as champion. Were he to do so, some posited, it would wreck havoc with boxing. Hey, if Tyson won, street crime might rise by 10 percent. One got the impression that, if he'd thought of it, Iron Mike would have gone to Graceland and masturbated on the toilet where Elvis Presley died.

By contrast, the Lewis camp hosted an elaborate buffet luncheon for the media followed by a full press conference and light workout by the champion. And no one talked about smearing brains on the canvas or called anyone a "pussy bitch."

"My mother brought me up a good boy," said Lennox. "It was important for me to grow up and be the best that I can to make her proud. You know, when she goes to the store and people say to her, 'You've got a good son,' that kind of thing makes her feel good."

"I don't hold no hate for Mike Tyson," Lewis continued. "We're two competitors. The way I look at it, I'm going to be fighting within the rules. If he's coming in with something else, I'll deal with it. But I'll fight him within the rules of my sport because, for me, there's nothing in winning as a dirty fighter. I'm not interested in that. I'm a gentleman boxer. I fight with honor. I know there's people out there who love a train wreck. But, sorry, I can't be a train wreck for them."

All of this took place in Memphis, Tennessee. But once everyone got past the issue of whether Lewis-Tyson would take place at all, there were questions regarding how many people would be there to watch it. Initially, the promotion announced that all 19,185 tickets had been sold at prices ranging from $250 to $2,400. But soon, that pronouncement took on the look of a pyramid scam.

There's a time-honored promotional tactic. Create a buzz that a particular sporting event or concert is where everyone wants to be and, suddenly, because of the buzz, everyone wants to be there. Lewis-Tyson fascinated the boxing community. Sports editors were in a frenzy over it. But ticket sales weren't exactly what they were reported to be.

Initially, it was announced that the fight had quickly sold out. Then came some interesting news. Several brokers who had been shut out of the ticket distribution were approached by other brokers with tickets to sell. Some brokers were even reported to have forfeited deposit money rather than pay full price for tickets that had been assigned to them. That led one broker who normally does a thriving business on big fights to acknowledge, "The Lewis fans have always traveled well, but they're not traveling to Memphis the way we thought they would. And the other fans aren't traveling there either."

Why not?

"It's a combination of things," explained the broker. The tickets are unusually expensive. Twenty-four hundred dollars is a lot of money for a fight. There was a short lead time between when the tickets went on sale and the fight itself. Given Tyson's erratic behavior, there's uncertainty as to whether the fight will actually take place. The World Cup soccer tournament is competing for customers. And Memphis isn't a particularly attractive destination."

Suddenly modern-day Paul Reveres were shouting, "The British aren't coming! The British aren't coming!" And the Lewis camp was particularly hard hit. It had purchased $4-million worth of tickets with the intent of reselling them as part of tour packages. Three thousand sales were expected. But the number wound up at 400.

At one point, the Lewis camp went so far as to seek to return $1-million worth of tickets that it had bought on a non-refundable basis. In so doing, it claimed that it had the exclusive right to sell fight tickets in the United Kingdom and that this right had been breached by various ticket brokers. But no such exclusivity existed and the request was denied. Meanwhile, rumors began circulating that local promoters had held back several thousand tickets in the hope of scalping them.

On May 23rd, it was announced that 1,000 previously unavailable tickets would go on sale to the general public. The official explanation was that additional seats had been freed up once the television production set-up in the arena was finalized. Then, on May 29, the sellout fantasy-bubble burst when 3,500 newly released tickets went on sale to the public at the Pyramid. As the fight approached, ducats were selling at discount. By noon on June 8, $1,400 seats were available on the streets of Memphis for $500, and $900 tickets could be had for $300. The final announced paid attendance was 15,327. Almost 4,000 seats were empty. The reported live gate was $17.5-million; still a record, but well below the previously trumpeted total of $23-million.

Meanwhile, during fight week, things were getting dicey. Boxing in Tennessee is regulated by the Tennessee Board of Boxing and Racing, which is one of seven divisions within the Tennessee Department of Commerce and Insurance. But Tennessee has very little experience with big fights, and both camps felt that outside help was desirable. Thus, Larry Hazzard (commissioner of the New Jersey Board of Athletic Control) was brought in to deal with certain contingencies, and Eddie Cotton of New Jersey was designated as the referee.

Not everyone was comfortable with the choice of Hazzard. The last time he'd supervised a heavyweight "title" fight was in Atlantic City in 1997, when Shannon Briggs was awarded a 12-round decision over George Foreman in one of the most egregious examples of judicial indiscretion ever witnessed in boxing. Hazzard was also the final authority when Roy Jones, Jr. was disqualified for striking Montell Griffin, who was counted out by referee Tony Perez after taking a knee in their 1997 title bout. That ruling raised eyebrows because, under similar circumstances in 1994, referee Arthur Mercante had disqualified Riddick Bowe for whacking Buster Mathis, Jr., who had taken a knee, but Hazzard then overruled Mercante and declared the bout "no contest." Adding to the discontent was the fact the referee for Foreman-Briggs had been Cotton.

The Lewis camp okayed Hazzard and Cotton in part because of the long-time relationship between Hazzard and Gary Shaw. Since October 1999, Shaw had been chief operating officer for Main Events (Lewis' American promoter). Prior to that, he had worked with Hazzard. But 10 days before the fight, the Lewis camp learned that Shaw would be leaving Main Events after Lewis-Tyson and intended to set up his own promotional company. One of his first fighters, it was believed, could be Mike Tyson.

Once segments of the Lewis camp lost confidence in Shaw, Hazzard was viewed with greater suspicion and it was decided that Greg Sirb (chairman of the Pennsylvania State Athletic Commission and former president of the Association of Boxing Commissions) should be imported to help oversee the fight. The Tyson camp objected to Sirb's involvement because, after the Nevada State Athletic Commission denied Tyson a license, Sirb had urged other states to follow suit. But the Lewis camp threatened a walkout, and Sirb came to Memphis.

Meanwhile, things had grown uglier in the Tyson camp with the addition of Stephen Fitch and Panama Lewis. Fitch goes by the name of "Crocodile." He wears combat fatigues, shouts a lot, and is basically a motivator.

Panama Lewis is something else. Once a successful trainer, he spent time in prison and is banned from boxing for life as a consequence of having tampered with a fighter's gloves, an act that led to permanently impaired vision for the fighter's opponent.

"Panama Lewis is famous for dirty," acknowledged Zab Judah, a Tyson friend and confidante.

Some people felt that the presence of Fitch and Panama was par for the course. "When you invite the circus to town," said Lou DiBella, "you shouldn't be surprised when wild animals and clowns appear."

But Emanuel Steward was displeased. "Crocodile is back from the swamp," he told the media two days before the fight. "And then they went to the swamp and got Panama Lewis. That's too bad because it brings things back in the direction of it being a freak show. We have a big enough problem with Mike's reputation and integrity without bringing in Panama Lewis. I don't want Panama Lewis or Crocodile anywhere near the ring on Saturday night because, when they realize that Mike is about to get knocked out, they could resort to anything."

The fighters weighed in separately on Thursday. Tyson tipped the scales at 234-1/2 pounds and Lewis at 246-1/2. There was a school of thought that the scales were five pounds heavy, but neither camp made an issue of it. However, there was another matter that the Lewis camp saw as a big issue—drug testing.

Prior to the fight, Tyson's primary adviser Shelly Finkel and the rest of Team Tyson refused to answer questions from the media regarding drugs that Tyson might have been on during the preceding months, or was still on. Tyson's trainer Ronnie Shields said he was in the dark. And Tyson's previous trainer, Tommy Brooks, acknowledged, "When I was working with Mike, I didn't know if he was on medication or not."

However, it was known that one of the medications Tyson had been on in the past was neurontin.

Neurontin is commonly used to treat mood disorders. But it was originally developed as an anti-seizure drug and acts on the receptors along the spinal cord so that pain is not perceived as acutely as it otherwise would be. In other words, neurontin can help a fighter "fight through pain" because there is less pain to deal with.

Tennessee doesn't have its own rules on drug testing so, after much debate, it was agreed that the state would follow standards set by the Association of Boxing Commissions. That was significant because the ABC's rules require steroid testing, and there were those in the Lewis camp who suspected that Tyson was on steroids. Thus, if Tyson won and tested positive for steroids, he could be stripped of the title, which would have had enormous financial implications vis-a-vis a rematch.

As for neurontin, the subject was addressed in conversations with Tennessee authorities and at the World Boxing Council rules meeting the day before the fight. And it was ruled that there would be no test for neurontin. However, by then, the Lewis camp had done its medical homework and determined that, in addition to deadening pain, neurontin slows reflexes. "I don't know if Tyson is on neurontin or not," said Pat English, the attorney for Main Events. "But if he is, we'll take that trade-off."

Thus, only one medical battle remained to be fought. It was important to the Lewis camp that drug testing be conducted after the fight; not before it. Emanuel Steward was insistent on that point, and he prevailed. Part of his motivation was founded on reports that, when Aaron Pryor devastated Alexis Arguello in 1982, Panama Lewis had prepared a "black bottle" for Pryor that contained a mixture of orange juice, honey, and cocaine.

As the final hours ticked away, both camps expressed confidence. Normally, Tyson wears Everlast gloves. But for this fight, Lewis had demanded Reyes (which are known as "punchers' gloves"). According to Shelly Finkel, "The first time Mike tried a pair on, his eyes lit up."

"I could kill him with these," Tyson told Finkel.

"I fought on a lot of Mike's undercards," Zab Judah added. "And most times, he wasn't that interested in the fight. He was out shopping and going places. But here, Mike is living the fight. He's sleeping it, he's talking it, he wants it bad. Mike is looking to hurt this guy."

Still, for all the talk, there was no hard evidence that Tyson had gotten himself into fighting shape. Thus, Emanuel Steward was concerned but confident.

"I haven't slept too good," Steward admitted shortly before the fight. "I'm more nervous about this fight than any fight I've ever been involved with.

Mike didn't get to where he is, being as small as he is, without being a very good fighter. And I think that Mike will go to the top of his game and use whatever he has left in this fight. Either guy could land a big punch in the first 10 or 20 seconds and this fight could be over. I worry about Tyson cold-cocking Lennox. Anybody who fights Tyson and doesn't worry about that is crazy. So, yes, there's a possibility that Lennox will get hurt in this fight, and we've discussed that. You don't beat Mike Tyson easy."

However, Steward went on to say, "Everyone is holding onto the image of Mike Tyson from 10 or 15 years ago. But that Mike Tyson is gone. The natural instinctive moves are gone. To be honest with you, I don't think that Mike Tyson deserves to be fighting for the heavyweight championship of the world. There's only one thing that Tyson can do based on his skills and physical structure; just come out and attack. And when a fighter rushes you from the opening bell, you have to fight with him. But if you look at the record, big fights, tough fights, dangerous fights, that's where Lennox is at his best. Plus, to beat Mike Tyson, you have to challenge him. You have to pressure Tyson and not give him time to set his traps, make him fight when he doesn't want to fight. And Lennox is prepared to do that. Lennox Lewis has not been intimidated by Mike Tyson. Never has been, never will be. Lennox went out of his way to make this fight. You don't go out of your way to make a fight with a guy you're afraid of. Lennox has no fear at all of Mike Tyson."

Said Lewis, "The talking is done; it's time for action. Lions don't run from hyenas."

Still, there was the matter of those one-punch knockout losses to Oliver McCall and Hasim Rahman. Achilles had his heel, and Lennox has his chin. The prevailing view was that Tyson could afford to make a mistake and Lewis couldn't. By fight time, the Las Vegas odds in favor of the champion had dropped from 2 to 1 down to 8 to 5.

"Whatever happens," Lewis' mother said shortly before the bout, "Lennox will always be a champion to me."

The fighters were scheduled to enter the ring on fight night at 10:15 p.m. But at nine o'clock, the Pyramid was two-thirds empty and long lines of ticket holders were backed up outside at security checkpoints. That raised the fear of lawsuits by fans who had paid thousands of dollars to come to Memphis and might miss the fight. There was also concern that civil disturbances could result. But delaying the start of the action would dramatically increase the cost of satellite time and, in some areas of the world, it was possible that the satellite feed would be lost altogether. Thus, at a hurried meeting attended by the mayor, police chief, security personnel, and representatives of both camps, it was decided that the settings on the checkpoint magnatometers should be changed. "We're looking for guns, not nail files," one attendee explained later.

Walking to the ring, Tyson looked like an unhappy child. Once, Iron Mike stood for the proposition, "Don't go near that flame because you'll be badly burned." But the smouldering fires that burned within have long since been replaced by a deadness inside. Waiting for Lewis to enter the squared circle, Tyson stood passively and stared down. It was a far cry from the young Mike Tyson, who snarled and paced angrily like a tiger eager for the kill.

By contrast, Lewis entered the ring looking belligerent and defiant.

A historic beating followed. Like Buster Douglas and Evander Holyfield, Lennox fought, not the myth, but the Mike Tyson he found in front of him. He kept Tyson at a distance, where he could fight and Tyson couldn't, and totally dominated him.

In round one, Lewis jabbed tentatively and let Tyson dictate the pace, tieing up the smaller man when he got inside. Then, in the second stanza, Lewis began working his uppercut and jab.

The Tyson camp had promised the Tyson of old but, instead, the world saw an old Tyson. A fighter can't disrespect his body for the better part of 10 years and make it up in 10 weeks. Tyson might have been in shape, but he wasn't in fighting shape. To get him into the ring, a lot of people lied to him. He showed no head movement, threw virtually no combinations, and landed an average of six punches per round. To the extent that he tried to get inside, he did so by lunging forward rather than working his way in behind a jab, slipping punches, and countering.

In round three, Lewis began landing straight right hands and Tyson started making silent compacts on the inside, allowing Lennox to tie him up. He looked very much like a man who understood that he was going to lose. By round four, Lewis was trading with abandon and Tyson was out of gas.

From that point on, Lewis beat up Tyson the way Tyson used to beat people up. In the vernacular of Memphis, he turned Tyson into "wet ribs"—a slab of beef oozing red.

For most of round five, Tyson wasn't throwing punches anymore, just catching them. Round six was more of the same. In round seven, Lewis turned it up a notch. And in round eight, he destroyed Tyson with a roundhouse right that left him stretched out on the canvas with blood streaming from his mouth, nose, and cuts above both eyes.

All totaled, Lewis landed 191 punches (including 84 power shots) to Tyson's 49. And this was a night when the term "power" punch was more than mere nomenclature. Against Lennox, Tyson was Joe Louis knocked through the ropes by Rocky Marciano, and Muhammad Ali taking a blow to the kidneys from Larry Holmes.

"That was one of the most thorough and systematic beatings a heavyweight champion has given to a legitimate challenger in the history of boxing," Steward said afterward. "Lennox just played with him. If Mike had been a sparring partner in camp, we would have gotten rid of him."

The only sour note as far as Steward was concerned was the conduct of the fight by the referee, Eddie Cotton.

"I thought it was bad, and I thought it was obvious," Steward said later. "The whole night, Eddie Cotton was looking to protect Tyson and for an excuse to act against Lennox. He was a bigger threat to Lennox than Tyson ever was. It's like he was on a mission to give the title to Tyson from the opening bell. The warnings he gave Lennox early on for tieing Mike up inside were ridiculous. Then he took a point away on what should have been called a knockdown for no good reason at all. He gave Mike time to recover a bit in the eighth round when he called a knockdown that wasn't; not that it made a difference. And on the final knockdown, when Lennox took Mike out with that big right hand, it looked like Cotton was getting ready to penalize Lennox again for pushing Mike down. All that talking I did in the corner—'He's dangerous; don't fool around; take him out now'—Mike wasn't dangerous. By that time, Tyson was gone. It's the referee who was dangerous. As long as Tyson was standing, I was afraid that Cotton would find a way to give him the fight. That's why I was so frantic. 'Get him out of here, please!' I was afraid Cotton would find an excuse to take another point away from Lennox and disqualify him."

"I agree with Emanuel," concurred HBO commentator Larry Merchant. "I thought that Cotton's mis-officiating of the fight was blatant and brazen. What it amounted to, really, was a failed coup."

Still, Lewis-Tyson was good for boxing. The fight engendered 1.8-million pay-per-view buys, second only to Holyfield-Tyson II. The $105-million pay-per-view gross was a record. And, more significantly, the sport now has a dominant heavyweight champion.

Whether or not Lewis will continue in that role is subject to speculation. After the bout, he told reporters, "Basically, I believe it's a good time for me to retire. I can see that, but preparing for Tyson was not the time to give it much thought. I didn't have time for saying 'what if this' or 'what if that.' I have some more thinking to do. Nothing is going to happen in the next two weeks or so which can change anything. I'm still going to be the greatest boxer in the world for a little while. I know there could be no better time for me to go, after beating the man who overshadowed me for so long without fighting real fights for 10 years. But then, I also think that maybe I don't need to go just yet. There's a lot of money to be earned out there, fighting people I know I can beat. The good thing is that I'm now free to retire any time. Beating Tyson has given me that option."

Lewis is obligated by court order to defend his IBF title against Chris Byrd by December or relinquish the belt. But at this point, the belts are largely extraneous and he has other options. If Kirk Johnson beats John Ruiz for the WBA crown in July, Lewis and Johnson (both of whom grew up in Canada) could face off in a showdown north-of-the-border. Alternatively, if Wladimir Klitschko triumphs over Ray Mercer in their WBO title bout later this month, Lennox could take on the Ukrainian giant and eliminate the one fighter who is seen as a legitimate potential successor to his throne.

And then there's the possibility of Lewis-Tyson II. After the fight, Tyson conceded, "He was too big and too strong. I don't know if I could beat him if he fights like that. I'm just happy he didn't kill me." But in the next breath, Iron Mike asked for a rematch, adding, "If the price is right, I'll fight anybody."

Then Tyson kissed Lennox's mum and wiped a smear of his own blood off of Lewis' cheek. But before one gets carried away in praising his "gracious" behavior, it should be remembered that, after Holyfield-Tyson I, Tyson lavishly praised Holyfield and all but caressed his arm, saying, "I just want to touch you." Then, in Holyfield-Tyson II, he bit off part of Evander's ear.

One can only begin to imagine what the world would have heard if Tyson had done to Lewis what Lewis did to him—"Every time I hit him, he cried like a woman . . . I tried to push the bone of his nose into his brain . . . How dare he challenge me with his primitive skills."

Maybe now Tyson can threaten to eat Frans Botha's children.

But having said that, it should be noted that this is a dangerous time for Tyson. Prior to the fight, Tommy Brooks observed, "Mike is a cat with nine lives, and he's on eight-and-a-half."

Make that eight-and-three-quarters now.

Tyson's reign as the true heavyweight champion of the world was brutally sweet. It began in November 1986 when, at age 20, he dismantled Trevor Berbick to win the WBC crown and ended in February 1990 when he lost to Buster Douglas. For those 39 months, he was the dominant heavyweight on the planet. It wasn't who he beat; it was how he beat them that was so impressive.

But Tyson has now been beaten, and beaten up, by three different fighters. And, more damaging to his legacy, in boxing the great ones hit back when hit. Yet when Tyson is hit, he stops fighting. So yes, Tyson can still knock out a lot of heavyweights. And on a given night, he has a chance against anyone. But if Tyson keeps fighting, the toll on his body and mind will be considerable.

"I'm scared of some things Mike does," Shelly Finkel admitted recently. "I worry about him after boxing."

But that time might be near. What will Tyson do next? He could easily make $500,000 a year from personal appearances and memorabilia signings. But that's not his style and might not be enough money to satisfy him. Thus, Tommy Brooks sounds a somber note when he opines, "I think Mike wants to go back to jail. He's not pressured there. He knows what he has to do. In jail, it's 'do this' and 'do that.' No one will throw curve balls at Mike in jail; only fastballs down the middle. And in jail, he won't be taking punches. So as sad as it seems, I think, before too long, Mike will be in jail again or in the mortuary."

Meanwhile, as for Lewis, the future looks bright. The past 12 months have been kind to him. A year ago, Lennox had been deposed by Hasim Rahman, he was being demeaned as a fighter, and Rahman was refusing to give him a rematch. But then he won a court battle that forced Rahman back into the ring with him and emerged victorious on a fourth-round knockout. Now he has beaten Mike Tyson.

Lewis is an unusual man. In public, he's controlled and never lets go of his emotions. Occasionally, he reveals a bit of his thinking. "I have a rage to win," he told reporters the day after dismantling Tyson. "But for me, that should never replace the need to think deeply about what you're doing and trying to develop all your skills. Violence will always be a big part of boxing. But it has beauty, too, and I like to bring that out a bit."

Lewis-Tyson was Lennox's coronation. There were places where he would never have been regarded as number one until he beat Iron Mike. Now, for everyone, it truly feels as though Lennox Lewis is the undisputed heavyweight champion of the world.

Where does Lewis fit into the historical rankings? That's hard to say. His standing has been diminished by knockout losses to Oliver McCall and Hasim Rahman and the fact that he was unable to knock Evander Holyfield down over the course of 24 rounds of boxing. But to his credit, Lewis defeated McCall and Rahman in rematches. And as Tyson, Rahman, George Foreman, Ray Mercer, and others have learned, Holyfield isn't so easy to put on the canvas.

Lewis has taken on all comers. He has never avoided the best available foe. He won an Olympic gold medal in 1988 and has been competing in the spotlight for 14 years. But lest he grow too self-satisfied, Lennox should recall the thoughts of Mike Tyson, spoken less than two months ago.

"The title is like a woman," said Tyson. "It's like love. It doesn't care for anything but itself. It doesn't care who possesses it. It's always going to be loved. The title's going to be loved until the day it dies, so it doesn't care about me, about you. It's like a woman—'Fuck you, I'm so beautiful, I can get the next man with more money, with a better body. He has a prettier way for me to go.' " ❑

*Tokunbo and Michael Olajide embody the best in boxing, but they also carry scars that will always be with them.*

# TOKUNBO AND MICHAEL

It's part of what fuels boxing. A young fighter comes along. In the ring, he does things right. He has genuine knockout power. People take notice. And the storyline is better if the young man is thoughtful, articulate, and smart. Tokunbo Olajide is that kind of person and fighter.

Michael Olajide, Sr. (Tokunbo's father) was born in Lagos, Nigeria. In the 1950s, at age 17, he moved to England. There, he worked as a manual laborer and pursued a career in boxing that encompassed 65 pro fights. His first son, Michael Olajide, Jr., one of four children, was born in Liverpool in 1963. In 1970, the family moved to Vancouver. One year later, Olajide, Sr. and his wife divorced. Tokunbo was born in 1976, the only child of his father's second marriage.

Michael, Jr. was the first son to follow in his father's footsteps. "I grew up pretty much without my father," Michael remembers. "I didn't see much of him until I decided to box. That's how I built a relationship with my father. I started to know him through boxing."

Michael turned pro in 1981 and won his first 23 fights. In 1985, with his son's career on the rise, Olajide, Sr. moved to New York and opened a gym. Then, in 1987, Michael challenged Frank Tate for the IBF middleweight crown and was floored twice en route to losing a unanimous 15-round decision. That was the beginning of the end.

Michael lost five of his last nine fights and retired in 1991. But more significantly, he lost the use of his right eye. "Back in 1986," he explains, "I was sparring at Gleason's Gym and got hit with an uppercut that damaged the orbital socket, the bone the eye sits on. That started it. Then I was sparring with Merqui Sosa and got thumbed in the eye and needed surgery. After that, I fought Tommy Hearns and suffered a vitreous hemorrhage. I can see shadows now and that's all. I'm legally blind in my right eye."

As Michael's career soured, so did his relationship with his father. "My father is easy to like," says Michael. "He can turn the charm on when he wants, but he's a very strong domineering individual. My losing to Frank Tate was a big blow to our relationship. I shouldn't have gone into the ring for that fight. I had 12 stitches in my hand and some other injuries. But I was a fighter and it was a championship opportunity so I went ahead with it. But losing that fight woke up some individuality in me. I realized that I had to take more responsibility for myself. After that, I started butting heads with my father, but I was still dependent. I was living at home, even though I could afford my own apartment. I paid rent, but it was always my father's place and my father's rules. My father was always belittling me and doing all the things a person does to maintain control. One time, I remember, we had a confrontation in the kitchen where it was one step away from becoming physical. I wasn't becoming a man, so I moved out."

A long period of estrangement followed. Meanwhile, Tokunbo was trying his hand at the sweet science.

"Boxing kind of chose me," the youngest Olajide says. "After school, other kids would go to the playground but I'd go the gym. Then, around the time I turned 17, I got serious about boxing and told myself, 'If I'm going to do this, I'm going to do it right'."

Tokunbo turned pro in 1997. Like Michael, he had been trained by his father as an amateur. But when he entered the professional ranks, Tokunbo chose others to guide him. "My brother never had the opportunity to maximize his skills," he explains. "Michael went a long way with natural ability, a good work ethic, and not a lot of know-how. He entrusted his progress to our father, but our father was a boxer, not a trainer or manager. I wanted to give myself every opportunity to be successful and take responsibility for my own progress."

That led to another estrangement; this one between Michael Olajide, Sr. and his youngest son. And while there has been some softening on Olajide, Sr.'s part since then, his relationship with Tokunbo and Michael is still marked by distance.

Meanwhile, fighting as a junior-middleweight, Tokunbo has compiled a record of 16-0 with 14 knockouts. His most notable victory came on January 26, 2002, on the undercard of Shane Mosley versus Vernon Forrest, when he destroyed Marvin Smith in two rounds.

It was a "bad" knockout.

"I threw a right uppercut and he ducked into it," Tokunbo recalls. "He was out on his feet. In that moment, I could have stepped back, but my first thought was 'win', so I hit him again as hard as I could."

The second punch was a brutal left hook that landed flush on the jaw. Smith was unconscious as he fell and cracked his skull against the canvas for good measure. He was taken from the ring on a stretcher.

"I've knocked people out before," says Tokunbo. "I've knocked guys unconscious maybe eight or nine times. Each time, I'm happy to win, I'm happy to not get hurt, and I hope the other guy is all right. But I'm not in the ring to play games. That's what I come to do, and I know my opponent would be happy if he could do the same thing to me."

That leads to the question of whether a fighter needs a mean streak to be great.

"It doesn't hurt," Tokunbo acknowledges. "It makes the process easier. Yeah, I have it. I don't know for sure where it comes from, but I could guess. And I know it's there."

Meanwhile, as Tokunbo's ring career has blossomed, so has his relationship with Michael. When Tokunbo was 12, his father forbade any contact between the two brothers. "It was a heavy price for me to pay," says Michael. "Tokunbo and I had been close when he was growing up. I used to take him everywhere with me, and I missed him. Then, around the time Tokunbo turned pro, he asserted his own independence from our father. When he came back into my life, it was like getting my fingers back again."

"I've learned from Michael," says Tokunbo. "Knowing what happened to him in boxing, I'm definitely aware of the risks involved."

"We're brothers and friends. We respect one another," adds Michael. "And I can still beat his ass on PlayStation Ready To Rumble."

As the years have passed, Michael has carved out a new career outside the ring. In the 1990s, he created *AeroBox,* a fitness regimen taught in gyms. As part of that venture, he now produces videos, sells merchandise, and conducts workshops. He also choreographed the fight scenes for the recent New York City Center revival of *Golden Boy* and worked as a fight technician on the feature film *Ali.*

Tokunbo is planning for the future too, but his immediate career is pugilism. "One of the most important things to do in boxing," he says, "is to know who to listen to and consult with before making decisions. I don't really ask for advice as much as I ask for someone else's perspective. There are a number of people close to me whose opinions I respect."

Tokunbo is managed by Ed Kotite. Where training is concerned, Tommy Gallagher is the lead strategist, although Gallagher's strategizing often consists of looking across the ring at an opponent between rounds and instructing, "Get him the fuck out of here." Angel Rivera is actively involved in Tokunbo's day-to-day preparation. "And Kwame Asante has been with me since I was 14," Tokunbo says. "Kwame instilled a real work ethic in me. He's less active now, but he still means a lot to me."

"There are pieces missing in my development as a boxer," Tokunbo continues. "But as I become more seasoned, I think they'll be there. I've always relied on punching power; but if you're going to rise in this game, you need more than one trick up your sleeve. I'm learning now how to break down opponents. I don't try to chop down trees with one swing of the ax anymore. My bottom line is, I feel that what happens in the ring has a lot more to do with the choices I make and the things I do than with my opponent. Being a good boxer requires being able to adjust when you're presented with a particular set of circumstances. But most fighters are susceptible to the same sort of thing, and most people react to getting hit pretty much the same way."

So how good is Tokunbo?

"He has talent," says Teddy Atlas. "He has good punching power and hand-speed. He's a solid counterpuncher and he knows when to punch. He's technically sound and has good instincts in the ring. Now he has to start using his jab more to create offensive opportunities like the ones he has when he counterpunches. And he hasn't been tested yet," Atlas cautions. "You want to make promising predictions based on what we've seen so far, but he has to step up the level of opposition before we can make meaningful judgments. When he steps up to that next level, we'll see how he responds, but I think he can go far."

Tokunbo shares that assessment, although he has a vision for himself that goes beyond boxing. "Right now, I'm 16 and 0 with 14 knockouts," he says. "And that's great, but someday that will be over, so I don't define myself as a boxer. I have a balanced life. I do things besides boxing, because in 10 years I won't be boxing anymore."

What will he do in the future? Quite possibly, music will be involved. Tokunbo began playing trumpet six years ago. Since then, he has studied at the Brooklyn Conservatory of Music and played in a jazz band at Hunter College. "Right now, it's a real serious hobby," he says. "I practice four or five hours a day; trumpet and piano."

"I think I know what's important," Tokunbo says in closing. "The common thread that runs through my life is, I'm at peace when no one else is around. I march to my own drummer. I spend a lot of time by myself. My approach to life is, whatever happens, I'm going to take something good out of it. I have to be productive to be happy. I learn a great deal from other people, but I don't let other people dictate what I learn. I try to be my own best teacher. I read a lot. I always look at my own part in what's happening. If I'm involved in something and it doesn't go well, then I'm partly responsible. What's important to me is to not stay in the same place."

Or as Gallagher says, "I come to the gym with the racing form. Tokunbo walks in carrying the *Wall Street Journal*."

In sum, Tokunbo Olajide cares about the kind of person he is. It will be interesting to watch as he matures, particularly outside of boxing. ❏

*Five months after I wrote my first article about Tokunbo Olajide, the plans that had been carefully laid for him came crashing down.*

# AN UP AND DOWN DAY ON WALL STREET

Every fighter starts out his career as a prospect, but some fighters are more promising than others.

One month ago, Tokunbo Olajide was at the top of most lists designating boxing's future stars. He'd begun his career at 17-0 with 15 knockouts. Veteran trainer Tommy Gallagher called him "the best fighter I've worked with in my entire life." Writer extraordinaire Tom Gerbasi noted, "The kid can punch hard. Not ouch, let me stop the fight hard, but call the stretcher hard." And Olajide himself observed, "Power is a thing that I can count on to always be there. I don't have to try. It comes out when it wants to."

On Sunday, October 13, 2002, Olajide entered the ring for his 18th professional fight; this one at The Regent Wall Street Hotel. The Regent Ballroom is fashioned from Italian marble with Corinthian columns that rise seventy feet to a gilded domed ceiling featuring the largest Wedgewood panels in the world. Four of the panels represent north, south, east, and west. The other 12 embody the signs of the zodiac.

The stars were poorly aligned for Olajide. His scheduled opponent, Nicholas Cervera, fell out and a last-minute replacement was found. His name was Epifanio Mendoza, an unknown from Colombia with a record of 15-0 and 15 knockouts. That in itself wasn't cause for alarm. Mendoza's opponents had a combined verifiable record of 6-41. But there's always danger in facing an unknown. What if he's the real thing?

Mendoza turned out to be a well-conditioned 6-foot-2. In the third minute of the fight, a short left hook followed by a big right hand put Olajide on the canvas. As he fell, his right ankle snapped. He rose and staggered. Whether Tokunbo was wobbling from an injured ankle or a concussive episode was a moot at that point. The bout was stopped by referee Pete Santiago at 2:26 of the first round.

"Winning and losing aren't at the foundation of who I am," Olajide said afterward. "We all have a path. This won't change who I am."

But from now on, inside the ring, he might be different. That evening, X-rays revealed a devastating vertical fracture. Six months of physical therapy and rehabilitation lie ahead. ❏

*Audley Harrison is an enigma of sorts to a sporting public that wants more from him than he has been willing to give so far.*

# AUDLEY HARRISON

Audley Harrison has an attitude.

"I've always been opinionated," says the man who triumphed in the super-heavyweight division at Sydney to become the first British boxer in 32 years to win an Olympic gold medal. "I'll only do things on my own terms; never on anyone else's, unless their ideas match mine. Whatever social system or institution I've been in, I've rebelled against the authorities. I hate people telling me what to do. I could never be a middleweight and have people telling me I had to lose a certain number of pounds. Most people are afraid to speak out and put their neck on the line, but I'm true to myself. I'm a shepherd, not a sheep. I'm a non-conformist, a rebel. I love proving people in positions of authority wrong."

It's not lost on Harrison that, when he was younger, people would cross the street to avoid him. Now they cross over to ask for his autograph. "Being a public figure is a role," he says. "It's a game. Most people get tired of playing it after a while, but it's part of my job."

Harrison was born in London to parents of Jamaican heritage. When he was four, his mother left home to live with another man.

"I honestly couldn't tell you what she was like," Harrison says in his memoirs. "All I know is that she was a nurse, continues to live in northwest London, and has had three more children. It's a quarter-century since she left home, and I've seen her only three times since then. She has stuck with the guy she married second time around, so she can't be that bad. But there's no bond between us. She's just another woman."

Harrison's father, a plasterer, raised his four sons on his own. He considered giving them up for adoption, but decided not to when he learned that child welfare authorities would be likely to place them in separate homes.

"My dad is a decent hard-working man who has lived his life obeying the law," says Harrison. "He taught us all the difference between right and wrong."

Nonetheless, Harrison was a textbook example of a child from a broken home who went wrong. He was expelled from two schools, developed only meager academic skills, and was constantly in trouble with the law.

"When I was getting into trouble as a teenager," Harrison acknowledges, "I knew I was doing wrong. At first, it was about having fun and having an adventure. But as I grew older, mischief turned to misdemeanor and misdemeanor turned to crime. I never felt like a bad guy. I was a thrill-seeking bored teenager brought up in a tough street environment where trouble hung in the air. But the older I became, the more I lived on the edge and the more risks I took. Scraps turned from fistfights to serious assaults involving bottles, knives, and knuckledusters. Most of the trouble involved showdowns with other gangs, although I did go through a bad bullying stage as I got older."

Ultimately, Harrison was incarcerated for 18 months after a wave of offenses including vandalism, street robbery, and assault. "I knew guys who, in all honesty, were no worse than me," he says, looking back on that time. "But they had stabbed someone in a fight and the guy had died, and they ended up doing life for murder. I could easily have been one of those guys. I'd been in plenty of nasty fights, and it was just luck that no one came at me when I had my knife."

Released from prison at age 19, Harrison resolved to turn his life around. He went back to school—"I started at the bottom; got some basic qualifications"—and eventually earned a college degree. While in school, he held a series of jobs ranging from work as a forklift truck-driver to a stint as a lifeguard. Meanwhile, his younger brother Rodney was a member of a local boxing club, and one night Harrison went to watch him fight. Soon after, intrigued by what he'd seen, he decided to give it a try.

"I was as raw as a boxer can be," Harrison remembers. "But I had an instinctive feel for it. I could throw a natural jab and a natural cross. My movement around the ring and my timing were good. I had quick hands. I could think on my feet. Everything felt right, as if I'd been boxing for years."

Harrison's first amateur bout was a second-round knockout of a local policeman in May 1992. Over time, he progressed up the ladder, winning a gold medal at the 1998 Commonwealth Games in Kuala Lumpur. But his ultimate amateur goal was Olympic gold.

Only two British boxers qualified for the 2000 Olympics. Harrison was one of them. There were 16 super-heavyweights in Sydney, and he prevailed with victories over Alexei Lezin of Russia, Olekseii Mazikkin of the Ukraine, Paolo Vidoz of Italy, and Mukhtarkhan Dildabekov of Kazakhstan. At age 29, he had fulfilled his dream.

Then it was on to Dream Two. Riding the crest of his Olympic success, Harrison turned pro with a financial flourish. Granada Media paid a large advance for his autobiography, written with Niall Edworthy. Octagon (a global sports marketing company) took him on as a client. But the centerpiece of Harrison's financial portfolio was an an exclusive two-year, 10-fight deal with the BBC for live United Kingdom television and radio rights to his fights. That deal, signed in January 2001, pays Harrison more than one million pounds. But oddly, the BBC failed to incorporate quality control provisions with regard to Harrison's opponents in the contract.

Therein lies the rub. On May 19, 2001, Harrison made his professional debut by knocking out an inept punching bag named Mike Middleton in the first round. On September 22, after a period of inactivity due to a cracked rib, an overweight out-of-shape Harrison boxed six dreary rounds en route to a decision over Derek McCafferty. A second-round knockout of Piotr Jurczyk followed on October 22. After that, a damaged pectoral muscle sidelined Harrison for the rest of the year. He's now scheduled to return to action on April 20, 2002, at the Wembly Conference Center against an American club fighter named Julius Long.

There are questions regarding Harrison's motivation as a professional fighter. There's also concern that he might be too fragile for the professional demands of the sweet science, given the fact that, as an amateur, he suffered through three hernia operations, a ruptured knuckle, a torn tendon, stress fractures in both feet, and torn ligaments in his shoulder. Doubts have also been raised regarding his training regimen. Between bouts, Harrison works with his former amateur trainer. Then, as a fight approaches, Thell Torrence and Kenny Croom fly in from the United States to sharpen him up.

In sum, Harrison hopes to follow in the footsteps of Floyd Patterson, Muhammad Ali, Joe Frazier, George Foreman, the Spinks brothers, and Lennox Lewis as Olympic gold medallists who won the heavyweight crown. But there are those who believe that comparisons with Tyrell Biggs are more appropriate.

"The British media is an interesting bunch," Harrison says of his critics. "I think they want me to do well, but they want me to do it on their terms. At this stage, it's about learning. People want me to get to the top, but it's important that I do it properly, which means slowly. I'll take plenty of punches and be in plenty of hard fights as my career goes on.

"My biggest assets as a fighter are my mental strength and ability to perform under pressure," Harrison continues. "In the ring, you've got to be prepared to go places where normal people can't go. It's kill or be killed. I'm a respectable puncher. Not a big puncher. And for a big guy, I have good hand speed and good footwork. The guys I'm fighting now are the same level opponent that Joe Frazier, George Foreman, and Lennox Lewis fought early in their pro careers. Give me time. I'll get there."

And then Harrison is on a roll.

"The press can sway public opinion, but it's not necessarily an accurate reflection of public opinion. I'm okay with the public's reaction to me as a professional so far. It's a big thing, being a British heavyweight. British fans are patriotic. They support their own. They're the most loyal fans in the world. But before Lennox, British heavyweight boxing was about fighters who were courageous, gutsy, strong, and losers. I don't want to be just another British heavyweight contender. I want to be heavyweight champion of the world. If it doesn't happen, so be it. But I think I have the talent to reach my goal. I don't fantasize. I visualize and dream, and then I make my vision a goal and do my best to turn it into reality. I'm boxing now because I want to, not because I have to. I search for adventure, and right now, that adventure is boxing. But if there comes a time when I don't want to box, either because I'm losing or because my skills have plateaued beneath the level where I want them to be, then I'm on to other goals."

What's left then is the issue of Harrison's contract with the BBC. There's a school of thought that neither the network nor the public is getting its money's worth as Audley fights irregularly against the softest of touches.

Harrison responds. "In amateur boxing, there's a boy-scout mentality. 'Think this! Think that! Do what we tell you to do!' And nothing prepares the fighter for the pros. But I'm beyond that. I'm cool, calm, and rational about the way I go about my business. Everyone, no matter what their job, wants to make as much money as they can. If they can negotiate more, they will.

"I negotiated a good deal for myself, and that's what I got," Harrison says in closing. "But you can't put a price on what I did for England. What I did at the Olympics touched a nation. I was carrying other people's dreams. And I stayed amateur for 10 years pursuing my goal, because I needed a gold medal to do the business things I knew I'd want to do. But that medal wasn't guaranteed. I took the risks and put in the work, and it's only fair that now I reap the rewards. What's the point of boxing for 10 years and being the bravest gun-slinger on the block if, at the end of it all, you have nothing to show for it?"

In sum, Audley Harrison might have broken the law when he was young, but he's not breaking any law now. All he did was go out and make the best deal possible for himself.

Over the years, thousands of boxers have been financially exploited by the system. If a boxer can go out and exploit the system for his own gain without doing anything unlawful, more power to him. ❏

*Jameel McCline was on a roll for much of 2002 as he sought to separate himself from the ranks of journeyman heavyweights.*

# JAMEEL McCLINE: THE STEPPING STONE

Jameel McCline is easy to like. The 31-year-old heavyweight spent his early years in Harlem with his mother and five siblings, all of whom were on welfare. When Jameel was seven, his mother put him in a group home run by Little Flower Children Services in Port Jefferson, New York. "It was a great place," he remembers. "Even though I wound up in trouble later on, who knows what would have happened to me without it. I got to see what I saw there, and it gave me a vision of a better life."

McCline graduated from Comsewogue High School in Port Jefferson and attended college for three semesters. Then the "trouble" referenced above intervened. In 1989, he was arrested for transporting and selling stolen firearms. "I was 18 years old and running around crazy," McCline acknowledges. He spent the next five years in prison, including 14 months in solitary confinement.

But McCline seems to have learned life's lessons well. He's now married to the daughter of a police detective and dotes on his own daughter from a previous relationship. He's a reader and very interested in politics. "I vote both sides of the aisle," he says when asked about his political preference. "I believe in the Democrat's idea of taking care of people, but I believe in the Republican's idea that you have to get out and make things happen for yourself."

In the ring, McCline is now making things happen for himself. At 6-foot-6, 260 pounds, he's a "big" heavyweight with promise. But very few fighters who take up boxing in their twenties reach the upper echelons of the sport, and Jameel turned pro at age 25.

The early signs weren't promising. After one round of amateur experience (a first-round knockout triumph), McCline began his professional career with a 2-2-1 record. "I didn't doubt myself after the early losses," he remembers. "I just kept at it. The doubts came later. I'd talk about being at the top of the heavyweight division, but a fight would fall out or I'd look bad in a win. And it was the same with fear. I was a little nervous before my amateur fight, but not much. The fear came later, when there was more at stake, when boxing became all I had in the way of my livelihood. And to be honest, there were times when I didn't prepare myself properly. I'd have a great fight, and then I'd get lazy and not do what I had to do to get ready for the next one."

McCline's record is now 27-2-3. The additional draws came against Ron Guerrero and Sherman Williams on Heavyweight Explosion cards two years ago in New York and cast further doubt on his credentials. But at the same time, Jameel was learning his trade as a sparring partner for Lennox Lewis, Hasim Rahman, Larry Holmes, Henry Akinwande, Tim Witherspoon, Ray Mercer, Larry Donald, and Andrew Golota. Some fighters in that position develop a sparring partner mentality. Others take advantage of the experience to become better boxers. McCline fit into the latter category. "I didn't know how to fight a lick," he remembers. "And I was sparring with some of the best heavyweights in boxing. They'd beat me because they were better fighters, but I never quit and I was learning."

Thus, it came to pass that, in the first two defining fights of his career, McCline was regarded as a stepping stone for better-known opponents. On July 21, 2001, he fought Michael Grant and floored Grant with the first punch of the fight. In a freak occurrence, Michael broke his ankle as he fell, rose, but was unable to place any weight on the foot. The bout was halted after 43 seconds. Then, on December 1, 2001, McCline pounded out a 12-round decision win over Lance Whitaker at the Javits Convention Center in New York. That led to McCline versus Shannon Briggs at Madison Square Garden on April 27, 2002.

Meanwhile, as McCline was progressing, Briggs was floundering. The 6-foot-4 Briggs, now age 30 with a 36-3-1 record, is personable, articulate, and bright. And a complainer. "People criticize me for having brains," he moans. "And they treat me differently now that I'm not on top."

"On top" refers to the early years when Briggs was a well-marketed potential superstar. But in the four defining fights of his career, Shannon was knocked out twice (by Darroll Wilson and Lennox Lewis), won an undeserved decision over George Foreman, and fought to a draw against Frans Botha (described by some as a human meatball). The low-point for Briggs came on April 27, 2000, when he lost an eight-round decision to Sedrick Fields on a Heavyweight Explosion card in New York. Thereafter, Shannon had four bouts against creampuff opponents and won them all by first-round knockout. But to put matters in perspective, in the past 4-1/2 years, he has won only one fight that went past the first round. It's a classic example of squandered talent.

In the days leading up to McCline versus Briggs, Shannon seemed to be trying hard to alienate the media. And he was successful, evincing a sense of entitlement that went far beyond the norm for fighters. The business of boxing has been pretty good to Shannon, but he pronounced it "demoralizing" and added, "I can't say 1,000 percent that my heart is in the game. There's a band-wagon now to dump on Shannon Briggs. There's no respect. When I go to a fight, they put me in the nose-bleed seats."

Clearly, Briggs was feeling sorry for himself. And at the final press conference, he verged on self-parody. "Every fight I fight, I have the edge," he told reporters. "I'm Shannon Briggs." That was followed by, "You guys have been slandering me, talking bad about me. Shannon Briggs this and Shannon Briggs that. Shannon Briggs got no heart. Well, guess what. I'm still here. I'm not a yes man. I'm not a house nigger. So people hate on me. I've been reading all this crap you've been writing about me. You people smile to my face and bad-mouth me behind my back. Well, I'm through kissing babies and walking old ladies across the street and sucking up to people so I can kiss their ass."

Meanwhile, McCline had been getting ready for the fight. "I love the beginning of training camp," he said. "I'm happy then, but I'm not happy now. Right now, I'm miserable. I've been stuck in a room away from home for 11 weeks. I don't get to see much of my wife and daughter. I'm eating food that's healthy, but it doesn't taste good. And my state of mind is like, a fight doesn't start for me when the bell rings. It starts weeks before, so I'm fighting now. Everything I do, all day every day, is geared toward fight night."

McCline also knew that a fighter has to go out and win a fight. He can't rely on something in his opponent (in this instance, Briggs' supposed lack of character) to give the fight to him. Thus, in a reflective moment, McCline said, "Everyone tells me, 'You'll walk through this guy; he has no heart; he'll quit.' People are taking him lightly, and there's nothing light about him. Shannon has fast hands. Shannon can punch. He's experienced. He's been in with the best. This guy is a fighter. He's not just a big lug who comes at you."

"Big lug" was a reference to Lance Whitaker. McCline had watched Whitaker (his own signature opponent) stagger to a draw against Ray Austin on April 13. And it troubled him. "You can look at it two ways," Jameel said. "You can say that I totally demoralized Whitaker and he gained 30 pounds afterward. But when I watched him fight Austin, and I don't mean to be disrespectful, I said to myself, 'This guy is a bum.' I try to be realistic, and watching that fight took away a lot of what I did against him. It put more urgency in my mind for the Briggs fight. Because yes, Whitaker is big; and yes, Whitaker is strong, but he's not a good fighter."

McCline was also painfully aware that, had Michael Grant not broken his ankle, McCline-Grant, regardless of its outcome, would have been a different fight.

In sum, McCline-Briggs was an interesting match-up; a hungry fighter on the way up hoping to continue his climb against a fighter on the way down looking to reverse the slide. McCline was a 2-to-1 favorite. The assumption was that Shannon had better skills and figured to be dangerous early, but that Jameel had the better corner and figured to be in better shape. "Jimmy is like a father to me," McCline said of his trainer, the widely respected Jimmy Glenn. "It's a father-son sort of relationship. He brings stability and calm to my preparation for a fight, and I trust him once the fight begins."

Then, the day before the bout, McCline received an unexpected gift when Briggs tipped the scales at a whopping 268 pounds (40 pounds more than he had weighed against Lennox Lewis). "I'm fighting a bigger guy [264 pounds], so I want to be bigger," was Shannon's explanation. But in truth, Briggs' training regimen seemed to have been based on the principle, "No pain, no pain."

The fight itself was basic boxing. Jameel established his jab early and fought cautiously, which allowed Shannon to set the pace throughout the night. That was important to Briggs' survival since, at 268 pounds, he was expected to fade down the stretch as he has in past outings. McCline, despite his size, isn't a big puncher, and Shannon fought like the larger man with Jameel trying to outbox him. In round six, a right-left combination put Briggs on the canvas, but he rose quickly and McCline continued to box cautiously. He rarely engaged, kept his jab going, and fought a calm measured fight. In sum, Briggs sold himself short. He had quicker hands and was the bigger puncher. But Jameel did what he had to do in training camp to get ready for the fight, and Shannon didn't. All three judges scored the contest 99-90 for McCline, which reflected the 150 to 67 disparity in punches landed. After the bout, Briggs told reporters, "I'm going to take off 30 pounds and come back." He should have lost the 30 pounds before the fight, not after it.

Meanwhile, McCline is optimistic about the future. He's a good athlete and is adjusting well to the demands of the sweet science, both in and out of the ring. "I sparred with Lennox Lewis before he fought Michael Grant and again before he fought David Tua," Jameel says by way of explanation. "And I learned so much from that guy about what to do in the ring and also how to have a professional organization. With Lennox, everybody has a job to do, everybody does their job, and everything runs smoothly. Lennox taught me how to prepare for a fight on a professional level.

"Boxing is a business," McCline continues. "It's how I make my living, so I have a very structured organization around me. It's a professional team, and I'm proud of it. Alan Wartski is my manager; Michael Borao, my attorney. My wife Tina sets up meetings and interviews, handles the rest of my schedule, and does marketing. My promoter is Cedric Kushner. I have a staff for strength, running, yoga, hypnosis. I'm faster and stronger now than ever. My body is so much more prepared for fighting, and there's no cap on my ability to learn."

"I'm impressed with Jameel," observes Emanuel Steward. "When Lennox had him in camp as a sparring partner, he wasn't the most talented kid in the world, because he didn't have any amateur background. But he was much tougher inside than I thought at first. He never complained; he never quit. Whenever Lennox wanted to go a few more rounds, no matter how tired Jameel was, he always said "yes'. He was humble but he had a lot of pride. Mentally and spiritually, he's on a good road. He's not burned out from too many amateur fights like a lot of fighters today. He has the size to compete with today's big heavyweights. And Jimmy Glenn is bringing him along nicely."

Glenn, in turn, says of his charge, "Jameel tries his hardest to do everything I ask him to do, in training and in the fights."

A lot of people in boxing are rooting hard for Jimmy Glenn, who's one of the good guys in the sport. And in today's heavyweight division, the door is wide open. Lennox Lewis is 36 and will be retiring soon. Mike Tyson is capable of self-destructing at any moment. John Ruiz lasted all of 19 seconds against David Tua, who can be outboxed as demonstrated by Chris Byrd, who in turn is vulnerable because of his size. Kirk Johnson has a suspect chin and has beaten one less world-class heavyweight than Hasim Rahman, who has been knocked out by three of them. Wladimir Klitschko remains a question mark and has lost to Ross Puritty. Meanwhile, the most sobering numbers attach to Evander Holyfield. Evander has won only nine of his last 16 fights. The last time he fought three times in a year was 1989. He hasn't knocked anyone out since Michael Moorer in 1997 and has won only two fights (Vaughn Bean and Ruiz) in the past 4-1/2 years.

In other words, as noted by Teddy Atlas, "The heavyweight landscape keeps changing, and it's getting weaker every day. Joe Louis ain't here. Muhammad Ali ain't here. Larry Holmes ain't here. Anything can happen."

"I don't want to sit around and play games," says Jameel McCline. "I want to fight every three or four months."

The stepping stone might be turning into a boulder. ❏

*David Tua has flaws as a boxer. But he hits hard, and as long as the money is right, he'll fight anyone at anytime.*

# MAFAUFAU TAVITA LIO MAFAUFAU SANERIVI TALIMATASI AND THE HEAVYWEIGHT PICTURE

Okay, I'm being a wise-ass. But, hey, it's David Tua's real name. And on August 17, 2002, in Atlantic City, Tua moved a step closer to stage center in the heavyweight division when he annihilated Michael Moorer in 30 seconds.

Tua-Moorer shaped up as a credible heavyweight fight pitting one generation against another. Moorer had remarkable power at 175 pounds. He began his career with 26 consecutive knockouts and an impressive run as WBO light-heavyweight champion. Putting the generational aspect of the bout in perspective, by the time Tua turned pro, Michael was 30-0 with 28 knockouts.

Moorer's impact as a heavyweight was compressed into six bouts he fought in the mid-1990s. In 1994, he won a 12-round decision over Evander Holyfield to capture the WBA and IBF titles and become the first southpaw heavyweight champion of the world. Six months later, he was knocked out by George Foreman in the 10th round. Then, after Foreman was stripped of his titles, Moorer won 12-round IBF title-bout decisions against Axel Schulz, Frans Botha, and Vaughn Bean. That reign came to an end in 1997, when he was stopped by Holyfield in eight rounds.

Tua won a bronze medal as a heavyweight at the 1992 Olympics and reached the spotlight as a pro on March 15, 1996. That was when HBO telecast a "Night of the Young Heavyweights" and Tua obliterated John Ruiz at 19 seconds of the first round. It was the signature bout for both men and has followed them throughout their respective careers.

The key to Tua's success is his power. His weakness is that he can be outboxed. His left hook is fast; but at 5-foot-9, 245 pounds, the rest of him is slow. Other than the Ruiz bout, in all of Tua's big wins prior to facing Moorer, he was trailing on points when he stopped his opponent late. Oleg Maskaev jumped off to an early lead, but fell in round 11. Hasim Rahman was well ahead on the judges' scorecards when Tua stopped him in the 10th round. And earlier this year, Fres Oquendo was leading Tua 80-72, 78-74, and 78-74 when he was KO'd in round nine. In each instance, a single punch turned the fight around.

As for the losses, Ike Ibeabuche was just as strong as Tua and a bit more skilled. "The President" prevailed on a 12-round decision. Against Lennox Lewis, Tua fought a safety-first fight, which isn't a good idea when you're challenging for the heavyweight championship of the world and the champion is putting round after round in the bank. Lewis won 119-109, 118-110, 117-111. And last summer, Tua was outboxed by Chris Byrd over 12 rounds.

But in boxing, as in baseball, three strikes and you get another at bat. Hence, Tua-Moorer. Handicapping the bout, pundits noted that Moorer had only been beaten twice. But he's always had trouble with punchers and has avoided them for most of his career. Meanwhile, although Tua has experienced difficulty with southpaws, he's had more trouble with opponents who are quick and fast on their feet. Moorer has always been a relatively slow immobile target who fights in spurts. He's a lazy fighter. And even when lazy fighters are ahead on points, they get hit.

Kevin Barry (Tua's trainer and manager) put the matter in perspective when he said, "We've trained for the very best Michael Moorer; the Moorer we saw in the mid-90s. But personally, I don't think that's the guy who will enter the ring. Michael is a good boxer with a well-educated jab. He puts punches together nicely on the inside and has a lot of strengths. But Michael is 35 years old. There's a lot of mileage on the clock. I see David catching up with Michael and knocking him out. If you let us pick our opponent," Barry added, "it would be Michael Moorer."

Two of Moorer's past trainers expressed reservations of their own about the bout. "Michael can win this fight," said Emanuel Steward (who developed Moorer as a light-heavyweight at the Kronk Gym in Detroit and worked with him for two weeks prior to the Tua bout). "But he has to hurt Tua. Not necessarily knock him down, but hurt him to get his respect. If he does that, then he can outbox him. But Michael's inactivity in recent years will work against him. I'd say the odds in Tua's favor—3 to 1, 4 to 1—are about right."

And Teddy Atlas (who trained Moorer during his championship reign) was more blunt. "This is a fight where Michael can't make any mistakes," said Atlas. "And you're talking about a guy who, throughout his career, has always made mistakes. So if I'm in Michael's camp and really on his side, the question I have to ask is 'Why?' Michael doesn't need this fight. He's a name. There are lots of guys easier to beat than Tua who Michael can fight and, if Michael beats them, he leapfrogs up in the rankings and becomes an opponent for some belt-holder. So to me, it's all about certain guys on the inside cashing in before they get out."

Moorer weighed in for the fight at 224 pounds. He looked to be in shape, but not necessarily in fighting shape. Meanwhile, Tua tipped the scales at 243 pounds and resembled a miniature sumo wrestler.

The fight itself was shorter than some sumo matches. Moorer offered no opposition. Tua drove him into the ropes almost immediately with body shots and finished him off with a picture-perfect right hand. Moorer landed one punch.

So much for Saturday night. As for the future . . .

Lennox Lewis might be the heavyweight champion of the world right now. But if sports fans engaged in rotisserie boxing the way they play rotisserie baseball, the two heavyweights most people would want on their roster over the next five years are Wladimir Klitschko and Tua. Tua has power. He has never been knocked down or cut as a pro. And he's 29 years old. Among today's top heavyweights, only Klitschko is younger.

Who does Tua fight next? Let's look at the possibilities and impossibilities among the heavyweight elite.

Lewis fought Tua two years ago. It was a boring fight, and they aren't going to fight each other again.

Tua versus Mike Tyson is the best styles fight imaginable in boxing and also the most explosive. Tua's performance against Moorer was Tysonesque. And it doesn't hurt that David is gracious, charming, and a genuinely nice guy, the quintessential anti-Tyson. Iron Mike won't go near Tua. Tyson-Tua won't happen.

WBO champion Wladimir Klitschko is currently being touted as the heir apparent to Lennox Lewis. This makes Klitschko the successor to Michael Grant, who was the previous heir apparent. There are a lot of unanswered questions about Klitschko. But most great heavyweights have had question marks attached to their name when they challenged for the crown. Muhammad Ali [then Cassius Clay] was considered a light-punching pretty boy with an amateurish defense. George Foreman was regarded as a clumsy novice. Larry Holmes supposedly had no heart. In recent decades, only Mike Tyson was conceded greatness before he won the title. With Tyson, the questions came later. If Klitschko fought Tua and beat him, it would give him real credentials. Look for the Ukrainian giant to head straight for the big money against Lewis or go in softer against Jameel McCline.

Evander Holyfield won't venture anywhere near Tua unless there's a championship at stake.

John Ruiz won what is humorously referred to as the WBA heavyweight title in a bout in which Holyfield knocked him out with a legitimate body shot. But Ruiz's corner claimed it was a low blow. Referee Joe Cortez mistakenly concurred, and Ruiz eventually won a close 12-round decision. Their rematch, which Holyfield dominated, was scored a draw allowing Ruiz to retain his crown. Then, in his most recent defense, the Boston Strongboy raised crying to a new art form and held onto his title when Kirk Johnson was disqualified (by Joe Cortez) for low blows. It's embarrassing for boxing (and boxing isn't easily embarrassed) when a title claimant wins fights by lying on the canvas and moaning like a beached whale.

Right now, Ruiz wants to fight Mike Tyson for a reported $12.5-million. Ruiz's promoter (Don King) has refused to make that bout unless Tyson drops his $100-million lawsuit against King or, in the alternative, gives King five options. Hence, Ruiz is suing King and seeking an injunction that would allow him to fight Tyson. If that bout can't be made, Ruiz would like to fight Lennox Lewis. Lewis (the real champion) has said of that bout, "I don't want to fight Ruiz, but I'm not saying I won't. He's not deserving of a legitimate title opportunity. But if the deal is right and it's the only deal that is, I'll fight him."

It will be hard for Ruiz to be taken seriously as a fighter until he erases the stigma of his 19-second demolition at the hands of Tua. But Ruiz will do everything possible to avoid getting into the ring again with his conqueror.

Chris Byrd is another possible but unlikely Tua opponent. Byrd is the IBF's mandatory challenger by virtue of his earlier decision victory over the Samoan. Tua-Byrd II won't happen. Either Lewis or Holyfield will step up to the plate against the light-hitting southpaw.

Complicated? You bet it is. Meanwhile, Tua is everyone's last option. The most realistic big-name opponent for him at the moment is Hasim Rahman. There's still controversy regarding their 1998 fight in which at least one damaging Tua blow landed after the bell. And if Rahman's promoter (Don King) balks at a rematch between the two men, Hasim could threaten to abandon HBO for Court TV and sue King over reported accounting irregularities dating to Rahman-Lewis II.

In sum, for the moment, David Tua is in a waiting mode. He wants what all of the aforementioned fighters have or once had—a piece of the heavyweight championship of the world. Someday, he might get it. ❑

*The vagaries of boxing economics were on display when David Tua fought Hasim Rahman on a card that included Bernard Hopkins.*

## HASIM RAHMAN AND BERNARD HOPKINS: THREE SMART FOR THEIR OWN GOOD

Mickey Duff, the venerable British boxing promoter, once said of a fellow who was giving him a hard time, "You've heard of someone being too smart for his own good. Well, this guy is three smart."

Eighteen months ago, Hasim Rahman and Bernard Hopkins were on top of the boxing world. But they were three smart for their own good.

There's something inherently likeable about Rahman, whose roller coaster ride through the bigtime began when he dethroned Lennox Lewis in South Africa on April 22, 2001. The new champion promptly began planning to put his three children in the best schools he could find and set up real estate trusts to guarantee their college education.

"My kids understand that daddy is gonna win and daddy is gonna lose," said Rahman. "But daddy is still daddy, whether or not he's the champ. And my kids will know that their daddy looked after them when he could."

Riding the crest of his championship-victory wave, Rahman turned down a $20-million offer to fight Mike Tyson on Showtime and a $14.15-million offer for a Lewis rematch on HBO. Then he abandoned his longtime promoter Cedric Kushner and accepted a $5-million bonus to sign with Don King.

From the beginning, it looked as though King was trying to outhustle Rahman and Rahman was trying to outhustle King. The smart money was on King.

A series of lawsuits followed. When the dust cleared, Rahman found himself in the ring again against Lewis, who knocked him out in the fourth round. Rahman's purse for the rematch was $5-million against a percentage of net revenue. When the accounting was done, the percentage amounted to a pittance. In June 2002, Rahman lost again, this time to Evander Holyfield. His total purses since signing with King have been less than he would have received for one bout had he stayed with Kushner.

Rahman is a good fighter, who got a great break and failed to capitalize on it to the fullest. By contrast, Hopkins is a great fighter who made it to the top and then undermined his own economic potential.

Hopkins reached his professional peak on September 29, 2001, when he knocked out Felix Trinidad to claim the undisputed middleweight championship of the world. Then he learned that beating The Man doesn't necessarily make a fighter The Man.

After conquering Trinidad, Hopkins fought only once in the succeeding 18 months; against Carl Daniels on February 2, 2002. He broke with Bouie Fisher (who had trained him from his second professional fight) and jettisoned Lou DiBella (who engineered his entry into the middleweight championship tournament). DiBella subsequently won a $610,000 court judgment against Hopkins for libel, and Fisher is suing the fighter for breach of contract.

"I believe that Bernard is the best middleweight to come along since Sugar Ray Robinson," Fisher said recently. "But he thinks he's the smartest guy in the world. He thinks he'll be on top forever, and it's all backfiring on him now. Bernard beat the odds. He got to the top, but he's destroying what he won."

On March 29, 2003, Hopkins and Rahman returned to the spotlight in separate bouts at the First Union Spectrum in Bernard's hometown of Philadelphia. Placing the fights in Philly was not the result of an outpouring of support for a favored local son. King would much rather have promoted them in Atlantic City. It was Hopkins who demanded the homecoming, which he considered his due; much like a beautiful girl insisting that the school administration organize a dance after a big football game so she can be named homecoming queen.

The first co-feature of the evening was Rahman versus David Tua. Next up was Hopkins defending his crown against Morrade Hakkar of France, the mandatory WBC challenger. There were those who thought of Hopkins-Hakkar as the walk-out bout for Rahman-Tua.

The heavyweights offered an interesting match-up. Officially, their fight was an IBF title elimination contest with the winner to become the mandatory challenger to Chris Byrd.

Over the past year, Tua has been on a bit of a roll. After losses to Lewis and Byrd, he pieced together knockout victories over Garing Lane, Fres Oquendo, Michael Moorer, and Russell Chasteen. He was ranked fifth by the WBC, second by the WBA, third by the IBF, and number one by the WBO. Meanwhile, Rahman was coming off the aforementioned losses to Lewis and Holyfield, and hadn't won a fight in almost two years. Still, in a testament to Don King's formidable powers of persuasion, Hasim was ranked second by the WBC, third by the WBA, and fourth by the IBF.

One interesting facet of Rahman-Tua was the manner in which the boxing intelligentsia regarded their first encounter. The two men had met previously on December 19, 1998. Rahman was leading by seven points on two of the judges' scorecards and by five on the third. Then Tua landed a hellacious left hook after the bell ending round nine. Hasim never fully recovered from the blow, and the fight was stopped early in round 10.

Thus, everyone knew that Rahman had the ability to outbox Tua. "I feel good about this one," Hasim said several days before the rematch. "I can win every round. I'm faster, stronger, and have better boxing ability. His only chance is to hit me with a big shot and knock me out." But most observers thought that Tua would do just that. The assumption was that, somewhere along the line, he would hit Rahman with a few good shots and Hasim would fold. A pre-fight media poll showed forty votes for Tua and only two for Rahman.

Moreover, there were times when Rahman sounded like a man who was in the game for one last payday. "I can't complain about the career I've had," he reflected at the final pre-fight press conference. "If I can't win this fight, there's no need to go on. I don't want to stop yet. But if I lose, I'm going to call it quits."

When the fighters weighed in the day before the fight, the final nail seemed ready to be hammered into Rahman's coffin. Hasim had weighed 234 pounds for his first bout against Tua and 238 when he dethroned Lennox Lewis. The only time he'd weighed more than that was when he came in at 245 for a May 20, 2000 contest against Corrie Sanders.

Normally, when Greg Sirb (Executive Director of the Pennsylvania State Athletic Commission) weighs in a fighter, he sets the scale at the contract weight and adjusts it downward from there. With heavyweights, he asks for guidance. When Rahman stepped on the scale, Sirb queried what he weighed, and Rahman answered, "I don't know; 250, 260."

The correct number was 259-1/2. Much had been made of the fact that Rahman had worked with three trainers while preparing for the fight. He'd begun with Fisher; fired him in favor of Buddy McGirt; and turned to Miguel Diaz when Main Events invoked an exclusivity clause in its contract with McGirt. Now, suddenly, it seemed as though Rahman had been trained by Ronald MacDonald.

Tua was far from svelt. He had weighed 224 for the first Rahman bout and has fought his own battle of the bulge since then. For the Rahman rematch, he came in at 245. That led Hasim to proclaim, "I'm 6-2, 259 pounds. Tua is 5-3 [actually 5-9], 245. You tell me, who's fat."

Regardless, after the weigh-in, the odds in Tua's favor jumped from 8-to-5 to 3-to-1.

As for Hopkins-Hakkar, the prefight outlook was "uggh!" Hakkar had fought twice in the past 21 months, winning once and losing once against an opponent named Cristian Sanavia. His record revealed five fights against someone named Philippe Cazeaux, who had knocked him out in one of their encounters. For this, the WBC designated Hakkar as its mandatory middleweight challenger.

Hakkar's hobby, the media was told, is playing with his dog. "And I'm crazy about pasta," the Frenchman was quoted as saying, although presumably he said it in French.

What kind of pasta?

"All kinds of pasta and all kinds of sauces. I like a plain pomodoro with fresh basil, marinara, Bolognese, clam, seafood, even a plain pasta with oil and garlic."

Not surprisingly, there were a lot of empty seats at the Spectrum on fight night. In the first co-feature, Rahman kept Tua at the end of his jab for the first four rounds. Then he started to tire. His jab lost its sting and he began to hold. Tua landed some good shots in the middle rounds and appeared to be breaking Hasim down. But Rahman didn't fold, and Tua also grew weary. The resulting draw was fair in the eyes of this observer.

Rahman benefited from the draw. The feeling coming into the fight had been that Tua was a fighter on the way up, whereas The Rock was on the way down. Now that perception has been reversed. Tua was exposed again as a one-dimensional fighter, and Hasim turned in a credible performance that restores his status as a heavyweight contender. It's hard to escape the conclusion that, had Rahman been in better shape, he would have been able to do what he did during the first four rounds for the entire fight.

Meanwhile, Hopkins versus Hakkar was an ugly ritual slaughter along the lines of an encounter between one of Roy Jones' roosters and a Mike Tyson pigeon.

Hakkar's strategy seemed to be that, whatever side of the ring Hopkins was on, Morrade wanted to be on the other. At times, he resembled a fighter hiding behind the referee in an old Charlie Chaplin movie. He landed zero punches in round one and only three in the second stanza. After eight rounds, perhaps fearing a lawsuit for wrongful death, Hakkar's European promoter Michel Acaries went to the corner and stopped the bout. If John McCain wants to delve further into corruption in boxing, Hakkar's status as the WBC's mandatory challenger would be a good place to start.

After the fight, Hopkins called out Oscar De La Hoya, Fernando Vargas, Vernon Forrest, and a lot of other guys who are smaller than he is. Conspicuously absent from the list was Roy Jones, Jr.

Jones-Hopkins II won't happen. Jones has gotten too big and is too good for Hopkins. Bernard's next fight of note could be for a 168-pound title against Joe Calzaghe or Sven Ottke (both of whom he would beat). It would be more interesting if he went up to 175 pounds and challenged Dariusz Michalczewski or the winner of Antonio Tarver versus Montell Griffin.

Meanwhile, it should be noted that fights like Hopkins-Hakkar might not kill boxing, but they'll certainly give it a bad case of food poisoning.❏

*Prior to the rematch between Micky Ward and Arturo Gatti, I profiled Ward for* Irish America *magazine.*

# "IRISH" MICKY WARD

Micky Ward is a fighter. That's the first thing to know about him.

Ward was born in Lowell, Massachusetts, on October 4, 1965. Outside the ring, he's soft-spoken and likeable. Inside the squared circle, he's something else. Ward is the quintessential club fighter—an honest, straight-ahead, no-frills warrior. What he lacks in talent, he makes up for with heart.

As an amateur, Ward won three New England Golden Gloves titles. He turned pro in 1985 and won 18 of his first 19 bouts. Then he hit a rough stretch and lost six of nine fights. In 1991, after four losses in a row, he retired from boxing. "I was burned out," he remembers. "I had nothing left to give."

As an ex-fighter, Ward paved streets for three years, a job he'd held part-time since the age of 16. Then, in 1994, he returned to the ring and, after nine consecutive wins, got a title shot against Vince Phillips (the IBF 140-pound champion). Early in the bout, Ward suffered an ugly cut and the fight was stopped after three rounds. It was the ultimate frustration. Micky Ward, a warrior to the core, hadn't been able to do his thing.

Ward received $30,000 for the Phillips fight, his largest purse up until that point in his career. Other bouts for respectable money followed. Then, on May 18, 2002, Ward stepped into the ring against Arturo Gatti.

Like Ward, Gatti is a warrior. In the mid-1990s, he held the IBF junior-lightweight crown. Then he went up in weight and fought a series of wars culminating in a 2001 loss to Oscar De La Hoya.

Ward-Gatti was a memorable fight. There were moments when it seemed to defy reality, marked as it was by unremitting punishment and an extraordinary ebb and flow. Ward was cut badly in round one and bled throughout the night. In round nine, Gatti sank to the canvas from a vicious body shot, rose, took more punishment, turned the tide, and had Ward in trouble. Then Ward rallied, leaving Gatti out on his feet at the bell. Somehow, Gatti rallied again to win the 10th round.

It was more than the fight of the year. Some onlookers called it the best fight they'd ever seen. Others put it on a par with Muhammad Ali versus Joe Frazier in Manila for sustained action, albeit at a lesser level of skill.

Ward won on the judges' scorecards by a narrow margin. "When I was in it," he said later, "I knew it was a tough fight. I was never hurt, but I was very drained, as tired as I've ever been. The night after the fight, I sat down and watched the tape. That's when I knew it was something special. That's also when I said to myself, 'These two guys are nuts.' "

Ward-Gatti struck a responsive chord with the boxing public. Virtually everyone who follows the sweet science wanted to see the two men in the ring again. But what could entice them to endure that kind of punishment a second time? Money, of course.

Ward-Gatti II was a fight that HBO had to have, and the cable giant opened its checkbook wide. Micky Ward and Arturo Gatti are now scheduled to do battle for the second time on November 23, 2002, at Boardwalk Hall in Atlantic City. Each man will be paid the mind-boggling sum of $1.2-million. To put that number in perspective, it's almost triple the largest purse that Rocky Marciano (another Boston-area resident) ever earned.

Rematches in boxing rarely live up to the drama of a first fight, but expectations for this one are running high. Ward himself downplays the moment, saying, "It's just another day, a hard day, but just another day at work. If I fight for the crowd and try to duplicate the last fight, I'll lose focus." But then he adds, "My style is no secret. I do what I do. I fight hard and tough whether I'm making a thousand dollars or a million. That's the way I am. I fight as best I can with my skills. Then heart and will take over. So I'll just go in there and fight hard again. How Arturo responds will dictate the fight."

Unlike most boxers, Ward is experiencing his time of glory at the end of his career. He'll be 37 when he enters the ring in November. As for the future, "I'm still paving streets," he acknowledges. "Not every day, but from time to time. Hey, a couple of fights like this and I won't have to pave streets anymore.

"This is a good time for me," Ward says reflectively. "Things are going well with my fiancee. My daughter [age 13 from a previous marriage] is doing fine. Everyone is healthy. November will be the first time I've had some big money to put aside. And don't worry, I'll be careful with it. I wasn't born yesterday. I know that anyone who tells me they can double my money can lose all of it. They can go double their own money."

Then Ward adds, "If someone had told me 10 years ago when I'd lost all those fights and retired from boxing that someday I'd make a million bucks from one fight, I'd have thought they were crazy. But good things happen when you don't give up." ❑

*The second encounter between Micky Ward and Arturo Gatti fell short of the first. But that's an unfair standard. Ward-Gatti II was a very good fight.*

# WARD-GATTI II

It was only a 10-round fight. There was no title on the line. Micky Ward was never a world champion, and Arturo Gatti only briefly held the IBF junior-lightweight crown. Unlike most high-profile bouts, this one wasn't going to affect the balance of power in boxing. Yet on November 23, 2002, Boardwalk Hall was jammed to the rafters. For the first time since the 1980s, Atlantic City's flagship arena was sold out for a fight. And the reason was simple. Ward-Gatti II promised boxing fans the spectacle of throwback fighters in a throwback fight.

Ward and Gatti have no qualms about going in tough. In the last 6-1/2 years, Ward has fought 14 bouts against opponents with a combined record of 352 wins, 72 losses, and 11 draws. Over the same period, Gatti has fought 16 times against opponents with a combined record of 544 wins, 63 losses, and 9 draws. In other words, both of these guys have been in the trenches. And their first fight was a boxing classic, a brutal all-out war. Ward dug deep and Gatti matched him. Ward dug deeper and Gatti matched him again. In the end, that first encounter turned on one memorable moment. Early in round nine, Ward landed a horrific hook to the body. Gatti grimaced in pain and went down.

"That left hook was the hardest I've ever been hit," Arturo said later. "Lots of guys can take a head shot, but a well-placed body shot is something else. I don't care who you are or how strong you are. If a good body shot is well placed, you're gonna get hurt. The pain from that blow, I couldn't hide it. That fight was the toughest I've ever been in."

Should the bout have been stopped?

"If it was anyone else, maybe," Gatti answered. "But I'm Arturo Gatti; my fights are like that. I get hurt and come back, get hurt and come back."

"It was a tough fight," Ward said later. "Two guys with a lot of heart, two guys with the will to win. When I was in it, I knew it was a tough fight. Did you ever have a real bad hangover? The day after, it was like that doubled."

Ward emerged victorious on the judges' scorecards in that classic earlier this year. But as he acknowledged in the ring after the decision was announced, "It was a close fight that could have gone either way."

Gatti was in accord. "I thought the judging was wrong," he said. "But Micky fought a good fight. Both of us deserved to win."

And they both did win. If Ward-Gatti I was "Fight of the Year," then Ward-Gatti II was "Payment of the Year." For the rematch, each man received $1.2-million. Gatti had been to those financial heights before. But Ward? Never before in boxing history had a fighter lost 11 fights and received a purse in excess of $1-million. Suddenly, Ward was a million-dollar club fighter.

Like Ward, Gatti is a warrior. He began his career at 29-1 but, over the past five years, had suffered five losses against only five wins. Still, a strong argument can be made that Gatti is the most exciting boxer in the world. Win or lose, he's a "human highlight reel" who always delivers action.

"Everyone knows what I bring to the table," Gatti said recently. "A lot of fighters have been through a lot less than I've been through and are gone now. I've showed a lot of people what a fighter should be. In the ring, I've never let nobody down."

The build-up to Ward-Gatti II took place against a backdrop of mutual respect between the combatants. Ward is an unpretentious man, perhaps a bit shy. "Some people like a lot of attention," he says. "I don't. I'm quiet; at least until I get a few drinks in me."

Gatti is more outgoing than his rival, but the fondness between them is clear.

Six months ago, after their first battle, Ward and Gatti found themselves lying in adjacent beds in a hospital emergency room chatting with one another. Gatti lives in New Jersey, while Ward hails from the Boston suburb of Lowell. The Boston Celtics were slated to face the New Jersey Nets in an Eastern Conference championship game later that day. The warriors promised one another that, if one of them had to stay in the hospital, the other would come back to watch the basketball game with him on television.

Three days before their rematch in Atlantic City, Ward and Gatti were again side by side, sitting on folding metal chairs at the final pre-fight press conference. "In the ring, we tried to kill each other," Ward acknowledged. "But I have a lot of respect for Arturo. I like him; he's a nice person. I'd never say anything bad about him, and I think that he feels the same way about me."

"Micky is a great guy," Gatti responded. "I can't say anything bad about him. Even if I wanted to, I couldn't find anything bad to say."

Would their rematch equal the drama of their first encounter?

"It took me a while to watch the tape of our last fight," Gatti admitted. "I didn't want to. But when I did, I saw a lot of things that have to be corrected. In the last fight, I was supposed to box but I got tired from all the body shots. I was boxing well, but Micky was stronger than me physically. And the accumulation of body punches got to me, so I wound up staying in front of him. I don't want that kind of war again. I'm stronger this time and I'll use the whole ring."

And there was one other factor to consider. How much pain would each man be willing to absorb when they met in the ring again?

In the days leading up to the fight, retirement was a repeating theme at Ward's press conferences. "I've been doing this for a long time," he told reporters. "It's been a long road, and sometimes it's seemed like too long a road. I just turned 37. At some point, enough is enough. You start to get tired. My plan is to fight two more fights, including this one, and then I'm done. Fighters stay in there longer than they should. I gave my heart and soul to boxing, and I don't want to stay in there one punch too long. I want to be healthy when I'm done. And once I'm done, I'm done. I'm not coming back no more."

Some took that as a sign that, for Ward, the hunger and will to leave everything in the ring were gone. By contrast, Gatti said simply, "Boxing is dangerous; especially with fights like I have. But it's my business how long I fight."

In the end, Ward-Gatti II didn't measure up to its predecessor but it was a remarkable fight. Like the first encounter between the two men, it was brutal, only this time the brutality was one-sided.

The bout boiled down to a few basics. Gatti had faster hands, a quicker jab, and better footwork. Ward moved forward for much of the night, but it was ineffective aggression. And when Ward did manage to get inside, Gatti bent low to avoid body shots and tied his opponent up.

The fight turned unalterably in Gatti's favor in the first minute of the third round. And ironically, it turned on a fluke. Gatti missed with a big right hand that landed on Ward's shoulder and slid up against the back of his ear. The punch hurt Ward badly. He lost his equilibrium, pitched head first into the vertical pads in Gatti's corner, and slid to the canvas. When he rose, his whole body wobbled and Gatti was all over him. At one point, the pounding was so fierce that Dick Eklund (Ward's brother and trainer) jumped onto the ring apron ready to stop the fight. Somehow, Ward survived but, for all intents and purposes, the fight was over. The pounding had robbed him of the strength necessary to win. He continued to move forward for the rest of the night, but it was Gatti who teed off consistently and landed.

The judges' scores were on the mark: 98-91, 98-91, and 98-90. Gatti fought beautifully, mixing intelligence, discipline, ferocity, and guts. As for Ward, let it be said that many fighters have taken a lot less punishment than he endured against Gatti and called it an early night.

Both men appeared at the post-fight press conference. "It was his night tonight," Ward said simply. "It was up to me to win the fight, and I didn't. He beat me; that's all."

Gatti, for his part, was a bit more expansive: "I was surprised I hurt him the way I did. No doubt about it, I knew he'd get up and finish the fight. Micky is the toughest guy that I ever fought in my life. There aren't many guys like him around. The sport needs people like me and Micky Ward. Me and Micky make the sport look good, and we make other fighters work harder when they see us fight. Micky is unbelievable. He has the heart of a lion. He's my twin, I think."

Then they were asked if there would be a third fight.

"If we can get it together, I'd give it another shot," Ward answered.

"It's one and one now," Gatti offered. "So a third one, I wouldn't mind."

Micky Ward and Arturo Gatti. They've left their mark on each other and on boxing forever. ❏

*When I look back over the years I've spent writing about boxing, a few quiet moments stand out in my mind.*

# PRELUDE TO GATTI-WARD III

On the night before the last fight of his career as a professional boxer, Micky Ward sat on a bench on the Boardwalk in Atlantic City. His fiancee, Charlene, was at his side. It was nine o'clock on the evening of June 6, 2003. Micky and Charlene were indistinguishable from hundreds of other young couples sitting on benches nearby, save for the navy-blue-and-white "Team Ward" jogging suits they wore.

Ward is 37 years old. He has been fighting as a pro since age 19. In 24 hours, he would step into the ring with Arturo Gatti for the third time.

Ward is more of a listener than a talker. His laugh, like everything else about him, is genuine. Since age 16, when not in school or training for a fight, he has operated a steamroller, paving roads. Often, he stepped into the ring for a purse of $500 or $600. His gross for the three Gatti fights exceeded $2-million. For the first time in his life, Ward is financially secure.

"After this fight, I'll go back to the roller," Micky said quietly. "Not every day, but two days a week. I'd go crazy without some kind of job."

The conversation turned to the house that Micky and Charlene live in, their cat, and two dogs. "The dogs are huge and gentle," said Micky. "There's a mastiff and a Saint Bernard. The cat is different. Every morning, it meows and claws at the door like it's demanding to go out. So I let it out, and every afternoon, it comes back looking like it was in a war." Ward laughed a soft laugh. "Some animals are gentle, and some are born to fight."

It was 9:30 p.m. The ocean breeze was getting colder. "I guess we should go upstairs," Ward acknowledged. "No sense in coming down with a cold right before my last fight." ❑

*The Gatti-Ward trilogy came to an end in Atlantic City with another non-stop action brawl. But first there was Michael Grant versus Dominick Guinn.*

# GRANT-GUINN AND GATTI-WARD III

Two careers ended in Atlantic City on June 7. One began with high expectations but ended in bitter disappointment. The other once looked as though it wouldn't amount to much but closed with a blaze of glory.

There was a time when Michael Grant was regarded by many as the heir apparent to the heavyweight throne. A talented athlete with awesome physical gifts, he won his first 31 fights before being annihilated by Lennox Lewis. In his next outing, he suffered a broken ankle leading to a first-round stoppage against Jameel McCline. After the loss to McCline, Grant did what he could to rebuild his career. He worked hard in the gym. He took seven fights for small money. Every step was aimed at getting back on HBO in a fight he could win.

Enter Dominick Guinn. A veteran of 300 amateur matches, Guinn was 21-0 against soft opposition as a pro. It was a crossroads bout for both men, and Guinn prevailed.

Ten seconds into the fight, there was a clinch and Grant had an opportunity to assert himself. Given his strength and 36-pound weight advantage, he should have manhandled his opponent, shaken him like a rag doll. Instead, he passively tied Guinn up, giving away the physical and psychological edge that his size and strength offered.

Thereafter, Grant looked painfully slow and ponderous. Guinn knocked him down in the third, fourth, and seventh rounds. After the fourth knockdown, referee Benji Estevez stopped the fight. As Guinn's trainer Ronnie Shields noted, "Michael is a nice guy, but we're talking about fighting."

Grant doesn't have the instincts or the personality for boxing. His chin, if he ever had one, is gone. He has no future in the sweet science, and there's no point in his fighting any longer. Still, it should be noted that, whenever Grant was knocked down in the ring (by Lewis and Guinn, four times each, and also by McCline and Andrew Golota) he got up, always.

Then came Part Three of the Gatti-Ward "Thrillogy".

Ward had fought for small purses throughout his career en route to a 38-12 record. His gross for the three Gatti fights exceeds $2-million. Micky is an honest fighter. And it's a mark of his honesty that, when he said this was going to be his last fight, people believed him.

Gatti is a better fighter now than he used to be. One of the great "what ifs" in boxing is, "What if Arturo hadn't undermined his early years with cocaine, booze, and all that womanizing?" But Gatti himself is philosophical with regard to the lifestyle of his younger days. "I'm not the only one," he said recently. "A lot of athletes feel that way after it's over."

There's something inside both Ward and Gatti that very few fighters have.

"It's great to end my career against a warrior like Arturo," Micky said at the final pre-fight press conference. "I like Arturo a lot. But if he hits me, I'm going to hit him back."

"There's no one tougher than Micky Ward," Gatti said in response. "I wasn't sure I wanted to fight him again. But I gave him my word, and here we are."

Boardwalk Hall was sold out. The feeling among those in attendance was that Gatti could win a boxing match or a slugfest, whereas Ward could win only the latter. The seven-year age difference between the two was seen as a big plus for Arturo. Minutes before the fight, Ward adviser Al Valenti likened his charge to another Boston hero. "It would be nice," said Valenti, "if Micky could go out like Ted Williams, hitting a home run in his last at bat in Fenway Park."

It wasn't to be.

Ward outboxed Gatti in round one, but Gatti turned the tables in rounds two and three and did some pretty good body work as well. Round four was one of those time-capsule rounds. Thirty seconds into the stanza, Arturo fired a hard right hand that landed on Micky's hip and recoiled in pain. His hand was broken, and both men knew it. The war was on.

In round five, a cut opened up over Ward's left eye. Then, just before the bell ending round six, Ward decked Gatti with a looping right hand to the top of the skull. Round seven was another time-capsule stanza and the most important round of the fight. Micky came out hard, and Arturo gave him the slugfest he wanted, hurting Ward in the process. At that point, those who cared about either man could have been forgiven for thinking that the brutality of their encounters was simply too much.

Gatti was the pursuer for most of the last three rounds. Each fighter showed such valor that an argument could have been made for tearing up the judges' scorecards and saying that no verdict would be rendered. But that wouldn't have been fair to Arturo.

The honest fighters got honest scoring: 96-93, 96-93, and 97-92 in Gatti's favor. Afterward, as was the case following their first encounter, they found themselves side-by-side in a hospital emergency room.

But first, they spoke briefly about the fight.

Gatti's entire face was distorted. Both of his lips protruded grotesquely, his nose looked like raw beef, and there was swelling around both eyes. Ward's face was scraped, bruised, and swollen, and he would need six stitches to close the gash above his left eye.

"This fight was harder than the first," Arturo acknowledged. "Micky stunned me. I went down because I was stunned."

"Who do you want to fight next?" he was asked.

"Not Micky Ward," Gatti answered.

Ward, for his part, was equally gracious. "It's not about who's tougher," he said. "We're both tough guys. It's about respect. I did the best I could, and Arturo did the best he could. I wanted to beat him more than anything in the world; but outside the ring, he's a beautiful guy."

Micky Ward never won a world championship belt. But he ends his career a true champion. ❑

*Gerry Cooney has turned his life around in a positive way. Now he's helping other former fighters do the same thing.*

# GERRY COONEY AND FIST

When Gerry Cooney stepped into the ring to fight Larry Holmes 20 years ago, it was the high point of what appeared to be a storybook career.

Cooney was raised in Huntington, Long Island. "My father had a heavy bag in the basement," he remembers. "I used to work out on it and thought I was pretty good. And I used to spend some time with one of my brothers in a gym. One day, I said I wanted to box, so they put me in with this little Italian guy about half my size and he punched me around the ring. I went home and told myself, "This isn't for me; the heavy bag never hit back like that kid did." But a few months later, I went back to the gym and boxed with him again. I knew then that I wanted to box."

Starting in 1971, Cooney established a name for himself en route to a 55-3 amateur record. One of his greatest triumphs came in the championship round of the New York City Golden Gloves at Madison Square Garden on St. Patrick's Day 1973. Gerry was a gangly 16-year-old, 6-foot-4, 160 pounds.

"There were 21,000 screaming fans," he recalls. "I got in the ring. It was pitch black. Then they put a spotlight on me and the place went wild. I knocked out Larry Derrick in the third round. The next day, my picture was on the back page of the *New York Daily News*. I loved it."

Cooney turned pro in 1977 and obliterated his first 25 opponents. The last two bouts in that streak were first-round knockouts of Ron Lyle and Ken Norton. Like it or not (and Gerry always maintained that he didn't), he was marketed to the American public as the "Great White Hope." Then he fought Larry Holmes.

"I met Larry for the first time in Gleasons Gym when I was 20," Cooney remembers. "I introduced myself, and we started playing the game right away. Larry is a serious guy when it comes to fighting and, early on, he started trying to intimidate me. We didn't like each other at all back then."

If Cooney had beaten Holmes, he would have become an unprecedented sports money-making machine. But he lost in 13 rounds. "I peaked two weeks early," he says. "I overtrained. And once the fight started, I held back in the early rounds because I was worried about going the distance. I was a guy who fought best when I fought from my heart. When the bell rang, I wanted to do my thing, but I didn't fight that way against Holmes."

After the loss, there were people who treated Cooney as though he had won. After all, he had fought valiantly in defeat and tested the heavyweight champion of the world on a night when Holmes was as good as he ever was. Thus, the rollercoaster ride continued. "Life was so fast for me," Gerry remembers. "I never got it. I didn't know who to trust, where to go, what was real. Everyone had the best story."

And there was another problem. "After I knocked out Norton," Cooney acknowledges, "I'd gotten involved with cocaine. When you're young, you think you can handle anything."

After Holmes, Cooney had just three fights over five years. Then, in June 1987, he challenged Michael Spinks for the "lineal" heavyweight title and was stopped in five rounds. "Going into the Spinks fight," Gerry remembers, "I was at the low point in my life. I was drinking heavily. I was taking drugs. To this day, I'm ashamed of my performance against Michael Spinks. If I was whole, he wouldn't have belonged in the ring with me. But I was a walking dead man that night."

Gerry Cooney today is a recovering alcoholic who has been sober and off drugs since 1988. He dabbles in the ownership of minor-league baseball teams, plays golf, and works on behalf of dozens of charities each year. He even has a cordial relationship with Larry Holmes. "A few years after the fight," he explains, "we started to get friendly and see the human side in each other. Then we began showing up for each other at different events. The way I look at it now is, hey, I went 13 rounds with The Man. And if I'd beaten Larry, who knows what would have happened. I could have straightened out or I could be dead now."

The centerpiece of Cooney's life today is his family. He and his wife Jennifer have three children—Christopher (age 14), Jackson (4-1/2), and Sarah Elizabeth (15 months old). One gets the impression that, when Gerry's children wrap their arms around his neck, it feels better to him than a championship belt being fastened around his waist.

"I grew up in a tumultuous house," Cooney says reflectively. "My father was a rough guy, very nasty, an angry drinker who took all his frustrations out on his children. That's the kind of home he grew up in, so that's the way he was. I grew up in fear of my father. I was always hiding, and it became a way of life. In school, I sat in the back of the room and never raised my hand. I never explored. I learned to survive. When my father died of cancer in 1976, I was still angry at him. It wasn't until after the Spinks fight that I bottomed out and realized that the way I was living my life wasn't working anymore and hadn't worked for a long time.

"I spend a lot of time with kids today," Cooney continues. "In helping them, I'm also healing myself. I try to explain to them that there are no do-overs in life, but there are second chances. I tell them to take care of themselves because life goes by fast. I only wish that, when I was a kid, I had someone to talk with. And I'm sad that my father didn't have someone to talk with, that he didn't experience more joy in his life."

As for his own children, Cooney says, "I talk with them all the time. I tell them I love them a hundred times a day." Meanwhile, there's another endeavor that's also close to Gerry's heart. In 1998, he founded FIST (Fighters' Initiative for Support and Training).

FIST is a non-profit corporation designed to help retired fighters make the transition to life after the ring. Its services are extended free of charge to all former boxers.

"People like to imagine boxers as a self-sustaining warriors," says Cooney. "And we're not. I've been around former world champions who are ashamed. They have nothing to show for their careers, nowhere to go, and no one to help them when the roar of the crowd is gone. Unlike baseball, football, and basketball, boxing has no pension fund or support system. There are no college scholarships for boxers. I was one of the lucky ones. I made good money and put some of it aside. The truth is, I took more punishment from drinking and drugs than I did from boxing. But even I didn't know what to do after boxing."

FIST has a six-stage case management process that's deliniated as follows:

(1) Outreach—Identify potential clients (former boxers) and make them aware of services offered.

(2) Initial intake—Conduct an informal interview to gather preliminary information on a potential client.

(3) Comprehensive intake interview—An assigned case manager has an in-depth discussion with the client to determine realistic goals and eligibility for various services.

(4) Client service plan—The case manager maps out a program for attaining the aforementioned realistic goals.

(5) Referral of client to specific service areas—These include (a) Medical: general examination and neurological testing; (b) Psychological: emotional counseling and substance abuse treatment; (c) Financial: emergency housing, food stamps, and medical benefits; (d) Educational: general equivalency diplomas; and (e) Vocational: job training and job placement programs with emphasis on employment that provides worker's compensation, health and pension plans, and other employment-related benefits.

(6) Follow-up evaluation and mentoring.

This isn't pie in the sky. It's a sincere effort to do some good with the real world in mind. Not everyone is receptive. Some fighters come to FIST expecting a handout rather than a nine-to-five job. But to date, FIST has worked with roughly 150 fighters in one capacity or another.

FIST got Carl Williams a job as a security guard. Williams had received a $1.6-million purse for fighting Mike Tyson and earned well into six figures for a bout against Larry Holmes. "I never thought I'd have to work," says

Williams. "To me, working was unrealistic. I'm a guy who had house servants." But a lavish lifestyle and an expensive divorce changed all that. "This job I have now," Williams admits, "it's not really what I want to do, but it's what I have to do. It can be humbling, but it's a paycheck."

FIST got jobs for Simon Brown and Alex Stewart. It put Saoul Mamby in computer school. It has arranged for apartments, medical insurance, and other necessities of a decent life for dozens of former fighters. After Greg Page was knocked out by Robert Davis in 2000 at the Hammerstein Ballroom in New York, Cooney gave Page his business card and said, "Please, call me." Despite Gerry's plea, Page fought on with disastrous results.

"I'm trying to make a difference," Cooney says in closing. "I want these guys to be able to appreciate the lives they lived in the ring and enjoy their past, not regret it."

As for himself, Cooney says simply, "I love every second of my life now. It's not a race anymore. I've stumbled and fallen and gotten up. I'm happy." ❏

*The members of Team Ruiz might be delusional. But they're also dedicated and loyal.*

# TEAM RUIZ

On March 1, 2003, John Ruiz and Roy Jones, Jr. will do battle at the Thomas & Mack Arena in Las Vegas for the WBA heavyweight crown.

Ruiz has taken a lot of criticism, much of it centered on his 19-second knockout defeat at the hands of David Tua seven years ago. But Ruiz isn't a bum. He deserves credit for coming back from the Tua debacle. And more to the point, over the past three years, Ruiz has had three fights with Evander Holyfield and one with Kirk Johnson. Officially, his record in these fights is 2-1-1. Whether one agrees with the official results or not, even Ruiz's most vocal critics acknowledge that all four bouts were contested on even terms. And one can argue that three fights against Evander Holyfield should be weighed more heavily than 19 seconds against David Tua in taking the fistic measure of the man.

Thus, even Lennox Lewis opines, "I don't think much of John Ruiz as a fighter, but there's one thing I'll say for him. You should never underestimate someone who goes 36 rounds with Evander Holyfield."

Still, let's keep matters in perspective. Ruiz versus Roy Jones is an entertaining match-up. It's a happening. But it's not a true heavyweight championship fight. When other great light-heavyweight champions ventured into heavyweight title territory, they went up against the best. Billy Conn fought Joe Louis. Archie Moore challenged Rocky Marciano and Floyd Patterson. Bob Foster took on Joe Frazier (and Muhammad Ali in a non-title bout). Michael Spinks defeated Larry Holmes. By contrast, Jones is going up against a man who would be a betting underdog against Lennox Lewis, Wladimir Klitschko, David Tua, Mike Tyson, Hasim Rahman, and Chris Byrd.

Nor is the expected 45-pound weight differential between the fighters as significant as it might seem. Jess Willard outweighed Jack Dempsey by 60 pounds, and Dempsey destroyed him. Billy Conn weighed 169 pounds when he challenged Joe Louis, and he was beating the Brown Bomber on points when he got careless in the 13th round. Rocky Marciano fought at 184 pounds. That's roughly what Jones is expected to weigh on March 1. Ruiz ain't Joe Louis, and most people would make him an underdog against Dempsey or Marciano.

So why the fuss?

Clearly, no matter what people say, the alphabet-soup titles mean something. Without the WBA crown, John Ruiz would be just another good heavyweight. But with it, he's on the verge of fulfilling several dreams; his own and those of his team.

Ruiz was introduced to the sweet science at the Somerville Boxing Club, a community gym in a blue-collar neighborhood just outside Boston. Norman Stone and Gabe LaMarca were working as volunteer trainers at the club when Ruiz began boxing there at age 15. LaMarca drove a truck as his day job. Stone was a supervisor for the Massachusetts Day Transit Authority. LaMarco is now Ruiz's trainer, and Stone is his manager of record. Say what you will, these two guys didn't latch onto a fighter who was already at the top. They helped him get there.

The Ruiz camp is populated by true believers. "Team Ruiz" is accurate nomenclature. Its members are stubborn and obstinate and their dominant trait is fierce loyalty to one another.

"I remember the first time I saw Johnny in the gym," says Stone. "He was a tall quiet skinny kid, who came in, did what he had to do, and left. It was always that way with Johnny. Gabe trained him, and I was more of a mentor to him."

In many ways, Stone was a surrogate father for Ruiz. John's natural father was estranged from the family, had a bad drinking problem, and died when John was young. "I didn't have the money to do for Johnny what other managers can do for their fighters," Stone recalls. "So I tried to make up for that with friendship and love."

Managing Ruiz has been Stone's day job since 1991. "After he lost to Tua, no one wanted anything to do with us," Stone remembers. "But we stayed together as a team. No one blamed anyone else, and we did what had to be done."

It's an article of faith with Stone that his fighter is virtually unbeatable. Ruiz has lost four fights in his career; three of them by decision. "Against Sergei Kobazev," Stone says, "Johnny got robbed. Against Dannell Nicholson, Johnny got robbed. Against Holyfield, Johnny got robbed."

And Tua?

"Against Tua, Johnny got caught."

"I'm very delicate about Johnny," Stone continues. "I don't like anybody to say anything bad about him. It's important to me that Johnny gets the respect he deserves and, after this fight, he'll get it. Everyone is surprised when they get in the ring with Johnny. We have sparring partners who come into camp and the first question they ask is, 'Should I go all out?' Hell, yes, go all out. They don't realize how strong Johnny is. He mauls people on the inside. They try to hold, but he wears them down and tears them apart. If Johnny has a weakness, it's that he doesn't throw enough punches. And he might not be the hardest punching guy in the world, but he hits hard enough to knock a light-heavyweight out. People knock Johnny. And I tell them, 'Fuck you, just watch. The final smile will be ours.' "

LaMarca is on the quiet side compared to Stone. Of course, there are times when Don King is on the quiet side compared to Norman. Cornerman Bobby Covino and photographer Angie Carlino are the fourth and fifth members of Team Ruiz. The final piece of the puzzle is attorney Tony Cardinale, who has been advising the fighter since shortly after the Tua loss.

Cardinale was born in 1950 in the coal-mining town of Wilkes-Barre, Pennsylvania. When he was one, his family moved to Ninth Avenue and 47th Street in New York, an area then known as Hell's Kitchen. Cardinale returned to Pennsylvania to attend Wilkes College. Then he got a law degree from Suffolk University and worked for five years with F. Lee Bailey before going out on his own. Ninety percent of his legal practice is criminal defense work for a list of clients that was once headlined by John Gotti.

"I've been around boxing all my life," says Cardinale. "Two of my uncles were professional fighters, and my father was a pro in the late '30s and '40s. My father was the classic opponent. He was tough, went in against anybody, fought the guys nobody else wanted to fight. He fought Artie Levine four times."

In the 1980s, Cardinale co-managed junior-middleweight Sean Mannion. Then he got involved with the Somerville Boxing Club.

"John Ruiz the person is a wonderful, warm, modest, quiet, hardworking, unassuming guy," the attorney posits. "John the fighter is very determined, very focused. He's able to overcome a lot of opponents who have superior physical skills by virtue of sheer will. All of us on Team Ruiz believe in each other and trust each other. We think John will win every fight. Take my word for it, John will find a way to break Roy Jones down. He might not look good doing it, but the job will get done. It might not be the prettiest fight you've ever seen, but John will win."

Team Ruiz is certain of victory; so certain that it has taken what it considers a "bold" step and others consider foolish in order to make the economics of the fight work.

Roy Jones has been guaranteed a $10-million purse by promoter Don King against 60 percent of net revenue from the fight. Insiders say that, out of that total, Jones will pay his own promoter (Murad Muhammad) $150,000. After various training expenses, the rest is Roy's to keep. If Jones wins, King will have options on one future heavyweight title defense.

Ruiz, by contrast, has no guarantee. Team Ruiz and King are supposed to split the remaining 40 percent of net revenue equally. Cardinale says that "net revenue" is defined as the income to the promoter from pay-per-view sales, the site fee, international sales, and closed-circuit income minus undercard costs and on-site hotel expenses. All other expenses are to be paid for out of revenue from delayed broadcast rights, sponsorships, and merchandising.

"The deal is fair," says Cardinale. "We pushed Don hard to make this fight and he's giving Jones a $10 million guarantee."

But Roy Jones' last two pay-per-view shows have generated fewer than 400,000 buys combined, and Ruiz has never been a pay-per-view attraction. At the end of the day, the economics of the fight will probably only make sense for Ruiz if he wins. If he does, his future might be bright. But this is a fight where it's not just who wins but also how he wins that counts. If Ruiz prevails in a slow sluggish mauling fight, it won't mean much. And if Jones wins by dancing away for 12 rounds, it will turn a lot of people off.

Still, if one of the combatants turns in a truly dominating performance, it will raise some eyebrows at a time when the WBA title is becoming a bit more valuable. Folks in boxing are getting tired of Lennox Lewis sitting on the sidelines, keeping the rest of the heavyweight division on hold.

"I'm not worried," says Stone. "Pound for pound, Roy Jones is the best fighter in the world, but John is too big and strong for him. We've been studying the tapes. Jones is a good fighter, but he makes mistakes. And this is a fight where Johnny can take more risks than he normally does, because he's not in there with a guy who has heavyweight power. Eventually, Johnny will catch up to him and knock him out."

"My main thing will be to work the body," Ruiz adds confidently. "I don't want to go head-hunting and miss all over the place. My strength is my strength. I'm a lot stronger than anyone Jones has fought, and it will be a new experience for him to be in the ring with someone like me. His flurries and pitty-pat punching won't work at heavyweight."

Ruiz and Stone are right when they say that size matters in boxing. A boxer has to be able to hurt his opponent. But Roy Jones is a unique fighter. And while Ruiz will present certain problems for Jones, there's a school of thought that Jones will present greater problems for Ruiz.

"Roy will see Ruiz's punches coming," says Jones' trainer, Alton Merkerson. "But Ruiz won't see Roy's punches coming. And when Ruiz watches the tape after the fight, he'll realize that he was hit with things that no one ever threw at him before."

Also, Team Ruiz might be underestimating Jones' punching power. That point is made by Jones himself, who acknowledges, "Sure, he can hurt me. Anyone who hurts Evander Holyfied can punch. But I hit hard enough to hurt him too. And a great little man beats a good big one every time." ❏

*Roy Jones let me spend the hours before his fight against John Ruiz in the dressing room with him, which led to an interesting perspective.*

# JONES-RUIZ AND THE ROY JONES LEGACY

For ten years, Roy Jones Jr. has been a dominant force in professional boxing.

Jones captured his first world title in 1993 with a unanimous decision win over Bernard Hopkins. Since then, he has dominated the middleweight, super-middleweight, and light-heavyweight divisions. The sole blot on his record is a 1997 disqualification against Montell Griffin. In their rematch, Jones knocked out Griffin in the first round.

Words come out of Jones' mouth like rapid machine-gun fire. His punches seem just as fast. To a degree, Jones has been a victim of his own success. There hasn't been anyone between 160 and 190 pounds good enough to test him. But Jones has contributed to his own image problems to the extent that many of his opponents have been mediocre.

Prior to Jones' last title defense, against Clinton Woods, Steve Bunce of *The Guardian* wrote, "This is not part of a sporting tradition. It's just the latest Jones fight where he has taken the most money for the least risk. Larry Merchant of HBO observed, "Roy Jones seems to think that stiff competition means fighting only stiffs." And Thom Loverro of the *Washington Times* added, "Roy Jones is an artist, but he doesn't want to get any paint on himself."

Jones has long been aware of the criticism. And he has kept an eye on the heavyweight division as a source of rebuttal since the mid-1990s when he first considered fighting Evander Holyfield and Mike Tyson. In late 2002, he signed to fight WBA heavyweight champion John Ruiz.

The fight was promoted by Don King as a modern-day version of David versus Goliath, although at times it was Jones who seemed like the giant. "Roy Jones is challenging destiny," King declared at the December 3 kick-off press conference. "He's undaunted in spirit. He has indomitable courage. He's not ordinary Roy Jones; he's Superman Roy Jones. Roy is faster than a speeding bullet and more powerful than a locomotive. He can leap tall buildings in a single bound."

Jones concurred, adding, "I've accomplished all that I can at light heavy-weight. People are tired of seeing races between a Porsche and a Volkswagen. They have to take me out of my weight class to even consider someone beating me."

The bout was Jones' first in Las Vegas since he defeated James Toney in 1994. The odds were 9 to 5 in his favor, and clearly, he was the attraction. But despite an endorsement deal with Nike, a best-selling rap CD, and a featured role in *Matrix II*, Jones chose to cast himself as unloved in the days leading up to the fight. "People want to see me get hurt, bleed, get knocked out," he complained at the final pre-fight press conference.

Why was he talking that way?

"Ego can take you down if you believe the hype," Jones explained that night. "Talking about being knocked down and bleeding keeps me in tune with reality."

One of the attractions of the fight was that boxing insiders were evenly divided on the outcome. In fact, a lot of people who considered Jones number one in the world "pound-for-pound" thought that Ruiz would inexorably wear him down. That belief rested in large measure on the logic that, in Jones' previous four bouts, he had fought Derrick Harmon, Julio Gonzalez, Glen Kelly, and Clinton Woods, while Ruiz had been up against Kirk Johnson once and Evander Holyfield three times. "John Ruiz is easy to beat when you're watching him on television in your living room," Holyfield opined.

"People say that Johnny has never seen anyone like Roy Jones," Ruiz's manager, Norman Stone added. "But there's nothing in Jones' background that can prepare him for Johnny. I've watched every fight that Roy Jones has fought. And you know what? He hasn't changed a bit from his amateur days. He's like Shane Mosley. Mosley got away with it until someone caught up with him. It was the same way with Naseem Hamed. Then you get a big tough guy in front of you who can take what you give, but you can't take back. I see Johnny knocking Jones out within seven rounds."

At times, Jones himself added to the doubts. "I didn't take a lot of light-heavyweights down with one punch," he acknowledged. "And this guy can take a lot more than those guys could. The average fan with any sense can't expect me to knock this big guy out. People have to look at the realistic picture, which is a big guy pounding on me. Can I take it for 12 rounds? Can I take it if he hits me on the chin? How well will I stand up under that type of punch? This is a big-ass dude. I can't be stupid. I've been in fights when I was dazed. I know how it feels to be dazed, and you just deal with it. I'm a survivor, but Ruiz is a big guy. He's capable of knocking me down. I may have to recompose myself at some point."

Still, when all was said and done, Jones remained confident. "I'll do what I have to do to win," he promised. "If I need to attack, I'll attack. If I need to box, I'll box. A lot of people say that Ruiz's punching power will change my mind, but I'm going to be asking chin questions too. The surprise will come when I hit him hard. Ruiz is measuring me against Evander Holyfield and Kirk Johnson, but I ain't them."

Two days before the fight, Ruiz weighed in at 226 pounds. Jones tipped the scales at 193 wearing an estimated three pounds of clothes. That was well above his previous high fighting weight of 175 pounds. But as conditioner Mackie Shilstone, who helped Jones prepare for Ruiz, explained, "Roy came to me at 192 pounds with 8.7 percent body fat. All we did was change the composition; bring his body fat down to six percent."

"This is the first time I've worked with Mackie, but not the last," Jones said after the weigh-in. "Look at me. The little man ain't so damn little."

And Dr. Margaret Goodman, who administered the pre-fight physicals, observed, "I've never seen a fighter in better condition than Roy Jones is in now. He's got the head of a middleweight on the neck and body of a heavyweight. His body is absolutely phenomenal."

Meanwhile, tempers in the Ruiz camp were rising. Team Ruiz was worried about money. Ruiz and Stone had entered into a deal with Don King whereby their purse was largely dependent upon pay-per-view sales. Ultimately, the fight would do well, engendering 525,000 buys. But in the days leading up to the bout, the prognosis was poor and the feeling was that Jones had done little to promote the fight.

"Roy hasn't done his job," Ruiz complained just prior to the weigh in. "I guess he has his money and couldn't care less about my end of it."

"I feel like Roy has gypped us," Stone added. "He's taken advantage of us, and that's not right."

On Thursday afternoon, the frustrations boiled over. It wasn't unexpected. Stone is a man whose passions are on the surface, and slights to his fighter bother him more than they bother Ruiz. Nothing is ever "just business" with Stone. Everything becomes personal.

Jones was aware of the situation. Before he and his entourage left his suite for the weigh-in, he gathered everyone together and said, "I don't want any fuss. Don't make physical contact with any of their guys; no touching or in-your-face stuff. Stone is looking for trouble. Don't give it to him."

Nonetheless, the weigh-in turned ugly. As soon as the fighters got off the scale, Stone accused Jones' trainer, Alton Merkerson, of tampering with Jones' gloves by removing them from their shrink-wrapping without a representative of the Ruiz camp being present. In truth, Marc Ratner (executive director of the Nevada State Athletic Commission) had done it. Regardless, one word led to another. Most of the words were Stone's. Then Stone grabbed Merkerson by the shirt; Merkerson whacked him with a pretty good righthand; and the two men toppled off the weigh-in platform into the crowd.

Merkerson was no worse for wear and, initially, Stone seemed to have suffered nothing worse than a cut lip. Then Stone began complaining of chest pains, had trouble breathing, and was taken to Valley Hospital as a precaution.

"Stone shouldn't have been in Merk's face," Jones said afterward. "What happened to him was long overdue, but I didn't want to be the one to do it."

Twenty-four hours later, Stone and Merkerson came face to face again in the same ballroom at Caesars Palace when the fighters' gloves were chosen. Stone had a swollen lip and broken pinky and was a bit stiff in the ribs from events of the preceding afternoon.

"I owe you bigtime," Stone told Merkerson.

"Don't start," Merkerson countered.

"It ain't over. My lawyer is gonna get you, and I will too."

There was no response.

"Fuck you," Stone added.

Merkerson turned to Ratner. "Are we here for a glove meeting?"

"Shut up, you piece of shit," Stone snapped.

Both fighters would be wearing 10-ounce gloves. It had been agreed that Ruiz would wear size "XL" and Jones would wear "large." Each camp had chosen two pairs the previous afternoon. But now, Stone had come to the conclusion that "large" gloves were tighter and thus more likely to cut an opponent than size "XL." "Give us a pair of the Roy Jones gloves," he demanded. "We'll fight with them."

"Fine," Merkerson responded.

"I want pair number one."

"Okay."

"No! I want number two."

"No problem."

"Fuck you, faggot."

Ratner was a calming influence. Pointing to a plastic bag holding eight pairs of shrink-wrapped 10-ounce "large" gloves, he offered Stone first choice. Stone selected two pairs for his fighter. Merkerson followed suit. Then Ratner sat the two men down at opposite ends of a table with three security personnel in between and reviewed the rules that would govern the fight. "There's some hard feelings here," he said in closing. "I don't want them to get out of hand. Don't do anything that would take away from the fight."

Meanwhile, upstairs in his suite, Roy Jones was about to deviate from ritual. Usually, the night before a fight, Jones watches martial arts action films. Calling them "B flicks" would be grading them kindly.

"The movies get my mind right," Jones explained. "They help me visualize. The people in them move in a way that's very precise. They never get tired. Their breathing is controlled. Their focus stays the same. He who loses form first loses."

Jones had brought 18 martial-arts videos to Las Vegas. However, now, on the night before the biggest fight of his professional career, he chose to watch tapes of himself as an amateur. "I want to remind myself that Roy Jones is still Roy Jones," he said. "Tomorrow night, I might be fighting like I did when I was young."

Translation: Jones was planning to set down more on his punches than he had in recent fights.

"Roy is hitting hard now," said Jones' stablemate Billy Lewis. "His punches have upgraded from an M-16 to an M-60."

But would those punches be enough to fend off Ruiz? The answer would come the following night.

Jones arrived at the Thomas & Mack Center on Saturday March 1 at 6:25 p.m. He was wearing a blue-and-white North Carolina basketball warm-up suit over jersey number 23 (Michael Jordan's old number).

Soon after Jones' arrival, his dressing room was jammed. Alton Merkerson was there, as were Roy's other cornermen. Two Nevada State Athletic Commission inspectors sat near a group of fighters that included Billy Lewis, Derrick Gainer, Vince Phillips, and Gabe Brown. Al Cole and David Izon had faced one another in the day's first preliminary bout. Now they sat side-by-side with Izon holding an icepack to reduce the swelling around his right eye.

The room seemed as hot as a sauna. Jones opened a folding metal chair and sat down facing away from his locker. Rap music blared. Occasionally, Roy drank from a bottle of mineral water. Now and then, he intoned the lyrics of the music and glanced at preliminary fights on the television monitor in a corner of the room. Mostly, he alternated between quiet contemplation and relaxed conversation.

Tami Cotel, the production coordinator for HBO Boxing, entered the room and asked Jones if he'd be willing to weigh-in on an HBO scale on camera.

"Tell me why I should do it," Jones queried.

"We always do it before a big fight."

"That's not good enough."

Cotel tried again.

"We want to compare your weight with what other great champions like Jack Dempsey, Joe Louis, and Rocky Marciano weighed when they won the heavyweight title."

Jones agreed to get on the scale. It registered 199. Subtract three pounds for clothes, and Jones weighed 196. That's more than Dempsey or Marciano ever weighed in the ring and a pound less than Joe Louis weighed when he captured the heavyweight crown.

"It's out now," Merkerson chortled. "I knew the scale at the official weigh-in was light."

Given the personalities involved, Merkerson is the ideal trainer for Jones. "Coach Merk" strategizes with his fighter, provides a disciplined framework during training camp, watches Jones' back in tight situations, and lets Roy be Roy. Each day when Jones comes to the gym, Merkerson asks him what he wants to do.

"I'm not gonna lie," Merkerson said in the dressing room as the music grew louder. "It's been a joyful ride."

At 7:38 p.m, with a member of the Ruiz camp present, Merkerson began to wrap Jones' hands. As that task progressed, Jay Nady, who had been assigned to referee the fight, entered with Marc Ratner to offer the normal pre-fight instructions.

"Any questions?" Nady asked at the close of his remarks.

"We want to fight clean," Merkerson responded. "I know you'll do your best, sir."

"I'll stay on top of it," Nady assured him.

When the taping was done, an inspector initialed the wraps. Then Jones put on a protective cup, brown trunks, and tasseled brown-and-white ring shoes. At 7:50 p.m, he turned off the music and summoned everyone to room center. Hands joined together in prayer, asking first that no one be hurt in the fight, and only then for victory.

After the prayer, Jones turned the music on again and stood in front of his chair. Slowly, he shifted his weight from one foot to the other. Then he sat down and began silently mouthing the lyrics to the music.

Jones, not Merkerson or anyone else, was dictating the pace of everything. And throughout his time in the dressing room, he rarely left his chair. He never warmed up in the conventional sense; never stretched, shadow-boxed, or hit any pads.

"It's known as 'the slows'," Merkerson explained. "The theory is that muscles work better if the body is hot but, at the same time, energy should be conserved."

At eight o'clock, Ratner returned with the gloves that Jones would wear during the fight. Fifteen minutes later, Jones gloved up with a Ruiz cornerman present.

Then Merkerson moved to the center of the room. "What time is it?" he shouted.

"Jones time," the chorus responded.

"What time is it?"

"Jones time."

"What time is it?"

"Jones time."

Then the Q and A changed.

"Whose house?"

"Jones house."

"Whose house?"

"Jones house."

"Whose house?"

"Jones house."

"And the new!"

"Heavyweight champion of the world."

"And the new!"

"Heavyweight champion of the world."

"And the new!"

"Heavyweight champion of the world."

Merkerson turned to Jones. "Let's go to work," he told the fighter.

What followed wasn't a great fight, but it was a great performance. Roy Jones asked a lot of questions, and John Ruiz didn't have the answers.

For most of round one, the combatants fought on even terms. Then toward the end of the round, Ruiz landed a clubbing right hand and Jones fired back harder. As early as round two, Ruiz had stopped bulling forward and was fighting a more cautious fight.

Jones didn't run. Instead, he stood in the center of the ring, often directly in front of Ruiz, feinting, looking to counter, getting off first when he wanted to, setting down on his punches more than in recent fights, and controlling the flow of the action. In recent years, Jones has averaged only eight jabs per round. Against Ruiz, it was 19.

As the rounds went by, Jones-Ruiz took on the look of a Roy Jones light-heavyweight title defense. Jones broke Ruiz's nose in round four. Then, with 18 seconds left in the round, he landed a lightning-bolt right to the temple that staggered Ruiz enough that Stone asked his fighter between rounds, "Are you all right?"

At that point, Ruiz looked like a beaten fighter. And for the rest of the night, he looked like a fighter who knew he was beaten. There were times when Jones fought more like a heavyweight than Ruiz did.

Stone's antics at the weigh-in and his inflammatory words the day after probably hurt his fighter in that they reinforced the view that the referee had to run a tight ship. Nady did just that, warning early and often against rough-house tactics. That upset the Ruiz camp. After round 11, when Nady came to the corner and announced "one more round," Stone shouted, "Get out of our corner. I'm gonna find out you bet on him. You're in the bag." It was a charge that Ruiz himself echoed after the fight, when he declared, "The referee should be investigated. He didn't let me fight my fight. I don't know what rules he was following. It's tough to fight two people in the ring. I guess he was following Jones' instructions."

This is known as sour grapes. Nady did an excellent job.

Overall, Jones landed 50 percent more punches than Ruiz, 134 to 89. Ruiz scored single-digit connects in 11 of the 12 rounds. This writer scored the bout 118-111, and the only reason it was that close is that Jones took off the final three rounds. People had expected an ugly fight, but Jones' performance was beautiful. It left no doubt that he's a great fighter, nor is there any doubt that right now he's number one in the world "pound for pound."

As for who Jones fights next, his options are plentiful. "Truthfully, I don't feel like I'm a heavyweight," he said at the press conference following the fight. But then Jones declared, "Show me the money! If the money is right, I'll fight another heavyweight. If it's not right, I'll go back down to light-heavyweight. That's not hard to figure out."

That means Jones could step into the ring next against Evander Holyfield, Mike Tyson, Chris Byrd, or a lesser heavyweight like Joe Mesi. He could return to 175 pounds and fight the winner of Montell Griffin versus Antonio Tarver or position himself at cruiserweight for a title fight against the survivor of Vassiliy Jirov versus James Toney.

But whatever Jones does, his style is likely to stay the same. "Why change?" he asked after dismantling Ruiz. "If I get beat, I want to get beat doing what I do well. After you beat that, then I might change something. Until someone can beat that, why should I change?"

It's a rhetorical question. No change is necessary. Roy Jones isn't the true heavyweight champion of the world. That honor belongs to Lennox Lewis. But the Roy Jones who fought John Ruiz on March 1 would have beaten most heavyweight champions in history.

Athletes today are better and better conditioned than their predecessors. Jones is far superior to heavyweight titleholders like James J. Braddock and Floyd Patterson. And no less an authority than Emanuel Steward says that, if you could transport Jones back in a time capsule, he would beat the smaller heavyweight greats like Jack Dempsey and Rocky Marciano.

Jones lives in a strange world. He channels his violence. Lest one forget, owning 700 fighting cocks and living with 40 pit bulls chained to stakes outside your front door is a bit unusual. But in the ring, Roy Jones is a unique talent who deserves comparison with boxing's immortals.

Sugar Ray Robinson, for whom the phrase "pound for pound" was invented, was a classic fighter. Robinson fought conventionally. He just did it better than anyone else. Roy Jones is different. He breaks the mold and moves beyond the framework of convention. Like Muhammad Ali, Jones deconstructs the art and science of boxing and reassembles the pieces to his liking. ❏

# ROUND 2

# NON-COMBATANTS

*LeRoy Neiman has had a front-row seat on the sports scene for almost 50 years.*

# A SPORTS FAN IS PAINTED BY LEROY NEIMAN

Actually, it isn't a painting. He used pastels.

But it's more than a sketch. "A study," he called it.

And with a simple act of kindness, LeRoy Neiman added to the good deeds he has performed over a lifetime.

Neiman was born in Minnesota on June 8, 1921. His father (Charles Runquist) was an unskilled laborer who abandoned the family when LeRoy was young. His mother remarried twice, and LeRoy took the surname of one of his stepfathers.

As a child, Neiman was drawn to art. In grade school, he put pen and-ink tattoos on the arms of fellow students. In high school, although lacking in formal training, he created posters for athletic events and earned pocket cash by painting images of meat, fruit, and vegetables on grocery store windows. Later, as a mess sergeant in the army during World War II, he designed posters, painted sexually suggestive murals in mess halls, and otherwise served the Allied cause.

After the war, Neiman studied at the St. Paul Art Center and the Art Institute of Chicago. Then he began work as a fashion illustrator and, while freelancing in Chicago, met a young copywriter named Hugh Hefner.

In 1953, Hefner launched *Playboy*, and Neiman became the magazine's "official" artist. His first noteworthy contribution was the creation of "Femlin"—a tiny character who has appeared on the *Playboy* jokes page in every issue since August 1955. Then, beginning in 1958 and continuing for the next fifteen years, Neiman traveled around the globe for *Playboy* to paint a monthly feature entitled "Man At His Leisure". His artwork celebrated the privileged world of "beautiful people" and gave his audience an intimate look at the most elite places and events on the planet, all from a glorifying point of view.

"When I paint," LeRoy acknowledged, "I consider the public presence of a person, the surface facade. I'm less concerned with how people look when they wake up or how they act at home. A person's public presence reflects his own efforts at image development. I focus on the beauty and the best. Sure, I'd rather paint a Rolls Royce than a Volkswagen."

Meanwhile, Neiman was carefully cultivating his own image to make himself famous and wealthy. As Hefner later observed, "LeRoy quite intentionally invented himself as a flamboyant artist in much the same way that I became Mr. Playboy." Neiman agrees, saying, "I guess I created LeRoy Neiman. Nobody else told me how to do it."

Neiman was the first artist to successfully tap into the mass media. And, over time, the Neiman style, with its splashes of intense color and sense of motion, became nationally known. In the late 1960s, he appeared regularly on New York Jets football telecasts as the team's "official artist in residence." At the 1972 Munich Olympics, he sketched live for ABC's cameras. Four years later at the Montreal games, he painted a huge mural for a national television audience and entered into a deal with Burger King for the distribution of five Neiman posters in conjunction with an Olympics promotion. Purists groaned, but LeRoy himself later said, "Those posters were distributed to kids who had never seen a painting before in their lives. And the Burger King project exposed my work to millions of people, so it was not a bad thing."

In his most prolific years, Neiman created as many as a thousand pieces annually. "I work fast," he said. "Sometimes I do forty sketches at one event. A painting generally takes me from two to three weeks."

It's a point of pride for LeRoy that no one but the artist himself has ever put a brush to one of his canvases. He has painted everything from nudes backstage at the Lido in Paris to the CD box for Frank Sinatra's recording of "Duets". However, he's best known for his sports scenes and portraits of athletes.

"Concentrating on sports helped me," Neiman admits. "There hasn't been any sports art to speak of, so I've had the field pretty much to myself." And he has made the most of that exclusivity, elevating himself to a special status in the world of sports.

When LeRoy Neiman paints an athlete or an event, it's a stamp of importance. He has been the official artist for five Olympics and crafted images of countless Super Bowls, NBA playoffs, the World Series, the Grand Prix at Monaco, Oxford versus Cambridge on the Thames, horseracing, cricket, bullfights, tennis, golf, hockey, billiards, yachting, cycling, and of course, boxing.

It has been said in pugilistic circles that Neiman has a great right hand. Dozens of fight posters and program covers bear his work. At big fights, he has long been a flamboyant presence in a front-row seat, his Salvador-Dali-like mustache every bit as distinctive as Don King's hair.

"I had a mustache before I went into the army and they made me shave it off," LeRoy recounts. "It was a Clark Gable mustache. Clark Gable was one of my heroes. They don't have movie stars like that anymore. Anyway, after the war, I grew it back. Then, in the early 1960s, I had the same publisher as Salvador Dali. We spent some time together, and Dali's wife told me, 'Make up your mind; either cut it shorter or grow it out.' So I let it grow.

Sometimes I tell people it's a virgin mustache, but that's not true. It's a prop, really. That's all."

Because of the mustache, LeRoy is easily recognizable in any setting. Stan Isaacs of *Newsday* once wrote, "Whether one approves of Neiman's work or not, one must agree that he himself is a work of art."

My own experience with LeRoy dates to 1989 when I interviewed him for a biography I was writing about Muhammad Ali. I arrived at his studio as per our appointment and was met with the question, "How do I know you're for real?"

Apparently, someone had recently interviewed LeRoy for what turned out to be a non-existent project and walked out of his studio with several sketches. I produced a letter of authorization from Ali that I had brought with me for verification, and the interview began.

"I saw him in person for the first time in 1962," LeRoy reminisced, thinking back on his introduction to Muhammad. "It was when he fought Billy Daniels at St. Nick's Arena. I went back to this dingy dressing room, opened the door, and there was Ali—he was Cassius Clay then —sitting by himself on a table. I asked if I could draw him and he seemed to think that was a good idea, so I sat down and started to sketch. He was golden, no hair on his body, just beautiful. He looked like a piece of sculpture with no flaw or imperfection. His features and limbs were perfectly proportioned. He was an extraordinarily handsome charismatic man."

Over time, Neiman became a fixture at Ali fights. On one occasion in the dressing room before a bout, Ali asked his trainer Angelo Dundee to turn off the lights because he wanted to see if LeRoy could sketch in the dark.

Meanwhile, after interviewing LeRoy, I saw him frequently at fights and occasional social functions. He was always pleasant and polite. Despite his status in the world of art, he carried himself in a way that made him seem approachable. Thus, on the night of January 15, 2000, when Roy Jones fought David Telesco at Radio City Music Hall, I approached him with a request.

The University of Arkansas Press was about to publish a novel I had written entitled *Finding The Princess*. University presses are notoriously lacking in funds to publicize their books. And a sketch of the author by LeRoy Neiman on the back of the dust jacket would . . . Well, you get the picture.

LeRoy told me to call him at his studio on Monday. A week later, I was sitting in front of the master.

"It bothers me that people don't go to museums," LeRoy said as he sketched. "Painters read books. Maybe you can tell me, why don't more writers go to museums?" Ten minutes after starting, he decided that he didn't like the direction he was going in, put the first sheet of paper aside, and began anew . . . An orange pastel . . . Burnt umber . . . "Got to get the hair right," he said. "And I want a serious look."

*Finding the Princess* was published later that year. I smile whenever I look at the dust jacket.

Meanwhile, like Old Man River, LeRoy keeps rolling along. He is, simply put, the most commercially successful contemporary artist in America. His work is more popular now than ever. To his adoring followers, he can do no wrong. And his level of sustained activity is extraordinary.

LeRoy's artwork has appeared as etchings, sketches, lithographs, silkscreen prints, and paintings. Original Neiman paintings (acrylics, oil, or a mix) can be found for as little as $20,000 but most sell for multiples more. It costs in the neighborhood of $150,000 to commission a 24-by-36-inch Neiman portrait. The 18-by-30-inch "study" he did for me as a favor would run roughly $10,000.

Some favor.

For over a quarter-century, LeRoy has created limited-edition serigraphs (silkscreen prints) which are distributed by Knoedler Publishing. These serigraphs are printed in limited editions (usually 250 to 500 copies), then numbered and signed by the artist. Six years ago, it was calculated that more than 150,000 LeRoy Neiman serigraphs had been purchased and that these prints had an estimated market value exceeding $400-million.

The numbers have gone higher since then.

Several years ago, Neiman created a 6-by-4-foot "Athlete of the Century" painting of Muhammad Ali. One thousand limited-edition serigraphs were signed by Ali and the artist. Five hundred of the serigraphs had tiny additional drawings by LeRoy and Muhammad near the border and are now marketed at $8,000 each. The other five hundred are listed at $6,000. To date, over 700 "Athlete of the Century" serigraphs have been sold. Hammer Galleries, which handles much of Neiman's output, values the original painting at $2-million.

In truth, there has been criticism of Neiman's work. He has been called "the artist who critics love to hate" and "the most belittled artist of our time." Art critic Hilton Kramer was once asked to share a few thoughts on LeRoy Neiman and answered, "That might be difficult. I never think of him."

But the other side of the coin is that Neiman has brought art into more homes than any American artist ever. And it's worth noting that the Smithsonian Institution happily accepted the donation of his archives to its own Archives of American Art. Thus, Neiman is able to say, "I get enough applause that I don't mind the negative things that are said and written about me. Maybe the critics are right, but what am I supposed to do about it? Stop painting? Change my work completely? I go into the studio. There I am at the easel. I enjoy what I'm doing and feel good working. If anyone tarnished my reputation as a serious artist, it was myself by playing around *Playboy*. But I learned a lot from those folks, and I don't regret it." Then he adds, "I'm doing the best work of my life right now. I've never said that before, but now it's true. I've become more reflective."

So there you have it. I've sat on the sofa in my living room next to Muhammad Ali, watching tapes of Ali-Liston, the Rumble in the Jungle, and the Thrilla in Manila. I've walked 18 holes with Arnold Palmer and been interviewed by Howard Cosell. Now I've had my likeness drawn by LeRoy Neiman. What more could any sports fan want?

Maybe someday Michael Jordan will shoot hoops with me. ❏

*For much of the world, by virtue of his position with HBO, Jim Lampley is now the voice of boxing.*

# JIM LAMPLEY IN DEPTH

"In some ways, I'm a mass of contradictions," says Jim Lampley. "The people around me would say that I'm a driven workaholic and largely successful. I see myself as lazy, undermotivated, and largely unfulfilled. When I consider how much some people accomplish in 24 hours, I feel as though I hardly scratch the surface. My sportscasting career is like an accidental gift from the universe. Prominence and upward mobility were given to me. By any objective standard, I'm seen as productive, but I know how much more I could accomplish if I were more disciplined. I have so many different things going on at any given time that I approach almost everything like a kid who crams for final exams. The gap between what I do and what I think I could do if I pushed myself harder is enormous."

In other words, Robert Redford as golden boy Hubbell Gardner in *The Way We Were*. As American as apple pie, everything came so easily to him. Except along the way, there were problems.

"I was an alcoholic at age 17," Lampley acknowledges. "I was a college dropout and eventually a college flunk-out. I was arrested for drugs and had to scramble through correspondence courses to get back into school and pull my life together. There were some difficult times."

Lampley's mother had been married to a military man who was killed in the crash of a transport plane in 1945. "The man who would become my father was my mother's husband's best friend," Lampley explains. "After the accident, he brought my mother a trunk with some of her deceased husband's belongings including his war medals in it. Their relationship evolved from there."

Lampley was born in Hendersonville, North Carolina, on April 8, 1949. Five years later, his father died of cancer. When Jim was 11, he moved with his mother and an older half-brother to Miami. "I grew up as a latch-key kid," Lampley remembers. "My mother sold life insurance to military personnel by going out and banging on doors day and night. We'd have breakfast together every morning and, other than that, I saw her on Friday nights and on weekends. She did the best she could, but I was largely unsupervised."

Lampley's mother was also a sports fan who tried to fill the gaps in her son's life with sports. "She took me to watch the Hendersonville High School

Bearcats," he reminisces. "Football, basketball, and baseball. She got me into reading the Chip Hilton stories. She turned on the television for NFL games and for Dizzy Dean and Pee Wee Reese on Saturday afternoon baseball telecasts. She competed with me to pick winners for the Triple Crown races. And way back in the 1950s, she sat down with me to watch *Gillette Friday Night Fights* on television."

"And the other big thing in our household," Lampley continues, "was reading out loud. It was a family tradition. For reasons I couldn't specify, whenever you wanted someone to know about something you had read, you didn't just tell them about it. You read it to them out loud. So the two basic building blocks of my sports broadcasting career come right out of my childhood, although I never actually identified sportscasting as a career goal."

After graduating from high school, Lampley enrolled at the University of North Carolina. He was an indifferent student, who lost a car and "one of the best collections of rhythm-and-blues recordings ever assembled" in an all-night poker game. He also drank heavily and in 1969, after flunking out of college, was arrested for possession of marijuana.

"That was rock bottom for me," Lampley recalls. "When my mother bailed me out of jail that night, she informed me that she had just spent the last of my father's insurance money to post bail."

Thereafter, Lampley turned his life around. He sobered up, returned to college at UNC, and graduated in 1971. Then he went to work for a three-term congressman named Nick Galifianakis, who was running for the Senate against Jesse Helms.

"No matter what I do," Lampley acknowledges, "I'll never work as hard as that again. The job lasted for 16 months and was the key formative experience in my life. I discovered a lot about myself in that time, and I proved to myself that I could be important."

After the campaign, Lampley returned to the University of North Carolina, where he earned a masters degree in communications in 1974. Then he got lucky. ABC wanted to hire an announcer who was close to college age for side-line reporting on its college football broadcasts. There were national auditions and Lampley prevailed. Suddenly, at age 25, he was on network television, having landed on top of a ladder that most people in the industry spend years trying to climb.

Since then, to use Lampley's words, "It's just been a matter of trying to keep my toes on the surfboard." By 1986, he had been at ABC for 12 years, rising through the ranks to become host of the network's college football telecasts, a frequent studio host for *Wide World of Sports* and the Olympics heir apparent to Jim McKay. Then Howard Cosell abandoned boxing, and ABC worked its way through Don Chevrier, Keith Jackson, and Al Michaels for blow-by-blow commentary. Finally, producer Alex Wallau asked Lampley if he knew anything about boxing. His first fistic assignment, Mike Tyson versus Jesse

Ferguson, came later that year.

In 1987, Dennis Swanson replaced Roone Arledge as president of ABC Sports. Swanson didn't like Lampley's style or salary, so he moved to CBS. There, in addition to sports, Lampley co-anchored the evening news for KCBS-TV in Los Angeles and served as a correspondent for *CBS This Morning*. Next came a stint at NBC involving NFL football, Wimbledon, and the Olympics.

Meanwhile, in March 1988, Lampley began calling fights for HBO and has been doing it ever since. Many in the industry feel that he is under utilized by the cable giant. Still, he's the glue that holds HBO's boxing telecasts together.

Lampley has a lot to do during fights. Sandwiched in between welcoming the audience at the top of the show and signing off at the end, he reads promos, clarifies George Foreman's comments, mediates disputes between Foreman and Larry Merchant, and, most importantly, handles the blow-by-blow commentary.

Former HBO Sports president Seth Abraham, who hired Lampley, declares, "Jim is incredibly utilitarian in terms of the range of things he does well. He has a superb work ethic. He's passionate about his performance. He's one of those rare individuals who lifts the level of everyone else on the telecast by setting them up and then finishing strong himself. He's the star of HBO Boxing."

"Jim raises blow-by-blow to an art form," adds Abraham's successor, Ross Greenburg. "You don't want any other announcer at the microphone for a big fight."

Lampley, for his part, opines, "Calling a fight is the single most subjective job in sportscasting. There are no point counts while the action is going on, no first downs or yard-markers. But beyond that, I try to be what I call a synthesist sportscaster. That means communicating both the details of the event and the societal backdrop. The single thing I'm proudest of with regard to my work at HBO is that, in 15 years, I've never stopped improving in my ability to see the fights and understand what's happening in them."

Meanwhile, Lampley's broadcasting partner Larry Merchant observes, "Jim has a terrific understanding of the broad picture and near total recall of minutiae like obscure names and dates. And I've never been on a telecast with him where I thought he just mailed it in. It's like that old line from Joe DiMaggio about how he worked as hard as he did all the time because there might be someone in the stands that day who had never seen him play baseball before and might never see him play again. That's Jim. He might not get it completely right every time; none of us do. But I've never seen him get it wrong either. He's a true professional, who makes what's really a very complicated job look effortless. There are very few people in any sport who can do what he does as well as he does."

Lampley, in turn, says simply, "When I go on the air at HBO, I'm backed by

90 people who are working to make me look good. That makes it relatively easy for me to do a good job."

Lampley has been married three times. His first marriage (1970-1978) was to his college sweetheart. "After we split up," he notes, "she married my attorney and best friend, and he's still my best friend." Then he wed a "nice Jewish girl from Brooklyn" (1979-1989) and had two daughters. Brooke, age 23, graduated from Harvard in 2002 and is in a fine arts PhD. program at Yale. Victoria, age 16, is a high-school student.

TV news anchorwoman Bree Walker was Lampley's third wife (1990-2000). Bree has a daughter, Andrea, age 14, from a previous marriage. She and Jim also have a son, Aaron, age 11.

Lampley and Walker were divorced three years ago, but remain close friends. He believes that, at some point in the not-too-distant future, they'll remarry. "For once in my life," he says hopefully, "I'd like to make a relationship work; not just for Bree and myself, but also to set an example for my children.

"Through all my divorces," Lampley continues, "I'm pleased to say that I've remained in my children's lives in a meaningful way and I think I've done a good job of parenting. That's the most important thing in life to me. I ask myself sometimes, 'If it were to all end tomorrow, what would I need to feel that my life has been worthwhile?' And my answer is always, 'I'd be satisfied if my children have self-esteem and productive lives.'"

That consideration has special meaning where Andrea and Aaron are concerned. Bree Walker has a hand and foot condition known as ectrodactyly that caused her to be born with her digits in jumbled clumps instead of the common assortment of fingers and toes. Both of her children inherited the condition from their mother.

"I've spent 30 years in a world covering the pursuit of physical perfection," Lampley says. "And I live in a family where physical perfection is out of the question. But Andrea and Aaron are wonderful people. And in addition to being wonderful, they win spelling bees and speech contests. Andrea is a terrific soccer player. Aaron is an avid fisherman. How he ties knots, I don't know; but he does it and does it well. So there's spiritual and emotional satisfaction for all of us and it creates a balancing perspective in my life."

Lampley's political principles are also important to him. "I come from white racist southern stock," he acknowledges. "There were Ku Klux Klan members on my family tree. But I came of age in the 1960s, which was an era when liberal politics were respected. I have a well-developed sense of justice that was nurtured by living my formative years in the south during the civil rights movement. My heroes when I was growing up were Martin Luther King Jr. and others who were part of that dramatic pageant.

"I hate the notion that race is an omnipresent backdrop to American life," Lampley continues. "Exploitation of the weak angers me. I believe in government for all the people, not just some of them. I believe in the redistribution of wealth rather than its concentration in the hands of the rich and powerful. The minimum wage should be higher, and so should taxes on rich people. Whenever I hear rich people complaining about taxes, I think they must have never visited any place else. We're the most under-taxed people in the world. It's not an imposition on my personal place in the culture to pay taxes. At the end of the day, it's all about, Do we want to share, or do we not want to share? We're the richest nation on earth. Why are so many people poor here?

"Gun control is, to me, the single most irrational element of American society and politics," Lampley posits. "We're the only nation in the world that thinks there's something good about the proliferation of guns. I'm in favor of gun control and don't understand why everybody else isn't. I have very powerful mixed feelings on the issue of abortion. I've paid for two abortions in my life and lost a lot of sleep over them, although I'm sure the women lost a lot more. But at the end of the day, I support a woman's right to choose. Where Iraq is concerned, I care deeply about the wellbeing of the men and women in our armed forces, but no one has proven to my satisfaction that immediate combat was necessary.

"I'm a 1960s liberal," Lampley says, summing up his political perspective. "And I think that one of the great things about the Bush Administration is that it's going to make liberalism respectable again. We need system fallout here in America. We need something that will shake our government to its core."

Lampley seems to be a man in constant motion. Longtime friend and boxing publicist Bill Caplan notes, "I've never seen him relax. He's always primed and ready to fire."

As part of that active swirl, Lampley will serve as NBC's daytime host for the 2004 Olympics in Athens, his twelfth Olympics assignment (six winter and six summer). He also recently signed a four-year contract extension with HBO that ensures his presence as the network's blow-by-blow commentator through May 2007.

Meanwhile, in recent years, Lampley has devoted an increasing amount of time and energy to Crystal Spring, a production company that he founded in 1995. Lampley likens running the company to "the daily chore of pushing boulders up a hill." Still, Crystal Spring has produced one film, is in production on another, and has development deals for three more.

(Journalistic ethics require the notation here that I'm the author of a novel entitled *Mark Twain Remembers*. At Lampley's suggestion, Steven Spielberg read the book and purchased film rights for DreamWorks. Crystal Spring is involved with the project.)

Meanwhile, with regard to the sweet science, Lampley declares, "Boxing on HBO has become my primary sportscasting identity and now virtually my only one. I expect the rest of my sportscasting career to consist of calling fights."

And what might that lead to?

"The honesty of my relationship with the audience is important to me," Lampley answers. "Someone asked me recently whether I ever got so fed up with boxing that I thought of pulling a Howard Cosell and just walking away. The answer is, 'Yes, every week.' I'd like to figure out now how to be more of a positive force in the sport and not just part of the scene. I want to be able to give back to boxing, and particularly to the fighters. By the end of next year, Crystal Spring should provide the bulk of my income. And the better my production company does, the braver my commentary will be in terms of resisting the political pressures of boxing and of HBO.

"I'm privileged to work for a company where honesty on the air is a valued and important tradition," Lampley continues. "But I can see where I might push the envelope a bit more in the future, and I'm excited about what that might mean to the content of the show. Sports journalism in general is bigger, broader, and more varied than ever before. But there's a crisis in the print media's coverage of boxing in that the gatekeepers consider the audience for boxing too small to commit the resources necessary for responsible journalistic coverage. That means, for the great mass of consumers, televised boxing is boxing. And for many people, HBO Boxing is boxing, with the result that HBO's role in the sport is of distorted public significance. If we do something right at HBO, it's good for boxing. But if we mess up, it has the potential to cause considerable harm. I can't think of another telecast in any sport that has as much influence within the sports world as HBO Boxing. That's a great privilege, but the opportunity it gives us comes with the responsibility to do our job right." ❏

*Larry Merchant fills the number-two slot in one of the best announcing teams in sports.*

# LARRY MERCHANT

Another HBO boxing telecast has begun. Everything is hot. Pulsating theme music, computer-generated graphics, sizzling video clips, the electric voice of Jim Lampley. Then Lampley delivers the familiar words, "Working with me tonight, as always, HBO boxing analyst Larry Merchant." And suddenly, the screen is given over to a white-haired man in his early seventies who speaks in a slow measured cadence and seems like a period piece from another era. Larry Merchant is on the air.

Merchant is man of personal idiosyncrasies who, by his own account, has never smoked a cigarette, had a cup of coffee, or eaten a peanut butter and jelly sandwich in his life. He's a commentator with a self described "built-in bullshit detector" who declares, "Despite the reality of what goes on inside the ring, the business of boxing is based on illusion. And if you want an example, I'll give you an example. The last big fight that Mike Tyson won was against Michael Spinks 15 years ago."

Merchant is also one of the best in the world at what he does for HBO.

Merchant was born in New York on February 11, 1931. His father ran a laundry and dry-cleaning business. His mother was a legal secretary. As a boy, he was interested in astronomy and opera. More conventionally, he played football for Lafayette High School in Brooklyn and fondly recalls a 62-yard touchdown run at Ebbetts Field in his final high school game.

"When I was a kid, "Merchant says, "my heroes were sportswriters. Dan Parker, W. C. Heinz, Red Smith, Jimmy Cannon, Jack McKinney, A. J. Liebling. And I was kind of romantic about wanting to leave New York and go far away. My imagination took me as far as Oklahoma."

Merchant enrolled at the University of Oklahoma, and was a walk on for an Oklahoma football team that was in the midst of a 31-game winning streak. In his sophomore year, he went to the Sugar Bowl as a last-string halfback and watched from the bench as the Sooners beat North Carolina 14-6. The following season, he injured his shoulder in a scrimmage, cried for three days, and decided to refocus his energies on journalism.

Ultimately, Merchant became editor-in-chief of *The Oklahoma Daily*, one of the best college newspapers in the country. "But a week before my term expired," he remembers, "I was removed as editor because of a series of articles I was running about McCarthyism and a loyalty-oath requirement that had been passed by the state legislature."

After graduating from college with a degree in journalism, Merchant returned to Brooklyn where he received token payment as backfield coach for the Lafayette High School football team. "My brother was captain of the team," he recalls. "And a fellow named Sandy Koufax, who played basketball for Lafayette, was one of his friends. Sandy was in our home a lot, and I saw him play basketball from time to time. Baseball was his second sport then."

After that, it was two years in the United States Army highlighted by a year in Germany as a sportswriter for *Stars and Stripes*. Then, in 1953, Merchant was discharged from the military and took a job as sports editor for the *Wilmington News* in Wilmington, North Carolina. "Not long after I started," he remembers, "the managing editor told me, 'The only time you can put a picture of a Negro in the paper is if Jackie Robinson hits five home runs.' I didn't stay around long after that."

A six-month stint with The Associated Press followed. Then, Merchant went to work as an assistant photo editor for the *Philadelphia Daily News* and, at age 26, was named sports editor.

"I probably did the best work of my life in Philadelphia," says Merchant. "I hired some terrific writers and wrote a column five days a week. One of the things I'd learned from reading Hemingway is that the losers are often more interesting than the winners and sometimes even more noble, and I put that philosophy to work. I was one of the new, young, irreverent, hands-on writers, who got in the trenches and wanted to know how things really worked. Philadelphia is also where I got my education in the culture of boxing. Archie Moore used to write me long letters filled with philosophical musings and historical insights. Archie was an extraordinary character in addition to being a great fighter, and he helped me to see boxing through a larger prism."

Eventually, Merchant relinquished the role of sports editor to concentrate on his column and a morning radio show. Then, in 1965, he moved to New York with a significant increase in salary to replace Leonard Shecter, who was retiring as a columnist for the *New York Post*.

Over the next 10 years, while at the *Post*, Merchant wrote three books, hosted a radio show, and did some television commentary in Boston (his first TV work). "But there came a time when I started to feel burnt out as far as the column was concerned," he acknowledges. "And I became less and less eager to go to the ballpark."

In 1975, Merchant left the *Post* with the intention of writing books about Muhammad Ali and Oklahoma football. "But the next day," he remembers, "I got telephone calls from CBS and NBC and wound up as a reporter and commentator for one of NBC's weekend sports shows." Two years later, he was named producer of the network's Sunday-afternoon NFL studio program.

"By then," Merchant continues, "I had a girlfriend who was an actress and had gone out to California. For a while we were bi-coastal, but eventually I moved to the west coast. I wrote a general-interest column for the *Los Angeles Herald-Examiner* for a year. Then the cable revolution began and, in 1978, I started commuting to New York two or three times a month to host a show on USA Network called *Sports Probe*. That same year, I got a call from Ross Greenburg, who asked if I was interested in trying my hand at boxing commentary."

Merchant's first fight for HBO was James Scott versus Eddie Gregory at Rahway State Prison on October 12, 1978. He has been a presence on the cable network ever since.

"My philosophy of commentary," Merchant explains, "is to try to convey who the fighters are and what the event is about. It's not my job to be a cheerleader. I'm skeptical of hype and false narrative. I don't avoid talking about corruption in boxing. When a fighter performs poorly, I tell the audience that I think it's so. I have a lot of respect for the courage it takes to be a fighter, and I never lose sight of the fact that the fighters are the stars of the show. But when a young man enters boxing, he promises to take great risks and make great sacrifices in exchange for commensurate rewards, and he has to be judged on his performance. I look at the sports world as perfect with its imperfections. I don't make things up. My goal is to get viewers involved and be honest at the same time. And I have to say, it's both rare and precious to me that the people who run HBO Sports have always encouraged me to be myself and say my say even when that makes things more difficult for HBO."

There have been two rough spots in Merchant's tenure at HBO. The first came in 1990, when Don King and Mike Tyson demanded that he be removed from HBO telecasts of Tyson's fights.

By Merchant's recollection, "After Tyson lost to Buster Douglas, King tried to overturn the knockout and Tyson went along with him. My view was that it wasn't HBO's mission to promote and market Mike Tyson, so I asked a lot of painful questions. Mike and Don didn't like it. And Tyson at that time was hanging out with people like Eddie Murphy, who could snap their fingers and get a director fired on the spot. So when Tyson and King were renegotiating their contract, Tyson decided to flex his muscles and told HBO that he didn't want me to do his fights. HBO, to its credit, stood by me, and Tyson left."

Seth Abraham (the person at HBO primarily responsible for the King-Tyson negotiations) recalls, "For 16 months, [HBO Sports vice president] Bob Greenway and I had been negotiating with Don King and his lawyer for an extension of Tyson's contract. On a number of occasions during those negotiations, Don referred to getting rid of Larry. And each time, we told him, 'That's not on the table. Let's move on to the next issue.' So the question disappeared. Finally, in October of 1990, we reached a tentative agreement on a 10-fight deal for $100-million. King and I had dinner in Chinatown. I gave Don the contract, which he said he'd bring to Atlantic City to review with

Tyson. And the next morning at 10 o'clock, my telephone rang. It was Don on the phone with Mike and John Horne. Tyson began the conversation by saying, 'I'm so happy I'm staying with HBO and that I won't have to deal with Larry Merchant anymore.' I said, 'Mike, that's not in the deal.' Then the screaming began. Don, Mike, and John Horne shouted and yelled at me for a half hour. I wouldn't budge, and a deal that had taken 16 months to negotiate blew up in 30 minutes."

Ross Greenburg (Abraham's successor as president of HBO Sports) expresses the view that, "It wasn't really about Larry. King was looking for an exit strategy because he wanted to start his own pay-per-view operation to make more money for himself. And to do that, he had to take Tyson to Showtime. Larry was a convenient excuse, that's all."

But Abraham has a different belief and states, "I think that Tyson made his feelings about Larry known to Don early in the game and that Don misread both Mike and HBO. He thought that getting rid of Larry wouldn't be a big deal to us as part of a $100-million contract extension or, if it was, that it wouldn't matter much to Tyson in the face of a $100-million deal. I honestly believe that it was Mike who killed the contract."

The second rough spot for Merchant involved the now-famous mariachi band incident.

As Merchant recalls, "In 1997, Oscar De La Hoya challenged Pernell Whitaker for Whitaker's welterweight title, and the whole promotion was about Oscar. That was understandable, since Oscar is such a big attraction. But then I found out that they were going to bring a mariachi band into the ring to play music for him and do nothing for Pernell. I thought that was unfair to Whitaker, and the way I expressed that thought was to say, 'As wonderful as mariachi music is, in this setting it sucks.' Anyway, Bob Arum was in negotiations with HBO at the time and he was also trying to ingratiate De La Hoya with all the Mexican fans who didn't root for him. Arum decided that my remark was something he could exploit to his own economic advantage, so he turned it into a cause celebre. I had some conversations afterward with Seth Abraham and Ross Greenburg and made a public apology, and that was the end of it."

"Larry could have chosen his words differently," says Lou DiBella, who was senior vice president for HBO Sports at the time. "And if he had it to do over again, he'd probably use different verbiage. But in the end, it was much ado about nothing. Larry wasn't demeaning anybody's culture. He was expressing the view that, in a fight between a great champion and a charismatic challenger, the champion should get his due. The whole thing was blown out of proportion by Arum as a negotiating ploy. That's what really sucked."

Abraham concurs with DiBella and adds, "I was sitting at the fight with Arum, so obviously, neither of us heard the broadcast live. But it didn't take long for us to hear about it. And what happened, really, was Arum saw Larry's comment as giving him the opportunity to renegotiate Oscar's contract with HBO. And we did renegotiate, not by changing the fights that were already in place, but by extending the contract with a higher license fee for the additional fights. You know, boxing promoters are incredibly resourceful. Larry gave Arum a hammer, and Bob hit HBO over the head with it."

And there was one more repercussion.

"Oscar's next fight was against David Kamau in San Antonio," Abraham remembers. "Things were pretty inflamed down there. There were some threats, and we thought there might be a security risk for Larry and the entire HBO Boxing crew. So I made the decision that, as a precautionary measure, Larry should sit out that one show. I wanted to let tempers cool down a bit."

Merchant is always willing to speak his mind. Thus, when asked to provide capsule IDs, he attaches the following labels to key participants in the aforementioned incidents:

Don King—"An evil genius"

Mike Tyson—"An emotionally-disturbed washed-up sociopath"

Bob Arum—"A brilliant scorpion"

Oscar De La Hoya—"A terrific fighter and an interesting kid"

Lou DiBella—"The kind of guy we'd all like to be if we had the time"

Ross Greenburg—"To the television manor born"

Seth Abraham—"A visionary executive and a friend"

Meanwhile, Merchant's contract runs through June 2007, at which time he'll be 76 years old. And the people who have worked most closely with him at HBO are full of admiration for him:

● Seth Abraham: "There are very few people who know as much about boxing as Larry, and I'd be hard-pressed to name anybody who knows more. I'm not talking now about rattling off statistics. I'm talking about the essence of the sport. And Larry never gets in the way of the story. He lets the fight carry the show."

● Ross Greenburg: "Larry is capable of turning a phrase in the heat of battle in a way that makes a broadcast even more dramatic than it might otherwise be. HBO has always felt that we have to give our talent the ability to speak their mind. And Larry's tell-it-like-it-is journalistic attitude is enormously important to us."

● Lou DiBella: "Larry has been the most consistent commentator in the business over the past generation. He knows the business. He conveys the truth. He's television with a journalistic sensitivity; the best of both worlds. In fact, I'll go one step further and say that Larry and Jim Lampley are the best broadcast combination in the history of boxing."

● Jim Lampley: "Larry is one of the most intellectually disciplined people I've ever met. He's a creative skeptic who expresses the unexpressed doubt and guides our telecast in a way that increases our integrity. By his commentary, Larry assures the audience that we, as announcers, won't be improperly influenced by the business interests that surround us. And he knows as much about the truths of boxing as any person I know."

And Merchant's thoughts?

"I find it a little surprising that I still love to do this," he says in closing. "But I'm not anywhere near to being burned out. It's all still fascinating and exciting to me." ❑

*The public-at-large doesn't know Tami Cotel. But she's integral to HBO's boxing telecasts and has seen more of the sweet science than most fight fans ever will.*

# TAMI COTEL

When Lennox Lewis and Vitali Klitschko meet in the ring on June 21, 2003, one of the most important people in the arena will be a 48-year-old woman with long brown hair wearing jeans and a form-fitting top. Tami Cotel is the production coordinator for HBO Boxing, and virtually everything that happens on fight night will bear her imprint.

Cotel was born in Chicago and grew up in Phoenix. Her father was a jeweler; her mother a real estate broker. "I had a rough childhood that I don't talk about much," she acknowledges. "In high school, I got into theater to help overcome my insecurities. To pay for college, I worked as an actress and a dental assistant."

In 1975, Cotel left Phoenix for Las Vegas, which she regarded as the entertainment capital of the world. "I auditioned for some of the girlie shows," she recalls. "Follies Bergiere, Hallelujah Hollywood, Lido De Paris. If you made the top-10 cut at a dance audition, the next thing that happened was someone would say, 'Okay, everything off from the waist up.' You couldn't be just a dancer. You had to be a topless dancer, and you had to have a decent cup size. I made it to the final cut for every show I auditioned for, but I wouldn't take my top off. I was afraid my mother would find out and kill me, so I had to do something else to support myself."

Thus began a career in the hotel industry that ranged from accounting to sales to a front-desk job. Cotel even took sports bets at the Stardust Hotel and Casino. Then, in 1982, things got scary. A benign tumor was removed from the back of her neck. In the process, seven nerves were severed from Tami's spine, leaving her partially paralyzed from the waist up. "I could use my hands, but not my upper arms," she remembers. "I could move my head up and down, but not from side to side."

Three years of intensive therapy, six days a week, followed. Some muscles never came back, but other muscles were trained to compensate for their loss. "By 1985, I was healthy again," Cotel continues. "But as my physical condition improved, I realized I was unhappy because I wasn't doing anything creative anymore. I was making good money, but I felt like a robot."

In 1985, Cotel left the hotel industry to work as a runner for a local production company called Mr. Camera. "My mother always told me that the most important qualities to succeed at any job are reliability, honesty, and common sense," she explains. "I figured I had those qualities, so why not give it a try."

One of Mr. Camera's clients was HBO. In 1985, Larry Holmes defended his heavyweight title against David Bey, and the cable network hired Mr. Camera to prepare a short profile piece on Holmes. While the piece was in production, Ross Greenburg (then executive producer of HBO Sports) met Cotel and asked if she would work the fighters' dressing rooms on fight night.

"I said 'yes,' " Cotel remembers. "Then Ross decided that HBO shouldn't use me in the locker room because I was a woman. So, instead, they let me work the holding area, where the fighters stand after they leave the locker room and are waiting to start their ring walk. The first fighter I tried to hold back was David Bey, who knocked me over and pushed his way to the ring. That was my introduction to boxing. I thought I'd never work for HBO again. But after that, every time HBO did a fight in Las Vegas, Ross hired me for the holding area. And I started doing all the other things that no one else wanted to do; little parts of everybody else's job. Getting stats on fighters, making telephone calls. If Ross or anyone else screamed for something, I'd run and get it. Ross was the first producer I worked for in live television. He scared me to death, but I learned from him what live television is all about.

"Then, in 1986," Cotel continues, "Larry Holmes fought a rematch against Michael Spinks. Larry lost on a decision and left the ring before he was interviewed. Ross was screaming, 'Somebody fucking get Larry Holmes. He's leaving the ring.' So I ran to the locker room, got there before Larry, and picked up a headset. Larry came in. Someone closed the door behind him and said no interviews. Larry was crying. His family was crying. I felt so bad for them that I started crying too. Larry looked at me and said, 'Tami, don't cry, honey. Tell HBO I'll give them an interview.' From that point on, it was okay with HBO if I was in the locker room."

Cotel now has a company of her own. She does a variety of production work apart from boxing, but HBO is her primary client. The network hires her as an independent contractor, and she books everything else around their boxing schedule. She has worked all but two of HBO's fight cards since 1985.

Cotel's position is variously described as stage manager, floor director, or production coordinator. Generally, she arrives on site on Thursday evening for a Saturday night fight. After checking into her hotel, she touches base with the local state athletic commission, confirms the names of the referees and judges who will work the televised fights, and contacts each fighter's camp regarding the fighter meetings that will take place on Friday with Jim Lampley, Larry Merchant, and George Foreman.

Friday is more hectic. Tami makes sure that everyone shows up at the fighter meetings; attends the weigh-in; talks with each fighter's camp about

HBO coming into the dressing room with a camera on fight night; advises each camp as to when the fighters have to be in the ring; determines which trainers will be hooked up to microphones; arranges for the judges to be on camera the following night; and gets the information necessary for HBO's on-air graphics. Then comes an evening meeting attended by the entire HBO production crew.

On Saturday, things turn from hectic to frantic. Cotel arrives at the arena six hours before a fight. The first thing she does is check out the location of the dressing rooms. Then she times each fighter's ring-walk and, if it's a circuitous route, tapes arrows on the floor. This can be complicated when Naseem Hamed is planning to fly down to the ring in a harness from the upper reaches of the MGM Grand Arena. She also explains to security personnel that a cameraman will be walking backward in front of the fighters and that no one should get in the cameraman's way or block his view.

During the next five hours, Cotel makes certain that the house public address system has a properly-labeled audiotape with each fighter's ring walk music; puts the judges on videotape so their faces can be shown on air at the same time as their introduction by the ring announcer; reviews the timing of the referee's dressing room instructions with the local commission; talks with the ring announcer to ensure that what he says in the ring will have matching graphics on screen for home viewers; reminds each fighters' camp of the required time for the fighter to be ready to walk to the ring; and gets each fighter to weigh-in on HBO's fight-night scale. All of these tasks are complicated by the fact that every fight card involves different variables depending on the site and identity of the fighters and promoter.

Then comes the actual broadcast. Cotel puts this part of her job in perspective when she observes, "There are certain things that television needs and certain things that fighters need. Timing is crucial to a live broadcast. But a lot of television people don't understand how important timing is for an athlete. It always amazes me how, at every event, everyone at HBO works together and the fighters cooperate to form this puzzle that comes together so perfectly the minute we go on the air."

Meanwhile, Roy Jones speaks for his ring brethren when he says, "Tami's got a job where the person who has it can be a nuisance and a bother and in everybody's way, but she's not like that. Tami makes you want to help her."

Once a broadcast is underway, Cotel walks the first TV fight to the ring. While it's in progress, she alternates between watching from the HBO production area and revisiting the dressing rooms of the fighters who will be in the next televised fight. After the bout ends, she climbs into the ring and, if the fight has gone the distance, looks at the ring announcer's cue card. Then she whispers the result to the production truck over her headset so a fight-result graphic can be prepared in advance. Next, she brings the winner, and sometimes the loser, to Merchant for a post-fight interview. And while Merchant's interview is going on, she races back to the dressing room to repeat the process for fight number two.

At times, things get physical, particularly in the ring after a fight when it seems as though every hanger-on is rushing to get on camera. Tami has blocked, pushed, and pulled countless entourage members out of view. She has crawled between people's legs to force a sight-line between Merchant and the HBO television monitor. She has been knocked down, shoved, tripped, put in armlocks, and suffered bruises, sprained wrists, and cracked ribs. On one occasion, away from the ring, she was urinated upon. That occurred in Tijuana, where inebriated fans relieved themselves by pissing over a railing onto the floor of the fighter holding area below. Tami simply got a tarpaulin, put it over her head, and continued with her work.

Over the years, Cotel has earned the trust of virtually everyone in boxing. Before each fight, she's in dressing rooms where things get pretty raw. There are dozens of lurid stories she could tell, but she never tells them. It's almost as though there's a fighter-Tami privilege along the lines of the confidentiality one expects from a doctor, lawyer, or priest.

Cotel's most memorable moment in boxing came when George Foreman knocked out Michael Moorer to reclaim the heavyweight championship of the world. "I remember going into George's dressing room before that fight," she recounts. "His protective cup had ripped; and George was sitting there with a needle and thread, very patiently sewing it himself. George is one of my favorite people. He has a such a huge heart. When he won; oh my God, what an exciting wonderful moment that was.

"The riot at Madison Square Garden after the first Bowe-Golota fight was very scary," Cotel says, continuing her review of memorable moments. "I was afraid something horrible was going to happen that night."

And of course, there was Lennox Lewis versus Mike Tyson in Memphis. As Iron Mike entered the arena, millions of people watched on television as he grabbed Tami by the arm, yanked her forward, and kissed her before she could pull away.

"That wasn't what it seemed," Cotel says. "I've worked with Mike since he started on HBO years ago. He knows that one of the rules of my job is, I'm never ever supposed to be on camera. So when he came in, he saw me, pulled me into the shot, kissed me, and said like a little kid, 'I got you on camera.' "

Meanwhile, ask people at HBO about Cotel and the accolades flow like wine at a Roman orgy.

● Ross Greenburg: "Tami does the job of five people; and she gets HBO into places we simply wouldn't get into without her. On the night of a fight, fighters aren't in the mood to do interviews. Trainers don't want cameras in the locker room. We get access because of Tami and the respect that the fighters and everyone around them has for her."

● Rick Bernstein [executive producer]: "We're stuck in the truck on the night of a fight, so Tami is our eyes and ears in the arena. And we trust her completely. I'll never forget the sense of urgency yet control in her voice during the Bowe-Golota riot at Madison Square Garden. All hell broke loose. Announcers' headsets were flying. And through it all, Tami weathered the storm, got the right people on camera, and helped keep the telecast seamless."

● Dave Harmon [senior producer]: "Tami is one of the classic behind the scenes mechanics who the people at home don't know about who makes HBO what it is. There are times when it seems like she can arrange anything. I don't know anyone else who can do what she does."

● Jon Crystal [producer]: "Tami is a marvel. She makes things happen. Every time someone tells me over my headset that we can't do something, I go to Tami and she says, 'Okay; I'll handle it.' And she does. She gets along with everyone. Fighters, trainers, managers, promoters, referees, judges, state commissioners, world sanctioning body personnel. Having her onboard brings peace of mind to a very difficult production process."

● Thomas Odelfelt [producer]: "Tami never complains; she never moans. She's like a ray of sunshine on our telecasts. And she can get people to do almost anything. We used to talk to the fighters about getting on our unofficial scale right before a fight, and they'd say, 'No way.' Then Tami would talk to them and, 10 seconds later, they were on the scale. She's amazing."

● Marc Payton [director]: "Tami is reliable, tireless, polite, and thoroughly professional. You've heard the expression that everyone is replaceable. That might not apply to Tami. I depend on her so much. We all do."

● Jim Lampley: "Tami is the one totally indispensable element of HBO's boxing telecasts. If Larry Merchant goes off to his daughter's college graduation, if I'm indisposed, if the producer is in jail; all of that can be covered. The one thing that can't be covered is if Tami isn't there. She's integral and vital to our telecasts. And the primary reason is that, on top of everything else she does, the fighters trust Tami. From the moment HBO arrives on site to the moment we leave the air, the face the fighters look for is Tami's."

● Larry Merchant: "Tami does an amazing job of dealing with fighters, trainers, promoters, and God knows who else, most of whom are in states of emotion ranging from high tension to crisis when she deals with them. There's fight stuff; there's television stuff. There are time crunches and raging egos. You're talking about live television so things have to happen on a certain schedule, and Tami makes them happen. She gets jostled around physically and verbally, but always manages to keep the show together. And after a fight, when I go into the ring in the midst of what's sometimes absolute chaos, I know that she'll have everything the way it should be. The fact that HBO puts Tami on planes and sends her all over the world to do what she does tells you how important she is to our telecasts."

● Harold Lederman: "Tami brings so many intangibles to the table and does so many things that most people never see. She works long hours. She's terrific at everything. There are even rumors that Tami scores the fights for me, but I categorically deny that."

At the close of each HBO Boxing telecast, Jim Lampley reads the primary production credits. Then the silent credits appear on the screen. "Tami Cotel, Production Coordinator" is the first of the non-spoken credits. "I would love it," says Lampley, "if some day in the very near future, the powers that-be at HBO instructed me to read Tami's credit out loud. She deserves it." ❏

*Flip Homansky is one of the people behind the scenes who make boxing work.*

# FLIP HOMANSKY

In the world of boxing, a handful of men and women adhere to a standard of excellence that separates them from the pack. Edwin "Flip" Homansky is one of those people.

Homansky was born in Savannah, Georgia, on July 7, 1950. His father owned a small liquor store in a rough part of town and opened regularly at six a.m. to accommodate the longshoremen who were going to and from work. Flip grew up in and around Savannah, went to college at Tulane, and graduated from the Medical College of Georgia. In 1979, after finishing his residency, he moved to Las Vegas to, in his words, "spend a year, have a good time, and make some money." He never left.

Homansky's first job in Las Vegas was in the emergency room at Valley Hospital. "Being in a good emergency room is a great experience," he says. "There's the adrenaline factor, and I enjoy the team aspect of it. In an emergency room, everyone has to work together. There are times when it's hard emotionally, but I'm pretty good at compartmentalizing. There's no way you can dwell on any one case that went well or poorly when someone in the next room needs you immediately."

Over time, Homansky rose through the ranks to become director of the emergency room at Valley Hospital. He's now chief of staff for the entire facility and the administrator for three other area hospitals. He has overseen the transition from emergency rooms that were run in haphazard fashion staffed by doctors who couldn't succeed in other positions to emergency rooms that are characterized by state-of-the-art procedures, practices, and standards of care. But his public image has been shaped largely by professional boxing.

"I'd always loved boxing," explains Homansky. "And if I was going to be in Las Vegas, what better world to be involved with?"

That involvement began when someone gave him a ticket for a fight at Caesar's Palace. "It was one of those Saturday afternoon network television cards," Homansky reminisces. "I don't remember who was fighting. I went and waited until it was over. Then I went down to the ringside area and told several people that I wanted to get involved. I met Donald Romeo, who was the Nevada State Athletic Commission medical director. And from that day on, I just hung around. Back then, the fights were run by a very inbred group, and they didn't seem to think there was a place for me. But I figured I'd wait them out. I went to every open meeting. I worked the amateurs. I knew that, if I learned the fights and fighters and all the other aspects of being a ring physician, eventually they'd call on me. That's the secret to everything I've done, really. Be available; never say no; and when you get an opportunity, do the best job you can."

In the early 1980s, only one physician was assigned to ringside for most fights. In Nevada, that physician was Donald Romeo.

"But I was always there for him," Homansky remembers. "Anything he needed, I did. And I was constantly running back to the dressing rooms to see if anyone needed help. As a doctor, you can learn a lot about boxing in dressing rooms after a fight if you sit down and talk with the fighters about what happened and why. You understand handwraps much better when you see them cut off after a four-round fight and witness first hand how they're molded and what a bad handwrap does to a kid's hands. You understand why a fighter should keep his hands up when you look at a left eye that's been blasted by jabs all night."

Homansky's first opportunity to serve as an actual ring physician for a professional bout came at the Silver Slipper; a small casino on a plot of land that's now The Mirage. Every Wednesday night, the Silver Slipper hosted club fights; no TV, just a couple of hundred fans. One evening, Romeo was out of town and Homansky got the nod. Thereafter, he continued to learn from the older doctor and began getting assignments of his own. His breakthrough bout came on May 15, 1983, when Bobby Chacon successfully defended the WBC junior-lightweight title on a 12-round decision over Cornelius Boza-Edwards.

"It was a beautiful brutal bloody fight," Homansky remembers. "Back and forth the whole 12 rounds. Both fighters were bleeding profusely. There were times when I could have stopped it. And I found out later that Ferdie Pacheco, who was the color commentator for NBC, blasted me for letting the fight go on. But I allowed them to continue and I'm glad I did. It was the right call for both fighters and the right call for boxing because it was a historic memorable wonderful fight. After that," Homansky continues, "I was treated very differently by the boxing establishment. In boxing, either you're accepted as someone who can handle a situation or you're not; and that fight was a turning point for me."

Several years later, Romeo suffered a stroke and Homansky became chief ringside physician and de facto medical director for the Nevada State Athletic Commission. He held those positions until two years ago, when he was elevated to the Commission itself by Nevada Governor Kenny Guinn. The longevity of Homansky's ring career is best demonstrated by noting that he has served during the tenure of four executive directors (Roy Tennyson, Harold Buck, Chuck Minker, and Marc Ratner) and six chairmen (Sig Rogich, Duke Durden, Duane Ford, Elias Ghanem, Jim Nave, and Luther Mack).

Of the fights he has seen, several stand out in Homansky's mind. "The first Leonard-Hearns bout was memorable for the intensity of it and the effort of both boxers," he recalls. "The saddest fight I was ever at was Muhammad Ali against Larry Holmes. Many of Mike Tyson early fights left an indelible impression because of Mike's ferocity."

And then there are the ring deaths, most notably, Jimmy Garcia at the hands of Gabriel Ruelas in 1995. Homansky was the ring physician assigned to Garcia's corner.

"I believe that acute injuries are going to happen in boxing no matter what safeguards are in place," Homansky says reflectively. "But they can be minimized; and every time there's a catastrophe, I try to learn from it. When a tragedy happens, initially I treat the situation clinically and analytically. I compartmentalize; I second guess myself. It's a personal process. Then later, when it's easier to deal with, I open up little bits and pieces and deal with it emotionally; but only in bits and pieces, never in toto. It's a long hard personal process."

Over the past two years, Homansky has become a significant presence as a boxing regulator. His vote against licensing Mike Tyson to fight Lennox Lewis in Las Vegas was considered a crucial factor in swaying the votes of two other commissioners en route to the final 4-1 tally against Tyson. "I'm a political animal," Homansky acknowledges, discussing that decision and others he has been called upon to make. "I read the players and size up situations to determine where the strengths and weaknesses are and how I fit into things. But none of that is worth anything unless you use it to advance what's right. That's important to me. I try to do the right thing. I know that sounds trite. But in any situation, I want to know what the right thing to do is and then get as close to that as possible."

Homansky is often frustrated by the overall quality of boxing regulation in the United States. "You can't handle boxing the way you handle a state dairy commission," he says. "No one can function as a regulator in this sport unless he or she fully understands the nature of the sport, the complexity of the financial arrangements, and what the participants go through before, during, and after every fight. The Association of Boxing Commissions is well intentioned but has no true enforcement power. The Ali Act approaches boxing piecemeal with an eye toward tasks that are thought to be doable. But the truth is, most states have so little boxing that their commissions can't hope to achieve the level of competence that we have in Nevada."

The solution?

"A federal imprint won't make everything right," Homansky answers. "But boxing needs an ultimate arbiter. Boxing needs some sort of federal control."

And then Homansky is on a roll. "We need better training for ring doctors," he says, "including mentoring and a standardized curriculum. There was a time when ring physicians were put in the same grouping as the timekeeper and whoever counted for knockdowns. They were part of a checklist of what was needed to get ready for a fight. The physician was only there in case a problem occurred, not to prevent problems. Thankfully, that has changed, and not just in Nevada. But there are still some states where a ring physician is chosen on the basis of, 'We need a doctor, any doctor, for some fights tonight.' And that's awful. Ring physicians can't just show up at ringside cold. They need certain medical skills. But they also need knowledge of boxing and they should know the fighters. A good ring physician studies fight records to learn who a fighter has fought. If a fighter is 15 and 3, were those three losses early in his career or by knockout in his last three fights? Has he gone more than four rounds before this fight, which is scheduled for eight? Who are his trainer and cutman?

"We need a national medical data bank," Homansky continues. "And also, national standards for medical testing and baseline tests for every fighter who enters the ring. That way, we can intervene before a fighter develops significant problems, not afterward. Every fighter should have an MRI as a baseline. It's not enough just to have an MRI after a tough fight. You need something to compare it with. Once an MRI is abnormal, there's already a problem. But if we see subtle changes, we can identify fighters who shouldn't be in the ring before there's a serious problem."

The list goes on. "It's a conflict of interest for a ringside physician to be involved as the attending physician for any fighter," Homansky posits. "No ring physician should receive any compensation in any form for the treatment of any fighter other than the payment he receives from the commission for his work at a fight. And I'm particularly troubled by fighters who disrespect their bodies, don't take care of themselves, and don't understand that, while they might still be able to sell tickets, they can't properly defend themselves anymore.

"Let's be honest," Homansky says. "Boxing is governed by money. And too many of the decision-makers look at fighters as nothing but meat from the time they're amateurs until the day they retire. Most fighters are encased in a cocoon of enablers who have an agenda of their own. Even after a fighter loses his belt and can't punch, can't defend himself, and can't perform like he used to, he's surrounded by a trainer and manager and television networks and all the hangers-on who keep calling him 'champ' and see only dollar signs when they look at him. Very few fighters have true insight into their deteriorating skills and the dangers they face every day in the gym and every time they step into the ring for a fight. The governmental regulators have to be more forceful in making the tough decisions regarding what's best for fighters. Too many state commissions simply look the other way and hope that a fighter who shouldn't fight anymore will retire on his own. I'm blown away by the number of people who say that fighters are aware of the risks involved and that you can't take away a person's right to earn a living. I disagree vehemently with that. A license to fight is not an absolute right. We have a responsibility to say 'no' to fighters when it's appropriate to say 'no.' Fighters deserve more than they're getting from the regulators of the sport."

The United States Congress is now considering legislation that would create a United States Boxing Administration to oversee the sport. Current proposals envision an "administrator" appointed by the president as the point man in this regulatory set-up.

Flip Homansky is on the short list of knowledgeable men and women who would make a superb administrator. Will he get the job in today's highly charged political climate?

Boxing should be so lucky. ❏

*In recent years, an increasing number of fighters have shared center stage with their attorneys. During that time, no lawyer has been more visible than Judd Burstein.*

# JUDD BURSTEIN: THE LAWYER OF THE MOMENT

Bernard Hopkins thought his next fight would be an easy one: on August 17, 2002, against Morrade Hakkar. Now that bout has fallen through and the schedule looks a lot tougher. On November 4, "The Executioner" is slated to face off against Lou DiBella in federal court. And when that battle takes place, Judd Burstein will be in DiBella's corner.

Burstein, age 48, was born and raised on Long Island. His father was a successful attorney, best known as a management-side labor lawyer but with a wide range of legal interests. "He was also an insane workaholic," Burstein recalls, "and worked seven days a week his entire adult life." Burstein's mother raised six children and somehow found the time to become a New York State Supreme Court judge.

In high school, Burstein was an indifferent student. He spent two years in college at Antioch before transfering to Brandeis and graduating summa cum laude in 1975. After that, he went to graduate school at McGill, where he got a masters degree and taught philosophy for two years. Then he got bored and enrolled in law school at NYU. "I hated law school with a passion," he remembers. "And I was a streaky student. If I was interested in a subject, I got an 'A'. Otherwise, I'd get a 'C' in it."

The subject that most interested Burstein was criminal law. After graduating from NYU in 1981, he went to work for Gerald Shargel (a noted criminal defense lawyer, whose client roster was studded with members of organized crime families). While with Shargel, Burstein represented the likes of Tony Provenzano and Roy DiMeo. The DiMeo representation ended when the body of Burstein's client was found in the trunk of a car.

In January 1984, Burstein became Shargel's partner. "But I was starting to get very uncomfortable," he acknowledges. "I was making a lot of money, but I wasn't where I wanted to be in life. So I left Gerry to set up my own practice and, at the same time, became counsel to another small firm. My practice was heavily weighted toward criminal appeals. And the truth is, I got a lot of appellate work from the world of organized crime. But it didn't pose the same moral questions as trial work because I was dealing almost exclusively with legal principles on appeal."

"Then," Burstein continues, "I met Jay Goldberg, who later became counsel for Donald Trump. At the time, Jay was representing a lot of Mafia types, and I got more business from Jay. Also, around that time, the federal government started bringing large civil racketeering lawsuits against organized crime and unions. And while I knew nothing about civil procedure, I knew everything about the racketeering statutes, so I started doing a fair amount of civil litigation."

1990 marked a turning point in Burstein's professional life. He was having what he describes as "a torrid affair" with a lawyer who was prosecuting organized crime cases for the United States Attorney's office in the Southern District of New York. Then, by his recollection, "One of my clients came to me and said that John Gotti was displeased; that either I end the romance or I'd be banned from representing organized crime clients. It's the only time I was ever afraid as a result of the OC connection. So I took a walk. The romance ended soon after that, but I never told them. I had soured on criminal law. I don't knock anybody who does it. I have clear perceptions about what it means to be a lawyer and the requirement that the state prove its case beyond a reasonable doubt lest an innocent person go to jail. And I believe that the legal principles, the institutional values involved in criminal cases, are more important than the outcome of any one individual case. But it would make me uncomfortable to handle organized crime cases now. And I couldn't represent my other clients properly if I did because, when I went into court for them, fairly or unfairly I'd have the label of being a mob lawyer attached to me."

Burstein got into boxing not long after he began developing a commercial practice. "Jay Goldberg hooked me up with Rock Newman in a dispute between Riddick Bowe and Evander Holyfield," he remembers. "And the result was a stunning loss."

But then Burstein did battle with Don King in separate cases on behalf of Terry Norris and Frans Botha. Bob Arum encouraged Julio Cesar Chavez to hire Burstein in litigation against King so he could proceed with the second fight between Chavez and Oscar De La Hoya. And suddenly, Burstein was on a roll.

His biggest break came in December 2000. "A Malaysian woman hired me to put together a Lewis-Tyson fight," he recalls. "She claimed she had $60-million to split between the two fighters. The idea was for her to pay Lennox $1-million for a 45-day option and then sign Tyson. I was negotiating with Adrian Ogun and an attorney for Lennox, when it became clear to me that my client wasn't on the level, so I stopped representing her. That and the negotiations preceding my decision must have impressed Adrian because, when Lennox's relationship with Panos Eliades [Lewis' former promoter] blew up, Adrian and Lennox began casting about for a new lawyer and I was hired."

Thus began a remarkable stretch of legal activity. On April 22, 2001, Lewis lost the heavyweight title when he was knocked out in South Africa by Hasim

Rahman. There had been a rematch clause in the fighters' contracts. But rather than live up to it, Rahman bolted from his promoter (Cedric Kushner), signed with Don King, and began planning for a series of matches against opponents other than Lewis. Burstein took the new champion to court and won an injunction forbidding Rahman to fight anyone before Lewis had his rematch, which Lennox won in November 2001.

Then, in February 2002, Burstein won a $7.4-million federal court judgment for Lewis against Panos for racketeering and fraud. In December, he's scheduled to represent Lennox again in federal court, this time against Milt Chwasky (Lewis' former attorney) in a lawsuit that alleges negligence, unjust enrichment, and breach of fiduciary duty.

"Milt Chwasky is exactly what's wrong with boxing," Burstein says, offering a preview of his case. "Milt was paid $1.4-million in legal fees, directly and indirectly by Lennox. And then he looked the other way when bad things started happening because he had embraced every conflict imaginable. I know boxing is an incestuous sport. But there's no way that a lawyer should represent a fighter and his promoter at the same time on transactional work. And when Lennox fought Zelko Mavrovic at Foxwoods, Milt represented the venue too."

Chwasky vigorously denies that he acted improperly and has termed the accusations against him "a crock of shit."

Time will tell.

[Author's note: In December 2002, Burstein and Lewis won a $1,175,000 jury verdict against Chwasky.]

In the courtroom, Burstein radiates energy, focus, and brilliance. There's also an aura of confidence about him, like a fighter who knows he's good. "I think I have another five years of trying cases before I get to be as good as I can be," he says. "A lawyer's skill is based on talent and experience. I expect those two things to peak for me when I'm in my early fifties. That's when I should be at my best."

Burstein has no partners. His office staff consists of five associate lawyers and five administrative personnel. "Litigation requires a certain degree of applying pressure and being relentless," he says. "There are times when a large firm on the other side might try to bury me with motion papers or documents. But I have affiliations with other firms that enable me to bring in more support if necessary." Then, continuing on his subject, Burstein acknowledges, "In many respects, litigation is like war. And I model myself more on Ulysses Grant than on George McClellan. McClellan was paralyzed at the thought of taking action. Grant was more of a risk taker and seized the moment in battle."

As for fees, Burstein's time is billed at rates as high as $600 an hour. "But I do a lot of partial contingency work," he elaborates. "If it's a case I like, I'm happy to bet on my talents."

And right now, Burstein likes boxing cases. "I loved the sport from the moment I got involved," he says. "In fact, that was the only time in my career that I made a real effort to cultivate business. Any time you get together large amounts of money and uneducated minority athletes, you have a breeding ground for exploitation and corruption. Golf and tennis have a totally different social demographic. The team sports have unions. But the stuff that goes on in boxing is mind-boggling to me. Look at the way Don King exploits fighters. Look at what's happening to Manny Pacquaio. Most fighters are treated like indentured servants. And when someone like Lou DiBella comes along and tries to do right by the fighters, the resistance to him is extraordinary. The exploitation of fighters angers me, and I think I can make a difference." ❏

*There's a fraternity among great athletes that transcends any one particular sport.*

# TED WILLIAMS: A TRIBUTE

A boxing website headquartered in England is an unusual forum to write about an American baseball player. But there's a special bond among great athletes. The death of one is felt by all. Death is a reminder that, no matter how young and strong an athlete might be, the body that serves as a vehicle to glory will ultimately fail.

Ted Williams was a great athlete. That's the first thing to be said about him. By most reckonings, he was the greatest pure hitter of all time. Five men in the history of major league baseball had a higher batting average. Others hit more home runs. But no one combined the two like Williams did.

William made hitting an art and a science. He was able to estimate that, from the moment a ball leaves the pitcher's hand, the batter has 1/10 of a second to recognize the pitch, another 15/100th of a second to decide whether to swing, and a final 15/100th of a second to do it. "That's what you're working with," Williams proclaimed. "Four-tenths of a second with a round ball and a round bat."

It was his opinion, often voiced, that hitting a baseball is the hardest thing in sports to do.

The world has grown accustomed to books "by" athletes. Invariably, these books are written "with" someone else. Often, the athlete never reads them. He simply talks into a tape recorder, answering questions for a day or two. Then the real author fills in the rest from press clippings. When Ted Williams finally got around to writing a book, he worked with John Underwood but the end product was vintage Williams.

*The Science of Hitting*, published in 1970, remains the classic work on hitting a baseball. Among the thoughts Williams offered were:

- "All they ever write about the great hitters is what great reflexes they have, what great style, what strength, what quickness; but never how smart the guy is at the plate, and that's fifty percent of it."

- "I was known as a hitter who guessed a lot. But for me, guessing was observing."

- "The single most important thing for a hitter is to get a good pitch to hit. A good hitter can hit a pitch that's over the plate three times better than a great hitter with a ball in a tough spot."

● "If a pitcher is throwing fast balls and curves and only the fast balls are in the strike zone, you'd be silly to look for a curve, wouldn't you?"

● "My preference was a light bat [33 ounces]. When we started using pine tar or resin and oil on the handles to improve the grip, I cleaned my bats with alcohol every night. I took them to the post office to check their weights. Finally, I got the Red Sox to put a scale in the clubhouse. I wanted them checked because bats pick up condensation and dirt being on the ground. They can gain an ounce or more in a surprisingly short time."

Williams came up to the major leagues as a 20-year-old prodigy in 1939 when baseball was truly the national pastime and the sport was deeply ingrained in the fabric of America. When he first donned a Boston Red Sox uniform (the only one he wore during his career), Lou Gehrig and Carl Hubbel were still active players. He retired in 1960, having played through three revolutions that changed the game—the advent of television, the arrival of Jackie Robinson, and westward expansion.

His records stand as a testament to his prowess. Despite losing three full seasons [1943-1945] in his prime to serve as a Navy pilot in World War II and two more [1952-1953] as a Marine pilot during the Korean War, he played up to a standard that today's hitters can only dream about.

"The days pile one on another to make a career," Williams once said. And what a career it was! 521 home runs . . . 2,654 hits . . . 1,839 RBIs . . . 1,798 runs . . . 2,161 walks . . . a slugging percentage of .690 . . . an on-base percentage of .483 [the highest ever] . . . and a .344 career batting average [unequaled since his day].

Along the way, he won six batting titles and led the league in home runs four times, runs scored six times, RBI's four times, walks eight times, slugging percentage eight times, and on base percentage 12 times. He won two triple crowns, was voted the American League's most valuable player twice, and was chosen as an All-Star on 16 occasions (all but his rookie season and the years he missed because of military service). In 1957, at age 39, he became the oldest man to win a batting title in either league. He won the batting crown again at age forty. If World War II and Korea hadn't intervened, his accomplishments would have been even more formidable.

Williams was also the last man to bat .400 for an entire season, and the way he did it shed light on his character. In 1941 (his third year in the major leagues) his average stood at .39955 going into the final day of the season. Because of the manner in which baseball keeps statistics, that number would have been rounded off to .400. Red Sox manager Joe Cronin offered to let him sit out a doubleheader against the Philadelphia Athletics. But Williams insisted on playing that day and got six hits in eight at bats to raise his average to .406.

That's a champion.

"No hitter has it all," Williams later wrote. "There probably never has been what you would call the complete hitter. Babe Ruth struck out more than he should have. Ty Cobb didn't have power."

But Ted Williams had it all. When Pete Rose was chasing the immortal Cobb's record of 4,191 career base hits, Rose opined, "No one can tell me that Ty Cobb would have hit .367 if he started playing ball in 1963. Don't even figure in night ball and relief pitchers. Just look at the gloves the players had back then; short fingers held together at the end by rawhide." Then Rose added, "But Ted Williams could have hit .344 in any era."

Williams was more than a great hitter. He was also a humanitarian. His work on behalf of various charities made the efforts of his contemporaries in sports pale by comparison. And when he was inducted into the Baseball Hall of Fame in 1966, he used the occasion to voice the view, "I hope that some day Satchel Paige and Josh Gibson will be voted into the Hall of Fame as symbols of the great Negro players who are not here only because they weren't given the chance."

Five years later, Satchel Paige was inducted at Cooperstown. Gibson and other greats from the Negro League followed.

Williams also had a soft spot in his heart for boxing. "I feel the greatest prize in sports is the heavyweight championship of the world," he said. "I happen to have been successful in baseball, but if you want to talk about dedication, take a fighter who climbs to the top and stays there."

Williams placed Joe Louis at the top of his rankings. "I think that Joe Louis was the greatest heavyweight fighter who ever lived," he reminisced. "I loved his style, his punch, his aggressiveness. He was moving in all the time; stalking you, stalking you. He fought everybody. He fought more often than anybody. To me, nobody will be a greater heavyweight than Joe Louis."

But Williams also spoke fondly of Muhammad Ali. "As for Vietnam and the political side of things," he said during an interview in 1989, "I served in two wars as a pilot. My career was interrupted several times, and I didn't agree with what Ali did, but I respected him for it. Ali's faith was important to him. He was sincere, and he acted in accord with his convictions.

"I have great admiration for Ali," Williams continued. "My first experience meeting him came [in 1966] at the airport in Tampa. I saw him from quite a distance, maybe 200 feet. Ali looked in my direction, and apparently he recognized me because he started to walk toward me. He got right up to me, and I don't remember exactly how he said it, but the gist of it was, 'I'm Muhammad Ali.' I said, 'I know who you are,' and we started talking. He was going to Canada to fight George Chuvalo, and he told me, 'Chuvalo's a tough guy, but I won't have any trouble with him.' I always admired his confidence; saying he was going to do something, and then, by God, going out and doing it."

"Ali was absolutely devoted to being the best, and he was one of the greatest fighters who ever lived," Williams said in closing. "I've seen him fight live; I've seen all his films. And what always amazes me is the way he maneuvered in the ring. There's no question in my mind that he was the fastest big man ever in boxing. And I think he got as much out of his physical ability as possible, which is another reason I admire him. He came as close as any athlete I know to getting the most out of his potential. I've been a fan of his for a long, long time."

Ali, for his part, responded in kind, saying simply, "Ted Williams was as great in his sport as I was in mine." ❏

*The past few years have been difficult for Cedric Kushner, but he has kept doing what he does best—promote fights.*

# CEDRIC KUSHNER SOLDIERS ON

These are difficult times for Cedric Kushner. Eighteen months ago, he seemed on the verge of unqualified success. Hasim Rahman had knocked out Lennox Lewis to capture the heavyweight championship. Shane Mosley was regarded by some as "pound-for-pound" the best fighter in the world. And Kushner promoted both of them. However, since then, in addition to losing twice each, Rahman and Mosley have gone on to other promoters. Kushner is being sued by myriad plaintiffs, and whatever the outcome of these cases, his debts are huge.

Still, Kushner has five-dozen boxers under contract. During the past year [2002], he promoted 40 fight cards, including a dozen of his trademark "Heavyweight Explosion" shows. And his roster of fighters includes Jameel McCline, Michael Grant, Joel Casamayor, and Anthony Thompson.

Boxing promoters are not known as men of virtue, but Kushner is fair with his fighters. He's also refreshingly pleasant and polite, and recently expressed his philosophy of deal-making as follows: "You don't have to like someone to do business with them. My motto is, 'Business with my enemies, dinner with my friends.' And because this is boxing, I often dine with my enemies as well."

It would be a loss for boxing if Cedric Kushner folded. He doesn't intend to.

"I've had some difficulties," the eternally optimistic Kushner said recently. "This is the worst period for boxing that I can remember in terms of opportunities on television, and virtually everyone in the business has been adversely affected. But we've reached a point commercially where people are starting to understand that the business can't go on like it has in the past and that the promoter isn't always the bad guy. So yes, I have obligations that are weighing upon me and I intend to honor them. And I intend to be a major player in boxing for a long time." ❑

*In 2003, Cedric Kushner became one of boxing's more compelling human-interest stories.*

# CEDRIC KUSHNER: SAVING A LIFE

*Cedric Kushner looks healthier these days than he has in years. There's more color in his face. His skin has a shine. His voice is livelier. His eyes sparkle. He walks with a faster gait. On April 7, the 5-foot-8 Kushner underwent gastric bypass surgery. To the layperson, it's known as stapling one's stomach. In reality, it's reconstructive surgery that creates a small pouch and reduces the size of a patient's intestines to enforce a smaller intake of food.*

*During the two weeks immediately after surgery, Kushner was allowed to ingest three ounces of liquid (juice or broth) three times per day. Then came phase two, during which dinner consisted of two tablespoons of pureed carrots, two table-spoons of mashed potatoes, and an ounce of pureed chicken. He's now in phase three. During this period, Cedric's lunch duplicates his dinner. If all goes as planned, sometime around June 1, Kushner will graduate to phase four. His break-fast will consist of a half-cup of fruit and a quarter-cup of cereal. Lunch and dinner will be four ounces of food each. In every stage, there are vitamin supplements.*

*Phase four is for life. The surgery is not reversible.*

*One month after the surgery, Kushner has lost 45 pounds.*

*What would drive someone to commit to such a radically different way of life? Here, in Cedric's own words, is his story.*

"In 1984, when I first got into the boxing business, I was 36 years old. I didn't smoke or drink. I didn't eat red meat. I enjoyed exercising. My weight fluctuated between 220 and 235 pounds, and I ran six to eight miles a day. I had a fighter named Teddy Mann, who would come to New York to visit me. We'd jog together in Central Park, and I could outrun him. Then, in 1985, I moved out of Manhattan to East Hampton. And it seemed like, after that, I couldn't control my weight. I remember once, after playing tennis, I weighed myself and saw that I was up to 255 pounds. From that point on, I was caught in a horrible upward spiral that I couldn't control.

"Over the years, I tried various diets. At one point, for six months, I ate nothing but soup. Then it was a lot of vegetables and fruit. When liquid protein was the treatment of choice, I tried that. I went to Duke University for six weeks. But there was a fundamental problem. Like most people who are overweight, I'd lose some pounds. But the moment I went off the diet and was in a less structured mode, the weight came back more quickly than I'd lost it and there were always a few more pounds.

"When I was on a diet, I weighed myself every day. When I wasn't, I got on a scale maybe once or twice a week. For a while, I lied to myself. I didn't look like I weighed as much as I did, so I told myself that I was a well-packed 250 or 260 or 270. I don't remember when I broke 300. Five years ago, I was up to 350 pounds. By then, I couldn't convince myself or anyone else that I wasn't grossly obese. But strangely enough, my medical condition was relatively good. I developed type-2 diabetes, but my blood pressure was excellent. I could play a decent game of tennis. But I was caught in a trap. As much as I wanted to do something about the problem, I couldn't. The obstacles were too great for me. My nickname evolved from Big Ced, which was rather affectionate, to Fat Man and other things people said behind my back. You turn away from the snide comments, but there's nothing that hurts more than something you can't conceal or control that you know is true. From time to time, a friend or business associate would say something to me in a kind way about my physical condition, but it only aggravated me. They weren't experiencing what I was experiencing. I felt that there wasn't anyone I could really explain my situation to.

"Then my problems worsened. I developed a terrible condition called sleep apnea, which causes a person to nod off without being able to control it. There were times when I was conducting a meeting at the highest level of my business and I'd fall asleep during the meeting, even though it might only be one o'clock in the afternoon. I'd fall asleep on the telephone. It happened while I was driving. And the condition kept getting worse.

"Last year, I consulted with a doctor who specializes in obesity, and he recommended a gastric bypass. I scheduled the operation, and then I changed my mind. I told myself that I had the willpower to lose weight and that I was a sissy for considering an alternative to dieting. But my condition continued to worsen. I was out of control. My weight ascended to 385 pounds. I could only sleep for two hours a night because I was more comfortable sitting upright than lying down. Life was a constant nightmare for me. It was an effort to get up in the morning and put on my socks. If I went to a store to buy a pair of pants, getting them on and off caused me to perspire. Even if people weren't watching me, I thought they were. I was uncomfortable sitting in regular chairs. Booths in restaurants were difficult to fit into if the table wasn't moveable. I was in a perpetually exhausted bloated condition. And to be honest, at times I was resigned to just letting things take their natural course. I started thinking that one doesn't see many obese 70-year-olds, and the difference between 54 and 70 wasn't that great.

"Then, one night, I was at home reading a magazine with the television on in the background, and there was a segment on TV about Al Roker. He's the NBC weatherman who had a gastric bypass operation. I listened to the questions that the interviewer was asking him. 'Isn't it an extreme operation? Why didn't you just go on a diet?' Roker responded that he'd tried many diets, which he listed and which were many of the same diets I'd been on. He'd gone to Duke University. He'd lost weight at various times and then gained it all back again. And I said to myself, 'That's my script. His problems are identical to mine.'

"I'd known in my heart for some time that I had to do something about my obesity. The interview with Al Roker convinced me that a person wasn't weak-minded just because he had the operation. So I went through the physical tests that are required for the procedure. There was also a visit with a psychiatrist, because there are numerous instances of people who've had the bypass and then can't deal with being limited to eating such small portions of food. And what happens then is, they stuff themselves to the point where they cause their stomach pouch to expand, which allows them to have a larger intake of food but can also cause a rupture and severe hemorrhaging that necessitates a repair operation.

"On the first Monday in February in the midst of a blizzard, I checked into the hospital. I was hooked up to an intravenous line, taken into the operating room, and given an injection in my stomach preparatory to the administration of anesthesia. Then the operation was postponed because my surgeon was unable to make his way to the hospital through the snow. The operation was rescheduled and postponed again when I contracted bronchitis. On the third try, I made it as far as the operating room, but the anesthesiologist said my lungs were still congested. Someone else might have seen an omen in all of this, but I remained convinced that the operation was the right thing for me to do.

"In the past, I drank eight to 12 diet Cokes a day. I'll never have a diet Coke again. The carbonation would cause problems with my digestive process. My favorite dessert used to be ice cream. I can forget about ice cream for the rest of my life. The concentration of sugar in it would have an adverse effect on me.

"But the truth is, I feel a great deal of relief; as though an enormous physical and mental weight has been lifted from me. I'm stronger, more energetic, sharper, and more focused mentally now than I've been in years. I still eat out every night, only now I eat less. I don't know if I'll ever get the same satisfaction from eating a limited quantity of food that I got from eating in the past, but that's an adjustment I'll have to make.

"I can't stress enough how good I feel just a month after the operation. From an elephant to a greyhound, is what I say. For the first time in years, I'm optimistic about my life. I can't tell you how much gratitude I feel toward the people who cared enough about me to comment constructively on my physical condition in the past, even though, at times, their comments aggravated me. And I can't tell you how inspired I am now by the positive things that people are saying to me. I've been given a second chance at life that, a month ago, I didn't think I'd ever have.

"You know; for years, I wanted to wear a red sport jacket. But I never got one because I thought it wouldn't look right on me. For obvious reasons, I made my clothes as inconspicuous as possible. But I expect to break 300 pounds sometime in July. People tell me that eventually I'll get down to 200, although I know I'll be comfortable at 225. I don't know if I'll ever actually wear a red sport jacket, but it's nice to know that, sometime in the not-too-distant future, I'll have the option." ❑

*In some families, boxing is a tradition.*

# THE MERCANTES OF BOXING

There was a time when they were known as Arthur Mercante and Arthur Mercante, Jr. But Arthur the Son didn't like being designated as "junior", which makes things complicated because now we have two Arthur Mercantes. Call them "Arthur the First" and "Arthur the Second." Or "Arthur the Elder" and "Arthur the Younger." Or perhaps simply "The Mercantes of Boxing."

The Arthur Mercante with silver hair is now 82 years old. During a career that ran from mid-century to the new millennium, he refereed 145 world championship bouts including the historic first meeting between Muhammad Ali and Joe Frazier at Madison Square Garden. First and foremost, he's a gentleman.

"Not many people know this," the elder Mercante says of his son. "But Arthur was a very good amateur fighter. In fact, he fought Juan LaPorte in the Golden Gloves and lost a decision in a very close bout that I thought he won. I'm proud of my son. He's very giving, very kind, always trying to make himself better in every way. He was the referee in that fight when Beethavean Scotland was killed. And I will tell you; after Scotland died, Arthur cried for days."

The younger Mercante was born in 1959 and has been the third man in the ring for 20 world championship fights, including Holyfield-Lewis I. "When I was growing up," he says, "my father was my role model and my idol. The greatest honor I've ever had was presenting him for his Boxing Hall of Fame induction. He was a hands-on father, always there for me and my brothers when we needed him. And he taught me almost everything I know about conducting myself in life, inside the ring and out of it." ❏

*To paraphrase: In boxing, everybody doesn't like someone. But nobody doesn't like Al Gavin.*

# AL GAVIN

On June 7, 2003, Arturo Gatti and Micky Ward will face off for Part Three of their Club Fight Trilogy. Gatti-Ward I captivated the boxing world and was universally recognized as boxing's "fight of the year." Ward-Gatti II sold out Boardwalk Hall in Atlantic City and led to demands for Gatti-Ward III. Each fighter has made millions of dollars from their encounters. But their rivalry came perilously close to being nothing more than a single round of action. That's because, in round one of their first fight, Ward was badly cut. Under different circumstances, the bout might have been stopped. But Ward had Al Gavin in his corner.

Gavin was born in Brooklyn. "Quite a while ago," he says. His father came to the United States from Wicklow, Ireland, and found employment as a plumber. Al grew up in Brooklyn with his parents, two sisters, and a brother.

"My father always had an interest in boxing," Gavin remembers. "That's how I got interested in it. I boxed in the amateurs and was strong enough mentally, but I didn't have the physical strength to do the things I wanted to do. I could box pretty well. My jab was okay and I had a pretty good idea of how things should be done. I just didn't have the tools. I wasn't a puncher. I wish I could say I had a rock-solid chin, but I didn't. I had maybe 20 fights and won 14 of them. Then I thought about turning pro and went to Al Braverman, who was managing at the time. Al was always nice to me. A lot of managers would have put me in the ring, and maybe I would have gotten hurt. But Al was honest. He told me, 'You don't have it.' And he was right. I took a look at the middleweight division. Sugar Ray Robinson was champion. In my wildest dreams, I couldn't beat him. Then I looked at some of the other guys like Gene Fullmer and Rocky Castellani. No way I could beat fighters like that. So to stay in the sport I cared about, I had to find another way."

Gavin was working in landscaping and gardening for the New York City Parks Department by then; a job he would hold for 35 years. Meanwhile, he started going to Stillman's Gym.

"Going to Stillman's was like going to college," he remembers. "In those days, it was a palace for fighters. Walk in and you saw elite trainers like Ray Arcel, Whitey Bimstein, Chickie Ferrara, and Freddie Brown. If you couldn't learn from watching those guys, you couldn't learn, period. I went to Stillman's almost every night and started coaching kids in the ring for the Police Athletic League. The first pro fighter I trained was a welterweight from Trinidad named Winston Nole in the 1970s. I managed Nole too, but decided that there were people who were better qualified to be a manager than I was, so I stopped managing."

Over the years, Gavin has trained dozens of fighters. On a personal note, he has been married for 48 years to a woman he calls "the strength of my life." Together, they have a son and two daughters. "My family, my religion, and my health are what's important to me," Gavin acknowledges. He's universally recognized as one of boxing's good guys, fair and even-tempered. But Gavin's fame within the boxing community comes from his skill as a cutman.

A good cut man is invaluable to a fighter. Sometimes, he's the difference between winning and losing.

Gavin works roughly 30 fight cards annually for anonymous preliminary fighters on up the ladder to Lennox Lewis. Over the years, he has been in the corner with Oscar De La Hoya, Vito Antuofermo, Bruce Seldon, Kevin Kelley, Junior Jones, and Arturo Gatti.

"What I get paid is up to the people I work with," Gavin explains. "No one makes me do the job; so if I feel like I'm being treated unfairly, I don't do it. Obviously, Lennox pays more than a four-round fighter. I've been with Lennox since he fought Gary Mason in 1991, and he's always fair with me."

When Gavin works a fight, one of the first things he does is find out who the ring doctor assigned to his fighter's corner will be. "The majority of ring doctors understand cuts," he says. "They know that fighters bleed sometimes, and they give the cutman a chance. But if it's a ring doctor I haven't seen before, maybe I get a little worried."

While a fight is in progress, Gavin watches intently from the corner, looking for signs of trouble that might presage a cut. A good cutman knows his fighters. He knows when and where they've been cut in the past and if their face has been swollen in the gym. He doesn't wait for blood to begin treating an area of concern. In fact, if a cutman waits for blood, he might be starting too late.

"The two trainers I learned the most from about stopping cuts were Tony Canzi and Johnny Zullo," says Gavin. "As for what I do, I just have a feel for it. It's a combination of art, science, and luck. Time is important. If there's a problem, I go to work as soon as the fighter reaches the corner. I don't get excited. I know where to put the pressure. Pressure is the most important element. That begins the process of stopping the bleeding."

Gavin's work over the decades has earned him the respect of his peers.

"Al is a pro," says trainer-commentator Teddy Atlas. "Ninety percent of the people around now are frauds, but Al is for real. He doesn't panic. He always comes prepared. He takes pride in what he does. When you hire Al, you're not just getting a guy who puts a swab on a fighter's face. Sure, he can stop a cut.

Once you've hired him, you don't have to worry about that part of the fight but you get a lot more. Al understands all the aspects and angles of boxing. You can ask him for strategy during a fight. He knows better than most people what both fighters are thinking as a fight goes on. He's not just a cutman; he's a co-pilot. And whether you need to rely on him or not during a particular fight, it's reassuring to know he's there. He's a great great boxing guy."

Emanuel Steward concurs, adding, "When I started working with Lennox eight years ago, Al Gavin was already there. Lennox's people asked me if I wanted to keep him. And I said, 'Without doubt, yes.' Al is one of the best people in boxing. He's technically good as a cutman, but it goes way beyond that. He lays back; he never interferes. He's never out blowing his own horn. He's easy to work with. He blends in perfectly with the personality of Lennox's camp. And he's a much better trainer than most people give him credit for."

Dr. Flip Homansky (former medical director for the Nevada State Athletic Commission) compounds the praise. "The ring is the most unlikely operating room that I can imagine," says Homansky. "And a medical degree is no guarantee that its holder knows much about jagged lacerations that are acutely bleeding. I've seen I don't know how many fights that were stopped because no one in the corner knew how to prevent a simple cut from getting worse. Al Gavin is everything that a cutman should be."

And Dr. Margaret Goodman (Homansky's successor in Nevada) observes, "I've learned a lot from Al, and other people should learn from him too. Al is the quintessential cutman. He knows what he's doing and works at his craft constantly. If there's a cut, Al can handle it. He keeps his fighter calm and, no matter how bad the bleeding, never does anything to undermine his fighter's confidence. And yet, there have been times when Al looks at me with just the right look to tell me that, in his view, his fighter has had enough. And I respect that a lot."

"I try not to be too brave in the corner," Gavin says in response to Goodman's comment. "My motto is, 'Don't be braver with the fighter than I would be with myself.' I'm nothing special. I just go out and do my job. I'm not a big-shot. I'm just a guy who likes boxing."

Maybe so. But if a fighter is cut, in those 60 seconds between rounds, Al Gavin is the most important man in boxing. Micky Ward said as much when he looked back on the start of his trilogy against Arturo Gatti and declared, "In that first round when I got cut, I knew I had the best cutman in the business. I knew that, if anyone could stop the bleeding, Al could. And I was right; Al kept me in the fight. Al Gavin means everything to me." ❑

# ROUND 3

# ISSUES AND ANSWERS

*September 11 will be a day of remembrance for a long time.*

# SEPTEMBER 11: ONE YEAR LATER

One year ago, we put aside our games.

The United States was attacked by terrorists who commandeered four civilian airplanes and turned them into weapons of mass destruction. Three thousand people died. The carnage brought a diminished sense of security for all of us coupled with anger and sadness at such an ugly turn of the world.

Within the boxing community, the impact of the attack was felt immediately with the postponement of the championship bout between Felix Trinidad and Bernard Hopkins. Then the horror of the tragedy became more personal as the names of the dead were revealed.

Vernon Cherry was a firefighter assigned to a ladder company beneath the Brooklyn Bridge, not far from the World Trade Center. He loved boxing and often sang the National Anthem at club fights in New York.

Gregg Atlas (the nephew of trainer and ESPN commentator Teddy Atlas) was assigned to a fire battalion in close proximity to the World Trade Center.

Pat Brown was a battalion captain and one of the first firefighters to arrive on the scene. For years, he had worked out at Gleason's Gym.

These and thousands of other innocents died on September 11.

In due course, the games resumed. Trinidad-Hopkins took place and is now recalled as Hopkins-Trinidad. Outside the ring, most of us returned to our daily routine. But Steve Farhood spent hundreds of hours working with former fighters to promote a fundraiser that generated $52,000 for the Twin Towers Fund. Lou DiBella took a $70,000 loss to turn one of his fight cards into a fundraiser that contributed an additional $55,000 to victims of the attack plus $6,000 to the Dr. Theodore A. Atlas Foundation.

Now, a year later, "9/11" is part of the vernacular. The land where the Twin Towers stood is a vacant lot. The New York skyline has been forever changed.

This year, September 11 is sandwiched between two championship bouts. Roy Jones faced off against Clinton Woods in Portland on September 7. Oscar De La Hoya and Fernando Vargas will do battle in Las Vegas on the 14. Most people who travel to the latter fight will make a point of not being in the air on 9/11.

Meanwhile, it should be noted that Secondsout is a British website. Since September 11, more than any other people, the Brits have stood by us. So, from the colonies, thank you.

*Like a lot of people, I once believed in Bernard Hopkins as a fighter and as a person. I still think he's a great fighter.*

# DiBELLA V. HOPKINS

Lou DiBella has won a $610,000 libel judgment against Bernard Hopkins in a jury trial in the United States District Court for the Southern District of New York. DiBella's lawsuit was filed in December 2001, shortly after Hopkins accused him of soliciting and accepting a $50,000 bribe while DiBella was still a senior vice president at HBO Sports.

The jury's verdict was a significant victory and marked the end of a long and winding road for DiBella. For Hopkins, one of the great fighters in ring history, there is damaged credibility and a large chunk of money won in the ring has been lost.

DiBella and Hopkins joined forces as advisor and fighter on a handshake agreement in early 2000, two months after "The Executioner" received $100,000 for defending his IBF middleweight title against Antwun Echols. With DiBella's support, Hopkins made $525,000 for a May 2000 defense against Syd Vanderpool and $650,000 for a December 2000 rematch against Echols. Then, in 2001, DiBella engineered Hopkins' entry into Don King's middleweight championship tournament. For that bit of business, Hopkins received $1-million for fighting Keith Holmes, $2.75-million for fighting Felix Trinidad, $50,000 in expenses for each fight, and a $200,000 signing bonus. In sum, before DiBella, Hopkins was an extremely talented fighter with limited name recognition who rarely made big money. With DiBella in his camp, he became a star.

DiBella believed in Hopkins. Sitting in Madison Square Garden moments before Bernard was to enter the ring for his historic bout against Trinidad, DiBella declared, "Tonight is important to my company financially, but it's hugely important to me personally because Bernard will always be hugely important to me. I cherish the relationship I have with Bernard."

But once Hopkins beat Trinidad, he figured he didn't need DiBella anymore. So he dumped him. If Hopkins had simply said, "Lou did a good job, but I don't want to work with him in the future," DiBella would have been hurt and angry, but there wouldn't have been a lawsuit. However, Hopkins went further. In late December 2001, stung by media criticism that he was an ingrate, he gave an interview to Internet writer Steve Kim in which he accused DiBella of demanding and receiving a $50,000 bribe to put him on HBO at a time when

DiBella was still employed by HBO.

Mike Trainer, who handled Sugar Ray Leonard's business affairs during the fighter's ring career, once said, "To survive in boxing, you take on the characteristics of those you abhor. You become like them."

Throughout his years in boxing, DiBella has defied that trend. He's one of the honorable people in the sport. And his passion for fairness didn't end when he left HBO and the checkbook he was balancing became his own.

When the Association of Boxing Commissions set up a fighters relief fund, DiBella donated $5,000. No other donor, corporate or individual, contributed more than $1,000. In November 2001, DiBella took a $70,000 loss to turn one of his fight cards into a fundraiser for the Twin Towers Fund. Earlier this year, he paid travel and hotel expenses for Gerald McClellan and McClellan's sister to attend a dinner in New York where Teddy Blackburn was honored for his work with the disabled fighter.

As of late, DiBella, like many others in boxing, has been struggling. "I knew the impediments I'd face when I set up my own business," he said recently. "I understood that the entrenched powers would line up against me. What I didn't count on, and maybe I was naive, was that the fighters—and I won't even say the fighters; I'll limit myself to one particular fighter—would react the way they did. The only reason I'm not where I want to be today is Bernard Hopkins. Bernard has poisoned the well for me with a lot of fighters. And Bernard should have fought two major fights this year instead of one minor one. If he had, I could have made $800,000 instead of paying hundreds of thousands of dollars in legal fees."

In truth, DiBella's lawsuit almost didn't proceed to trial. On October 24, 2002, Hopkins' lawyers drafted and forwarded a proposed settlement agreement to Judd Burstein (DiBella's attorney). The document, if signed, would have required Hopkins to pay DiBella $170,000 in three payments spread over the next 14 months and release the following statement to the media: "Lou DiBella and Bernard Hopkins have settled Mr. DiBella's lawsuit against Mr. Hopkins on confidential terms. Mr. Hopkins states, 'At no time did Lou DiBella request or receive a bribe or under the table payment from me or do anything wrong.' "

But there were problems with the proposal. Hopkins refused to put teeth in the payment provision, and DiBella envisioned spending additional money on attorneys fees to collect. And perhaps more important, the proposed settlement contained the following provision: "Except for the statement set forth above, the parties shall not make any statement about this settlement, the transactions and occurrences giving rise to the action, or the action to anyone and shall keep the terms of this agreement absolutely confidential."

That was the deal-breaker. DiBella's case was primarily about damage to his reputation. Laying aside the irony of Bernard Hopkins requesting a gag order, DiBella wanted to be able to speak freely once the case was over. He didn't want Hopkins to "spin" the settlement with comments like "I signed it to save money on lawyers and get rid of the case and I'm not allowed to say anything more; but people in boxing know what this was all about." DiBella was opposed to a gag order of any kind. His view was that Hopkins is good at dishing it out when it comes to someone else's reputation and Bernard should be able to take it as well. So rather than accept a settlement that he viewed as equivalent to a draw, DiBella went for the knockout.

The trial began on Monday, November 4, before Judge Denny Chin, a former assistant United States Attorney who has been on the bench for seven years. That morning, the jury was chosen; four men and four women including one African-American. For the next two days, Burstein lay the groundwork for DiBella's case. His first three witnesses were Kery Davis (senior vice president of programming for HBO Sports), Peter Mozarsky (vice president and senior counsel for sports and original programming at HBO), and Dave Itskowitch (vice president of DiBella Entertainment). Through their testimony, the following timeline was pieced together.

In late 1999, DiBella decided to leave HBO and began negotiating his termination agreement with the cable company. Then, in January 2000, Roy Jones decided to make a May 2000 defense of his light-heavyweight title against Richard Hall. HBO was contractually bound to televise the fight. And by contract, the undercard fight had to be approved by Square Ring (Jones' promotional company) and Murad Muhammad (Jones' promoter). DiBella and Kery Davis wanted to put Hopkins on the undercard, and it was agreed by all concerned that Bernard would fight Brian Barbosa (one of Muhammad's fighters).

Meanwhile, in February and March 2000, DiBella was meeting at HBO with Hopkins and two of Bernard's attorneys (Arnold Joseph and Scott Magargee), and an agreement for a future working relationship between DiBella and Hopkins was reached. As part of that agreement, Hopkins was to pay DiBella $50,000.

The focus of the lawsuit was on that $50,000 payment. Hopkins said it was a bribe to get on HBO; that DiBella performed no services for him prior to his entry into the 2001 middleweight championship tournament (for which DiBella was paid by Don King); and that, in any event, it would have been unethical for DiBella to enter into a business arrangement with a fighter while he was still in a position of authority at HBO. DiBella said the payment was for services to be rendered after he left HBO and that he'd disclosed his relationship with Hopkins to Seth Abraham (president of Time Warner Sports), Kery Davis, and Peter Mozarsky.

In mid-March 2000, in anticipation of the Barbosa fight, DiBella lent Hopkins $30,000 for training expenses. Then, on March 26, 2000, Barbosa was cut in a tune-up bout and a replacement opponent had to be found. The nod went to Syd Vanderpool, who was also promoted by Murad Muhammad.

On May 12, 2000, DiBella signed his termination agreement and left HBO. The key to the agreement was a clause that gave him 15 dates on which he was to provide fights to be televised by the cable network.

The night after DiBella left HBO, Hopkins won a 12-round decision over Vanderpool. On December 1, in a rematch against Antwun Echols, he stopped his opponent in the 10th round. Then, at DiBella's urging, he entered Don King's middleweight championship tournament and, on April 14, 2001, decisioned Keith Holmes. The Echols and Holmes fights were televised by HBO on dates that "belonged" to DiBella.

Three weeks after defeating Holmes, Hopkins voiced his feelings about DiBella to Internet writer Paul Upham. "It was a great choice that I made working with Lou DiBella," Hopkins said. "He showed me what kind of man he was. He not only invested in me as a person and a human being; he didn't let any advice that might of come through his ears in the last seven or eight years influence his thinking on treating [me] as a person. Lou DiBella has been snow on Easter Day to me. He's been Santa Claus for kids waiting for December because he delivered what he said he would. That's big fights, more belts, and better promotion from when I never had it with the people I was with formerly who didn't care. Lou DiBella played a good part, and I will never forget him for that."

On September 29, 2001, Hopkins reached the pinnacle of his career when he knocked out Felix Trinidad in the 12th round. When Larry Merchant stuck a microphone in front of him immediately after the bout, the first person Bernard thanked was DiBella.

During the first two days of trial, the jurors saw Hopkins and DiBella but, except for a brief tape excerpt, did not hear them. What they saw worked in Bernard's favor. Each day, he entered the courtroom impeccably dressed in a conservative suit. With his regal profile and calm exterior that revealed little of his emotions, he looked like Denzel Washington on Wall Street. DiBella, by contrast, squirmed constantly in his seat and resembled a bit player on *The Sopranos*.

All that changed on Wednesday, November 6. Late in the morning, Judd Burstein gave each of the jurors a transcript of the interview between Hopkins and Steve Kim. Then he played a tape of the interview [excerpts of which follow] and the ugliness in Bernard's character became clear.

"I want you to write it," Hopkins told Kim. "Now don't bullshit. Ain't nothing off the record. Me and you talk. You know how to fix it up in there. You got the tape recorder and you can't be held accountable for nothing because you're protected by the Constitution of America and you understand that Bernard said this. Every time I fought, Lou DiBella got paid, even when he was with HBO, which is fucking wrong. What I'm saying is, Steve, is that the bottom line is, Syd Vanderpool fight; now you tell me; do an HBO employee accept $50,000 while he's still working for HBO? So the thing is, everybody is trying to make Lou out as this fucking angel and that Bernard Hopkins is a fucking devil and they trying to make me look like the bad guy. So if they want to let the fucking cat out of the bag; then let's come on, let the fucking cat out of the bag. Ask HBO why an employee of their company asked me to give him $50,000. And I paid him too. I gave him $50,000. Now I'm asking Steve Kim; is that ethically right for HBO? You think Time Warner want to hear about that?"

"Who did you have to give $50,000 to?" Kim queried.

"Lou DiBella. Listen man. Listen to what I'm saying. What I'm telling you right now, Steve, is some serious, serious allegations. Wouldn't you agree?"

"Oh, yeah! I'd call them very serious."

"Now listen to this," Hopkins continued. "I'm telling you right now that these motherfuckers—and you use my words—trying to make it seem like and trying to dance around and shit that I'm the bad guy; and you know Lou is whispering stuff probably around to people too; he just ain't saying nothing open. So why not let the fucking cat out of the bag now? What's on your mind, Bernard? What's on my mind is, if anybody influence behind the scenes about Bernard Hopkins crossing Lou DiBella, they gotta understand that it was money taken out of my career before I even fought Trinidad to pay to get on the card. So yes, there. Was the money wired or the check sent prior to that day he left? Yeah; [there] was a way of doing it to not be discovered. It wasn't a gift. I don't know him that well to give DiBella $50,000 way before he even start establishing his relationship with me as an advisor. You follow me? What I'm saying is, every time Lou DiBella did something for Bernard Hopkins or played a role for Bernard Hopkins, even when he was with HBO—that's what you put in there—even when he was with HBO, he got paid. That's how you do it, Steve, and you're gonna get calls. Listen to what I just said. This is how you do it. I became real good at this. Bernard claims or Bernard said or however you put it; everything Lou DiBella have done for me, he have gotten paid for it; even when he worked as an employee for HBO."

"That's saying he's taking money under the table," Kim responded. "Illegal."

"Okay," Hopkins answered. And then the tirade continued. "I can tell you right now that I can back up every goddamn thing I'm saying, and this here is going to make the motherfuckers, whoever it is, run under the fucking covers and wish I never said it. Because the bottom line is, other people is gonna ask questions. Ohhhh! Did he really do that? And then they're gonna start digging. You see, Steve. Let me tell you something, Steve. I got a lot of information. I just don't spill everything to you. I know a lot of shit that was going on even before I dealt with Lou DiBella, but I didn't say nothing long as I didn't get fucked. But let's be clear—and I'm going to keep repeating myself till you say, 'Bernard, okay; I got it.' Every time Lou DiBella have done something for me, including lobby for me to get me on the Roy Jones undercard starting from Syd Vanderpool—it ain't that many; you can count 'em up yourself; it ain't that many—he got paid even when he worked for HBO. I can prove it. So what I'm saying to you, Steve, you gonna slay the fucking bastard."

At 12:07 p.m., immediately after the tape was played, Burstein called DiBella to the witness stand. DiBella was a nervous wreck. He's a passionate man, and Bernard's betrayal had hurt him deeply. The court proceedings had become the emotional equivalent of a criminal trial for him. Even though he was the plaintiff in the case, he felt like the defendant because it was his reputation that was on trial. Now, his complexion was almost as green as his shirt. But because of his nerves, DiBella came across as aggrieved (which he was) and soft-spoken (which he normally isn't). It was a marked contrast to the stream of obscenity-laced vindictiveness that the jurors had just heard on tape from Hopkins.

What was the $50,000 payment for?

DiBella explained to the jurors that he knew the business of boxing and could offer sound advice to Hopkins. He had also been able to guarantee to Bernard that, once he left HBO, Hopkins would be showcased on the network through dates to be included in his termination contract. And he would spend to publicize and market the fighter.

DiBella confirmed Peter Mozarsky's testimony that he had properly disclosed to HBO that he had entered into a business relationship with Hopkins. He confirmed Kery Davis' testimony that the Hopkins-Echols rematch was the first card to use an HBO date granted to him under his termination contract. In fact, Davis had testified that Hopkins-Echols II was preconditioned on DiBella using one of his dates, and the same precondition was true of Hopkins-Holmes. Moreover, Davis had testified that, during the Hopkins-Echols II negotiations, he had thought of Team Hopkins as being Hopkins, DiBella, and Arnold Joseph.

Burstein asked DiBella if he had demanded $50,000 as a precondition to Hopkins appearing on HBO.

"Absolutely not," DiBella answered. "It's against everything I am and everything I stand for. I would never do anything like that."

Then came a moment of high drama. Burstein asked DiBella about the impact that Hopkins' charges and the Kim article had on him.

"It was devastating to me," DiBella responded. "It was one of the hardest things . . ." His voice faltered and then he broke down. "It killed me," he said, his words mingling with sobs. "I was ripped apart. I'm still ripped apart. I have to answer this allegation constantly. I've been lucky to have a pristine reputation in a filthy business. And to be portrayed as a television executive who sold dates to a fighter was devastating to me. It was a horrible lie."

DiBella's direct testimony ended with the introduction of a pair of boxing gloves. On October 1, 2001, two days after he defeated Trinidad, Bernard had invited Lou to his room at the St. Regis Hotel and, as a show of appreciation, given him what he said at the time were the gloves he'd used to knock out Trinidad.

Then Robert W. Hayes (Hopkins' attorney) began his cross examination of DiBella, but it didn't lead to much. The salient facts that unfolded were as follows.

Once Hopkins (on DiBella's advice) signed a promotional agreement with Don King and entered the middleweight championship tournament, Bernard was no longer obligated to pay DiBella out of his purses. Rather, DiBella was to collect his fee from King out of net revenue from each fight. DiBella was paid $390,000 by King out of revenue from Hopkins Holmes and $300,000 by King out of revenue from Hopkins-Trinidad. Neither number was unreasonable given the amount of money generated by each bout, the fact that Hopkins-Holmes had been televised on one of DiBella's HBO dates, and the fact that DiBella had been receiving a base salary of $600,000 with a guaranteed bonus of at least $300,000 annually when he left HBO.

After Hopkins-Trinidad, King had been slow to negotiate a contract to pay DiBella out of revenue on future fights. According to the defense, DiBella then asked Bernard to pay him out of his own purse. And when Bernard refused, Lou broke their agreement by pressuring Hopkins to breach his contractual obligations to King and manipulating the media to preclude King and Hopkins from entering into a long-term contract for Bernard's services with HBO. That caused Bernard to begin asking questions and view his entire relationship with DiBella in a different light.

But it didn't stick. DiBella testified that he had asked Hopkins to support him in his negotiations with King, nothing more. And Bernard had possessed the leverage to do that successfully if he'd chosen to exercise it. In fact, on December 20, 2001 (the day after the Kim interview), Hopkins had renegotiated his own contract with King to increase the minimum purses to which he would be entitled for certain fights by roughly $1-million per fight and gotten King to give him a $225,000 Bentley as part of the bargain.

By the end of the day, DiBella had begun to calm down; like a fighter who entered a fight doubting his ability to survive and has gone back to his corner saying to himself, "Hey; I'm winning this fight." The following morning, his cross-examination ended. Then, shortly after noon on Thursday, Burstein called Hopkins to the stand.

It was a shrewd decision. Conventional courtroom procedure would have been to wait for Hayes to call Hopkins as a defense witness. But that would have allowed Hopkins to tell his story in his way. Now the facts would come out the way Burstein wanted them to.

Bernard is a great fighter. He's also exceedingly verbal and smart, but his credentials as a businessman are suspect.

Since dumping DiBella, Hopkins has had only one fight (against Carl Daniels on February 2, 2002). His next bout is tentatively scheduled for January 11 against Morrade Hakker at the First Union Center in Philadelphia.

King won the right to promote the bout with a purse bid of $1,501,000. Hopkins' announced share of that total will be $1,125,750, although there are rumors that he made a side-deal with King to ensure DKP winning the purse bid that will reduce his take to $750,000. There are also persistent rumors that the fight won't take place at all. Both HBO and Showtime have declined to televise it, and King might be reluctant to promote a pay-per-view bout on the same night as a free National Football League playoff game.

Meanwhile, Hopkins has turned down an offer of $6-million plus a percentage of profits to fight Roy Jones on HBO Pay-Per-View and a three-fight multimillion-dollar package from Showtime for bouts against Hakkar, Joe Calzaghe, and Harry Simon. That led King to declare recently, "Bernard Hopkins is like a man who won the lottery and then waited to cash his ticket until after it expired."

On the witness stand, Hopkins didn't have control over his environment. And as Burstein's questioning progressed, the loss of control appeared to bother the fighter. His confident exterior melted away and he seemed to physically shrink, pulling his shoulders protectively inward. This wasn't something that could be settled with fists.

Hopkins denied to the jury that he had a business relationship with DiBella when the $50,000 payment was agreed upon in early 2000. "I was told that $50,000 would be the fee to get on the [Vanderpool] card," he said. That, of course, ignored the fact that Hopkins was locked into the card when the earlier deal was made for him to fight Brian Barbosa.

"I don't know if it was criminal or not that he took the $50,000," Hopkins continued. "At the time I said good things about Lou DiBella, I honestly believed he was the person I said he was . . . I'm a goldfish in a river with sharks."

It had been previously suggested to Burstein that he hand Hopkins the gloves that Bernard had given to DiBella at the St. Regis Hotel (the ones from the Trinidad fight) and ask him to try them on to see if they fit. The attorney had emphatically rejected the suggestion. But he did ask Bernard about the gift.

"They're not the gloves I fought in," Hopkins responded.

In reality, the gloves were a back-up pair that had been held by the state athletic commission for emergency use in case the gloves actually worn split during the fight. At day's end as the parties walked out of the courtroom, DiBella turned to a friend, lifted his right index finger, and ran it across his neck, emulating Hopkins' trademark slash of an executioner.

The trial resumed on Tuesday, November 12, after a four-day holiday-weekend. The day started with what Hopkins regarded as a good omen. He was sitting in the courtroom with his mother, waiting for the session to begin, when a Hispanic maintenance worker approached and asked for his autograph.

"I didn't think Spanish people wanted my autograph," Hopkins told his suitor.

"I do. I think you're great."

"What's your name?"

"Tito."

Hopkins smiled and turned to his mother. "That's a good way to start the day," he said. He signed. Then court began. And right away, Burstein was all over him.

Hopkins claimed that there had been no business relationship between him and DiBella other than payment of the alleged $50,000 bribe until after the second Echols fight, which took place on December 1, 2000. He also claimed he didn't learn until autumn 2000 that DiBella had left HBO. And he maintained that two of his attorneys (Arnold Joseph and Scott Magargee) had been party to the conference call in early 2000 during which DiBella demanded the alleged $50,000 bribe but that neither attorney suggested to him until months later that it had been improper for DiBella to ask for the $50,000. His testimony boiled down to the proposition that he didn't know it was wrong for DiBella to demand and receive the $50,000 until he learned in autumn 2001 (after the Trinidad fight) that it was against HBO policy for HBO employees to demand and receive bribes. "I thought that's the way business was normally done," he told the jury.

Burstein ran through a string of contradictions between Hopkins' deposition testimony, an affidavit that Bernard had signed in support of a failed motion for summary judgment, and his trial testimony. For example, at his deposition, Hopkins had stated under oath that his advisory relationship with DiBella began shortly after the Vanderpool fight.

Next, Burstein elicited the admission from Hopkins that DiBella had agreed to loan him $30,000 for training expenses in advance of the Vanderpool fight. Hopkins claimed that the loan had been negotiated in the same conversation that the disputed $50,000 payment was agreed upon. Why had DiBella loaned him the money?

"They needed this fight on HBO," Hopkins answered. "I wasn't going to fight on the card unless Lou loaned me the $30,000 for training expenses."

That, of course, raised the issue, if HBO needed the Hopkins-Vanderpool fight so badly that DiBella had to loan Hopkins $30,000, then why did Bernard feel that he had to pay a $50,000 bribe to get on the card?

As the noose tightened around his neck, Hopkins began to ramble evasively. Again and again, the judge admonished, "Mr. Hopkins; you're not answering the question . . . Mr. Hopkins; just answer the question 'yes' or 'no' . . . Mr. Hopkins, every time there's a question, you go way beyond the question. Just answer the question."

Then Burstein confronted Hopkins with the Kim interview. At his deposition and in an affidavit, Bernard had stated under oath that Kim had taken his words out of context. Now, after an excerpt from the tape was played for the jury, Hopkins became even more evasive and Judge Chin took over the questioning.

"Is the article accurate?" the judge demanded.

"Yes," Hopkins admitted.

"Are you quoted accurately?"

"Yes."

"Is anything taken out of context?"

"No."

"Was that an accurate recording of what you said to Mr. Kim?"

"Yes."

On Wednesday, November 13, Hopkins' testimony was interrupted so Burstein could question Kim, who had flown from Los Angeles to New York. Kim verified the transcript of the tape that Burstein had put into evidence and testified that Bernard made it clear to him during their interview that he wanted his allegations about DiBella to be published. He also testified that, several days after the article went online, Hopkins telephoned Kim and complimented him on the piece being "very, very, very, very accurate."

As for the damage to DiBella's reputation caused by the article, Kim acknowledged, "This one created a few ripples. If you're selling honor and integrity and your personal reputation is questioned, that would have to hurt."

Then Hopkins returned to the stand and it was Hayes' turn to question. First he led his client through a recitation about growing up on the mean streets of Philadelphia (omitting reference to the 46 months that Bernard spent in prison). After that, Hopkins talked about the sacrifices he had made to become a world champion.

As for the nitty-gritty of the case, Hopkins testified that DiBella told him in March or April 2000 that he would probably be leaving HBO and was interested in working with Bernard should that happen. But according to Hopkins, "We never talked about prepayment for anything." Then Bernard repeated the allegation that he took part in a speaker-phone conversation with DiBella at one end of the line and Hopkins with two of his attorneys at the other end. During this conversation, DiBella allegedly said that Roy Jones and Murad Muhammad didn't want Bernard on the May undercard but that Lou would get him on if Bernard gave him $50,000 immediately after the fight. According to Hopkins, there was no mention in that conversation of DiBella providing any other services and he had no business relationship with DiBella until after the December 2000 Echols rematch. In fact, according to Hopkins, DiBella didn't do anything for him after the Echols rematch either other than advise him to enter the middleweight championship tournament. Then, once Hopkins defeated Trinidad, the relationship between fighter and advisor fell apart because, in November 2001, Lou asked for 15 percent of Bernard's gross purses for the remainder of his career.

"He always said he wouldn't take nothing from me," Hopkins testified. "I seen him changing after the Trinidad fight. He continued to keep asking for the 15 percent. Then he started hollering and screaming and I stopped returning his telephone calls because I knew what he was calling for. I was prepared to work with Lou DiBella, but I wasn't willing to give him 15 percent."

Also, according to Hopkins, he learned for the first time on December 19, 2001 (when Arnold Joseph reported to him about a conversation with Kery Davis) that DiBella had violated HBO policy by demanding the $50,000 bribe. "I got betrayed; I got lied to," said Hopkins. So when Bernard talked with Steve Kim that same day, "I lost it a little bit," he acknowledged. "I was angry." But, said Hopkins, "My intention wasn't to hurt Lou. I was looking for answers."

However, the Hopkins-Kim interview tape spoke for itself. In truth, Hopkins was making accusations, not looking for answers.

On the morning of Thursday, November 14, Burstein got a chance to reexamine Hopkins and he exposed myriad contradictions between the fighter's trial testimony, his deposition testimony, and his affidavit in support of an earlier motion for summary judgment.

[Here, I should note that, after Hopkins' testimony was complete, I was called to the witness stand. Bernard had denied telling DiBella that the gloves he gave him on October 1, 2001, were the gloves he'd worn in the Trinidad fight. I was there when the gift-giving occurred, and Burstein made a last-minute decision to put what I saw on the record. My testimony was brief. I stated that, when Bernard gave the gift, he told DiBella, "These are the gloves I knocked out Trinidad with. Everything good that happened to me this year, I owe to you." The thrust of my testimony was not that the gloves were genuine, but rather what Hopkins told DiBella.]

Then the defense called its first witness; Scott Magargee.

Hopkins' entire legal team worked at Cozen O'Connor, a Philadelphia law firm with approximately 440 attorneys, 16 offices in the United States, and an office in London. Magargee was a senior associate at the firm. His background was primarily in criminal defense, although he also did some civil litigation.

Under questioning by Hayes, Magargee stated that he was in a conference room at Cozen O'Connor with Hopkins and Arnold Joseph on April 11, 2000, and overheard a conference call between them and DiBella. He then claimed he overheard DiBella saying that the May 13 Roy Jones card was one of his dates and that he could convince HBO to put Bernard on the undercard but that his fee for doing so would be $50,000. According to Magargee, he gave no thought to the propriety of DiBella's request and heard no further discussion about it until he learned much later that the $50,000 had been paid.

To call Burstein's cross-examination of the witness a 10-7 round would be charitable to Magargee. Among the points made were:

(1) Although Magargee had been admitted to practice in Pennsylvania and

New Jersey, he had subsequently been declared "administratively unautho-rized" to practice law by the Supreme Court of New Jersey.

(2) Hayes and Joseph will be among those voting in the future to determine whether or not Magargee is elevated to partner status at Cozen O'Connor.

(3) At Margargee's deposition, he had been unable to recall whether the supposed bribe conversation took place in March or April 2000.

(4) Also at his deposition, Magargee stated it was Arnold Joseph (not DiBella) who had told him that the Roy Jones card would be on one of DiBella's dates.

(5) Magargee couldn't remember the specific words used by DiBella when he'd demanded the alleged $50,000 bribe and couldn't remember whether or not Hopkins agreed to pay it in the same conversation.

(6) There was nothing in Magargee's billing printout for April 11, 2000, that indicated he had attended a meeting with Hopkins. Here, Hayes objected, stating that portions of the billing printout had been redacted—i.e. whited out. That angered the judge, who noted that it was Hopkins' own legal team that had whited out a portion of the billing printout on grounds that the redacted material was confidential and had nothing to do with the DiBella-Hopkins litigation. The judge then called Hayes' objection "unfair" and "misleading" and told the jury, "Mr. Burstein's point is that, if Mr. Magargee had met Mr. Hopkins, he would have written down that he met with Mr. Hopkins."

(7) Magargee claimed that he had been privy to a conversation that amounted to commercial bribery (which is a criminal offense). Magargee's background is primarily in criminal law. Yet he claimed that, at the time of the conversation, he didn't know that DiBella was doing anything illegal, unethical, or otherwise inappropriate.

On Thursday afternoon, portions of Don King's taped deposition testimony were played for the jury. Then Hayes called Arnold Joseph as a witness. Joseph repeated the story of the April 11, 2000, conference call in which DiBella allegedly demanded the $50,000 bribe. He also claimed that, despite having spent three years as an assistant district attorney in Manhattan prior to going to work at Cozen O'Connor, he didn't know at the time that there was anything improper about DiBella's demand because he thought that May 13 was one of DiBella's dates. Here, it's worth noting that, in his deposition, Joseph never said that Magargee was present during the alleged "bribe" conversation.

Then there was the matter of when Hopkins actually paid DiBella. Everyone agreed that, on May 19, 2000, Hopkins repaid the previously mentioned $30,000 dollar loan. However, the $50,000 payment was not made until January 2001. Hopkins had testified that, on May 13, minutes after the Vanderpool fight, he offered DiBella checks for $30,000 and $50,000 and that DiBella refused them, telling him that he was still working for HBO. [In truth, DiBella had already finalized his termination agreement and had left HBO.]

Then, according to Hopkins, DiBella went to Philadelphia on May 19 and picked up the $30,000 check but told Bernard that he was still working out the details of his termination contract and thus wanted to further defer the $50,000 payment. Joseph offered similar testimony, although his recitation of events immediately after the Vanderpool fight differed in significant respects from Hopkins' purported recollection.

The heart of the matter, according to Burstein, was that, in the year 2000, DiBella had given deposition testimony for use by Hopkins in a lawsuit in Denver between Hopkins and America Presents. Prior to the actual trial, the attorney for America Presents raised the question of whether DiBella had a business relationship with Hopkins that the court should be aware of, since that might have a bearing on how Lou's credibility would be weighed by the Denver jury. On August 18, 2000 (three months after the Vanderpool bout), Joseph (with Magargee at his side) denied to the judge in Denver that Hopkins and DiBella had any relationship. According to DiBella, it was Joseph who had requested that payment of the $50,000 be deferred. And according to Burstein, Joseph requested the deferral so he could lie to the judge in Denver about the existence of the DiBella-Hopkins relationship.

Joseph admitted on cross-examination that he had "in the back of my mind a slight concern" that the $50,000 might become an issue in the America Presents litigation. But under cross-examination, he continued to maintain that there was no business relationship between DiBella and Hopkins at that time. He also stated that he never questioned the propriety of DiBella's actions until December 2001 when DiBella allegedly asked for 15 percent of Hopkins' future purses and Kery Davis expressed surprise when Joseph told him the Cozen O'Connor version of the DiBella-Hopkins relationship. That, according to Joseph, caused him to reevaluate DiBella's conduct. Burstein then ran through a litany of inconsistencies between Joseph's trial testimony and his earlier deposition, and the day's session came to an end.

The defense rested on Friday morning after calling Bernard's wife and mother-in-law to testify with regard to minor bookkeeping matters. If anything, their testimony helped DiBella, since Hopkins had denied that he brought his wife to DiBella's 2000 Christmas party, and Jeanette Hopkins admitted that she had been there with her husband.

At 11:30 a.m. on Friday, Robert Hayes began his summation to the jury. Using Hopkins as a prop, he stood behind the fighter, occasionally putting his hands on Bernard's shoulders. Then he moved to the lectern directly in front of the jury and pounded away at the theme of his case —that Hopkins, Joseph, and Magargee had all been privy to an April 11, 2000, conference call in which DiBella demanded a $50,000 bribe.

At 1:30 p.m., it was Burstein's turn. But five minutes into Burstein's summation, the judge, who had been perusing some documents, halted the proceedings and asked counsel to come with him to the robing room. Minutes later, they returned to the courtroom and the judge addressed the jury. His remarks were stunning.

The judge had been given an unredacted copy of Scott Magargee's billing printout for April 11, 2000, the day that Magargee, Hopkins, and Joseph all claimed to have been present at Cozen O'Connor for the conference call during which DiBella purportedly demanded a $50,000 bribe. But contrary to the representation that Hayes had made in court the previous day, the redacted material did relate to DiBella v. Hopkins; it was not confidential; and it indicated that, while there had been telephone calls between Hopkins and Magargee that day, THERE HAD BEEN NO FACE-TO FACE MEETING BETWEEN THEM. In other words, the testimony that Hopkins, Magargee and Joseph had been together in a conference room listening to Lou DiBella demand a bribe on a speaker-phone was fiction. Moreover, it appeared as though someone at Cozen O'Connor had deliberately whited out portions of the billing printout with the intent of fraudulently supporting the defense contention that the meeting in question actually occurred.

Burstein knew a prime opportunity when he saw it. Holding the billing printout aloft, he walked over to Hopkins, pointed directly at him and, with all the indignation he could muster, declared, "This man is a liar. Bernard Hopkins makes it up as he goes along. He's a great athlete, but he's a terrible person. That kind of rampant dishonesty needs to be checked. Bernard Hopkins has told you all that, when it suits his purposes, he'll lie under oath."

Then, Burstein flashed chart after chart on a video screen. The first few charts each bore the legend "Arnold Joseph's Lies" above excerpts from Joseph's testimony. Next, came charts entitled "Scott Magargee's Lies". After that, Burstein read a statement by Judge Kane, who had presided over the America Presents litigation in Denver. On September 4 of this year, referring to Joseph's conduct, Judge Kane declared, "Now I find myself faced with serious allegations that there was never a fair presentation of facts in this case and that I may have been misled by factual omissions and possibly even outright misrepresentations."

By the time Burstein finished his summation, labeling Hopkins "a vicious petty man," the question wasn't whether the jury would find in favor of DiBella; it was "how much?"

During a brief interlude that followed, Hayes sought to explain his handling of the billing printout. But the judge responded, "I don't accept what you tell me. It's appalling. I am appalled." Then Judge Chin read his charge to the jury (an explanation of the law to be followed during deliberations) and court adjourned for the weekend.

Jury deliberations began shortly after 9:00 a.m. on Monday, November 18. At 9:25, the jurors sent a note to the judge asking for a flip chart, easel, masking tape, markers, pens, post-its, highlighters, coffee, and water.

"Too bad they didn't ask for a rope and noose," Burstein told DiBella.

The supplies were provided. Then, at 10:40 a.m., the judge called counsel back into the courtroom to address the issue of Magargee's billing printout.

"I was extremely troubled by events relating to the time-sheet," Judge Chin told the attorneys. "I have some questions. Whose decision was it to make the redaction? Who made the redaction?"

"I did, your honor," Hayes acknowledged.

"What was the basis for your decision? It seems to me that, on their face, the [redacted] words are relevant."

Hayes launched into a rambling response and, after a while, the judge interrupted.

"I don't see how you can make that argument with a straight face. It's ludicrous. It's all very, very troubling." Then, regarding the issue of sanctions against Hayes and possibly others at Cozen O'Connor, Chin said, "I'm reluctant to go down this road, but frankly, I don't think I have much choice. On the face of it, it appears to me that you withheld evidence that might be helpful to Mr. DiBella and that you tried to mislead the jury. It is the critical conversation in the case. It is during this conversation that Mr. DiBella supposedly [demanded] a bribe. It is extremely, extremely troubling. There are different ways to address the issue. But frankly, you should treat it as a serious matter."

Then came the waiting.

DiBella and his company (DiBella Entertainment, Inc) were both plaintiffs in the lawsuit and had raised two causes of action. The first claim was for libel. Here, DiBella had to prove by a preponderance of the evidence (that it was more likely true than not) that (1) the statements complained of were defamatory; (2) the statements complained of referred to DiBella and/or DiBella Entertainment; and (3) Hopkins made the statements. In addition, he had to prove by clear and convincing evidence (evidence establishing a high degree of probability) that (4) the statements complained of were false; and (5) Hopkins made them knowing that they were false or with reckless disregard as to truth.

DiBella's second claim had been made pursuant to a theory known as "quantum meruit" which requires the payment of fair value for services rendered in the absence of an express contract. Here, it was necessary to prove to the jury by a preponderance of the evidence that (1) DiBella and/or DiBella Entertainment performed services in good faith; (2) Hopkins accepted these services and was enriched by them; (3) DiBella had expected reasonable compensation for his services; (4) Hopkins did not pay reasonable value for the services; and (5) equity and conscience required further payment.

A unanimous verdict was required on each cause of action.

Shortly before 3:00 p.m. on Monday afternoon, the jury asked to hear the tape of an interview that Hopkins had given to Rich Marate of ESPN Radio in February 2002. The Marate interview and statements that Hopkins had made to Ron Borges of *The Boston Globe* and Bernard Fernandez of the *Philadelphia Daily News* were also at issue in the trial. Then, at 5:30 p.m., deliberations were halted for the night.

The jury reconvened on Tuesday morning, and the feel of a verdict was in the air. At 1:12 p.m., shortly after lunch, the judge received a note stating that a verdict had been reached. At 1:30 p.m., the jury entered the courtroom and the verdict was read.

DiBella was awarded $110,000 in compensatory damages and an additional $500,000 in punitive damages in conjunction with the interview that Hopkins gave to Steve Kim. The other libel claims were dismissed, in part because the jurors felt that they were duplicative of the first. The quantum meruit claim was also denied because the jurors felt that DiBella had been adequately compensated for the work he'd performed on Hopkins' behalf. "The numbers were a bit intimidating," one of the jurors said afterward. "None of us get millions of dollars for advising someone or signing a contract." Another juror added, "All this talk about dates and Echols I and Echols II; it was a bit confusing."

There will be post-trial motions and, perhaps, appeals. Also, requests for sanctions against Hopkins' counsel and possible disciplinary proceedings lie ahead. As far as DiBella is concerned, a criminal prosecution would also be appropriate.

"The most shocking thing to me about this experience," DiBella said after the verdict had been reached, "has been the moral bankruptcy of Bernard's lawyers. I'm repulsed by their conduct. They went far beyond the boundaries of acceptable advocacy. All they did was sit down with their client and piece together a pack of lies. If they aren't punished, there's no point in the legal system having rules to govern the conduct of lawyers."

Then DiBella turned pensive. "I'm sorry it came to this," he said. "But Bernard did what he did, and I did what I had to do in response to keep my reputation in tact. There hasn't been a day since the Kim article came out that I haven't thought about it. Every day, Bernard's accusations have been a dark cloud hanging over my life. His betrayal will always hurt; but at least now, I can put it behind me. I'm at peace with the fact that my side of the story has been told and the truth has won out."

Then DiBella reached into his pocket and pulled out a totem he'd been carrying around for months; the metal top from a small glass jar. The underside of the top was inscribed with a quotation from Mark Twain: "If you tell the truth, you don't have to remember anything."

That's what DiBella v. Hopkins was all about. Bernard Hopkins, for all his talents, couldn't turn an ugly lie into the truth. ❏

*Fighters often get the short end of the stick. But a 96-4 purse split? Subsequent to this column being written, Carl Daniels and his manager got cold feet and the referenced lawsuit was never filed.*

# THE 96-4 PURSE SPLIT

Carl Daniels is on the verge of filing a lawsuit against AOL-TimeWarner and Don King Productions in the United States District Court for New Jersey. The suit will allege that the defendants tortuiously interfered with Daniels' business relationships and conspired to deprive him of just compensation in conjunction with a purse bid that was held for Daniels' February 2, 2002, bout against middleweight champion Bernard Hopkins. Hopkins was victorious in the bout when Daniels was unable to answer the bell for the 11th round.

More significantly for the business of boxing, the lawsuit will seek a declaratory judgment from the court that HBO is a "promoter" within the meaning of the Muhammad Ali Boxing Reform Act. If the court so rules and the ruling is upheld on appeal, it would limit HBO's long-term contracts with fighters, force HBO to make certain financial disclosures, and otherwise change the way it does business.

Daniels was the mandatory IBF challenger for Hopkins' crown. According to Nick Garone (Daniels' manager), after Hopkins defeated Felix Trinidad to unify the middleweight championship last September, Don King offered Daniels $400,000 to face Hopkins. Garone asked for $900,000. A purse bid was then scheduled for November 7.

The purpose of purse bids is to ensure that a champion and mandatory challenger receive fair compensation for their services. Any duly registered promoter who wants to promote the fight can submit a sealed bid; the highest bid is accepted; and the purse is then divided 75 percent to 25 percent in favor of the champion.

Under IBF rules, each promoter registered with the organization is notified by fax that a purse bid is about to take place. At the time of the Hopkins-Daniels purse bid, 11 promoters were so registered. The annual registration fee is $2,000.

"A week before the purse bid," Garone remembers, "Marian Muhammad called me up and said, 'Do you realize this is going to purse bid? I told her, 'Yeah, I'm in negotiations.'"

Finally, according to Garone, after long back-and-forth negotiations, he and

King shook hands on a purse of $800,000 for Daniels.

"We shook hands," Garone says. "That's a funny statement. I thought we had a deal because I shook hands on a contract with Don King. Don told me he'd call Joe Dwyer [chairman of the IBF Championship Committee] to postpone the purse bid, and I really thought I was going to get a written contract. Then Don never called me back."

As the day of the purse bid approached, Garone began to get nervous and took steps in an effort to protect his fighter. By his account, "I had Les Bonano and Dino Duva call [HBO Sports Vice President] Kery Davis and say, 'We're thinking of bidding. What are the particulars?' I was physically in the room with Dino when he called Kery and asked what HBO would pay as a license fee. Kery told him, 'I won't disclose what's on the table. We'd rather deal with Don King on this one. We'd rather you not get involved.'"

John Agnetti, the attorney for Carl Daniels, goes further. He quotes a third party as saying Davis told him, "If anyone else bids successfully on this fight, we're not going to televise it."

Davis acknowledges that HBO was trying to negotiate a long-term contract with Don King for Hopkins' services at the time of the purse bid. He doesn't remember talking with Bonano about the fight. As for his conversation with Duva, Davis says, "I told Dino that we were supporting King in the purse bid. Don had a number from us pursuant to contract terms that had been negotiated, although I don't think the contract had been signed yet. If another promoter had bid on the fight and won, I don't know what would have happened. But when we have a multi-fight contract with a promoter or a fighter, it's our practice not to support other promoters in a purse bid. That would be bidding against ourselves."

"It was a screwy situation," Dino Duva remembers. "We were considering going in to bid on the fight, but Kery said he was in an awkward position and couldn't talk about numbers before a purse bid because of confidentiality clauses in his dealings with King."

Les Bonano says simply, "It is a fact that I had a conversation with Kery, and I'm sure the things Nick is telling you about it are accurate and true because Nick is an honest guy. But I don't want to get involved in this at the present time for reasons I'm sure you can understand."

The purse bid was scheduled for November 6, 2001, at noon at the IBF office in New Jersey.

"That morning," says Garone, "Dino called Marian Muhammad and said he wanted to submit a bid through Duva Boxing, but she told him he couldn't because Duva Boxing wasn't licensed with the IBF. Dino asked her to hold off on the bid until later in the day so Duva Boxing could apply for a license, and she refused."

Under IBF rules, a promoter must be registered with the organization for at least 30 days prior to making a purse bid. There is a way around the 30-day requirement. A promoter can file a non-refundable $20,000 fee with a request for an exception and hope for the best. Don King himself followed that procedure in 2001, when he wanted to bid on the second fight between Vernon Forrest and Raul Frank. The IBF granted his request; King won the purse bid; and the two men fought at Madison Square Garden.

Be that as it may, Bobby Goodman of Don King Productions came to the Hopkins-Daniels purse bid with two envelopes. No other promoter was present to force a higher bid from King, so Goodman submitted a bid of $500,000. Daniels received 25 percent of that amount; $125,000. Meanwhile, according to Garone, HBO paid King a license fee of $3.5-million. King, in turn, paid Hopkins a reported $2.8-million.

Joe Dwyer says he's sorry that Daniels came out of the purse bid so poorly but opines, "I think it was incompetence on the part of Garone. It's up to the fighter and his management team not to put themselves in this sort of situation. Nick was trying to play in the big leagues, and he didn't belong."

Garone acknowledges that he could have handled things better and says he feels awful about the small purse paid to his fighter. But he also says that his handling of the situation doesn't justify what he claims was misconduct by others. His bottom line is, a winning purse bid of $500,000 makes no sense when HBO is paying a license fee that's so much larger.

Certainly, if Daniels had a promoter of his own, the purse bid would have been significantly higher. Promoter Dan Goossen says that a competitive situation could have resulted in a purse bid of $2.5-million.

Cedric Kushner is more cautious. "No one thought Daniels could win," Kushner notes. "So you're really talking about a one-fight situation, because Don King has Hopkins. At best, if you put the site fee, foreign television, and sponsorships together, you have about $1-million. Then, let's say, HBO bids $2-million, because that $3.5-million was by no means guaranteed. That gives a promoter $3-million to work with, but you have expenses in promoting the fight and you want to make a profit. So a promoter might bid between $2-million and $2.25-million."

What would have happened then? If another promoter had bid $2-million, Hopkins might have refused to fight for his 75 percent share ($1.5-million). In that event, the fight would have fallen apart, and Bernard would have been stripped of his title by the IBF. Certainly, as Kushner notes, the $3.5-million HBO license fee would have dropped, since that number was contingent on Hopkins-Daniels being part of an HBO-King-Hopkins contract. But suppose, to the dismay of the promoter, HBO didn't bid $2-million either?

Pat English, the attorney for Main Events, answers that question with the thought, "There is no answer." According to English, "No one discouraged us from bidding on the fight; and frankly, we should have, but a lot of these purse bids slip by. There's a tendency not to bid on another promoter's fighter, because of the assumption that the other promoter will find a way to structure a deal with his fighter that allows him to win the purse bid." Also, English continues, "there were really only two networks to sell the fight to: HBO and Showtime. So it all depends on what TV was willing to pay."

Here, the thoughts of Showtime's Jay Larkin are instructive. "No one came to us with the fight," says Larkin. "If they had, we would have been interested, but only at the right price. As a stand-alone one-off fight, $500,000 is a lot closer to reality for Hopkins-Daniels than $3.5-million."

Thus, Dan Goossen speaks for his brethren when he says, "Sure, HBO wanted things to fall into place in a certain way. But Nick Garone let it happen. Nick is a nice guy. Nick means well, but he got outsmarted."

Still, as Garone notes, when HBO is paying a license fee of $3.5-million, the winning purse bid should be more than $500,000. He says that the integrity of the purse bid system was compromised; that the system didn't work properly.

The week before the fight, Garone sent a claim letter to HBO along with a copy of a draft complaint which he said he would file if an equitable financial adjustment was not forthcoming. Now Carl Daniels appears ready to make good on Garone's threat.

"The key here is HBO's conduct," says Garone. "HBO was scaring off other promoters. Don knew the numbers, and HBO refused to give the numbers to other promoters. And on top of that, Kery Davis was telling other promoters not to bother bidding on the fight, that HBO wanted to work with King. That's because HBO wanted to close a multi-fight deal with King and Hopkins. But Carl was forced to subsidize their deal. It's another example of the system allowing certain people and certain corporations to squeeze honest fighters as hard as they can while funneling fighters and money to each other."

John Agnetti, who will represent Daniels in the litigation, is obviously in accord. "I know we're in for a fight," says Agnetti. "Boxing is controlled by a small group of people, and if you buck the system, they'll come at you with a vengeance. Also, there's a conspiracy of silence in the industry, which means it will be very hard to get all of the people involved to testify. But Hopkins-Daniels is a microcosm of how business is conducted in boxing. This lawsuit isn't just about Carl Daniels. It's about the good of the game. Fighters should get a fair shake, and Carl didn't." ❑

*Mike Tyson provides endless copy, as this November 2002 article demonstrated.*

# TRAINING MIKE TYSON

Sooner or later, most people around Mike Tyson become "former." That's true of his wives, managers, television networks, and promoters. It's also true of his trainers.

Over the years, nine men have had a significant voice in training Tyson. Listed in chronological order, they are Cus D'Amato, Teddy Atlas, Kevin Rooney, Jay Bright, Aaron Snowell, Rich Giachetti, Tommy Brooks, Stacey McKinley, and Ronnie Shields.

Now Tyson is in search of trainer number ten. Buddy McGirt is one name that has been prominently mentioned. As the days pass, there may well be more. Meanwhile, yours truly has contacted ten of the best-known trainers in boxing.

Donald Turner trained Evander Holyfield for both of his victories over Tyson. Kevin Rooney trained Tyson through the Michael Spinks fight. Tyson's record with Rooney was a 35-0 with 31 knockouts. Teddy Atlas helped train Tyson as an amateur when he was with Cus D'Amato. Lou Duva trained Tyrell Biggs when he fought Tyson. Alton Merkerson has been with Roy Jones, Jr. dating back to Jones' days as an amateur. Angelo Dundee was in Trevor Berbick's corner the night Tyson won the WBC heavyweight title. Later, he trained Pinklon Thomas for his bout against Tyson. Floyd Mayweather, Sr. trains Oscar De La Hoya and describes himself as "the greatest trainer in the world." Emanuel Steward readied Lennox Lewis for Lewis-Tyson. Gil Clancy is a longtime trainer and one of the most respected voices in boxing. Bouie Fisher helped mold Bernard Hopkins, and he was briefly in the gym with Tyson when Mike was young.

Here's what each of these men had to say when asked how they'd respond if Tyson called and asked them to train him.

### Don Turner

Evander is my guy, and I'm not the type of person to be jumping around. So as long as Evander is fighting, it would be impossible. But if Evander retired and Tyson called, I'd give it a try. I wouldn't bother asking questions—"Are you gonna do this? Will you do that?"—because when you ask a guy questions like that, he'll tell you what you want to hear. And I wouldn't try to run his life outside the ring. Mike Tyson has been the same way outside the ring his whole career. These things you read about in the papers now didn't just start happening. As for what I'd do with him inside the ring, Tyson has been fighting for a long time. He knows what he has to do. Train hard; that's number one. Mike trained a lot harder when he was young than he does now. And in all honesty, I'd go to Kevin Rooney and ask him to help me. What you want, really, is to get Mike back to the way he was when he was with Kevin. Don't teach him anything new. When a guy already knows how to fight, a trainer is there to remind him of what he knows, not to reinvent the man as a fighter. If Mike went back to the program that Cus D'Amato started him on when he was young, he could be a top fighter again. In fact, very few people can beat him as he is now.

### Kevin Rooney

Yeah, if Mike called me, I'd do it. But I'd tell him, "You have to trust me." And we'd have to go back to the way things were. Mike's not the same fighter he used to be, and there are reasons for that. Mike's thing is, he's the boss. And I'd tell him, "You're the boss of your own life; but when you're in training camp, I'm the boss." Mike always had a tendency to be lazy, but I knew how to motivate him. And it's obvious that he doesn't train like he used to anymore. Against Lennox Lewis, in the biggest fight of his life, Mike was only in shape to fight one round. So I'd tell him, "When you're in training camp, you don't hang around strip clubs. Mike, get up and run. Mike, we're sparring 10 rounds today." And I'd get rid of the bums that are around him. None of them were there when he was on the road to greatness, and he doesn't need any of them now. He'd be better off spending time with Steve Lott, who was loyal and a true friend and wasn't just there for the money. But the key to it all is that Mike has lost his desire. Cus used to say that, once a fighter loses his desire, it's all downhill. Mike has to get his desire back, and he's got to get it back soon because things are getting near the end. It's not too late for him to beat the guys who are out there now, because there's not much out there. But in terms of being great again, it's close to over. And that's a shame, because Mike was on the road to being the greatest fighter who ever lived. The plan was for him to go 50 and 0, beat Rocky Marciano's record, and retire. But that didn't happen and he's a lost soul now.

### Teddy Atlas

I'd probably dismiss it and say I'm not interested. If Tyson called, if he kept me on the phone long enough, most likely I'd ask, "Why are you calling me? Why do you want me to train you? What's different now?" I'm hesitating a bit talking to you because I want to be certain about my answer. If he kept calling, if I believed he was sincere in seeking help, if we met face to face and so on and so on, I'd try to keep an open mind. But that's fantasy because I know Mike Tyson and that's not who he is. He's afraid to face the truth that his existence has no decent meaning the way he is now. There might be moments when he wishes he had certain qualities that he doesn't, but he never follows through on it. And he surrounds himself with enablers who steer him away from the truth because he wants it that way. So I'd say, "No, I'm not interested." The practical line for someone who wanted to take the job would be to detach from Tyson outside the gym and only worry about what he does inside the ring. But if you do that, you're closing your eyes to the fact that the things he does outside the gym effect him in the ring because they're connected to his discipline and state of mind. Tyson is weak in the ring because he's weak outside the ring. He compromises in the ring because he compromises outside the ring. You could bring back Ray Arcel and Eddie Futch, God bless them, and I could humbly assist them, and Tyson still wouldn't be a decent person or a great fighter. There's a lot of guys he can still beat. Against anyone, there's always a chance he'll get lucky. But count me out. I'd get a big payday if I trained him, but I'd be risking the loss of everything I've tried to stand for my entire life. I'd feel dirty. It has to do with where I am as a person now and the history between us and where Tyson is now both athletically and as a person. It wouldn't make me a hero to say no. It wouldn't make me better than anyone else, but it would make me who I am. People weigh things differently; I understand that. Someone else who's a decent honorable person might take the job, but I wouldn't.

### Lou Duva

I'd take a shot at it. At least, I'd see if I could. But first, I'd sit down with Mike and call it the way I see it. You know, it's a bad history for trainers and Tyson. My son-in-law [Tommy Brooks] had trouble with him. He didn't listen to Ronnie Shields before the Lewis fight or during the Lewis fight either. And if you can't get his attention, forget it, don't take the job, because there's no way you'll be able to handle him. I'm a pretty good motivator and I fight for my guys, but there's more to motivation than hollering at someone. So I'd sit down with Mike and ask, "What do you want out of yourself? What are you willing to do to get it? Let's make a deal. You listen to me and you do what I tell you to do." If he thinks he's down to his last chance, maybe he'd do it. But you have to understand, a new trainer isn't the answer. The changes have to start with Tyson. The only guy who can really help Mike Tyson is Mike Tyson. And one thing more; Mike Tyson is only part of the problem. The other part is the character of the people he has around him. Mike looks for crutches and, outside the ring, they provide them. Then, inside the ring, he's on his own where they can't help him. So I'd tell Mike to stand on his own two feet; get rid of the bums. And if he didn't, I'd walk. Would he do it? I don't know. I'm not sure Mike can be honest with anyone, including himself, about what has to be done to turn his life around. And even if I took the job, you have to figure that, with Mike's history, sooner or later something bad would happen.

*Alton Merkerson*

I'd have to talk with Roy first. I have an exclusive contract with Roy where I don't train anyone else without his consent. But if Roy said yes, I'd be interested. I think Tyson is great for boxing, and my feeling is Mike isn't a bad guy. For sure, he's not as bad as his image. Some of things he's done don't sit well with me. Biting Holyfield, hitting guys after the bell; you know the things I'm talking about. But everybody is a Dr. Jekyll and Mr. Hyde, including me. Some people just go off the deep end faster than others. I wouldn't ask Mike questions before we started. I'd tell him how things have to be and see what kind of feedback I got. I'd say to him, "This is the way we do things. You have to walk a straight line. If you want me to train you, you have to trust me." Then I'd see how we connected and if we could learn to read each other. I wouldn't insist that he come to Pensacola to train, but the atmosphere here would be good for him. Boxing isn't all done in the ring. The atmosphere he hangs around in and he people he socializes with take away from his success because they affect the attitude he brings to the gym. If we started working together, I wouldn't dictate to him, and I wouldn't let him dictate to me. There has to be compromise. I'll give you an example. If I told Mike to jump rope and he said, "Coach Merk, my ankle is hurting," I might say, "Okay, let's do the treadmill instead." That's a compromise. But if Mike told me, "I ain't jumping no damn rope," that would be a problem. As for the fighting end of things, Tyson has a lot of strong points and you have to work off what he does well. Roy thinks a lot during a fight. Tyson isn't like that. Mike's not going to change his fight plan during a fight. His strong point is delivering punishment, so you improve his defense, which has gotten sloppy lately, and let him fight the way he does. Expose him to a few new things, but go back to what he used to do well.

*Angelo Dundee*

There are things I used to do that I don't want to do anymore. I don't want every-day responsibilities, and training Mike Tyson is a fulltime job. He needs guidance all the time and, even then, you can't be with him every minute and Mike has that self-destruct thing that sometimes gets him in trouble. I don't say anything bad about anyone; never have and never will. But you know the old saying, "You can lead a horse to water, but you can't make him drink." Mike would have to prove to me that he wants to do things for himself. That's what makes a fighter. If he did that, I still wouldn't want the main responsibility, but I'd be willing to become part of a team. First though, I'd want to know if it was a good team and what the overall situation was. Hey, I wish the guy luck. I thought he was going to beat Lennox Lewis.

*Floyd Mayweather, Sr.*

Tyson has always been a nice guy to me. When I see him, we talk; he gives me a hug. But I can't say what he's really like. I know something is off-balance, but I don't know what the problem is. I haven't been with the top heavyweights before; but if you're a good trainer, you can train anyone. And I could make Mike a better fighter than he is now. I'd be able to train him because I got so many things to show him. I could get him enthusiastic again because he'd understand that he's learning again. I'd give him challenges. And if he's still a fighter, he'd want to meet those challenges. But fighting isn't just physical; it's mental too. A lot of boxing has to do with the way a person lives. The street life and boxing don't mix. If you're on the edge all the time, you can't focus to do what you have to do to be great. So I'd tell Mike, "I can't change your life, but I can make suggestions. And my number one suggestion is that you get some discipline. Some fighters are willing to make sacrifices, and some fighters aren't. I want to work with fighters who make sacrifices, so it's up to you." I'd also tell him, "Right now, you run your camp and you tell people what to do. My thing is, I run the camp. So you do it my way, or it's better for both of us if you find someone else." You gotta understand, it's not just about the money. I'm trying to establish myself and my own legacy.

*Emanuel Steward*

That's a very interesting question. I'd ask Lennox first, of course. And Lennox is an unusual person when it comes to things like that. He might say, "Mike and I aren't really going to fight each other again, so do it." If that was the case, I'd seriously consider it. Properly trained, Mike has a few good fights left in him. But I'd have to have control over a lot of things; who he fights, who's in camp with him. I wouldn't try to control his lifestyle. You can't do that with anyone, and particularly not with a fighter. What I'd do is spend a lot of time with him, talking, doing things together. I've done that with most of the fighters I've worked with, and I've never had a problem with supposedly troubled young men. In the ring, I'd go back to some of the things Mike did before. A lot of those things are gone forever because it was youth instinct that allowed Mike to do them. He'll never have the same speed and intensity that he had when he was young. But his punching power is still there. And some of what he's lost, he can make up for with experience and better use of his jab. Once you get beyond Lennox and Wladimir Klitschko, the heavyweight division isn't exactly laden with talent. There's still room for Tyson at the top.

*Gil Clancy*

I was asked once before, years ago, not by Tyson but by some of the people around him. I didn't want to do it then, and I wouldn't want to do it now. I don't think Tyson can control himself, and I don't think anyone else can control him either. It's as simple as that.

*Bouie Fisher*

If Mike asked, I'd be honored. I'd accept it. You know, I was in Mike's camp a long time ago, before he started having problems. I had a fighter, Jesse Ferguson, who became one of his sparring partners. Normally, they didn't let other trainers into Mike's camp. But I was allowed in because we all got along and they needed good sparring. Mike was always respectful to me, and I'd welcome the opportunity to spend some time with him again. He has a heart. He's not a monster. And if a relationship clicks, you can always work things out. So I'd start by suggesting, "Let's talk, and let's get some more people you can talk with so you have peace of mind." The professional term is "counseling." And I'd tell him, "You were once a dedicated fighter. You wanted to be a champion and you lived that lifestyle. Let's go back to living that way again." Maybe, somewhere down the line, it will happen. But Mike only has a few years left to salvage his legacy. ❏

*I've been critical of Don King on many occasions. But when King was sued by John Ruiz, I thought DK was in the right.*

# RUIZ VS. KING: THE VULTURES WERE CIRCLING

If one were to choose a handful of men who have shaped, molded, and personified professional boxing over the past century, Don King would be among them. King has put on some great shows and is a show unto himself, a man of Shakespearean proportions.

But in court this past Wednesday (August 21, 2002), King looked like an ageing lion. His suit was rumpled, his shoes were scuffed, and his face was weary. He's 71 years old and has been on a fast track for a long time.

King had been dragged into court by John Ruiz. On May 8, 1998, the two men entered into a contract that grants King "the sole and exclusive right to secure and arrange all professional boxing bouts" that require Ruiz's services. Thereafter, King paid Ruiz $6.5-million in purses plus expenses for a series of fights and guided him to the WBA heavyweight crown.

At the final press conference prior to Ruiz's July 27 title defense against Kirk Johnson, Tony Cardinale (the primary business advisor and attorney for Team Ruiz) thanked King for his efforts. "John Ruiz had a dream," Cardinale told the assembled media. "And he realized that dream because of Don King." Then Cardinale looked directly at King and said, "Don, we love you."

Immediately after the bout, Norman Stone (Ruiz's manager) declared, "We will not fight anybody unless Don King is with us. Believe me when I tell you that. This is the man we live with. This is the man we die with."

But the money-making potential of Mike Tyson is like the allure of an irresistibly beautiful woman. It makes men do strange things. The Ruiz camp wanted a Tyson bout. And King saw Ruiz-Tyson as a chance to settle some side business, thereby doing well for Ruiz and himself. More specifically, King indicated that he would not allow Ruiz-Tyson to happen unless Tyson settled his $100-million lawsuit against the promoter on terms favorable to King or gave King an unspecified number of bout options.

In response, Ruiz sued the promoter, seeking a temporary restraining order that would "enjoin Don King Productions and Don King, directly or indirectly, from in any way seeking to enforce the promotional agreement between DKP and plaintiff and from impeding, hindering, or interfering with the negotiation, arrangement, or promotion of a professional boxing bout between [Ruiz] and Mike Tyson."

King plays by a larger set of rules than most people. Court battles are a regular part of his plan. Over the years, he has spirited numerous fighters away from their managers and promoters. The Ruiz lawsuit was karmic payback. And it also played into the litigation strategy of Team Tyson in that it sought to weaken King by threatening his hold on the WBA crown.

King has been taking some knocks lately. The Tyson litigation is a source of considerable concern. Lennox Lewis has remained independent of Don King Productions and formed a competing promotional company that's about to receive multi-million-dollar television backing. The Hasim Rahman litigation and Rahman's subsequent loss to Lewis cost the promoter a bundle. Felix Trinidad is at least temporarily retired, and Bernard Hopkins is proving more difficult to deal with than King thought he'd be.

In boxing, all great championship reigns come to an end. When King entered the United States Courthouse on Wednesday, his aura of invincibility was at stake. The vultures were circling. Driving a stake through The Great One's heart won't solve boxing's problems, but a lot of people with business interests in the sport would be happy to see him go.

The hearing began before Judge Laura Swain at 2:15 p.m. Ruiz was represented by Aaron Marks. Peter Fleming appeared on behalf of King.

In his opening statement, Marks told the judge that "John Ruiz's ultimate career goal is to be recognized as one of the greatest fighters of all time." One hopes, for Ruiz's sake, that he has a backup career goal in mind. More to the point, Marks maintained that King had breached his contractual obligation to Ruiz by putting his own interests ahead of those of the fighter. "The only impediment to John Ruiz fighting Mike Tyson in the most important fight of his life," Marks told the judge, "is Ruiz's own promoter."

Fleming, in his opening statement, told the court that Ruiz was a fighter going nowhere, carrying the stigma of a 19-second knockout at the hands of David Tua, when he signed with King. The promoter then orchestrated and financed the litigation that led to Lennox Lewis being stripped of his WBA title; put Ruiz in three title bouts against Evander Holyfield and one against Kirk Johnson; and generated millions of dollars for the fighter.

Fleming also represented to the court that, "Don King is prepared to pursue negotiations for a Ruiz-Tyson bout with no preconditions whatsoever." And in terms of law, the attorney declared, "Mr. King is not a fiduciary. The Ruiz–King contract specifically states that Ruiz is an independent contractor. There's a contract here, and they just want to walk out on it."

Tony Cardinale was Ruiz's first and only witness. He testified that Showtime wanted to telecast Ruiz-Tyson as a pay-per-view bout on November 9 and that King had made unreasonable demands of Tyson. But more significantly, Cardinale acknowledged that Shelly Finkel (Tyson's advisor) and Dale Kinsella (Tyson's attorney) had told him that Tyson would not go forward with the bout if Don King were Ruiz's promoter. Cardinale also told the court, "Time is of the essence. If this window of opportunity is lost, Tyson will simply fight someone else."

Then King took the stand. He told of flying to Atlanta prior to Ruiz-Johnson in an attempt to settle his litigation with Tyson. That was followed by several meetings in New York with Finkel and Tyson's legal team and a final meeting at King's office in Florida. There was no settlement. King acknowledged that, like any good negotiator, he had initially asked for concessions from Tyson in conjunction with a proposed Ruiz-Tyson bout. But he stated that he subsequently told Finkel that the fight could be done unencumbered and that he was "ready, willing, and able to promote a fight between John Ruiz and Mike Tyson."

As for his overall relationship with Ruiz, the promoter declared, "Johnny was a hard sell because all people thought about was that 19-second knock-out. No one respected Johnny. The press wouldn't accept Johnny. I stood up for Johnny and the rest of his team because of what I thought was their love, affection, and loyalty, which I know now doesn't exist anymore." One half-expected King to close his testimony by quoting King Lear: "How sharper than a serpent's tooth it is to have a thankless child." Instead, he ended with, "You have to live up to your contracts. Here's a fighter I have under contract. And because he thinks he can make a lot of money, he just walks away from his contract."

Court was adjourned at 6:05 p.m. after some final words from Peter Fleming: "There is nothing more important in the business of boxing than the ability of a promoter to enforce his promotional contracts. The heart of this case is the contract. Mr. King has served Mr. Ruiz well, and now they want to cut him out."

Judge Swain issued her ruling on Thursday morning.

In order for a temporary restraining order to be granted, two standards must be met: (1) The moving party must be facing irreparable harm if the order is not granted. That harm must be actual, imminent, and not compensable by monetary damages; and (2) The moving party must show a likelihood of success on the merits.

The judge denied Ruiz's motion. She ruled that, although all contracts carry with them a duty of fair dealing and good faith, there is generally no fiduciary duty owed to a boxer by a promoter. In fact, she noted that the Ruiz-King promotional agreement contemplated instances where the interests of Ruiz and King might be inconsistent with one another. She also ruled that the Ruiz-King promotional agreement does not give Ruiz the right to unilaterally choose his opponents and held that King is not required to put aside his own commercial interests in fulfilling his contractual obligations. Her decision was not a final resolution of the matter, but it strongly indicates what the end result will be.

All of this, of course, leaves the question: "Will Don King make Mike Tyson versus John Ruiz?"

After the court's decision, King said that he would seek to arrange the bout. But during his trial testimony, he told the judge, "The numbers that are realistic aren't going to be acceptable to Mike." That could have been laying the groundwork for failure. Or maybe it was just the start of negotiations. Either way, King could seek to use Ruiz-Tyson as an opportunity to get his hooks into Iron Mike again. He could even make the fight and then, knowing which buttons to push, upset Tyson so much that the fight blows up and doesn't happen.

Meanwhile, hours after the judge's decision, the Ruiz camp released the following statement: "Team Ruiz looks forward to setting up this fall a bout between John Ruiz and Mike Tyson, and we also look forward to the court hearing on September 6 to ask that we be permanently excused from our promotional agreement with Mr. King if this fight is not made."

The folks at Team Ruiz are not going quietly. But there's a lot of fight left in the old lion.

Team Ruiz would be wise to remember the admonition of Ralph Waldo Emerson: "When you strike at a king, you must kill him or don't strike at all." ❏

*The world sanctioning organizations that rule boxing leave much to be desired. That was clear when the inner workings of the WBA were on display in New York.*

# THE WBA IN NEW YORK: A HOLE THE SIZE OF A QUARTER

Rats are adept at squeezing through small openings.

I once saw a rat trying to squeeze through a hole the size of a quarter. It got its head through, which is usually the determining factor. But it was a fat rat; and for whatever reason, the rest of it couldn't get through. It squeezed and pulled and grunted and tugged, but the hole was too small.

The WBA officials who assembled in New York on October 16, 2002, for an open hearing on the WBA's heavyweight ratings resembled rats trying to squeeze through a hole the size of a quarter. Some of them might have been well-intentioned. But overall, the hearing was a transparent effort at damage control.

Boxing's world sanctioning bodies aren't known for integrity. Indeed, Craig Hamilton, who once went to a WBA hearing in an effort to keep Lennox Lewis from being stripped of the title for fighting Michael Grant, said at the time, "Dealing with the WBA is like dealing with a drug cartel, not a legitimate ratings organization." But when the WBA released its most recent ratings in September, there was a firestorm of protest.

Larry Donald moved up three slots to # 3 despite the fact that he hadn't won since a 10-round decision over James Stanton 15 weeks earlier and Stanton had lost six of his previous seven bouts. Hasim Rahman moved up five places to #5 despite not having fought since a June loss to Evander Holyfield. The untested unskilled Nikolay Valuev was ranked # 6. Fres Oquendo was elevated four slots to #7 despite the fact that his previous fight had been an April knockout loss at the hands of David Tua. Jameel McCline, undefeated in his past 28 fights, dropped from #7 to #8. David Tua was demoted to #9. Kirk Johnson slipped from #5 to #10. And British heavyweight champion Danny Williams fell five places to #14 despite having won his previous 11 fights.

Donald, Rahman, and Oquendo are all promoted by Don King. Williams had been promoted by King but left DKP for Lion Promotions shortly before his demotion.

Ratings are at the heart of controlling which fighters get to fight for championships. Normally, the WBA and its brethren slough off complaints, but this time there was a twist. John McCain (the ranking Republican on the

Senate Commerce Committee) sent a letter to Attorney General John Ashcroft questioning whether the WBA is violating the ratings provisions of the Professional Boxing Safety Act. The California Athletic Commission withheld the WBA's sanctioning fee for the flyweight title fight between Eric Morel and Denkaosaen Kaowitchit. And the recent $31-million judgment in favor of Graciano Rocchigiani against the WBC made the powers that be at the WBA a bit skittish.

Thus, Wednesday's open hearing. WBA president Gilberto Mendoza and legal advisor James Binns (widely regarded as the WBA's controlling powers) were not present. The hearing was chaired by Gilberto Mendoza Jr. (international coordinator for the WBA Executive Committee). Also in attendance were Renzo Bagnariol (chairman of the World Championships Committee), Guy Jutras (chairman of the Officials Committee), Bolí 1var Icaza (chairman of the Ratings Committee), ratings committee members Jose Oliver Gomez, Stanley Christodolou, and George Martinez, and attorney Robert Mack.

Mendoza thanked the media for its constructive criticism. There was a discourse on the fact that Oliver McCall was unranked because he had gone to Yale ("yale" being the Spanish pronunciation of jail). Gary Shaw said that a fighter like Oquendo shouldn't be allowed to move up in the ratings by not fighting after a loss to which Mendoza responded, "That's your personal opinion and you're entitled to it." Then Mendoza announced that there had been some "technical problems" with the WBA's computers and that, on top of that, certain relevant information hadn't been fed into the computers. "We are all human beings," he explained before declaring that the WBA's most recent heavyweight ratings had been vacated in favor of a points system.

The points system is the WBA's fallback position when the Executive Committee determines that an officially-designated "controversy" exists. Or as Dino Duva put it, "The points system is a different set of rules that the WBA turns to when it can't justify its ratings."

The points system is idiotic on its face. For example, a fighter gets more points for successfully defending a regional championship than he does for successfully defending a world title. A fighter who is knocked out in the third round of a great fight (for example, Thomas Hearns against Marvin Hagler) loses more points than a fighter who runs for 12 rounds and is beaten by a mediocre opponent). But it's a moot point because the WBA doesn't follow the points system when it doesn't feel like following it.

During the course of the hearing, Dino Duva, Pat English, Butch Lewis, Gary Shaw, Don Majeski, Joe DeGuardia, Tony Cardinale, Norman Stone, Bobby Goodman, and Don King all had their say on behalf of various fighters. King was the day's most entertaining speaker. Among the points he made were, "The WBA should be applauded for its integrity in holding an open hearing on its ratings . . . Ratings are subjective . . . It's a promoter's obligation to lobby for his fighters to get the best rating possible. The day that lobbying is cut out is the end of boxing."

Then Mendoza announced the WBA's new heavyweight rankings (point totals in parenthesis):

1. Evander Holyfield (40)
2. Vacant
3. Vitali Klitschko (43)
4. David Tua (40)
5. Hasim Rahman (36)
6. Mike Tyson (35)
7. Jameel McCline (31)
8. Kirk Johnson (24)
9. Fres Oquendo (26)
10. Larry Donald (23)
11. Nikolay Valuev (29)
12. Faruq Saleem (21)
13. Lamon Brewster (20)
14. Joe Mesi (18)
15. Danny Williams (17)

Holyfield was granted the top slot despite having fewer points than Klitschko because of his victory over Rahman in an elimination bout. It was decreed that the winner of the scheduled November 23 fight between Klitschko and Donald would be ranked second. No one could explain why Fres Oquendo and Nikolay Valuev were ranked behind fighters who had fewer points. And more significantly, no one could explain why Chris Byrd (who had 36 points and has beaten both Klitschko and Tua) was absent from the ratings.

If this is what the WBA does with its heavyweight ratings, think what the other divisions are like. For example, Shane Mosley is absent from the WBA ratings.

Louis Brandeis once wrote, "Sunlight is the best disinfectant." In the case of the world sanctioning organizations, stronger remedies are necessary. ❏

*The New York State Athletic Commission has been an embarrassment for years. One reason for that has been an all-too-frequent lack of quality leadership.*

# THE NEXT CHAIRMAN OF THE NEW YORK STATE ATHLETIC COMMISSION

On May 21, 2002, a meeting of Ring 8 was held in New York. Ring 8 is the New York City arm of the Veteran Boxers Association, which has 41 chapters in the United States and England. Each chapter is designated as a "ring." The most active chapter is Ring 8 with 565 members.

The meeting began with the normal conduct of business. Then Bobby Bartels (president of Ring 8) read the following statement of principle with the approval of the organization's board of directors:

"In recent years, the New York State Athletic Commission has been rife with problems. Qualified personnel have been forced out of their positions and replaced by political appointees. This is detrimental to boxing and to boxers.

The chairmanship of the New York State Athletic Commission is now vacant. Most of the candidates currently mentioned for the chairman-ship are individuals who are under consideration primarily because of their political affiliation.

Ring 8 implores Governor George Pataki to appoint a qualified chairman who:

(1) Understands the sport and business of boxing and the people in boxing;

(2) Will run the commission for the benefit of the boxers and the sport of boxing;

(3) Will run the New York State Athletic Commission without regard to any political party affiliation; and

(4) Possesses the leadership, management, and administrative skills necessary to run the commission effectively.

This issue is not just about the sport of boxing, but also the safety of boxers. Ring 8 urges Governor Pataki to take the crucial aforementioned items into consideration when he appoints a new chairman."

In sum, Ring 8 understands what Governor Pataki doesn't; that the New York State Athletic Commission is in turmoil. Ring 8 also cares about an issue that the Governor seems to not care about; that the lives of fighters are in danger.

In recent years, incompetence and corruption have been hallmarks of the New York State Athletic Commission. A handful of good men and women still work there. But too many qualified personnel have been forced out of positions with the commission and replaced by unqualified political patronage employees. This has hurt the taxpayers of the State of New York, boxing, and boxers.

Last summer, after Beethavean Scottland was beaten to death and Joey Gamache was almost killed as a consequence of commission bungling, the governor bowed to media pressure. Mel Southard resigned as chairman of the NYSAC and Ray Kelly was named as his successor.

Kelly's appointment was a source of hope. The new chairman brought a reputation for ability and integrity to the job and openly acknowledged, "I found a commission that many years ago had a reputation for being the premier boxing commission in the country, and that has been lost. The reputation of the commission has diminished. There's a cloud over the commission, and we have to move that cloud aside. I want to get the best people here; and I'll chose people on the basis of merit, not political connections. That allegation is out there, and it's fair to say that's how some commission appointments came about. But from now on, it won't be a question of who knows who; I promise you that."

It would be nice if one could say that Kelly's tenure was a time when the NYSAC turned a corner. But in truth, it was a strange and unsatisfying interregnum. Kelly started the process of cleaning house but didn't go far enough. In November, he was named commissioner of the New York City Police Department, which severely limited the time that he could devote to NYSAC business. By and large, the personnel he brought into the commission knew virtually nothing about boxing. And equally upsetting, they evinced a disheartening lack of respect for people in the boxing industry and for the sport itself.

Then, on March 19, the first of two meetings devoted to the NYSAC took place at Ring 8. Four men who are helping to keep boxing alive in New York City (Cedric Kushner, Lou DiBella, Bob Duffy, and Joe DeGuardia) took part in a panel discussion with Charles DeRienzo (executive director of the NYSAC). The foursome voiced concern over the ignorance of commission employees and the belief that NYSAC personnel are disinterested in working cooperatively with the boxing community to ensure that fights are conducted in a safe and appropriate manner.

DiBella was particularly outspoken. DiBella cares deeply about boxing and is one of the most knowledgeable people in the sport. After announcing, "I'm not going to get excited," (which was a sure sign that he was going to get excited) DiBella unleashed a torrent of criticism against the NYSAC. Among the points he made were:

● "Ray Kelly is a good man, but that's not enough. In the real world, things have to get done. It's not enough to come in and say, 'We're going to clean up boxing.' You still have to do things; and to do that, you have to know how to do them. And the truth is, right now, almost no one at the commission knows anything about boxing."

● "The New York State Athletic Commission has become a national joke. They have no idea what the problems are, what the bad guys do, or even who the bad guys are. Why are a slew of ex cops who were probably all fine policeman but have no knowledge of professional boxing any better than what we had before?"

● "Joe DeGuardia was suspended by the commission for writing on its standard form Boxer-Promoter Contract. The contract has a provision in it that says it's the only contract that can exist between a fighter and a promoter for any given fight, and Joe amended one of the clauses to reflect his true agreement with the fighter. That shows you how out of touch the people who run the commission are. Every main-event promoter and every main event fighter who signs that contract is lying. Only an idiot would think that you can have a fight like Bernard Hopkins against Felix Trinidad at Madison Square Garden and the only contract Don King would ask them to sign is two pages that were drafted by someone at the New York State Athletic Commission decades ago."

● "The same doctors who participated in the death of Beethavean Scottland are still overseeing health and safety for the New York State Athletic Commission. That's frightening."

On March 20 (the day after the Ring 8 session), DeRienzo resigned as executive director of the NYSAC. One day after that, Dave Itskowitch of DiBella Entertainment received what he considered to be a threatening telephone call. Picking up the phone late in the afternoon, he was greeted by a voice that said simply, "Tell Lou he didn't do himself any favors on Tuesday night." Then, after refusing to give his name, the caller hung up. The call was traced to a cell phone belonging to Southard.

"I confronted Southard about it," DiBella said later. "Initially, he was evasive about making the call. Then he gave me some kind of double-talk about wanting to help me by warning me."

When this writer contacted Southard about the incident, Southard said, "I called to tell Lou that I thought he'd put himself on the right side of some of the issues. I don't remember if I left my telephone number or not when I called. My best recollection is that I did."

Finally, on May 6, Ray Kelly was forced to resign as chairman of the New York State Athletic Commission because of a provision in the city charter that precludes a person from working for both the City and State of New York at the same time.

Thereafter, Ruby Marin (a staff attorney with little background in boxing) served briefly as de facto executive director of the commission. Then, on May 16, NYSAC employees were summoned to a meeting presided over by Jerry Becker (one of two remaining NYSAC commissioners) and were informed that Becker would be overseeing the office "at the present time."

Becker says he's not a candidate to chair the commission. "With guys like you," he told this reporter last week, "do you think I'd put my name in the ring? I've already been circumcised once." Then Becker added, "I'd appreciate it if you recognized that I know a lot about boxing. And I'd also appreciate it if you understood that the staff and I are trying to do a good job."

Still, as one commission employee notes, "Things are worse now than ever, because the people in charge know less and they're consumed by trivialities. Go to a fight, and these guys are more concerned with who sits where than they are with properly regulating the fights."

It's bizarre. One day, the commission announces a "zero tolerance" weigh-in policy. That is, if a fighter fails to make weight when he steps on the scales for the first time, he won't be given an opportunity to lose the excess poundage. Then, in the next breath, it decrees that any fighter who gets on an HBO scale the night of a fight will be subject to discipline including possible suspension. HBO has been weighing fighters to show the disparity between a fighter's weight of record and his actual weight when he steps into the ring. In support of their policy, commission officials cite NYSAC Rule 209.46 which states, "Scales used for any weigh-in shall be approved in advance by the commission." But logic dictates that this rule applies to *official* weigh-ins. The commission's edict makes no sense. Meanwhile, because of bureaucratic bungling, New York is becoming known in fight circles as the "home of the four-hour weigh-in."

The list of concerns goes on. One day, commission personnel turn down a tough opponent as "unqualified" for a local club fight. The next day, they approve a lesser boxer for a nationally televised main event. Sometimes, they do both.

Tommy Gallagher (whose wife, Maureen, is president of Thomas Gallagher Promotions) complained that TGP had to cancel a May 3, 2002, show in Manhattan when its main event fell out. "The commission approved Don Normand (25-13) as an opponent," says Gallager. "But Normand couldn't come to New York from Tennessee for his medicals within the time required by the commission, so we substituted John Randall (9-5) who had won five fights in a row and knocked Normand out last November. Everything was set. Then the commission told me it wouldn't approve Randall, so I got Normand to agree to take off from work and come to New York early. But after that, the commission told me that it had withdrawn its approval of Normand."

Ruby Marin says that the rulings on Normand and Randall were "collective decisions made by our staff," and adds, "Our primary concern is to avoid mismatches."

But another commission employee takes a contrary view. "I've come to the conclusion," this employee says "that the people in charge here actually want to kill the small shows because they don't want to be bothered with them. It's an aggravation for them, and they just don't want to do the work."

Meanwhile, the NYSAC continues to waste taxpayers dollars by "regulating" professional wrestling. And it flies inspectors into New York City from all over the state at taxpayer expense, gives them meal money, and puts them up in hotels, when local inspectors could work a fight card for the cost of two subway tokens.

Now the commission has scheduled a training seminar on ring officiating and is planning to bring in Joe Cortez to lecture on refereeing. "While they're at it," notes one commission official, "maybe they could bring in a competent commissioner to teach the commissioners how to do their job." But that thought aside; last year, Arthur Mercante, Sr. conducted the New York seminar. Cortez is a fine referee. But why pay all the costs associated with importing someone from Las Vegas when there's a qualified person in New York?

The conduct of the April 27, 2002, fight card at Madison Square Garden also warrants comment. That was the night Jameel McCline beat Shannon Briggs and Manuel Medina lost his IBF featherweight title to Johnny Tapia. No one from the commission attended any of the pre-fight press conferences, but that was expected since they hadn't attended any of the press conferences for Shane Mosley versus Vernon Forrest either. Then, on fight night, McCline wrapped his own hands and used 1-1/2-inch tape. That's illegal. One-inch tape is supposed to be used. In the old days, an NYSAC inspector would have intervened. That's what they're in the dressing room for. Indeed, the late Patsy Giovanelli is legendary for telling trainers, "His hands aren't being taped right. I don't care what the other side says; I'm not going to okay it." But on April 27, the violation went undetected.

Proper medical care is another problem. Since Scottland was killed last June, Arthur Mercante, Jr. (who refereed the fight) has been denied high-profile assignments and given only a few small club fights. But Dr. Barry Jordan, who sat passively at ringside that night and has consistently defended the commission's medical handling of the bout, remains as chief neurologist and de facto medical director of the commission.

Margaret Goodman is chief ringside physician and chairman of the medical advisory board for the Nevada State Athletic Commission. "What separates a great ring doctor from an adequate one," says Dr. Goodman, "is knowledge of the participants, a relationship with the individuals working that card, and experience." But New York has painfully few ringside physicians who are adequate, let alone great. And aftercare for the fighters in New York is horrifyingly lax.

On November 23 of last year, Richard Grant suffered multiple injuries during a vicious post-fight attack by James Butler, who he'd just defeated on a 10-round decision at Roseland Ballroom. Grant was admitted to a New York hospital, where he was diagnosed as having a cut on the inside of his mouth and a bruised jaw. But eight days later, he was still in pain, couldn't chew, and was having trouble opening his mouth. Thus, at a December 1 medical seminar, Grant approached Dr. Goodman and asked her for advice.

"There's nothing wrong with him," one of the NYSAC doctors told Goodman. "He had an X-ray."

But in instances of this nature, a special panoramic X-ray is called for. Goodman referred Grant to an oral surgeon. The following week, it was determined that he had suffered a broken jaw.

That raises a lot of questions. Did anyone from the medical staff of the New York State Athletic Commission accompany Grant to the hospital on the night of the fight? Did anyone from the medical staff of the NYSAC specify in writing what minimum tests should be performed in the emergency room? What sort of follow-up was there by the NYSAC medical staff?

"Jaw injuries are not uncommon in boxing," says one observer. "After all, the fighters are getting punched on the jaw. Richard Grant couldn't eat. Richard Grant was having trouble opening his mouth. Doesn't it strike you as scary that no one asked, "Gee, do you think maybe his jaw is broken?"

If the New York State Athletic Commission can't provide better medical care for fighters, it shouldn't sanction fights in New York.

Meanwhile, there's a growing sense within the boxing community that things are continuing to deteriorate at the NYSAC. Mike Silver is a boxing historian with hands-on experience. He was an inspector for the commission in the early 1980s and has served as a consultant to HBO and ESPN Classic on close to a dozen documentaries about the sweet science.

"The commission has always been a dumping ground for patronage employees," says Silver. "But in the old days, there were enough people there who knew what they were doing that, even if the chairman was a boob, his underlings could do the job. That's not the case anymore. Things are worse now than they ever were. You keep saying, 'It can't get any worse that this,' and then it does. Boxing is the most dangerous sport in the world. If you're a regulator, it's not okay not to know. But in New York, boxing is being supervised by people who have no idea what they're doing. This commission has failed fighters and failed boxing more miserably than any commission in history."

Last November, in response to the crisis, the New York State Assembly held hearings on the NYSAC. Its main legislative response to date has been the introduction of a bill that would increase the number of commissioners (and hence, the number of patronage jobs) from three to five.

What's the solution?

It's not enough just to have a good chairman. To function properly, a government agency needs quality people down the line. But leadership is important, and attention is now turning to the issue of who will be the next chairman of the NYSAC.

Boxers in the State of New York deserve a fulltime chairman who knows boxing and gives them 100 percent of his professional time. Yet with the notable exception of Joe Dwyer (a former chief inspector for the NYSAC), all of the names currently being floated as potential successors to Kelly belong to candidates who are unqualified for the job. That includes Bernard Kerik, the current front-runner, who might have been a fine police commissioner but isn't grounded in the sport and business of boxing the way someone who runs the commission should be.

George Pataki has a $60-million campaign war-chest and such a big lead in the polls that he can afford to be arrogant. Let's hope that, in this instance, he isn't. ❑

*The following article highlighted the absurdity of tax dollars being spent to "regulate" professional wrestling in the State of New York.*

# PROFESSIONAL WRESTLING AND THE NEW YORK STATE ATHLETIC COMMISSION

On June 29, 2002, World Wrestling Entertainment presented one of its trademark extravaganzas at Madison Square Garden. WWE was formerly known as the WWF (World Wrestling Federation). But the World Wildlife Fund (also known as the WWF) got touchy and legal action followed. Thus the name change.

The Garden lobby was mobbed on the night of the 29th. Vendors did a brisk business in T-shirts, programs, and other wrestling paraphernalia. The crowd was diverse with a young blue-collar demographic. A lot of the men in attendance looked like wanna-be wrestlers. They were big and burly with long-hair dyed varying colors of the rainbow. Some looked like Joey Buttafucco and others like Howard Stern. But there were also a lot of husbands and wives with young children in attendance. For many Americans, WWE events are family entertainment.

The first of the evening's 10 bouts was scheduled for 7:30 p.m. and most of the 20,000 seats were filled by then. The house lights went off, the attendees went wild, and a tuxedo-clad announcer bounded into the ring. The National Anthem was played. And not only did the crowd rise, they sang it. That was followed by flame throwers and explosions, and the games began.

WWE fans know what they're going to get when they buy a ticket, and they get it every time. Each of the matches constituted a battle between good and evil. There was non-stop action and unremitting mayhem. At various times, combatants crawled beneath the ring and emerged with a table, garbage can, ladder, or other implement of destruction. A great deal of combat took place after each bout, often with the loser rendering the winner unconscious.

Some of the wrestlers looked like pumped-up body-builders. Quite a few had pony-tails. One of them ("16-time world champion" Ric Flair) inspired thoughts of a cross between an aging Charles Atlas and Liberace. Another (Steven Richards) bore a faint resemblance to Steve Albert. There was also match between the reigning WWE women's champion (Molly Holly) and "Silicone" Trish Stratus.

Most of the wrestlers were quite strong, as evidenced by the fact that they were able to lift an opponent up in the air before slamming him to the canvas. There were also some pretty good acrobatics, including two men diving off a ladder at the same time. Every so often, bad guys would charge into the ring to interfere with the course of action and, on occasion, good guys would materialize to neutralize them.

One match quickly followed another. The crowd was enthusiastic but well behaved. It was theatre in the round, and true WWE believers (who constituted most of the audience) were in heaven.

Then it was time for the main event: The Undertaker defending his undisputed WWE championship against the one and only Hulk Hogan.

Hogan is an icon of professional wrestling. This was his first appearance at Madison Square Garden since the late 1980s, and the arena has special meaning for him. It was there, many moons ago, that he beat the Iron Sheik to capture his first undisputed wrestling crown.

Hogan was introduced first. He entered the ring wearing his trademark yellow and orange flower-child garb, and the crowd went wild. Words like "chaos" and "pandemonium" don't describe the frenzy. It was pure "Hulkamania."

Then, dressed in black, The Undertaker appeared. WWE promotional material describes him as 6-foot-10, 328 pounds, and "a one man street gang meting out vicious beatings for the perverse pleasure of it." However, as boxing promoter Don Elbaum once said of a 7-foot Bosnian fighter he was promoting who turned out to be only 6-foot-7, The Undertaker seemed "small for his size."

Hogan, meanwhile, is listed as 6-foot-7 and a mere 275 pounds. Several months shy of 49 years old, he's quite bald except for a fringe of long dyed-blonde hair. And he isn't as acrobatic as he once was. But in wrestling, old champions never succumb in the ring to the infirmities of age. Rather, they make up for lost youth with personality.

To the delight of the crowd, Hulk Hogan pinned The Undertaker. But in one of life's inequities, the referee had been knocked unconscious and didn't see it. Then, adding insult to injury, Hogan was on the verge of pinning The Undertaker again. But on the count of two-and-ninety-nine-one-hundredths, Vince McMahon (founder of the WWE) charged into the ring and knocked the referee unconscious again. Then, The Undertaker pinned Hogan.

The show was over at precisely 10:30 p.m. Good won five matches and evil won five matches. Armageddon continues at the next WWE show.

What does all of the above have to do with professional boxing (other than the fact that Madison Square Garden was where Muhammad Ali and Joe Frazier did battle and now the crowd has been roaring at the sight of grown men hitting each other in the head with a garbage can)?

Simply put, the WWE show casts light on the culture of lawlessness that has long pervaded the New York State Athletic Commission. For decades, professional wrestling in New York has been "regulated" by the commission. And if that isn't embarrassment enough, NYSAC rules state the following:

Rule 216.3: "All wrestlers are required to wrestle under the rules of this commission, and contracts between wrestlers for wrestling exhibitions must specify that the wrestling rules of this commission shall apply to such exhibitions."

Rule 216.11: "Wrestlers are forbidden from indulging in the following unfair or foul tactics: striking, scratching, gouging, butting, or unnecessarily punitive strangleholds."

Rule 216.12: "Seconds, managers, and coaches may not touch a wrestler during an exhibition, neither shall they give any advice or coaching until a rest period is declared."

Rule 216.17: "All wrestling must take place within the ropes. Wrestlers deliberately throwing opponents out of the ring are guilty of a foul and the referee may thereafter award the exhibition to the fouled wrestler."

Rule 216.19: "Wrestlers must provide themselves with such type and color of wearing apparel as the commission may require for each exhibition."

Rule 216.25: "No wrestler shall molest, hit, or abuse any spectator, referee, or judge, or engage in any unsportsmanlike conduct."

"Silly," you say?

Absolutely. But these rules are part of a system that has provided jobs and no-show jobs to commission employees as referees, judges, inspectors, and other per diem slots at professional wrestling matches for decades. This system is the reason that, over the years, New York has spent *11 times* more per fight card than Nevada to regulate boxing.

Not everyone at the NYSAC went along with the boondoggle. Former chief inspector Joe Dwyer recalls, "When I was with the commission, I refused to work the wrestling shows. A lot of guys considered wrestling a plum assignment. But I felt we shouldn't be spending the taxpayers' money on foolishness like that, and I didn't want to be a part of it."

But Dwyer was the exception. Until recently, the New York State Athletic Commission had a fulltime director of wrestling. It still has at least one employee who covers the fights at an overtime pay-rate from the time he leaves home [a two-hour drive to Madison Square Garden] till the time he returns to his residence. Add in mileage, meals, and far greater office administrative costs, and the cost to taxpayers is imposing.

Recently, the New York State legislature passed the Professional Wrestling Health And Safety Act. The law, if signed by Governor George Pataki, will do away with the pretense that professional wrestling is an athletic competition that should be regulated by the state. However, under the statute, promoters of professional wrestling must still be licensed by the state; certain personnel involved with wrestling will be required to apply to the NYSAC for temporary working permits; and there will be a requirement that promoters implement an anti-drug plan and file it with the commission.

Maybe next, the NYSAC can license Barnum & Bailey and require an anti-drug plan when the circus appears at Madison Square Garden.

Other legislation passed recently by the New York State Assembly and under consideration in the State Senate is more troubling. It increases the number of commissioners at the NYSAC (and hence, the number of patronage positions to be filled at taxpayer expense) from three to five. In listing the qualifications necessary for appointment as a commissioner, the legislation provides, "Persons designated or appointed to the commission shall have demonstrated long-standing interest, knowledge, and experience in boxing OR WRESTLING."

That's a thumb in the eye to the entire boxing community. What does knowledge of professional wrestling have to do with the very serious job of properly regulating boxing in New York?

Involvement with professional wrestling is just one of many things wrong with the NYSAC. Bernard Kerik (the newly appointed chairman) is stepping into a culture of lawlessness seeped in political patronage and the waste of taxpayers' dollars. If he changes that culture, more power to him. But if he doesn't, the New York State Athletic Commission will continue to be an embarrassment. ❏

*The "NYSAC Follies" continued under the leadership of Bernard Kerik, while good men like Joe Dwyer were left on the outside looking in.*

# JOE DWYER AND THE NEW YORK STATE ATHLETIC COMMISSION

On June 19, 2002, George Pataki formally designated Bernard Kerik as chairman of the New York State Athletic Commission. The following day, a hearing on the nomination was held by the Standing Committee on Finance of the New York State Senate.

The hearing was chaired by Ronald B. Stafford, a Republican whose district includes parts of six counties in upstate New York. Kerik was introduced and made the following remarks:

"Good morning. I thank the committee for the invitation to be here. A few weeks ago, the governor approached me and asked me to chair the athletic commission, and I told him I would. Many years ago, when I had a lot more hair and less pounds, I fought competitively in martial arts. I understand the challenges. I understand the dangers. I'm aware of what the commission is supposed to do. I'm committed and acquainted with the job as well as the fighters, the promoters, the judges, the doctors, the medical personnel. I would make sure that they do their jobs as well. I think my past experience in management would serve me well in doing this, and again I thank you for allowing me to be here."

Stafford then exclaimed, "Excellent statement," and told Kerik, "We can see why you are a success."

That was the entire hearing. No one asked Kerik the most basic questions. No one inquired into his assertion that he was "acquainted with the job as well as the fighters, the promoters, the judges, the doctors, the medical personnel." No one asked how much time, if any, he intended to devote to the job. No one inquired about his philosophy of regulation.

Kerik might have been a good police commissioner, but he has been a non-presence at the New York State Athletic Commission. As a gesture of noblesse oblige, Kerik waived his salary as chairman. Unfortunately, he has also waived the responsibilities of his chairmanship. At the time of his appointment, he had a lucrative job in the private sector, and he has kept it. Several fulltime commission employees say that they have yet to see him in the NYSAC office. "It would be wrong to call Kerik a disinterested spectator," says one of those employees. 'Spectator' implies that Bernie at least goes to the fights, and he doesn't." Nor has Kerik played any meaningful role in the operation of the commission.

Kerik is reported to have told commission insiders that he will leave the NYSAC after the November election. He is also reported to have told associates, "I didn't ask for this job." But he accepted the job. And if he intends to resign after the election, he has lent his name to an ongoing shell game that has left a government agency rudderless for another six months.

The New York State Athletic Commission is once again in turmoil. For over a year now, its primary feature has been a revolving door that has seen Kerik replace Ray Kelly as chairman, Hugo Spindola replace Ruby Marin as counsel, and Charles DeRienzo come and go as executive director. Significantly, none of these five individuals evidenced the most rudimentary knowledge of the business of professional boxing.

For much of 2002, the commission relied heavily on Ray Locasio. Locasio came to the NYSAC as a computer specialist with no boxing background, but he worked pretty hard to learn the boxing end of things. In 2000, after Bob Duffy resigned as director of boxing, Locasio took over most of Duffy's duties.

In early September, Locasio said he would leave the NYSAC for a job in private industry unless he was given a raise. In response, he was told that the secretary of state was thinking of doing away with the position of executive director (which has yet to be filled) and dividing the responsibilities of that job between Locasio and Spindola. Then, on September 13, Locasio was advised that the powers that be intended to create a new position for him (assistant to the chairman) at a salary of $78,000 a year. Four days later, Jerry Becker (one of three NYSAC commissioners and acting head of the office) told staff members that henceforth all persons were to report to Locasio and that Locasio would report to Becker. In addition to his salary, Locasio was to receive the use of a state car, parking shield, and gas credit card. Then Ralph Petrillo (a Becker loyalist whose primary duties with the commission involve medical paperwork) complained that, unless he got a raise and a car, he was leaving. At that point, Locasio was told that he had to relinquish the car to Petrillo. Locasio refused and left the NYSAC. His workload was initially divided between Petrillo (who now has the use of a state car) and Bob Limerick (who in recent years distinguished himself by supervising professional wrestling for the commission). Then, a week later, amidst fears that even the pretense of effective regulation was going down the drain, Locasio was designated a deputy commissioner. He will perform the duties of that position despite having a fulltime job in the private sector.

Last spring, before Kerik was appointed NYSAC chairman, trainer and ESPN commentator Teddy Atlas voiced concern regarding the future of the commission. "I'm scared right now," Atlas acknowledged. "I really am. I was scared before Kelly was announced and I'm even more scared now because they're going to go back to the political crony game, where they're just going to throw in a political hack that they owe a favor to. I'm scared to death that's going to happen now. It's going to be very damaging; so damaging that we may never overcome it. I'm petrified that they're going to get the wrong person in there. I have a fairly good pulse on it, and I know the echoes out there and the political people that are lobbying to get in there. Now is the time to act and not get any more of these phonies in there. We've had enough of that."

Four months later, Atlas' words are just as applicable. According to one NYSAC insider, "The game plan is to put everything on hold until after the election. If a job opens up before November 5, leave it vacant. Then it's back to the good old days."

Meanwhile, the lack of knowledge with regard to professional boxing at the commission is frightening, as is the disdain evidenced for virtually everyone in the industry including the fighters.

What's the solution?

Change starts at the top. When Kerik leaves the commission, the governor will name a successor. Designating Joe Dwyer as the next chairman of the NYSAC would be a clear signal that positive change is intended.

Dwyer was born and raised in the Bay Ridge section of Brooklyn. His father was a New York City Police Department detective, who fought professionally in the late 1920s but gave up boxing when he married Joe's mother. "My parents separated when I was young," Dwyer remembers. "My father was my idol and he was a great guy in many ways. But he never took responsibility and, because of that, my mother had a rough life. My mother raised us. And, believe me, we didn't come from money."

On his 16th birthday, Dwyer dropped out of high school and went to work as a mail clerk for American Express. At age 17, he joined the U.S. Navy Reserves and went on active duty a year later. While in the Navy, he got his high school graduation equivalency degree and served as a first mechanic for jet fighters onboard the U.S.S. FDR and U.S.S. Intrepid.

It's also worth mentioning that Dwyer was a fighter. In 59 amateur bouts, he had 56 wins, 2 losses, and one no contest with 27 knockouts. Fighting as a middleweight, he won the New York City Metropolitan AAU, New York State AAU, and U.S. Navy championships.

After leaving the Navy, Dwyer worked for two years as a cargo checker on the Brooklyn waterfront. Then, in 1961, he joined the New York City Police Department.

Dwyer served as a cop for 34 years, 15 of them as financial secretary for the Brooklyn-South sector of the Patrolmen's Benevolent Association. Along the way, he earned a degree from Regents College and received 14 citations for bravery. He also spent four years undercover investigating organized crime as a supposed rogue cop on the take from drug dealers. The latter assignment led to one terrifying moment.

"I was in a car with a drug dealer in Bay Ridge," Dwyer remembers. "I was wearing a wire and there was a photo op in progress when the battery in my tape recorder ran down and the machine started beeping. Right away, I grabbed my chest and told the perp, 'Take me to the hospital'."

"What?" the dealer demanded.

"I've got a pacemaker. Take me to Methodist Hospital now."

Fortunately, the suspect did as instructed. Meanwhile, in 1983, while still a cop, Dwyer became an inspector for the New York State Athletic Commission. A year later, he was elevated to chief inspector. In 1995, ring judging was added to his duties. He left the commission in July 2000 to become chairman of the International Boxing Federation championship committee. In that role, he has earned the respect of the boxing community and helped move the organization beyond the much-publicized criminal proceedings that toppled former IBF president Robert Lee.

It doesn't take a rocket scientist to know that the chairman of the New York State Athletic Commission should have a working knowledge of the sport and business of professional boxing. Dwyer meets that requirement. He's also a capable administrator and a straight-shooter with a reputation for integrity and aggressiveness in pursuing what he thinks is right. The fact that he had 59 amateur fights adds to his understanding of what goes on in a boxing ring.

As for his philosophy of regulation, Dwyer declares, "Right now, the commission is driving boxing away from New York. It's part of the problem when it should be part of the solution. There has to be a cooperative effort. It can't be us against them, which is how too many people at the commission view their jobs. Government employees, like everyone else, should treat people with dignity and respect; not just flaunt their authority and yell at them. The commission has to reach out and have a dialogue with all the elements in the sport. It has to have regular meetings with promoters, managers, and fighters to discuss their problems. It has to revamp the rules, which are outdated and too lax in some respects and too oppressive in others.

"What you have at the commission now," Dwyer continues, "is an attitude of indifference. That has to change. The staff at the commission is capable of doing a better job, but they need direction and they need more people who understand boxing to help them. There are a lot of people in this state who have a great feel for boxing because of the time and effort they've put into learning about the sport. But because of the way the selection process works, very few of these people work at the commission."

Unanimity is rare in the conflict-ridden world of professional boxing. One of the few things that virtually everyone seems to agree upon is that Dwyer would be an excellent chairman of the New York State Athletic Commission. Like Kerik and Kelly before him, he isn't asking for the job. But he'd take it; and he'd do it right. ❏

*When, at long last, the New York State Athletic Commission was shamed into abandoning the pretext that professional wrestling is a sport in need of regulation, I revisited the carnival.*

# PROFESSIONAL WRESTLING AND THE NYSAC REDUX

On August 20, 2002, Governor George Pataki signed the Professional Wrestling Health And Safety Act. The law did away with the pretense that professional wrestling is an athletic competition in need of regulation by the state. As a result, it's no longer illegal for combatants to "strike, scratch, gouge, butt, or employ unnecessarily punitive strangleholds (New York State Athletic Commission Rule 216.11)." In fact, it isn't even against the rules anymore for professional wrestlers to "deliberately throw opponents out of the ring (Rule 216.17)."

Over the years, the New York State Athletic Commission has spent hundreds of thousands of dollars to "regulate" professional wrestling. Were those tax dollars well-spent or were they part of a political patronage boondoggle?

Last June, while the NYSAC regulations were in full force and effect, I attended a World Wrestling Entertainment extravaganza at Madison Square Garden. Recently, for purposes of comparison, I scrutinized a WWE show at Nassau Coliseum. I wanted to know if anarchy is upon us now that dedicated public servants are no longer paid to watch Hulk Hogan do battle with The Undertaker. And to make certain that I didn't miss anything, I brought along an expert consultant.

Justin Zverin is 10 years old and attends fifth grade at PS 101 in Queens. He's a star forward for Grandstand, which compiled an 11 and 1 record this past autumn in the Forest Hills Soccer League. In fact, Justin scored two goals in Grandstand's 8-1 championship game victory over Score. He's one of the better young players at the famed West Side Tennis Club in Forest Hills and excels at football, basketball, and rollerblading. To top things off, he has a 4.0 grade average.

The Nassau Coliseum was half-empty for the show. The public address system wasn't working particularly well, so listening to the announcer was like trying to decipher the lyrics to "Louie Louie" being sung by The Kingsmen over the New York City subway messaging system. However, none of that impeded what went on in the ring.

The first match of the evening was Billy Kidman versus Jamie Noble. As the battle raged, Justin gave me a crash course in "wrestling for dummies" . . . "That's a suplex . . . That's a super-suplex . . . Every time Jamie Noble wrestles, he gets thrown headfirst into his girlfriend and their heads smash together." In due course, a large-breasted woman wearing extremely short cut-off jeans materialized on the ring apron to root Noble on. And sure enough—Whack!!! Kidman threw Noble headfirst into the poor young thing and their skulls collided. The victory went to Kidman.

Next up was a six-man tag-team match. "The bald guy is Albert," Justin offered. "He beat up Ray Mysterio so bad." That bit of information was relevant because Mysterio is Justin's favorite wrestler.

Albert is a big hairy guy. After a while, the crowd started chanting, "Shave your back! Shave your back!" In response, one of Albert's adversaries began pulling on his back hair. This appeared to cause great pain and poor Albert wailed loudly, but Justin explained that what I was watching wasn't real. Remember, Justin has a 4.0 grade average in addition to his athletic skills. I wonder if the New York State Athletic Commission personnel who received hundreds of thousands of dollars to ensure that "No wrestler shall engage in any unsportsmanlike conduct (Rule 216.25)" understood this at the time they were being paid.

In match number three, Chuck Palumbo pinned John Cena.

The fourth contest was another tag-team bout featuring muscular stunt men named Spanky, Nunzio, Shannon, and Crash. I'm not sure who was who but, then again, I'm not sure it mattered.

The fifth bout pitted Scott Steiner against Matt Hardy. "Scott Steiner is important," Justin advised me. Mr. Steiner's signature move is that he flexes his biceps and then kisses them. Adoring fans who came to the Coliseum hoping to see the "biceps kiss" were not disappointed.

Match number six saw the Guerreros (Eddie and Chavo) defending their WWE tag-team championship against Kurt Angle and Chris Benoit. The Guerreros won by disqualification when Angle hit one of them on the head with the coveted WWE tag-team championship belt. Apparently, under WWE rules, general mayhem is permitted but desecration of this sort will not be tolerated.

Then it was time for the women. Dawn Marie and Gail Kim did battle in a "bra and panties match." I'm not kidding; that's what the program said it was. The way one wins a bra and panties match is to rip off an opponent's blouse and slacks, thereby leaving her clad in nothing but a bra and panties. This might not be politically correct but, remember, bra and panties matches were previously approved and regulated by the New York State Athletic Commission. In this particular instance, Kim won. However, Justin had more important things on his mind. He was waiting for the Main Event: Brock Lesnar versus "7-foot-2-inch, 500-pound" Big Show in a steel cage match for the WWE championship.

Mr. Lesnar versus Mr. Show was of particular importance to wrestling fans, since Lesnar has been seeking a mixed martial arts encounter against Lennox Lewis. His chances of that happening are about the same as my chances of an assignation with Sophia Loren. Meanwhile, Big Show is described in WWE literature as "a man who terrorizes opponents and sends his antagonists home in broken pieces."

Steel cage matches are a variation on the normal WWE theme. The ring is encased in an eight-foot-high metal "cage," and the first man to escape from the cage wins. Normally, this is achieved by rendering an opponent unconscious and climbing over the top of the cage. However, the outcome of Lesnar versus Big Show hinged on a quirk of fate. Lesnar made a big mistake. He threw Big Show (all 500 pounds of him) against the side of the cage. The cage collapsed under Big Show's weight. Big Show went flying from the ring. And as the first man to escape from the cage, Big Show was declared the victor. Justin was somewhat disappointed with the result, but said that the evening had been "really cool." I should add that after the main event, in a fit of rage, Lesnar beat up Big Show's manager. Shelly Finkel beware.

Proponents of good government will be pleased to know that, in the absence of NYSAC regulation, there was no discernible decline in the skill level, sportsmanship, or moral values of WWE grapplers. Proponents of even better government will note that, under the Professional Wrestling Health And Safety Act, promoters of professional wrestling must still be licensed by the state and certain personnel involved with wrestling are required to apply to the NYSAC for temporary working permits. Also, there is a requirement that wrestling promoters implement an anti-drug plan and file it with the commission.

That's pretty stupid. If the Rolling Stones appear at Nassau Coliseum, the promoter doesn't have to file an anti-drug plan with the State of New York. ❏

*The articles I wrote on corruption at the New York State Athletic Commission led to my being invited to testify before Congress in early 2003.*

# TESTIFYING BEFORE CONGRESS

The call came on Wednesday, January 29 from a staff member for the United States Senate Committee on Commerce, Science, and Transportation. He wanted to know if I'd accept were I to be invited to testify regarding proposed legislation to combat corruption in professional boxing.

It reminded me of the letters that are sent out when a British citizen is under consideration for knighthood. As Sir Henry Cooper once told me, "The Queen doesn't like to be rejected, so first they make sure you'll accept and then they extend the honor."

Anyway, I said I'd accept, and the invitation came the following afternoon by fax:

Dear Mr. Hauser,

On Wednesday, February 5, 2003, at 2:30 p.m. in SR-253, the Senate Committee on Commerce, Science, and transportation will hold a Full Committee oversight hearing on professional boxing.

As Chairman of the Committee, I invite you to testify. At this hearing, the Committee will hear testimony on the current issues and problems surrounding professional boxing. The committee asks that you focus your testimony on the problems facing the sport; the success of federal regulations in solving those problems, and the recent legislative proposals to create a federal regulatory entity to oversee the sport, along with any other related issues you wish to bring to the attention of the Committee.

Sincerely,
John McCain

I formally accepted. Then the staff member called again to say that the hearing had been rescheduled for 9:30 a.m. That meant getting up a five o'clock in the morning to travel to Washington, D.C. from New York.

Yuk.

Still, I've always been interested in politics. I've interviewed Gerald Ford and Jimmy Carter and met Bill Clinton twice (once in the Oval Office). The

177

thought of being part of the political process appealed to me. Thus it was that I awoke at 5:00 a.m. on February 5 and was on the 7:30 a.m. Delta Shuttle to Washington.

The hearing was held in Room 253 of the Russell Senate Office Building. Initially, John McCain was the only Senator present, although Byron Dorgan of North Dakota joined him at the halfway mark. My mother would have preferred that I address a joint session of Congress. But the truth is, I enjoyed the proximity to McCain. I'm a liberal Democrat, and he's a fairly conservative Republican. But he has the aura of a thoroughly decent man who is troubled by the corruption of the once-honorable profession of politics, and I wish there were more people like him in positions of power.

The other invited guests were Bernard Hopkins (who testified that fighters are exploited); Ross Greenburg (who testified that HBO is not a promoter); some guy with a hat and cigar (who kept interrupting the other witnesses); and Patrick Panella of the Maryland State Athletic Commission (who said that the federal government should not enact legislation that preempts the state commissions).

My testimony was as follows:

*I'd like to thank the committee for the honor of being invited here today and get very quickly to the issues at hand.*

*We're far past the point where we can blame the world sanctioning organizations and a handful of promoters for all of the corruption in professional boxing. The entire system is corrupt, and some of the worst enablers are in positions of power at state athletic commissions.*

*For eight years, the New York State Athletic Commission has been shamelessly run as a slush fund for a political party. Data made available by the New York Department of State indicates that, prior to recent budget cuts, it cost $87,000 per fight card to regulate boxing in New York. By contrast, last year it cost Nevada only $5,400 per card to regulate professional boxing.*

*When Evander Holyfield fought Lennox Lewis at Madison Square Garden, the New York State Athletic Commission assigned 25 inspectors and demanded 67 ringside credentials. By contrast, Nevada employs only 16 inspectors statewide and assigns no more than six inspectors to any given fight card.*

*On the night of the Holyfield-Lewis fight at Madison Square Garden, Robert Duffy (who was the New York State Athletic Commission director of boxing) assigned two inspectors to each fighter's corner. Then he was overruled, and four different inspectors with strong political ties were given the assignment. One of those inspectors had never worked a fight before in his life. You don't start your career as a ring inspector in the corner at a unification fight for the undisputed heavyweight championship of the world. Duffy complained and was told—and this is a direct quote —"Hey, Duffy, you don't understand. We won the election."*

*Duffy was subsequently forced out of his job. The man who made that comment* to him now runs the New York State Athletic Commission on a daily basis.

Until recently, the Nevada State Athletic Commission was considered the best-run athletic commission in the country. A number of dedicated competent public servants like executive director Marc Ratner still work there. But the Nevada State Athletic Commission is now a textbook example of conflicts of interest run amok.

Tony Alamo is a senior vice president at Mandalay Bay Resort and Casino and the man primarily responsible for overseeing boxing at Mandalay Bay. Tony Alamo, Jr. sits on the Nevada State Athletic Commission, which is charged with regulating his father's boxing promotions. The situation was further exacerbated on January 13 of this year, when Edwin "Flip" Homansky (a nationally respected administrator) was removed as vice chairman of the Nevada Commission and replaced by Tony Alamo, Jr.

It might be that Tony Alamo, Jr. is totally independent of his father. But everyone in boxing who I've talked with doubts it. And his presence on the Nevada State Athletic Commission sends a powerful message regarding government-sanctioned conflicts of interest.

Also, nationwide, many state athletic commissions are afraid to enforce the laws that Congress has passed because they know that, if they do, big fights will simply go elsewhere.

I'll give you an example.

Section 11(d)(1) of the Muhammad Ali Boxing Reform Act requires all sanctioning organizations to submit a complete description of their ratings criteria to the Federal Trade Commission and the Association of Boxing Commissions. Each of the major sanctioning organizations purports to have filed this information. The problem is, most of their filings are fraudulent.

The World Boxing Organization had a dead man ranked in the top 10 of its super-middleweight division for four months. During that same four-month period, the dead man rose in the rankings from number seven to number five.

This past autumn, the World Boxing Association released rankings that were so outrageous and, in the heavyweight division, so tied to the interests of one promoter that Senator McCain of this Committee wrote a letter of protest.

Section 6 of the Ali Act provides that the chief law enforcement officer of any state may bring a civil action to enjoin the holding within its borders of any professional boxing match related to a false filing. No such civil action has ever been brought.

Section 6 of the Ali Act also provides that a world sanctioning organization that files incomplete or false information shall not be entitled to receive any compensation, directly or indirectly, in connection with a boxing match including sanctioning fees. That provision is not being enforced by any state.

And Section 6 of the Ali Act provides that violation of the disclosure requirements is a criminal offense punishable by up to one year in prison and a fine of up to $100,000. The Criminal Division of the Justice Department is responsible for these prosecutions, but no such indictment has ever been brought.

*Why have laws if no one is going to enforce them?*

*Boxing needs strong federal regulation by knowledgeable personnel who assume their positions of power without conflicts of interest. And while we're waiting for legislation to create this regulation, I respectfully suggest that it's imperative for the federal government to act now through criminal prosecutions as well as civil lawsuits brought by the Justice Department and Federal Trade Commission to enforce the laws as they're currently written.*

*This Committee cannot rely on state athletic commissions to clean up boxing. And the Association of Boxing Commissions is nothing but a collective of the same officials who have failed to enforce the law on the state level.*

Will any good come of it?

I don't know, but things went better than I thought they would. I doubt that my testimony (or anybody else's) will affect the proposed legislation. But it might impact upon enforcement of the laws that have already been passed.

The hearing lasted slightly less than two hours. McCain asked a number of questions that were right on point. And in his closing remarks, he declared, "We should light a fire under the Justice Department because there have been some egregious violations of the law."

If boxing is lucky, Congress will do just that. ❏

*As 2003 progressed, more and more corruption was revealed at the New York State Athletic Commission. That, in turn, led to change and hope that the NYSAC had turned a corner at last.*

# GOOD NEWS AND GOOD RIDDANCE AT THE NEW YORK STATE ATHLETIC COMMISSION

Ron Scott Stevens has been designated by Governor George Pataki as the new chairman of the New York State Athletic Commission. For the past eight years, the commission has been widely viewed as a slush fund for the Republican Party and a dumping ground for political patronage employees. Stevens replaces Bernard Kerik, who resigned as chairman on April 11, 2003. His appointment is a step in the right direction for an agency desperately in need of change.

The NYSAC has been a microcosm of incompetence and corruption throughout the Pataki administration. Under the chairmanship of Floyd Patterson (1995-1998) and Mel Southard (1998-2001), qualified employees were forced out of their jobs and often replaced by no-show personnel. The tragic death of Beethavean Scottland at what was treated as a social event for Republican-party loyalists was symbolic of their reign.

In September 2001, less than three months after Scottland's death, Ray Kelly was named chairman of the NYSAC. Kelly tried to turn things around and restore a sense of professionalism. But neither he nor his executive director, Charles DeRienzo, understood the sport or business of boxing. And Kelly was understandably preoccupied with his responsibilities as commissioner of the New York City Police Department. He resigned from the NYSAC in June 2002 and was succeeded as chairman by Bernard Kerik.

Kerik's chairmanship was a fraud. He served for a dollar a year and was overpaid. During his tenure at the NYSAC, there wasn't a single commission meeting. Several fulltime NYSAC employees said that they literally never saw him in the office. He attended only one fight (at which he arrived late), and his lack of interest in the sport became a national joke. In his absence, the commission was run on a day-to-day basis by Jerry Becker.

Becker is a former Bronx Criminal Court and Family Court judge who has been active for years in the Conservative Party. He is currently chairman of the New York State Housing Finance Agency and was designated a commissioner of the NYSAC by Pataki on June 14, 2000.

Becker sought to implement a series of reforms at the commission, particularly in the medical arena. But fundamental problems remained. Part of the problem was lack of knowledge. "Jerry Becker thinks he knows boxing, but he doesn't," one commission employee posited.

As if to prove that notion, Becker masterminded a move within the commission to approve or disapprove fights based on the won-loss records of fighters. "I've had people come to me with guys who are 1 and 6," Becker told Joe Gergen of *Newsday*. "I will not accept a 1 and 6 guy no matter how great he looks in the gym." But the problem with that policy is obvious to anyone who knows boxing. When Eric Esch a.k.a. "Butterbean" fought Mitchell Rose at Madison Square Garden, Butterbean was 14-0 and Rose's record was 1-6. Rose knocked Butterbean out in the second round.

Becker also spearheaded the hiring of Scott Crockett (whose wife performs public relations work at the Housing Finance Agency) as an assistant to the chairman at a reported salary of $77,000 a year. It might be that Crockett is an exemplary public servant. But to some, his most apparent qualification for the job was that he served as a campaign staffer for George Pataki during the governor's 2002 reelection campaign.

"I've come to the conclusion that the people in charge here actually want to kill the small shows because they don't want to be bothered with them," one NYSAC employee said last year. It's an aggravation for them, and they just don't want to do the work."

When that quote appeared, there were howls of protest from the commission hierarchy. But the facts speak for themselves. In 2002, there were no shows in the big arena at Madison Square Garden for the first time since the 1994 building renovation. There has been only one show in the entire State of New York so far this year.

All of the above led veteran boxing scribe Don Majeski to write, "The New York State Athletic Commission is the most highly-funded poorly-run boxing commission in the world. This is the worst boxing commission in New York since the advent of the Horton law in 1896. Not a single person there is qualified to sit on a boxing commission. No one has any experience in professional boxing. If boxing was dead in New York State, this commission buried it."

Still, it was business as usual at the commission until recent events spiraled beyond the control of political spin doctoring.

On February 21, 2003, Senator John McCain (chairman of the United States Senate Committee on Commerce, Science, and Transportation) wrote to George Pataki urging that the governor examine allegations that the New York State Athletic Commission is "corrupt from top to bottom" and is plagued by "many sinecures, allowing employees to incur exorbitant expenses at taxpayer expense and handing out inspector positions as political favors."

Meanwhile, behind the scenes, a greater crisis was brewing. On March 22,

2000, the Rackets Bureau of the New York County District Attorney's office referred allegations of improprieties involving the NYSAC to the Office of the Inspector General of the State of New York [OSIG]. The OSIG conducted an investigation that was concluded on January 21, 2003. Then it issued a report.

Anyone who wants to see how the Pataki administration has corrupted government in the State of New York should take a long hard look at the findings of the inspector general.

From 1995 through December 2001, James Polsinello was at various times executive director of the NYSAC, executive assistant to the chairman, and special assistant to the chairman. There were numerous public reports during his tenure that he had a "no-show" job. Yet these reports were ignored, and Polsinello was paid tens of thousands of dollars a year by the taxpayers of the State of New York.

The NYSAC is part of the New York Department of State. With regard to Polsinello, the OSIG report declares, "DOS personnel informed OSIG that Polsinello was present approximately two or three days a week for approximately one or two hours on each occasion. Polsinello acknowledged that, after [Anthony] Russo arrived [in May 1996], he had very little daily work to do. He confirmed that he was not present at the NYSAC office on a daily basis. In his view, he was performing his duties because he was available for assignments through contact at his home or on his cell phone. He insisted that he had inspected training facilities, but was unable to name any gym that he had inspected and admitted that he had never documented his inspection visits. In essence, Polsinello equated 'being available if sought out' to work. OSIG's investigation concluded that NYSAC's employment of Polsinello at a salary that has ranged from $55,000 to over $67,000 constituted a wasteful expenditure of state monies."

Anthony Russo was executive director of the NYSAC from May 1996 through September 15, 2000. With regard to Russo, the inspector general's report declared, "OSIG's investigation found substantial evidence that Russo regularly ignored his responsibilities and failed to provide full-time service to the NYSAC. It is difficult to see how Russo's compensation, which ranged from $50,000 to $65,000 annually, was justified by the work produced by him."

While on the job, Russo claimed to be operating out of the NYSAC's Poughkeepsie office. Here, information provided to the OSIG by Barbra Kozak (an assistant in that office from June 1995 until 1998) is instructive. The OSIG report states, "Kosak informed OSIG that Russo visited the Poughkeepsie office only to sign time-sheets and memoranda. In interviews with other NYSAC employees, OSIG found that Russo seldom visited the New York City office and may never have been to the NYSAC office in Albany. After Kozak resigned, large volumes of NYSAC mail went unopened for extended periods in Poughkeepsie despite notifications to Russo. Ultimately, the mailroom of the New York State office building in Poughkeepsie decided to return all mail received for NYSAC to the parties who had sent the mail."

It gets worse.

The OSIG report also documents the finding that, "Russo's monthly cell phone usage often exceeded $400 and, on one occasion, exceeded $1,500. OSIG's review of the cell phone bills showed that most of the telephone calls appeared personal, not NYSAC-related. At one point, DOS, after receiving Russo's $1,500 cell phone bill, directed Russo to identify his personal calls and submit a check covering those calls. Russo submitted a check for $500, which bounced when DOS tried to cash it. After OSIG began investigating Russo's telephone usage, OSIG learned that Russo resubmitted a $487.50 check to DOS which subsequently cleared."

Then there's Dr. Robin Scarlata, whose father had close ties to New York Senator Alphonse D'Amato. From 1995 through mid-2000, Scarlata was paid to perform the part-time duties of medical director and, later, co-medical director of the NYSAC.

"During her tenure with NYSAC," the OSIG report states, "Scarlata worked fulltime as a radiologist on Long Island. Scarlata maintained neither a desk nor a telephone number at any NYSAC office. Other than attending several Long Island boxing contests and some major New York City boxing matches, OSIG was unable to verify that Scarlata performed any additional work for NYSAC during her five-year tenure. Nonetheless, from 1995 through mid-2000, Scarlata was paid on the basis that she was spending 37.5 hours every two weeks working for NYSAC. She filed monthly time sheets in which she listed particular hours during each business day as periods during which she performed NYSAC work. According to her time sheets, this period was often listed as 8:00 a.m. to 12:00 p.m. or 9:00 a.m. to 1:00 p.m. Scarlata produced only time sheets in response to a request for documents documenting her activities as co-medical director. On the advice of her attorney, Scarlata declined to be interviewed by OSIG. The evidence indicates that Scarlata performed no discernible functions as medical director during her five years at NYSAC, yet received a salary ranging over the period from approximately $43,000 to $50,000."

The inspector general's report is just the tip of the iceberg. The logical question that it neither asks nor answers is, "Why were Polsinello, Russo and Scarlata given no-show jobs?" To repeat: WHY WERE POLSINELLO, RUSSO AND SCARLATA GIVEN NO-SHOW JOBS? One might also ask questions like:

● Who gave them their jobs?

● Why were there no criminal prosecutions?

● Why weren't they required to return any of the hundreds of thousands of dollars that they received for their "no show" jobs?

● Why were two of the three simply shifted to other "jobs" on the public payroll when things got too hot for them at the NYSAC?

Also, keep in mind that the OSIG's investigation and report are the work of an agency whose top personnel owe their jobs to George Pataki. And consider the fact that the report is riddled with false information given to the OSIG by NYSAC personnel. For example, in exonerating the NYSAC of wrongdoing in conjunction with charges that a phony weigh-in was conducted by Russo prior to the Arturo Gatti versus Joey Gamache fight, the report states, "NYSAC told OSIG that there had been no lawsuit filed or action requested by anyone involved in that bout." That statement is blatantly false. In truth, on February 20, 2002, Joey and Sissy Gamache filed a notice of claim against the NYSAC and the State of New York. The claim itself was filed on November 21, 2002.

The OSIG report was confidential. But by mid-March, word of its contents began to leak out. The Pataki administration had to defuse what had become a ticking time-bomb. In other words, the NYSAC needed a credible chairman.

For a long time, Jerry Becker had been viewed as the NYSAC's chairman in waiting. The theory was that Kerik would stay on as a figurehead until such time as Becker could be installed in the top job without arousing excessive media opposition. In his public statements, Becker consistently denied that he wanted the job. Others were skeptical of his protestations. Either way, the OSIG report made it clear that Becker's elevation to the chairmanship would have damning political consequences.

Becker became a commissioner on June 14, 2000. The OSIG report states, "During the period from 1995 to 2001 [when Ray Kelly was named chairman], NYSAC commissioners failed to exercise effective oversight of NYSAC professional staff resulting in poor performance on the part of the agency." In other words, 15 months of that wrongdoing occurred on Becker's watch.

Enter Ron Scott Stevens. Stevens is 56 years old and has been in boxing for much of his life. At various times, he has been involved with the sweet science as a writer, ring announcer, sportscaster, matchmaker, and promoter. He's honest and cares about the sport.

Stevens was courted for a job at the NYSAC on the understanding that he would be its executive director. Then that position was eliminated and Scott Crockett was hired at an executive-level salary as assistant to the chairman. Stevens came on board in December 2002 as director of boxing.

The obvious first question to be asked with regard to the new chairman is, "How much autonomy will he have?" There's a lot of work to be done at the commission. Stevens needs to determine which personnel on his staff are qualified and get rid of the rest. He has to upgrade inspector training and do more to develop top-notch referees and judges. The medical department has been beset by problems that require attention. And in addition to all the institutional problems, there will be day-to-day issues. Suppose, for example, Mike Tyson applies for a license to fight in New York?

It's not an easy job. The boxing community wishes Ron Scott Stevens the best. ❏

*Some issues in boxing are never resolved.*

# THE FIGHT OF THE CENTURY

Often, when there's a blockbuster fight, the boxing hype machine goes into overdrive.

"This match-up is the greatest ever . . . This is the biggest fight imaginable." And the magic words, "It's the fight of the century."

The consensus list for the fight of the last century boils down to three candidates:

> Jack Johnson vs. James Jeffries
> Joe Louis vs. Max Schmeling II
> Muhammad Ali vs. Joe Frazier I

Each of these fights was the most significant of its era. Each featured two great champions with at least one of them in his prime. Each was viewed in its day as an allegory of good versus evil. And each reached far beyond the sporting arena to involve social issues that went to the core of the American psyche.

Let's look at them one at a time.

*Jack Johnson vs. James Jeffries*

December 26, 1908, was the dawn of the Golden Age of Boxing; although at the time, many thought that Armageddon was at hand. In Sydney, Australia, Jack Johnson knocked out the undistinguished Tommy Burns in 14 rounds. A black man was heavyweight champion of the world. Worse; a black man who, by his conduct in and out of the ring, mocked the entire white race.

Not only did Johnson defeat white opponents; he humiliated them, laughing and taunting during fights. He consorted with white prostitutes and had the temerity to marry a white woman.

The cry went out for a white savior. James Jeffries had reigned as heavyweight champion from 1899 through his retirement in 1905. He was undefeated and, in his prime, had knocked out the likes of James Corbett, Bob Fitzsimmons, and Tom Sharkey.

Jack London, writing in the *New York Herald*, spoke for many when he implored, "Jeffries must now emerge from his alfalfa farm and remove that golden smile from Johnson's face. Jeff, it's up to you."

186

Jeffries had retired from boxing five years earlier and was living in quiet contentment on a California farm, where his weight had ballooned to 300 pounds. At first, he resisted the entreaties. Then, finally, he succumbed. The fight was to be a battle for racial supremacy. Jeffries himself acknowledged as much several days before the bout when he told reporters, "I realize full well just what depends on me, and I'm not going to disappoint the public. That portion of the white race that has been looking to me to defend its athletic superiority may rest assured that I am fit to do my very best."

He wasn't.

On July 4, 1910, in Reno, Nevada, Jack Johnson toyed with the chosen representative of the white race and knocked him out in 15 rounds.

### Joe Louis vs. Max Schmeling II

The Great Depression was ravaging America. War clouds were gathering in Europe. Boxing was at its peak. And Joe Louis was heavyweight champion of the world. But as Louis himself acknowledged, "It won't feel like I'm champion till I beat Schmeling."

In 1936, Schmeling had KO'd the Brown Bomber in 12 rounds. That same summer, despite the heroics of Jesse Owens, Adolf Hitler had turned the Berlin Olympics into a showcase for the doctrine of Aryan supremacy. After Louis defeated James Braddock for the heavyweight crown, Louis-Schmeling II became inevitable.

The rematch took place at Yankee Stadium on June 22, 1938, and was heard live on radio throughout the world. It lasted 124 seconds. On that night, 24-year-old Louis was the greatest fighter who ever lived. Bill Corum of the *New York Evening Journal* summed up the encounter with the words, "Someday, somebody will beat Joe Louis. But nobody will ever beat the Joe Louis you saw last night."

### Muhammad Ali vs. Joe Frazier I

The 1960s had exploded. America was torn apart by assassinations, urban riots, Vietnam, and counter-culture rebellion. Meanwhile, although no one knew it at the time, the sweet science stood on the edge of decline. This was the last gasp of New York's reign as the favored venue for big fights and the climax of boxing's prime.

On March 8, 1971, the eyes of the world were focused on a small square of illuminated canvas that was one of the great stages of modern times. "What you had that night," Bryant Gumbel later noted, "were two undefeated heavyweight champions. One was the very symbol of black pride, parading black feelings about black heritage, speaking out against racial injustice. And the other guy just kind of went along. He wasn't a proponent of the old order, but he didn't fight it either. One guy was dead set against the war. The other didn't seem to have much of a feeling about it. After a while, how you stood on Ali became a political and generational litmus test. And fairly or unfairly, because he was opposing Ali, Joe Frazier became the symbol of our oppressors."

It was the most anticipated, most heavily promoted event in the history of sports.

Frazier won over 15 brutal rounds.

● ● ●

So which of these bouts deserves recognition as the "Fight of the Century"?

Johnson-Jeffries and Louis-Schmeling II each featured a great performance by the victor. As competive fights, they didn't compare with Ali-Frazier I. Still, in choosing a "Fight of the Century," the quality of the bout itself is a secondary standard. Its historical significance is far more important. So let's look at each fight in its historical context.

### Muhammad Ali vs. Joe Frazier I

Ali's biggest fights and most significant accomplishments were outside the ring. His decision not to serve in the United States military and his outspoken embrace of black pride were far more important than any of his boxing matches.

Ali-Frazier I, of course, was also significant to Joe. But to the world at large, the fight was about Ali. Frazier engendered relatively little emotional response from people except insofar as he related to Muhammad.

Moreover, Ali-Frazier I is already receding into a historical grouping with Ali's other fights against Frazier, Sonny Liston, and George Foreman. So, yes, Ali-Frazier I captivated the world. And, yes, it changed the economics of sports. But in society at large, things stayed pretty much the same. And if Ali had won that night (which he did in his next two fights against Frazier), the world wouldn't have changed.

### Jack Johnson vs. James Jeffries

Arthur Ashe once observed, "Nothing that Frederick Douglass did; nothing that Booker T. Washington did; nothing that any African American had done up until that time had the same impact as Jack Johnson's fight against Jim Jeffries. It was the most awaited event in the history of African-Americans to that date. Virtually every black American knew that Johnson versus Jeffries was going to take place. They knew it; they knew what was at stake; and they also knew they could get the results almost immediately because of the advent of the telegraph. And when Johnson won, it completely destroyed one of the crucial pillars of white supremacy; the idea that the white man was superior in body and mind to the darker peoples of the earth. That was just not true as far as anybody was concerned anymore, because now a black man held the title symbolic of the world's most physically powerful human being. It had an emotional immediacy that went beyond what Ali or Louis did, because it was the first time anything like that had ever happened."

In truth, Johnson was interested more in doing for himself than for his people. Most of his friends were white, and he made a number of derogatory comments about blacks, particularly black women, throughout his life. He didn't have a highly developed racial consciousness.

But Jack Johnson, more than anyone else, shattered the myth of white physical superiority. And the impact of his performance in Johnson-Jeffries was complete with the fight itself. Johnson didn't need more big fights (like Ali) or World War II as a coda (like Louis) to put his triumph over Jeffries in its full context. History changed as a consequence of that fight.

### Joe Louis vs. Max Schmeling II

Joe Louis made a time of oppression more bearable for black people. When he began his ring career, there was literally not a single black person in the United States whose accomplishments were noted regularly in the white press. Not a single black person played a prominent role in the American establishment. As Arthur Ashe later noted, "Joe was the first black American of any discipline or endeavor to enjoy the overwhelming good feeling, sometimes bordering on idolatry, of all Americans regardless of color."

Louis was the symbol of his race to black people and to white. All of his fights encompassed the issue of color. But Louis-Schmeling II went beyond that. The bout also spoke to issues of democracy and totalitarianism. It was viewed as a test of decency and freedom versus Nazi philosophy. And while Johnson-Jeffries and Ali-Frazier I were contested against the backdrop of a bitterly divided nation, America was united in the hope that Louis would defeat Schmeling. Indeed, it was the first time that many white Americans, particularly in the south, openly rooted for a black man against a white opponent.

The fight itself was an annihilation rather than a competitive bout. But one-sided fights become larger through the prism of history. And with regard to Louis-Schmeling II , an annihilation was what America wanted.

The impact of Louis-Schmeling II was extraordinary. Within days, films of the contest were showing in theatres across America. The bout had an almost spiritual effect on the nation. And the fight benefits greatly from historical hindsight in that it ties into events like World War II and the Holocaust which give it international implications that Johnson-Jeffries didn't have.

● ● ●

So to repeat the question: Which of these three bouts deserves to be known as the "Fight of the Century"?

Three respected fight historians have stated their view. Randy Roberts is a professor of history at Purdue University and the author of biographies about Jack Johnson and Jack Dempsey. "It comes down to a choice between Johnson-Jeffries and Louis-Schmeling II," says Roberts. "And in my view, Johnson-Jeffries is a little more important. Without the world events that came later, Louis-Schmeling II loses some of its significance, but Johnson-Jeffries stands on its own."

Mike Silver is a boxing historian who has worked as a consultant for HBO and ESPN Classic on documentaries dealing with Joe Louis and his era and also on films such as *Shadow Boxing: The Journey of the Afro-American Fighter*. "You can make a strong argument for either Johnson-Jeffries or Louis-Schmeling II," Silver posits. "I think the answer lies in the future. It will depend on which of these seismic sporting events is still the object of research and analysis a hundred years from now."

Jeffrey Sammons is a professor of history at NYU and the author of *Beyond the Ring: The Role of Boxing in American Society*. Sammons is also undecided. "It's a difficult choice," he acknowledges. "To me, it's between Johnson-Jeffries and Louis-Schmeling. It's a toss-up, really. And it would be a disservice to both fights to consider ranking one above the other."

I'm inclined to agree with Sammons. But if a split ballot isn't allowed and I'm forced to choose, I'll go with Jack Johnson versus James Jeffries as the "Fight of the Century." ❑

*This article was written just before the rematch between Vernon Forrest and Ricardo Mayorga, which Mayorga won by decision.*

# A GOLDEN ERA

The heavyweight championship is considered by many to be the best barometer of the health of boxing. When Muhammad Ali reigned the second time around, when Mike Tyson was in his prime, the sport was considered alive and well. By contrast, when Frans Botha, Bruce Seldon, and Frank Bruno shared the alphabet-soup titles, boxing was thought to be on life support.

But some fight fans look to a different measure—great fights between great fighters. By that standard, two decades ago, the sweet science was in a golden age. Sugar Ray Leonard, Thomas Hearns, Marvin Hagler, Roberto Duran, and Wilfred Benitez engaged in 12 memorable fights against one another. Nine of them occurred in a 5-1/2-year period. Leonard-Hagler, Leonard-Hearns II and Leonard-Duran III were tacked on at the end; the latter two as an afterthought to the era. All 12 of these bouts were waged between 147 and 160 pounds.

Hey, gang, guess what! Oscar De La Hoya, Felix Trinidad, Vernon Forrest, Shane Mosley, Bernard Hopkins, and Fernando Vargas, have ushered in a new golden era. And recently, Ricardo Mayorga crashed the party. These men have fought eight memorable bouts against one another during the past 3-1/2 years. The Mayorga-Forrest and De La Hoya-Mosley rematches will bring that total to 10. Their encounters have been just as exciting as the superfights of 20 years ago. And, like their predecessors, these bouts have been, and will continue to be, contested at between 147 and 160 pounds.

Let's take a look at both eras, starting with the records of the fighters from 1980s against one another.

SUGAR RAY LEONARD 5-1-1

| | |
|---|---|
| 11/30/79 | Wilfred Benitez KO 15 |
| 6/20/80 | Roberto Duran L15 |
| 11/25/80 | Roberto Duran KO 8 |
| 9/16/81 | Thomas Hearns KO 14 |
| 4/6/87 | Marvin Hagler W12 |
| 6/12/89 | Thomas Hearns D12 |
| 12/7/89 | Roberto Duran W12 |

THOMAS HEARNS 2-2-1

| | |
|---|---|
| 9/16/81 | Sugar Ray Leonard L14 |

| 12/3/82 | Wilfred Benitez W12 |
| 6/15/84 | Roberto Duran KO 2 |
| 4/15/85 | Marvin Hagler KO by 3 |
| 6/12/89 | Sugar Ray Leonard D12 |

MARVIN HAGLER 2-1

| 11/10/83 | Roberto Duran W15 |
| 4/15/85 | Thomas Hearns KO3 |
| 4/6/87 | Sugar Ray Leonard L12 |

ROBERTO DURAN 1-5

| 6/20/80 | Sugar Ray Leonard W15 |
| 11/25/80 | Sugar Ray Leonard KO by 8 |
| 1/30/82 | Wilfred Benitez L15 |
| 11/10/83 | Marvin Hagler L15 |
| 6/15/84 | Thomas Hearns KO by 2 |
| 12/7/89 | Sugar Ray Leonard L12 |

WILFRED BENITEZ 1-2

| 11/30/79 | Sugar Ray Leonard KO by 15 |
| 1/30/82 | Roberto Duran W15 |
| 12/3/82 | Thomas Hearns L15 |

Now let's look at the current elite in the same weight divisions.

Oscar De La Hoya is one of two always-bankable fighters in boxing today. The other is Mike Tyson. Critics complain that De La Hoya has done everything but insist on a clause in fight contracts mandating that opponents enter the ring to the latest CD of Golden Boy love songs. But Oscar can fight.

Felix Trinidad did everything that was asked of him in the ring except beat Hopkins. If he had done that, his picture would be on the wall next to Jesus in every home in Puerto Rico. Tito may, or may not, stay retired.

Vernon Forrest surprised the world against Shane Mosley. Then he surprised the world again when he got knocked out by Ricardo Mayorga. Now the question is, "How will he do in the Mayorga rematch and against the other elite fighters?"

Sugar Shane lost twice to Forrest. But he's still the only man to have clearly beaten De La Hoya.

Bernard Hopkins has an attitude; and in the ring, he uses it to his advantage. Outside the ring, Bernard also has an attitude. Don King recently explained the difficulty in making big-money fights for Hopkins. "You have to understand," King wailed. "Bernard is crazy. I can't control him. Who ever controlled him?"

Unlike the other-mentioned fighters, Fernando Vargas probably won't be in the Hall of Fame. But he's a superb inquisitor. Emanuel Steward once said,

"Guys with tough insides make great fights." Vargas has tough insides. At age 25, he's also considerable younger than De La Hoya and Trinidad (both 30), Mosley (31), Forrest (32), and Hopkins (38). Still, Vargas took bad beatings against Trinidad and De La Hoya and was in worse shape after his fight against Oscar than most people realized.

Ricardo Mayorga is the upstart in the group, a fighter who came out of nowhere. And he can punch.

Here's how the members of today's elite have performed so far against one another:

OSCAR DE LA HOYA 1-2

9/18/99     Felix Trinidad L12
6/17/00     Shane Mosley L12
9/14/02     Ferdando Vargas KO 11

FELIX TRINIDAD 2-1

9/18/99     Oscar De La Hoya W12
12/2/00     Fernando Vargas KO 12
9/29/01     Bernard Hopkins KO by 12

VERNON FORREST 2- 1

1/26/02     Shane Mosley W12
7/20/02     Shane Mosley W12
1/25/03     Ricardo Mayorga KO by 3

SHANE MOSLEY 1-2

6/17/00     Oscar De La Hoya W12
1/26/02     Vernon Forrest L12
7/20/02     Vernon Forrest L12

BERNARD HOPKINS 1-0

9/29/01     Felix Trinidad KO 12

FERNANDO VARGAS 0-2

12/2/00     Felix Trinidad KO by 12
9/14/02     Oscar De La Hoya KO by 11

RICARDO MAYORGA 1-0

1/25/03     Vernon Forrest KO 3

There are a lot of dream matches against one another for today's elite if they want them. They also match up nicely in dream encounters against their predecessors.

So, fight fans, take note. You're witnessing some wonderful history in the making. ❏

*Diminished standards have removed the shine from the International Boxing Hall of Fame. Thus, it made sense to find out who the real experts thought deserved to be inducted.*

## WHO REALLY BELONGS IN THE BOXING HALL OF FAME ?

On June 8, 2002, the International Boxing Hall of Fame in Canastota, New York, will enshrine 18 inductees in four categories: (1) pioneers (boxers whose last contest was prior to 1893); (2) old-timers (boxers whose last contest was between 1893 and 1942); (3) moderns (boxers who have been retired for five or more years and whose last contest was no earlier than 1943); and (4) non-participants (others who have made a contribution to the sport).

The people who run the Hall of Fame are well-intentioned, but the process is flawed. Standards are so low that it's possible to be inducted with only four votes. Many of the electors are unqualified and others have conflicts of interest. For those reasons, I've declined to cast a ballot in recent years even though, as a member of the Boxing Writers Association of America, I'm eligible to vote.

This year's inductees in the "moderns" class prove the point. They are Jeff Fenech, Pipino Cuevas, Victor Galindez, and Ingemar Johansson. Each was a competent fighter. None of them belongs in the Hall of Fame. Yet they are about to join 236 other members of the boxing community who are enshrined in Canastota.

"It's ridiculous," says trainer and boxing commentator Teddy Atlas. "I don't want to take anything away from these guys. Each of them was a good fighter, but there are no standards for induction anymore. All that seems to matter now is that some new guys are inducted each year so the Hall can make money on its induction weekend. A lot of the guys who are in Canastota couldn't have been sparring partners for real hall of famers. Ingemar Johansson in the Hall of Fame? Ingemar Johansson was on a level with Frans Botha and Axel Schulz."

Watering down the standards for induction into the Hall of Fame is like having four "world champions" in each weight class. It diminishes the honor.

So who belongs?

Several years ago, I set out to answer that question. I surveyed two dozen experts: trainers like Atlas, Eddie Futch, Gil Clancy, Angelo Dundee, and Emanuel Steward; historians like Randy Roberts; writers like Jerry Izenberg, Michael Katz, and Steve Farhood; and others within the boxing community like Don Elbaum, Arthur Mercante, and Johnny Bos.

Each "elector" was asked to name 20 fighters. The only requirement was that the fighter had to have been retired for five years. Those polled could designate their own standards for induction. Common reference points apart from total wins and losses were (1) longevity, (2) a fighter's record against other great fighters, and (3) his historical importance.

The results were interesting. When the votes were tabulated, 24 boxers had separated themselves from the rest of the pack. Indeed, the 24th-place finisher received twice as many votes as the fighter who finished 25th. Six fighters were named on every ballot—Sugar Ray Robinson, Joe Louis, Muhammad Ali, Henry Armstrong, Benny Leonard, and Willie Pep. The top 24 finishers, in order, were:

> Sugar Ray Robinson
> Joe Louis
> Muhammad Ali
> Henry Armstrong
> Benny Leonard
> Willie Pep
> Jack Johnson
> Rocky Marciano
> Archie Moore
> Jack Dempsey
> Micky Walker
> Harry Greb
> Joe Gans
> John L. Sullivan
> Barney Ross
> Sandy Saddler
> Gene Tunney
> Ezzard Charles
> Sam Langford
> Tony Canzoneri
> Marvin Hagler
> Stanley Ketchel
> Carlos Monzon
> Eder Jofre

If I had my druthers, these 24 men would be the first inductees in a new Boxing Hall of Fame.

The following fighters, listed alphabetically, also received votes from the experts: Carmen Basilio, Nino Benvenuti, Jack Britton, Charlie Burley, Marcel Cerdan, Billy Conn, James Corbett, George Dixon, Bob Fitzsimmons, Bob

Foster, Joe Frazier, Kid Gavilan, Emile Griffith, Jim Jeffries, Jake LaMotta, Ted "Kid" Lewis, Sonny Liston, Benny Lynch, Jose Napoles, Reuben Olivares, Carlos Ortiz, Aaron Pryor, Luis Rodriguez, Salvador Sanchez, Michael Spinks, Jimmy Wilde, Ike Williams, Harry Wills, and Carlos Zarate. These men would be leading candidates for future induction.

Contemporary ring greats would also be eligible after being retired for five years. Listed alphabetically, they include the likes of Julio Cesar Chavez, Roberto Duran, George Foreman, Thomas Hearns, Larry Holmes, Evander Holyfield, Bernard Hopkins, Roy Jones, Sugar Ray Leonard, and Pernell Whitaker. And of course, it remains to be seen what happens in the future for fighters like Marco Antonio Barrera, Vernon Forrest, Shane Mosley, Felix Trinidad, and Mike Tyson.

Thus, a question for you the reader: "Who would be your 24 candidates for enshrinement?" Remember, for every fighter you add to the list, another fighter must be taken off. ❏

*On occasion, I like to step back and take a look at the overall state of boxing, as I did here in mid-2002.*

# THE STATE OF BOXING

"Boxing," says Lou DiBella, "is in the worst state that I can remember. It's now a cable/satellite-TV business on the verge of imploding from lack of corporate support. It's a money-losing business. It's not a major sport anymore. And in five years, unless something happens to cause a change in direction, it will be a fringe sport."

Those are strong words. After all, on the surface, boxing seems very much alive. There's more boxing on television now than ever before.

HBO will televise 26 shows this year (12 *Championship Boxing*, 10 *Boxing After Dark* and four pay-per-view fight cards). It just finished a five-week run featuring Klitschko-Mercer, Ruiz-Johnson, and the much anticipated Forrest-Mosley and Barrera-Morales rematches. The network is planning a 12-part series on the history of HBO Boxing to air in 2003. And on June 8, it joined with Showtime to produce record numbers for Lennox Lewis versus Mike Tyson.

Showtime, for its part, will air 51 fight cards in 2002 (22 *Showtime Championship Boxing*, 26 *ShoBox* and three SET pay-per-view). And ESPN plans to televise 70 shows this year (48 on *ESPN2 Friday Night Fights*, 10 on ESPN2 *Tuesday Night Fights* and 12 ESPN specials). Add in Fox, Univision, Telemundo, and spot programming, and things look good. But beneath the surface, there are problems.

In boxing today, as in the past, the world sanctioning bodies acting in concert with a handful of promoters wield enormous power. Several superstar fighters have formed promotional companies to control their own destiny. And there are other players. But the primary power rests with television.

One reason for boxing's distressed condition today is that ABC, CBS, and NBC stopped broadcasting fights due to a shortage of advertisers. And the situation was exacerbated when NBC made a decision to no longer broadcast Olympic boxing.

There was a time when the Olympics generated instant stardom, after which exposure on "free television" built further interest in a fighter. In 1976, many Americans actually planned several evenings around Ray Leonard, Howard Davis, Leon and Michael Spinks, and the rest of the United States boxing team at the Montreal Olympics. But now, the public-at-large is unfamiliar with most boxers. The last superstar to come out of the Olympics was Oscar De La Hoya 10 years ago. And there's little hope for change in the near future. Most network executives today are unfamiliar with the boxing business and wouldn't feel comfortable making deals to televise fights even if circumstances warranted. Thus, ABC, CBS, and NBC have been replaced by ESPN, Showtime, and HBO.

There's a school of thought that HBO saved boxing; that if it hadn't made a franchise out of boxing in the post-network era, the sport would have gone under years ago. That may, or may not, be true. However, it's undeniable that HBO gave the sweet science an enormous boost just as it was disappearing from network television.

HBO did for boxing what ABC did for pro football. Prior to 1970, NFL games were seen on Sunday afternoon and Thanksgiving. Then Roone Arledge took the same game with the same teams and the same rules, created *Monday Night Football*, and turned his broadcasts into a cultural phenomenon. Similarly, HBO undertook to televise fights in prime time. It made a financial commitment to production values, broadcast talent, and marketing that went beyond anything that had been done before. It became home for major fights. And it created an event that thrust boxing into the national spotlight.

HBO is the money tree of boxing. Unlike the broadcast networks, it's driven by a need for subscribers, not advertising revenue. It's the psychological leader in determining which fights matter most. And it's still televising the big fights that it's expected to televise. But there are questions regarding the future of boxing at HBO.

Taking HBO's signature boxers one at a time: Roy Jones won't fight the big fights. De La Hoya's hand injury is more serious than has been publicly acknowledged. Shane Mosley has lost twice to Vernon Forrest. Felix Trinidad has, at least temporarily, retired. Floyd Mayweather and Fernando Vargas have been beset by problems in and out of the ring. And Lennox Lewis is expected to retire in the not-too-distant future. The two new stars that HBO recently spotlighted (Bernard Hopkins and Forrest) aren't tied to long-term contracts. And HBO has been benefiting from fighters it developed on *Boxing After Dark* such as Arturo Gatti, Marco Antonio Barrera, Erik Morales, Junior Jones, and Kevin Kelley without replacing them.

Moreover, there's a perception that the new stars of HBO Sports are Bob Costas and Bryant Gumbel, not the fighters.

For years, boxing was the engine that drove HBO Sports. Now (HBO Sports president) Ross Greenburg seems to be seeking a broader image, and boxing is no longer assured of dominance in the mix. Seth Abrahman (Greenburg's predecessor) speaks to that issue when he says, "Ross brings a different sensibility and a different view regarding what HBO Sports should be. And I say that uncritically. Ross has every right to recreate HBO Sports the way he thinks it should be. Also, you have to remember, there's an ebb and flow to sports. So I would expect boxing to diminish as a percentage of HBO's overall sports programming in the future. In fact, the process has already begun."

Greenburg takes issue with Abraham's comment. "I respect Seth a lot," he says, "but that's not an accurate observation. I think he's mistaken. Boxing is still our number one franchise. We have an unwavering commitment to the sport."

HBO hopes to prove that commitment by re-signing Jim Lampley as its blow-by-blow commentator. Lampley has the ability to go on camera and, by virtue of his presence, add to the importance of a fight. To the viewing public, he is *the* authoritative blow-by-blow commentator in boxing. HBO is paying Costas $2.5-million a year to host *On The Record*. Given the fact that boxing is HBO's most important sports product, what will Lampley ask for? And what will he do if he doesn't get it?

Right now, Lampley and HBO are reported to be close to an agreement. Larry Merchant's contract expires the same day as Lampley's. Merchant and HBO are also in negotiations. On a parallel track, HBO has made overtures to Teddy Atlas about coming on board as an analyst for *Boxing After Dark,* although Atlas is expected to remain at ESPN2.

If HBO pulls back on its commitment to boxing, it will redefine the economics of the sport. There will be far more pay-per-view shows. And a lot of fighters, managers, and promoters will make less money.

Showtime is boxing's second television power broker. For years, it had its own version of multi-fight, long-term contracts when it allowed Don King to be its exclusive provider of boxing programming. Then it moved away from King and, in response to HBO's policy, started signing fighters to multi-fight contracts. That practice has now ended, although the network still has agreements with Kosta Tszyu, Acelino Freitas, and Joe Calzaghe under its old long-term-contract model.

"What we learned," says Showtime boxing czar Jay Larkin," is that multi-fight contracts don't work for us unless opponents are designated in advance. When you have them, you're constantly worrying, 'Will this hurt the fighter's feelings? Will that make the fighter angry?' And multi-fight contracts prevent good fights from happening. Showtime should have one constituency: its viewers. But with a multi-fight contract, your constituency becomes the fighter, his manager, the promoter, and the world sanctioning bodies. You get stuck with a lot of mismatches and mandatory defenses that no one cares about. And it clouds your mission, which is to deliver the most entertaining fights possible. So, eventually, we came to realize that we can get better fights for less money and far fewer headaches by cherry picking individual fights. We decided that Showtime is going to put on the fights it wants to put on, not fights that we're required to put on by contract."

Showtime is an important component of the boxing landscape. It funds its share of major fights. "But we try to do it on a rational basis," says Larkin. By

Larkin's reckoning, "What's happening to the industry now is partly the result of HBO saying, 'We'll pay whatever it takes to get everything we want.' That's what HBO has done over the years, and it's the same sort of irrational thinking that led to the boom and then the bubble bursting in high-tech stocks. Showtime was paying Naseem Hamed $125,000 a fight," Larkin continues. "Then HBO stepped in with ridiculous numbers. HBO is giving Roy Jones $6-million a fight to get into the ring with mailmen and cops. Their numbers are simply off the charts. So our view is, if two guys don't want to fight on Showtime Championship Boxing for $500,000, maybe they'll get lucky and HBO will pay them millions of dollars. Otherwise, they can fight on ESPN2 for $10,000 or $15,000 dollars each."

ESPN is also a player. Since the advent of its *Top Rank Boxing* series in 1980, the cable network has introduced a national television audience to thousands of fighters ranging from preliminary pugs to main event stars. It has telecast more than 1,000 fight cards and done more than its share to keep boxing in the public eye. Indeed, Mike Tyson's first nationally-televised bout was a scheduled four-rounder on ESPN. HBO and Showtime might be the ones who are putting big money into boxing today. But ESPN did yeoman's work in keeping the sport alive in the 1980s.

Unlike HBO and Showtime, ESPN has two revenue streams —advertising and subscriptions. Miller Beer is the flagship sponsor for *Friday Night Fights*. And ESPN's parent company is paid by local cable companies for each customer who receives ESPN, ESPN2, ESPN Classic, and other ESPN channels as part of a cable package. Thus, ESPN keeps a close eye on ratings because ratings dictate how much it can charge local cable companies.

"We're ratings driven; not just profit driven," says ESPN's director of boxing Bob Yalen. Thus, it's more than a matter of academic interest that *ESPN2 Friday Night Fights* averages about 600,000 homes, with that number occasionally exceeding one million.

ESPN has great cost controls. Its license fees are relatively low ($50,000 to $60,000 per show). It has a modest production budget. It gets advertising. Why don't the broadcast networks simply follow the ESPN formula?

The answer to that is simple. A broadcast network needs far more than a million viewers in prime time to make a program profitable. Still, ESPN2 is a plus for boxing. It gets the sport into a lot of homes on a regular basis. Teddy Atlas is great. And Max Kellerman appeals to a younger demographic that boxing needs to be successful.

Still, it's worth remembering that HBO, Showtime, and ESPN don't have any more of a moral obligation to support boxing than ABC, CBS, NBC, and Fox have to support the NFL or the National Basketball Association. Yes, boxing has been responsible for selling cable television to a lot of customers. But Milton Berle was responsible for selling many of the nation's first television sets, and the networks dumped him when his usefulness expired.

Thus, Greenburg, Larkin and Yalen each acknowledge that their fiduciary duty to their respective networks far outweighs any fiduciary duty that might exist with regard to the good of boxing. And that belief extends to calls that the networks help "clean up boxing." Greenburg speaks for his brethren when he says, "Our job as network executives is to put together the best fights and the fights that the public wants. There's no reason for us to obsess over the sanctioning bodies and state athletic commissions. We assume that they'll all take care of their business and we'll take care of ours."

That view was evident in the decision of HBO and Showtime to join forces in promoting Lewis versus Tyson. The Nevada State Athletic Commission made a decision based on law and principle to deny Tyson a license. Then other state commissions fought to get in line to ignore the Nevada ruling, and the bout took place in Tennessee.

Did the public want to see Lewis-Tyson? Apparently so. In fact, post-fight research indicates that an astonishing eighty percent of the fans who bought Lewis-Tyson I are interested in seeing Lewis-Tyson II.

Tyson has already exercised a clause in his bout contract and demanded a rematch. Under the terms of the original agreement, both Lewis and Tyson are allowed one interim fight. Then proceeds from their rematch, if it occurs, will be split 60 percent to the HBO-Lewis camp and 40 percent to the Showtime-Tyson camp.

Showtime would like Tyson's next bout to be against a genuine contender. David Tua, Vitali Klitschko, and Jameel McCline have been suggested by the network as worthy opponents. Team Tyson holds to an alternative view and is reported to be searching through intensive-care wards for Iron Mike's next foe.

One of the problems with all this is that boxing can get stuck on Lewis-Tyson. Tyson is an anomaly. The Tyson business is not treated like the rest of the boxing business at Showtime or anywhere else. Moreover, there's no evidence that Lewis-Tyson did anything to change the public perception of boxing in a way that would help the sport thrive again on a broader scale. As George Foreman notes, "Boxing has been good to Mike Tyson, but I don't think Mike Tyson has been good for boxing."

So what does the future hold for the sweet science?

Don King opines, "Boxing is going through a period right now where the superstars are fighting with diminishing regularity. That's temporarily hurting the sport, but it's not dying."

Ross Greenburg is a bit more expansive and declares, "Boxing has always been cyclical, but you're always just one superstar away from lifting the entire sport. In the 1970s, there was Muhammad Ali. Then Sugar Ray Leonard came along and inherited Ali's mantle. After that, there was the young Mike Tyson. We're waiting now for the next big superstar.

"The big thing for me philosophically," Greenburg continues, "is that boxing has to reclaim the average sports fan. We've lost the average guy who watches the World Series, the Final Four, the Kentucky Derby, and the Super Bowl. We have to find a way to get that guy back for the big fights. The best thing for the sport and business of boxing that could happen right now would be a return to free network television. And the fighters have to be willing to fight the tough fights. Ray Leonard didn't worry about the 'L' on his record when he was deciding who to fight next. Pernell Whitaker didn't worry about the 'L' on his record when he was deciding who to fight next. Those guys went from great fighter to great fighter. They understood that it doesn't destroy your career, you can always come back if you lose to another great fighter. And if you beat another great fighter, it makes you even greater. I'm not a boxer, so it's easy for me to say, 'Go in against the best.' But there's nothing better for the sport.

"Also," adds Greenburg, "I think it's time for promoters to start promoting again. A lot of promoters think their work is done once they sign a fight. Then they stop working and wait for the bell to ring. They should go to the dictionary and look up the definition of the word 'promoter'."

Meanwhile, in discussing the state of boxing, three more factors should be thrown into the mix.

The first of these is the Hispanic market. The Hispanic audience is boxing's fastest growing market. Univision and Telemundo have drawn consistently high ratings for boxing telecasts. Many pay-per-view shows do particularly well in Hispanic neighborhoods. ESPN has a fledgling Spanish-language station called ESPN Deportes. And starting in January 2003, HBO will televise 12 monthly shows promoted by Golden Boy Promotions on HBO-Latino.

Still, the fact that boxing people have been talking about the Hispanic market to the degree that they have been lately is proof that, for boxing to be healthy, its fan base has to be broadened. Major sports like football, baseball, and basketball don't have the same degree of fractionalization in caring about who's in their viewing audience.

Second, those in the know in boxing are keeping a close eye on the Internet.

Historically, the boxing beat was one of the most desirable jobs in sports journalism. But now, the public perception of boxing comes primarily from an ill-informed mainstream press. Most newspapers don't cover boxing on a regular basis. It's impossible to open a major daily in the United States anymore and get complete quality boxing coverage. When newspapers list sports today, boxing comes under the heading of "other sports." As publicist John Beyrooty notes, "The way things are now, I can send something to 10 newspapers and it won't run in any of them. Except for championship fights, most of the newspapers don't even carry fight results."

In April 2000, Michael Katz left the *New York Daily News* to write fulltime for Houseofboxing.com. When he did, it gave new credibility to Internet boxing coverage. Now, almost every major story in boxing is broken on the

Internet. The Internet brings improprieties to light far more aggressively than the mainstream media ever did, and Internet-links pages give every story national exposure.

The Internet has become the primary means of communicating information within the boxing industry and to hardcore boxing fans. More and more often, Internet articles are making their way to the desks of CEOs. The boxing dot-coms are sending ripples though the pond and, on occasion, waves across the ocean. As Ed Keenan of Media Works notes, "If you get something on the Internet, everyone in the industry is reading it."

There are a lot of problems with Internet boxing coverage. Many of the sites lack proper editorial oversight with regard to fact-checking and other issues of quality control. Also, to date, entrepreneurs have been unable to harness the economic potential of the medium. Ad revenue is scarce, subscription sales are rare, and most Internet boxing sites are losing money or barely breaking even. But no less a personage than Don King declares, "Boxing is moving now with the technology, and the Internet will be the next big new frontier. In about five years, you'll get millions of dollars from the Internet alone on the big fights."

And, last, no discussion about the state of boxing would be complete without reference to the need for a federal commission.

The business of boxing today is a perfect metaphor for a society that's being overrun by a tidal wave of white-collar crime that the authorities are powerless to stop.

There's a culture of corruption in boxing that's so powerful and so inbred that virtually everyone in the sport participates. And virtually everyone in a position of authority who might help improve the sport has washed his or her hands of trying. Most state regulators are incompetent and have glaring conflicts of interest. They sit back and do nothing while managers steal from their fighters and ring judges connive with promoters to fix fights. And if one state commission does its job properly, other states rush in to sully its work.

When Vernon Forrest fought Shane Mosley in Indianapolis on July 20, both camps had runners who relayed the judges' scorecards to their fighter's respective corners as the bout progressed. Three nights later, not to be outdone, the New York State Athletic Commission bungled its way into allowing Mario Diaz of ESPN2 to look at a judge's scorecard after round four of the Aaron Davis versus Ross Thompson fight to see if a trip to the canvas had cost Thompson a 10-8 round.

On the federal front, the Muhammad Ali Boxing Reform Act was a well-intentioned piece of legislation, but it suffers from three glaring flaws: (1) it accepts the present form of corrupt antiquated state regulation; (2) it has too many loopholes; and (3) no one is enforcing it.

Boxing needs a federal commission.

In May of this year, Senators John McCain and Byron Dorgon introduced legislation known as the Professional Boxing Amendments Act. This bill, if enacted into law, would create a United States Boxing Administration that would work in tandem with the various state and Native American commissions to oversee the boxing industry. Key personnel would be an administrator appointed by the President of the United States, an assistant administrator, and general counsel.

The United States Boxing Administration would (1) set minimum national standards regarding the health, safety, and general wellbeing of boxers; (2) license various personnel and corporate entities within the boxing industry; (3) suspend and revoke these licenses where warranted; (4) establish a national medical registry; (5) promulgate ratings criteria that the various world sanctioning organizations would be obligated to follow; and (6) develop guidelines for minimum contractual provisions to be included in boxer-promoter bout agreements and boxer-manager contracts.

The bill envisions a strange hybrid of state and federal regulation of boxing. Essentially, it says to the various state and Native American commissions, "You can run things within your own jurisdiction, but you have to meet minimum federal standards."

It will be interesting to see what new legislation, if any, is enacted by Congress and whether the new law is properly implemented by a knowledge-able administrator and staff.

Meanwhile, it would be nice on occasion to hear outrage expressed by the powers-that-be when something egregious happens in boxing. The exploitation of Manny Pacquaio and the concomitant silence from HBO and other leaders of the boxing establishment is a case in point. Why can't the "heart and soul of boxing" hold a press conference and demand fairness for the boxers who risk their lives for viewer enjoyment? At the very least, HBO, Showtime, and ESPN should publicly announce what they pay for fights. That's what happens with the sale of television rights for every other sport. But boxing doesn't make that information available. Also, governmental regulatory bodies should track how much of each fighter's purse actually winds up in the fighter's bank account. And the television networks should refuse to do business with promoters and managers who don't provide financial tracking information under oath in return for their TV license fees. It's not just about a legal fiduciary duty. It's about decency. ❏

*In early 2003, I took another overall look at professional boxing, concentrating on one aspect of the game.*

# CONFLICTS OF INTEREST

Boxing has a lot of problems. And its biggest problem is that there's no central authority to set definitive standards for the good of the sport. Other major sports such as baseball, football, basketball, tennis, and golf are structured to encourage legitimate championships and protect the integrity of the game. Boxing, by contrast, has petty dictators in competition with one another at every level. Unholy alliances are rampant. There's no union to protect the fighters. And the worst conflicts occur outside the ring.

Conflicts of interest constitute the biggest ethical problem in boxing today. Yet they've become so ingrained in the sport that hardly anyone cares about them. Too many people wearing too many hats play too many roles.

This is one facet of the sport where it's unfair to put all the blame on promoters. Certainly, promoters feed into unethical situations, and their relationship with the world sanctioning organizations is at the core of corruption in boxing. But for the most part, promoters don't have a fiduciary duty to fighters.

Conflicts of interest arise in situations where a party is supposed to be neutral (as in the case of sanctioning bodies, government regulators, and ring officials) or has a fiduciary duty to the fighter (as is the case with managers, trainers, and lawyers). That means there's not much of a conflict-of-interest problem at the television networks. Is it in HBO's interest that its signature fighters like Oscar De La Hoya and Roy Jones, Jr. win? Absolutely. But the networks aren't fiduciaries and they aren't required to be neutral.

Having said that, though, it should be noted that the television networks are the *de facto* promoters of big fights today. They make the matches and fund them. As HBO Sports president Ross Greenburg acknowledged when he testified before Congress, "We are the bank, and a powerful one at that."

HBO, Showtime, and ESPN, if they chose to do so, could leverage their economic power to eliminate many of boxing's conflicts of interest. Also, the networks have their own conflicts problems. For example, ESPN hired promoter Russell Peltz to put together shows for *ESPN2 Friday Night Fights*, and he promptly used that position to advance his own economic interests to the detriment of other promoters and fighters who refused to sign with him.

Money is at the root of most conflict of interest problems in boxing, although family ties and personal loyalty also play a role. Let's look at some of the players.

## THE WORLD SANCTIONING ORGANIZATIONS

"If you look up 'conflict of interest' in the dictionary," says Seth Abraham (now chief operating officer at Madison Square Garden), "you'll see the logos of the world sanctioning bodies. They have a no-shame policy."

The manner in which the world sanctioning organizations rate fighters is a classic example of conflicts of interest run amok. Ratings are supposed to be based on the ring performance of fighters. But, often, ratings are based on the influence within the organization of a particular promoter, manager, or other non-combatant.

Craig Hamilton (an adviser to Michael Grant) recalls attending a World Boxing Association dinner when Grant was a heavyweight on the rise. He asked Jimmy Binns (counsel for the WBA) what had to be done to get Grant rated by the WBA. According to Hamilton, Binns answered, "Hire me as a lawyer."

Binns calls Hamilton's allegation "absolutely absurd." But for whatever reason, many of the WBA's ratings are ludicrous, as are those of the other three world sanctioning bodies. When Frans Botha is the third-rated heavyweight in the world and Kali Meehan and Nicolay Valuev are ranked in the top 15, something is wrong. When Mike Tyson is rated as high as number three (by the WBC) and not at all by the WBO (which lists Sinan Simal Sam, Lou Savarese, and Attila Levin ahead of him), one can be forgiven for assuming that these discrepancies are based on something other than genuine differences of opinion regarding merit.

Ratings are often changed based on who a champion wants as an opponent. Fighters are frequently stripped of their titles and box-offs ordered based on questionable criteria.

Also, every major sanctioning body is based on an economic model with a built-in conflict of interest in that most of their revenue comes from championship-bout sanctioning fees. This means there's a huge incentive to rate bankable stars favorably and make certain that these stars get generous treatment from referees and judges.

So, yes, there are instances like the International Boxing Federation stripping Vernon Forrest of his 147-pound title at the behest of its championship committee chairman, Joe Dwyer. But in a decision-making process that is supposed to be based on merit, the revenue-producing nature of a fighter is often the determining factor. That much was made clear on March 12 of this year when IBF president Marian Muhammad fired Dwyer because she "lacked confidence" in his ability to effectively perform the duties of his job.

"There's a natural progression," says Jim Thomas (Evander Holyfield's attorney). "When a promoter buys five tables for a sanctioning body's annual dinner, don't you think that effects ratings?"

And that's just the start. Things go downhill from there.

Defenders of the system argue that, while a phony ranking might work to the detriment of one fighter, it's another fighter's gain. But that argument is specious. Phony rankings are unfair to the disadvantaged fighter. They undermine the sport. And the true beneficiary of a phony ranking is the promoter or manager who paid for it and uses it to gain extra leverage in his dealings with fighters.

### GOVERNMENT REGULATORS

Government regulators often serve political parties and specific economic interests rather than the good of the sport. Too often, money changes hands to create influence and alter the decision-making process.

The New York State Athletic Commission has been a slush fund for the state Republican party for years. The NYSAC is so oblivious to conflict-of-interest standards that it was left to HBO to draw the line and say that Harold Lederman could no longer judge fights for HBO and serve as a judge for the NYSAC at the same time.

The Tennessee Board of Boxing and Racing is a national joke. After an eight-day temper tantrum during which he refused to train, claimed flu-like symptoms, had a large tattoo etched on his face, and reportedly smoked marijuana for hours on end, Mike Tyson flew to Tennessee to fight Clifford Etienne. On February 21, the day before the fight, Iron Mike "passed" his pre-fight physical. However, pursuant to Tennessee law, the physical was conducted by a doctor hired by the promoter. When the Nevada State Athletic Commission (to which Tyson is expected to apply for a license) asked to see the test results, the Tennessee Board of Boxing and Racing refused to provide them.

Meanwhile, Nevada has its own problems. On January 13, Luther Mack (chairman of the Nevada State Athletic Commission) unilaterally designated Tony Alamo, Jr. as vice-chairman of the NSAC. Mr. Alamo's father, Tony Alamo, Sr., is the senior vice-president who oversees boxing for Mandalay Bay. Mandalay Resort Group is both a licensed promoter and *the* major player in boxing in Las Vegas. As Jim Lampley noted after Alamo's elevation was announced, "That's not the kind of progressive movement that the Nevada commission has been known for in recent years."

Alamo, Jr. says that he recuses himself from votes when necessary and adds, "We [he and his father] are completely independent. We don't talk about boxing. He happens to work in the hotel industry, and I'm a physician. If people are excluded from voluntary public service because they are related to someone in the hotel industry, that's not good for Nevada or any other state."

However, there's no record of Alamo, Jr. having recused himself on any matter that has come before the commission to date. It's hard to believe that he and his father never talk about boxing. And his father doesn't just "happen to work in the hotel industry." He happens to be the most important player in boxing in the entire state of Nevada. Nor is Alamo, Jr. simply a "voluntary public servant." He's vice chairman of the NSAC. The issue here isn't Tony Alamo, Jr.'s character. It's the obvious conflict of interest involved.

But that's just one of several burgeoning controversies in Nevada. In recent weeks, there have been reports that NSAC personnel accepted special room rates, free meals, and other gratuities from promoters. Initially, this controversy focused on a $115 room rate given to Luther Mack (chairman of the Nevada State Athletic Commission) at Mandalay Bay. The special rate was authorized by Tony Alamo, Sr.

Luther Mack is personable and charming. He says that, contrary to reports, he was given only a $15 discount on a room that would normally cost $130. "If it was a $400 room," Mack acknowledged recently, "that's a whole different story. I don't need a suite. This was a regular room. It was not a suite. That would certainly be in violation of the rule."

However, records from Mandalay Bay seem to tell a different story. They indicate that Mack stayed at Mandalay Bay on the following eight nights: November 15 and 16, 2002 (room 17233), December 6 and 7, 2002 (room 12334), December 27 and 28, 2002 (room 31201), January 31 and February 1, 2003 (room 27102). In each instance, Mack was billed $115 per night. Sources at Mandalay Bay say that each of these rooms is an "executive suite" that normally costs in the neighborhood of $400 a night.

Questions have also been raised about the receipt of fight tickets by members of the Nevada State Athletic Commission.

Under Nevada regulations, each of the state's five commissioners is given six tickets in addition to his own seat for every fight card held in Nevada. These tickets are provided by the promoter. Two of them must be ringside. The other four tickets may be anywhere in the arena. The goal of this rule is to eliminate the embarrassment and abuse that might otherwise flow from commissioners asking promoters for tickets. But ringside tickets can be in the first row or the last. "Anywhere in the arena" can mean more ringside tickets or nose-bleed seats. That leaves a lot of room for favors.

These tickets are no small item. Many of the issues surrounding the Nevada State Athletic Commission were first raised by Charles Jay of TotalAction.com. They began receiving national attention on January 31 when Teddy Atlas referenced them on *ESPN2 Friday Night Fights*. In the 29 days after Atlas' remarks, there were four major fight cards held in Las Vegas. The ticket range for these cards was as follows: Medina-Marquez ($50 to $250), Mosley-Marquez ($25 to $250), Austin-Marquez ($40 to $200), Jones-Ruiz ($100 to $1,200).

If the promoters of these fight cards gave each commissioner the least expensive tickets required by law, their face value would have been $4,660 for each commissioner. If the promoters gave each commissioner the most expensive tickets allowable under Nevada law, their face value would have been $11,400 for each commissioner.

And that's for one month alone.

Raymond Avansino, Jr. (the most recent appointee to the Nevada State Athletic Commission) was reportedly sufficiently concerned with the ticket issue that he asked the Nevada State Ethics Commission for a confidential opinion on the propriety of the system. Then, after some preliminary steps, his request for an opinion was withdrawn.

One might also ask whether the commissioners pay personal income tax on tickets that they receive and give to a family member or friends. According to the Internal Revenue Service, these tickets are taxable as items of personal income.

In dealing with the ticket issue, special room rates, and related matters, Nevada's chief deputy attorney general Keith Kizer (who represents the Nevada State Athletic Commission) cites Section 281.481(1) of the Nevada Revised Statutes, which states, "A public officer or employee shall not seek or accept any gift, service, favor, employment, engagement, emolument, or economic opportunity which would tend improperly to influence a reasonable person in his position to depart from the faithful and impartial discharge of his public duties."

The key loophole in this statute is the provision that gratuities are only forbidden if they "would tend improperly to influence a reasonable person." Kizer knows each of the commissioners. He believes that they are all honorable men and thus would not be improperly influenced by these perks of office.

However, Section 6308 of the federal Professional Boxing Safety Act is a different matter. This statute has a section entitled "Conflicts of Interest" that declares, "No member or employee of a boxing commission, no person who administers or enforces State boxing laws, and no member of the Association of Boxing Commissions may belong to, contract with, or receive any compensation from any person who sanctions, arranges, or promotes professional boxing matches."

In other words, the federal statute contains a flat prohibition. There's no "reasonable person" exemption. Moreover, under the federal law, "compensation" doesn't mean just money; it means anything of value.

The policies of the Nevada State Athletic Commission appear to violate the Professional Boxing Safety Act. That's a shame because, in many respects, the NSAC is the best-run commission in the country with the best executive director in the country.

It would be sad if the NSAC's signature standing were to end. Meanwhile, insofar as every state athletic commission is concerned, this isn't just a boxing issue. It's a good-government issue. When the government becomes a lawbreaker, it breeds disrespect for the law.

## REFEREES AND JUDGES

In other sports, the integrity of officials is taken for granted. In boxing, too often, bias is presumed to exist.

Where big fights are concerned, referees and judges receive huge officiating fees and generous travel allowances that flow directly or indirectly from the promoter. They've also been known to get other gratuities from promoters, including ringside tickets for family members and friends. Their assignments might come through world sanctioning organizations and state athletic commissions. But the true source of their perks is the promoter, who usually has a vested interest in the outcome of the fight.

As Lou DiBella notes, "When a judge or referee asks a promoter for another first-class ticket so he can fly to a fight with his girlfriend or wife, there's an implied quid pro quo. Anyone who refuses to admit that is lying."

When someone who is supposed to be a neutral official understands that he (or she) can receive something of value by ruling a particular way, it undermines the integrity of the process. Yet in some jurisdictions, major promoters even have the power to blackball referees and judges.

Also, referees and judges know which fighter is favored by a particular sanctioning body. And the practice of certain judges and referees aligning themselves with one or more sanctioning organizations further undermines the neutrality that state athletic commissions should be seeking to ensure.

Bad decisions in boxing virtually never go against the house fighter. Referees and judges frequently compromise their roles by favoring a hometown fighter. Indeed, hometown decisions are a staple of the sport, based on the premise that local promoters need local fighters to be successful in order for their promotional companies to succeed financially. The assumption is that a fighter who loses a split decision in another guy's home town would have won had the fight been on his own home turf.

Marco Antonio Barrera stated a view held by many when, after his controversial 2000 loss to Erik Morales in Las Vegas, he declared, "I would have won the fight if Don King was my promoter."

The scoring of ring judge Bob Logist in the 1999 bout between Felix Trinidad and Oscar De La Hoya is an even more compelling example. Trinidad won a controversial majority decision in that fight. But because De La Hoya ran so shamelessly for the final two rounds, the public outcry was muted. Still, Logist's scorecard was a horror. He voted for Trinidad but somehow, against all reason, gave the last round to Oscar. One can be forgiven for wondering whether Mr. Logist went to that fight with an agenda; and that once he had Trinidad safely ahead after 11 rounds, he decided to even out his card a bit by giving the last round to De La Hoya.

The greatest source of power in boxing today is television, which puts up most of the money for fights. It would be nice to hear HBO, Showtime, ESPN, and their brethren say, "From now on, the quality of judging will be a factor in deciding the venues from which we choose to telecast fights." The networks already exercise veto power over sites on the basis of ambiance and production costs for given fights. The integrity of decisions should also be a factor, since bad decisions impact negatively on the viewer experience.

## RING DOCTORS

"If you're a ring physician, you have to be neutral," declares Flip Homansky (former medical director for the Nevada State Athletic Commission). "But if you're a fighter's attending physician outside the ring, there's a whole different set of principles to follow. An attending physician is supposed to meet the needs of his patient, not be neutral."

Thus, Homansky posits, "It's a conflict of interest for a ringside physician to be involved as the attending physician for any fighter. No ring physician should receive any compensation in any form for the treatment of any fighter other than the payment he receives from the commission for his work at a fight."

In other words, if a doctor wants to be involved with taking care of a fighter outside the ring, he (or she) shouldn't be a ring physician. It's that simple. But too many doctors violate that principle today because they're largely anonymous and state athletic commissions don't care. To put the matter in perspective, suppose Ferdie Pacheco had been a physician working at ringside for a state athletic commission at the same time he was the personal physician for Muhammad Ali?

Commission-appointed ring physicians in some states rack up huges fees from insurance companies for the treatment of fighters. Other ring physicians refer fighters to themselves for lucrative physical therapy sessions.

In California, the same doctor (1) conducted pre-fight physicals in his office; (2) ran the pre-fight-physical lab tests through his office; (3) worked the fights; (4) handled fighter aftercare in his office; and (5) was the personal physician for the same fighters.

Referees and judges shouldn't make money off a fighter outside the ring, and ring doctors shouldn't either. They should be responsible to the state athletic commission that assigns them, period. They should not have business relationships with fighters.

## MANAGERS

A manager is a fiduciary. His loyalty belongs to the fighter. His most important function is to negotiate on behalf of his fighter and get the fighter the most money possible for each fight.

Yet some managers are subservient to certain promoters. The father-son relationship between Don and Carl King is a classic example, but by no means the only one. Other managers do business with only one promoter in return for what is presumed to be a piece of the promotional pie.

Attorney Judd Burstein states the obvious when he says, "The connection between certain managers and certain promoters is very troubling." And Jim Thomas adds, "There are too many instances where a manager's relationship with a particular promoter is more important to him than his relationship with the fighter."

There are times when managers put one of their fighters on the short end of a hopeless mismatch in order to curry favor with a particular promoter or get a good fight from the promoter for another one of their fighters. It's not unusual for a manager to say to himself, "Fighters come and go, but this promoter will be here for a long time."

No matter how one cuts it, a fighter's manager has to be independent of the promoter. Yet the situation is exacerbated overseas, where it's legal for the same person to promote and manage a fighter. How could Frank Maloney properly manage Lennox Lewis and work for Panos Eliades at the same time? Klaus-Peter Kohl manages and promotes both Klitschko brothers. A manager's job is to get as much money as possible for his fighter. A promoter's best interests dictate paying the fighter as little as possible. So when HBO offers Kohl "X" dollars for a Klitschko bout, which hat does Kohl wear when the fighter's purse is being negotiated?

Shelly Finkel declares, "There's no bigger inherent conflict in boxing than the same person being the manager and promoter for a fighter." That, of course, brings one to the issue of Finkel and Main Events. Shelly guided a lot of investment money to Main Events prior to the 1984 Olympics. That money enabled the promoter to evolve from a mom-and-pop organization to a major player in boxing. And with the exception of Mike Tyson, until recently when Gary Shaw left the company, Shelly took virtually every one of his fighters to Main Events.

Thus, the question frequently asked is, "How can Shelly Finkel deny being tied to a promoter when, for years, he brought virtually every fighter he had to that one promoter?"

"There have been accusations that I owned a piece of Main Events," Finkel says in response. "That's absolutely not true. Main Events didn't have the cash to sign the 1984 Olympians and I put them together with two builders in Connecticut, but I didn't get a penny from the financing. When you look around at the promoters in boxing, you don't have many options. I had strength at Main Events, and I knew that I could always count on Main Events to give my new fighters exposure."

"Yes, Shelly brought his fighters to us," adds Pat English (the attorney for Main Events). "And the reason was, he knew he'd always get a fair deal for his fighters."

It's natural to do business with someone who treats you fairly and who you trust and like. Relationships of that nature are particularly rare in boxing; so if a manager finds one, he's well advised to cultivate it. Deals made by virtue of good relationships aren't necessarily conflicts of interest.

But to inquire a bit further, it's generally believed that Showtime fronted the money for Finkel and Main Events to sign a quartet of 2000 Olympic fighters. The purported understanding was, Shelly would acquire the fighters as their manager; he would then sign the fighters to promotional contracts with Main Events; and Main Events would license their fights to Showtime. Contracts with Francisco Bojado, Juan Diaz, Rocky Juarez, and Jeff Lacy resulted.

Finkel is adamant in declaring, "There was no commitment from Showtime before the fighters were signed. Yes, I went to Sydney with Gary Shaw and we talked a lot about various contingencies. Then I signed the fighters and, about a month later after considering other promoters, the fighters signed with Main Events. We were talking with Showtime during that period, but the Showtime deal wasn't signed until November."

If commitments were made to Main Events and Showtime in advance, did that constitute a conflict of interest? Not if the fighters knew about the various deals before signing, understood them, and approved them. But in the absence of a knowing waiver, there would be an issue because Finkel wouldn't have been able to shop the fighters around for a better deal than Main Events was offering (even if it meant more money for the fighters), and Main Events wouldn't have been able to take the fighters to a competing network.

It should be noted that Lou DiBella had a deal with HBO prior to the 2000 Olympics that led to the signing of Ricardo Williams, Jermaine Taylor, Brian Villoria, Jose Navarro, Clarence Vinson, and Michael Bennett. But DiBella is quick to proclaim, "There were significant differences. I never said I was on the management end of the equation when I signed the fighters. The guys I signed knew in advance that I had a deal with HBO. And the six Olympians I signed were represented by five different management groups."

Questions have also been asked about the fact that, when Finkel was Evander Holyfield's de facto manager, he made a deal with John Davimos for a piece of Michael Moorer, who later defeated Holyfield for the heavyweight title.

Finkel's explanation for that bit of business is as follows: "After Evander fought and lost to Riddick Bowe the first time [in 1992], he indicated to me that he was retiring from boxing. Then Michael Moorer came to me and said he'd like me to manage him. Moorer still had a contract with John Davimos. So I called John, and John sold me a third of his piece, which gave me 10 percent of the fighter. Then Evander came back. It all predated Evander fighting Moorer, which came much later."

Well and good. But when Holyfield fought Moorer in 1994, losing his championship in the process, he should have known that Finkel had a financial interest in his opponent. And according to Evander, he didn't. Shelly says that he didn't take a cut of Moorer's purse from that fight. But after Moorer won the title, Finkel did receive his share from future purses.

Also, there's another point that should be noted with regard to managers. In order to be certified as a player agent pursuant to the collective bargaining agreement that governs the NBA, a player's agent can take no more than three percent of a client's contract compensation. In the NFL, the number is four percent. In boxing, in most jurisdictions, a manager can take up to 33-1/3 percent. Think about that for a moment. The manager gets half as much as the fighter.

## TRAINERS

Like managers, trainers have a fiduciary duty to the fighters they serve. Often, the trainer is a surrogate father. He has enormous input regarding a fighter's ring strategy and the choice of opponents. The trainer works for the fighter. But at times, the unambiguous nature of their relationship is compromised.

Main Events has a history of putting trainers together with fighters. The company did it with Lou Duva and George Benton in the past. It's doing it now with Buddy McGirt, who has a contract to train fighters for Main Events.

McGirt is a good guy, but where do his loyalties lie? Suppose Main Events has an average world champion and can get a promotional piece of a budding superstar by matching him against the Main Events fighter? Does McGirt counsel against the fight that Main Events wants? Or suppose the converse, that the Main Events champion wants to fight a Don King fighter who refuses to give options to Main Events. Does McGirt push for the fight even if Main Events doesn't want it? Suppose a fighter that McGirt is working with suffers a minor shoulder injury in training. And suppose further that Main Events needs this particular fighter to fight or the fight card will fall apart and a large TV license fee will be lost?

Enough said.

## LAWYERS

Lawyers often represent both a fighter and his manager. That might be appropriate under certain circumstances where there's a unity of interest between fighter and manager. But, too often, lawyers are inappropriately on both sides of the equation. Indeed, there are times when an attorney represents the fighter, his manager, the promoter, and even the venue in a single transaction. And the problem is exacerbated by the fact that there are very few capable attorneys with expertise in boxing to choose from and some of those attorneys are exclusively tied to one promoter.

Last year, a Manhattan jury returned a $1.175-million verdict in favor of heavyweight champion Lennox Lewis against his former attorney, Milt

Chwasky, who represented Lewis at the same time he was representing Panos Eliades (Lewis' promoter) and serving as an officer of the United States branch of Panix Promotions. Among other things, Lewis was awarded $1-million for breach of fiduciary duty. Chwasky's practice appears to have been unaffected by the verdict.

Judd Burstein, who represented Lewis in the Lewis-Chwasky litigation, says, "I've turned down a lot of fighters because of conflicts of interest that were a lot less severe than conflicts of interest that exist between certain other lawyers and their multi-client representation."

And Jim Thomas states the obvious when he declares, "A fighter needs a good lawyer who understands his fiduciary obligation to the fighter; not a lawyer who wants a piece of everything from everyone. A lawyer has a legal and ethical obligation to put his client's interests above all others including his own."

## CONCLUSION

The issues surrounding conflicts of interest aren't always clear-cut. Sometimes, it's a question of degree. It can even be argued that a manager shouldn't represent more than one world-class fighter in the same weight division because advancing the aspirations of one fighter might come at the expense of another. Nor are writers immune from criticism. Those of us who write for websites and other publications sponsored directly or indirectly by the boxing industry walk a fine line.

But the bottom line is that more has to be done to protect fighters, and no boxing reform movement will be successful unless it addresses the conflicts of interest that permeate the sport. Most conflicts of interest involve people putting money in their pockets at the expense of fighters. But right now, no one is seriously policing the sport; there's no real pressure to change the status quo; and virtually no one cares. Most onlookers simply view the exploitation, shrug their shoulders, and say, "That's boxing."

Fighters are risking their lives in the ring. At the very least, the people who are supposed to be working on their behalf should be completely loyal to them. ❏

*This article, written in August 2003, became part of the debate surrounding the proposed federal legislation to regulate professional boxing.*

# ARE HBO AND SHOWTIME "PROMOTERS"?

The United States Senate adjourned for its August recess last week without voting on legislation that would create a federal boxing commission.

At present, there is no real enforcement of the Professional Boxing Safety Act anywhere in the United States. Presumably, a federal commission would take steps to enforce it. But the proposed legislation has stumbled over issues relating to the relationship between the television networks, fighters, and promoters.

Senator John McCain, who has been a driving force for the reform of professional boxing, has leaned toward exempting the television networks from classification as "promoters." By contrast, Senator Harry Reid wants to label the networks as "promoters" and put restrictions on their conduct.

McCain is a Republican, and the Republicans control the Senate. But Reid is the Senate minority whip, and McCain needs help from the Democratic side of the aisle if the legislation is to pass. The network issue is a small part of the overall proposal. But the manner in which it is resolved (if it's resolved) will have a huge impact on the balance of power in boxing.

At present, the Professional Boxing Safety Act defines a promoter as "the person primarily responsible for organizing, promoting, and producing a professional boxing match." It then includes a broad exemption for casinos and other host sites. One can argue that, under this definition, HBO, Showtime, and several other networks are promoters. But to date, the Act hasn't been enforced against them as such.

The television networks (HBO and Showtime foremost among them) don't want to be classified as promoters for several reasons:

(1) In today's world, the term "boxing promoter" is synonymous with slime, and such a designation would be bad for their image;

(2) If the networks are designated as promoters, they will be subject to the financial disclosure requirements of the Professional Boxing Safety Act; and

(3) If the networks are designated as promoters, they will enter into the murky area of legal liability to fighters and others. Litigation is inherent in boxing. The networks have deep pockets. HBO, Showtime, and their brethren don't want to be targeted as defendants in lawsuits alleging causes of action

that range from breach of contract to wrongful death.

Traditionally, boxing promoters purchased all rights to a bout and then exploited them. In other words, the promoter was responsible for paying the fighters' purses and other expenses associated with a fight. The promoter's profit was the difference between these expenditures and revenue from the sale of tickets, television rights, and assorted ancillary rights such as merchandising and sponsorships.

But in boxing today, many people who call themselves "promoters" aren't; and others who say they aren't are. For many big fights, the promoter of record is simply a middle-man money manager. He doesn't even sell tickets. That chore is left to the site.

On February 5, 2003, HBO Sports president Ross Greenburg testified before a hearing of the United States Senate Committee on Commerce, Science, and Transportation and argued against legislation that would label HBO a promoter. The thrust of his argument was that HBO simply buys television rights to the best programming it can offer its subscribers and that the steps it takes in pursuit of this goal don't make it a promoter.

In relevant part, Greenburg declared, "We agree that any entity which in fact has a promotional agreement with a boxer and is primarily responsible for organizing and promoting a boxing match should be subject to the provisions of the Act. However, it would be patently unfair and wrong to define and regulate telecasters that televise boxing matches as 'promoters' per se. The view that television networks should be regulated as if they were promoters reflects a misperception that the television industry and boxing promoters perform roughly the same function and have similar relationships with and economic power over boxers. This simply is untrue. It would turn free market principles on their head to subject telecasters like HBO to regulation merely because, as the result of arms-length bargaining, they enter into agreements to pay large fixed license fees in exchange for the exclusive rights to televise a boxer's matches over a fixed period of time."

But a strong argument can be made that HBO and several other television networks are promoters. The network contract is the dominant piece in any big-fight promotional puzzle. Nothing else of consequence is finalized until the television license fee is in place. Greenburg has sought to downplay his network's role in the process. Testifying before Congress, he declared, "A boxing match cannot take place without a promoter. On the other hand, most boxing matches are not televised."

But in truth, television is a prerequisite for a big fight. In fact, it's not uncommon for a promoter to win a purse bid for the right to promote a championship fight and then default on the bid because he is unable to secure a television contract.

Let's look further at the issue of money.

HBO puts up most of the financial guarantee for virtually every big fight it televises. It's usually far more at risk financially than the promoter of record. HBO might not participate in revenue streams from a given fight except for income from pay-per-view buys. But it has had ancillary rights such as international sales written into long-term contracts with many fighters. Also, HBO is "paid" in the form of viewer ratings for its regular telecasts. Ratings translate into subscriber dollars.

HBO and Showtime co-promoted Lennox Lewis versus Mike Tyson no matter how one views it. And Showtime was Tyson's de facto promoter during the entire post-Don King period through the Clifford Etienne fight.

It's also worth taking a look at the scheduling of fights.

Greenburg testified that, "HBO's offering large license fees to a promoter to purchase the television rights to a boxing match between two top fighters is no different than a network offering large fees to purchase the television rights to a tennis match or golf match."

But that's not so. Everyone knows that the Masters will take place next April in Augusta and that there will be tennis at Wimbledon next summer. By contrast, HBO often determines both if and when a particular fight takes place and charts the course for many of its fighters.

After Vernon Forrest lost to Ricardo Mayorga, he wanted to take an interim bout before seeking to regain his title. But Forrest was told by HBO that he had to fight an immediate rematch against the man who had knocked him out or the network would cancel his contract. If Forrest had fought an interim fight, it would have improved his chances of beating Mayorga the second time around. The flow of the rematch was very different once six rounds passed and Vernon's crisis of confidence abated.

HBO wasn't necessarily wrong to demand that Forrest engage in an immediate rematch. It made for good television and was within the network's contractual rights. But the network was matchmaking with a heavy hand, not just bidding on a fight offered by a promoter.

And HBO does more than matchmake. There are times when HBO executives get on the telephone with managers, ask how much a fighter wants for a particular fight, and push and cajole when the answer isn't to their liking. HBO executives also ask site officials whether their arena is available on a given date and how much the site fee for a particular fight might be. On occasion, they become actively involved in site negotiations.

HBO imposed Madison Square Garden as the site for Lennox Lewis versus Michael Grant because it wanted a Manhattan media buzz to boost pay-per-view sales of the fight. More recently, it imposed Buffalo as the site for a September 27 heavyweight card headlined by Joe Mesi. Again, there's nothing wrong with either demand. But choice of site is traditionally a prerogative of the promoter.

Recent years have seen the phenomenon of superstar fighters supposedly acting as their own promoter. Thus, Roy Jones is "promoted" by Square Ring;

Lennox Lewis is "promoted" by Lion; and Naseem Hamed is "promoted" by Prince Promotions. But it's an illusion that these fighters promote themselves. The de facto promoters of their fights are the television networks. Often, they are assisted by the sites (usually casinos), which pay large site fees in exchange for the live gate.

The networks also prepare press kits, issue press releases, and organize promotional tours. On occasion, they even influence the choice of officials.

Showtime demanded that Harold Lederman be removed as a judge for the ill-fated Evander Holyfield versus Henry Akinwande fight that was slated for Madison Square Garden in 1998. Prior to the bout being cancelled, the New York State Athletic Commission complied. In Atlantic City on June 7 of this year, HBO suggested that Larry Hazzard remove Eugenia Williams as a judge for Michael Grant versus Dominick Guinn because of her role in the first Lewis-Holyfield fight. Williams was removed. HBO then more forcefully prevailed upon Hazzard not to designate Eddie Cotton as the referee for Grant versus Guinn because its production team had already prepared graphics listing Benji Estevez as the third man in the ring. There's an argument to be made that the television networks should try to influence the choice of officials and should refuse to televise fights from jurisdictions where ring officials are incompetent or corrupt. But, traditionally, that's an area reserved for managers and promoters.

If it walks like a duck and quacks like a duck and looks like a duck, most likely it's a duck. HBO and Showtime might not be promoters in the traditional sense. But on a big fight level, virtually no one in boxing is anymore. The networks are involved in every aspect of a big fight. They put up the money, control match-ups, organize press events, and approve (or dictate) various crucial elements such as fight date and site. Showtime even chooses the ring announcer, Jimmy Lennon, Jr.

That then brings us to the present impasse in Congress. Part of the problem in gaining passage of the proposal to create a federal boxing commission is that no corporate entity with clout is pushing for it and the networks would rather see the legislation die than be labeled promoters. Meanwhile, some very influential interested parties have gotten involved.

One of Harry Reid's largest campaign contributors is Bob Arum. Don King has also been a generous supporter. Arum and King want to discourage the networks from signing contracts directly with fighters. And they want to perpetuate the system that has given them so much control over boxing in recent decades.

Thus, among the positions Reid has pushed is the proviso that a network be branded a promoter if it has a direct contract with a fighter. That would give a competitive advantage to major promoters such as Arum and King because it would encourage the networks to go through them rather than deal directly with fighters. In other words, under the Reid proposal, the promoters would win both ways. There would be a firewall between the fighter and the network to protect the promoter's position. And it's less likely that a fighter would get financial data from the network to help him in negotiating with his own promoter.

Discussions between the McCain and Reid staffs have been extremely contentious. Then, just before the congressional recess, Reid suggested further limits on the networks' conduct. That raises the question of whether Reid wants to regulate the networks in a constructive way or simply strengthen certain promoters. And it's an important issue because, as Charles Jay notes in his groundbreaking *Operation Clean-Up* series, "When we talk about defining someone as a promoter, what we're really doing is defining their responsibilities. We're identifying them for the purposes of subjecting them to some kind of regulation, a constraint on behavior so that, if they do not conform to certain standards, they can be disciplined."

HBO has more influence over boxing today than any other entity. And it has more influence over boxing than any television network has ever had over any sport.

There are times when it seems as though a sense of entitlement permeates everything that HBO does. There are also moments when the network is perceived by some as coming dangerously close to anti-competitive conduct. Some of its counter-programming against Showtime has raised eyebrows. And given the fact that Showtime's annual budget for boxing is under $25-million, one boxing insider asks, "Why does HBO spend $100-million a year on boxing when it could accomplish the same thing for $60-million?"

HBO says that it spends as much as it does on the sweet science to give its subscribers the best programming possible. Another reason for the expenditures might be that HBO Sports is protecting its budget turf. That is, it doesn't want to give up anything within the AOL Time Warner empire. But the fact that HBO pays huge license fees also makes it harder for Showtime to attract quality fights. And whatever the motivation, HBO uses its checkbook to advance its own agenda.

Thus, Craig Hamilton, who has dealt extensively with HBO, observes, "HBO is usually fair to the fighter, very fair. But HBO tries to exercise control over every important aspect of a fight, and then it tries to insulate itself from being held accountable. If there's a problem, HBO wants to palm it off on a middleman promoter, who's often nothing more than a vehicle for the network to avoid liability. If something goes wrong, HBO wants to be able to say to the fighter or the fighter's estate, 'Gee, that's a shame, but it's not our fault.'

"And what happens," Hamilton queries, "if someone new comes in at HBO and says, 'I don't want to be fair?' What happens if HBO starts giving out dates the way Bob Yalen does it at ESPN? ESPN doesn't fairly distribute dates. ESPN has given dates to promoters who don't have a single fighter under contract. The networks can create a promoter anytime they want to simply by giving dates."

Charles Jay echoes Hamilton's thoughts and says, "What the public doesn't understand is that a television network can literally create a promoter out of thin air. It has happened. It is happening. As long as some TV executive says 'yes', virtually anyone can become a successful promoter."

Moreover, in exercising their power, television executives can be motivated by a desire to make money and provide the best entertainment possible to viewers. They can be motivated by an interest in doing what's good for boxing. Or they can be motivated by petty personal prejudices, financial kickbacks, and women on the side. And no matter how one cuts it, the people who exercise this power are dominant forces in an industry that has traditionally exploited fighters.

If one adheres to the view that professional boxing should be regulated by the government, then the television networks should be subject to some form of regulation. The networks have argued against this. They take the position that the legislation in question is designed to protect fighters against the predatory conduct commonly engaged in by traditional promoters, not the networks. And certainly, television hasn't been guilty of many of the abuses engaged in by promoters. But neither have some promoters. The promoter isn't always bad.

The ultimate issue then, is whether the television networks should be regulated given the dominant role they play in boxing. To achieve this, it's not necessary to define the networks as "promoters" within the meaning of the Professional Boxing Safety Act. The statute can carve out the same exception for television networks that currently exists for sites and then regulate any entity that puts up a television license fee that is more than a given amount or is estimated to be above a certain percentage of gross revenue for a particular fight.

If the networks are regulated, the ultimate goal of the legislation should be fairness, particularly for the fighter. In that regard, the most meaningful requirement that Congress can impose on the television networks is financial disclosure.

It's often said that there are no secrets in boxing. But in truth, there are. Fighters are frequently left in the dark when it comes to the size of the television license fee and other revenue that a promoter receives for a particular fight.

Under the present law, promoters are obligated to reveal certain financial data, but this requirement is largely ignored. Also, the mandatory disclosure doesn't have to occur until the day of a fight; no final accounting is required; and some promoters take the position that they will "show" the required financial information to fighters but not give them copies of documents or anything else in writing. Side-deals further undermine the disclosure process. Suppose, for example, instead of paying a license fee of $2-million for a particular fight, a television network gives the promoter a license fee of $1.5-million plus an additional $500,000 for the right to show tape excerpts from an unrelated bout.

Financial disclosure goes to the heart of the biggest problem in boxing today: the financial exploitation of fighters. Right now, if the promoter doesn't make disclosure or discloses phony numbers, the networks look the other way and say, "It's not our problem." That should change.

The United States Senate will reconvene in September. At that time, it will reconsider the formation of a federal boxing commission. John McCain wants the commission and will compromise to get it. There's a possibility that, to achieve his goal, he will agree to insert language in the statute that denominates the networks as they presently do business as "promoters."

If that happens, rather than be classified as promoters, the networks might pull back and cede some of their power to Bob Arum, Don King, and others. Or they might decide to go all out and jump into the promotional cesspool with both feet, rendering promoters even less relevant than they are now.

There's also a third option. HBO and Showtime might say, "We don't need this hassle," and abandon the sweet science altogether. Where would that leave boxing? ❏

*Some problems in boxing are more complex and more difficult to resolve than others. This was one of them.*

# THE STRANGE CASE OF STEVE SMOGER

Steve Smoger is universally recognized as one of the best referees in boxing. In recent years, he has also been a municipal court judge in Ventnor, Margate, Port Republic, and Pleasantville, New Jersey. Therein lies the quandary.

Two years ago, the New Jersey State Advisory Committee on Judicial Conduct filed a complaint charging Smoger with judicial misconduct. Smoger resigned his judgeships. The Advisory Committee continued its proceeding and, after a hearing, determined there was "clear and convincing" evidence that Smoger was guilty of four different types of misconduct:

The first finding against Smoger was that he had improperly issued bench warrants to defendants who came late to court and illegally set bail for defendants in cases he presided over. Among other things, this led to a $142,000 settlement being paid to a man who was wrongly arrested on a criminal warrant issued by Smoger after he arrived five minutes late for a court appearance. Another plaintiff received $50,000 in settlement of a lawsuit because Smoger inadvertently put him in jail for 94 days after he accidentally rode a bicycle into a cop. Smoger inaccurately filled out a court form with a guilty plea that resulted in the man being improperly incarcerated.

"I ran a conservative court," Smoger says in response. "When a defendant arrives late, it keeps the arresting officer from going home to his family and costs the taxpayers extra money for police overtime. Where the first settlement is concerned, I later lifted the warrant but there was a clerical error. In the second instance, I made a mistake. When I was a judge, I worked four days a week in four different courts. I saw hundreds of defendants each week. Mistakes happen."

Second, the Advisory Committee on Judicial Conduct ruled that Smoger had violated a court rule that bars municipal judges from practicing law in penal matters by serving as a prosecutor for the Atlantic City Board of Alcohol Beverage Control.

"Maybe I was remiss in not seeking an opinion from the Advisory Committee on that one," Smoger acknowledges. "I reviewed the statutes prior to taking my job with the Board of Beverage Control, and I determined that my duties there would be administrative rather than penal in nature. I suppose there was an error in my review, although reasonable minds can differ on the applicable opinions and case law."

Third, where the sweet science is concerned, Smoger refereed professional boxing matches in violation of a specific directive from the New Jersey Supreme Court that he stop. On July 29, 1992, the administrative director of the New Jersey court system advised Smoger in writing of a Supreme Court directive that, as a municipal judge, he could no longer referee professional fights. Smoger ignored the order. Thereafter, the administrative director sent Smoger a letter stating that he had been observed refereeing a professional boxing match and asked for an explanation. Smoger's response was evasive and misleading. He wrote back that the reporting party must have been watching television and seen "a re-broadcast of a professional match that I officiated [before the court's directive]."

Smoger later changed his explanation and stated in writing that he had understood the prohibition to apply only to boxing matches held in Atlantic City casinos and that he had "fastidiously" followed that portion of the directive. However, the prohibition clearly was not limited to fights in Atlantic City casinos. And more to the point, records showed that, subsequent to being advised of the prohibition, Smoger refereed 31 professional boxing matches in New Jersey, nine of which were in Atlantic City casinos. Confronted with this evidence, Smoger acknowledged that he had knowingly violated the directive. "It was all with complete knowledge," he conceded. "In the pit of your stomach, [you know that] you're doing something that's not quite according to Hoyle. But you do it and you hope that nobody knows. I thought I could slip through . . . I wanted to ply my trade. I love boxing and saw the situation through my own rose-colored glasses. My desire to referee clouded my judgment."

Here, it should be noted that boxing is Smoger's passion, but there was also considerable financial incentive for him to keep refereeing. He has been paid as much as $7,650 to referee a single fight.

The fourth finding against Smoger was that he had violated a state law that precludes judges from receiving compensation other than their salaries for the performance of official duties. The Advisory Committee on Judicial Conduct ruled that Smoger had indirectly received compensation for officiating over marriages by recommending that newlyweds make donations to an organization called the Hiltner Foundation. The Hiltner Foundation is not an officially registered or public charity. Rather, it is a fund that was set up by the Margate city clerk and the mayor's secretary to pay for the education of their deceased brother's children. Also, there was at least one instance where a New Jersey resident pled guilty to driving with a suspended license and Smoger reduced the fine that had been imposed against him by $100. More than coincidentally, the motorist had made a $100 contribution to the Hiltner Foundation at his wedding a day earlier.

It was also alleged that Smoger learned in his capacity as a municipal court judge that the Margate Police Department was conducting a drug investigation of Maria Hiltner (wife of the Margate city clerk) and alerted the clerk's sister as to the existence of the investigation. However, the Advisory Committee found that this charge had "not been proved by clear and convincing evidence."

After issuing its findings, the Advisory Committee on Judicial Conduct made a formal presentment to the New Jersey Supreme Court. In it, the committee requested that Smoger be barred for life from serving as a judge. Among other things, the presentment stated that Smoger had demonstrated "an egregious and persistent pattern of total disregard for judicial ethical obligations" and called him "a dishonest person totally indifferent to the standards governing judicial behavior."

In July 2002, the New Jersey Supreme Court followed the Advisory Committee's recommendation and barred Smoger from the bench for life. It then referred its file on him to the State Office of Attorney Ethics to determine what action should be taken against Smoger as an attorney now that he was no longer a judge.

In October 2002, Richard Engelhardt (counsel for the State Office of Attorney Ethics) asked the State Supreme Court Disciplinary Review Board to reprimand Smoger. A reprimand is the strongest penalty that can be administered against a lawyer short of suspension or disbarment. Smoger's attorney asked for the lesser penalty of an admonition.

In December 2002, the State Supreme Court Disciplinary Review Board agreed unanimously that Smoger should be reprimanded. The New Jersey Supreme Court heard argument on the recommendation in April 2003. One month later, it formally reprimanded Smoger.

The legal profession has now dealt with Steve Smoger's transgressions. The remaining issue is, "How should boxing deal with Steve Smoger?"

Smoger loves boxing. Some of his fondest childhood memories are of staying up late at night with his father to watch the *Gillette Friday Night Fights* on television. He boxed in a YMCA youth program ["It was more like physical conditioning," he says] and competed in intramural boxing matches at college. After graduating from law school, he put in four years as an associate with a small law firm in New Jersey. In 1975, he joined the office of the Atlantic City prosecutor. In 1992, he was designated a municipal court judge.

Municipal judges in New Jersey work part-time. They handle civil ordinance violations and small criminal matters. By 1994, Smoger was serving simultaneously as a municipal judge in Margate, Ventnor, Pleasantville, and Port Republic. Meanwhile, he had become increasingly involved with the sweet science.

Smoger's active participation in boxing began in the early 1970s when he served as a timekeeper, judge, and referee for the Police Athletic League. In

1978, casino gambling arrived in Atlantic City and boxing came with it. "One afternoon," Smoger recalls, "I was at the PAL center, and Jersey Joe Walcott called. He was chairman of the New Jersey State Boxing Commission, which was what they called it back then. There were fights scheduled for that night and Walcott said, 'We're shorthanded. Is there anyone at PAL who can help out as an inspector?'"

Smoger volunteered and, for the next five years, worked as an inspector. In 1983, he was granted a provisional referee license. "Those were the glory years for boxing in Atlantic City," he remembers fondly. "Don King was promoting here. Bob Arum was promoting here. Don Elbaum had a show every week at the Tropicana. One year, we had something like 163 fight cards in New Jersey."

Meanwhile, Smoger was moving up the ladder. His first world title fight was a 112-pound IBF championship bout in South Korea in 1986. Since then, he has refereed 50 major championship contests, including Roy Jones versus Bernard Hopkins, Hopkins versus Felix Trinidad, Holyfield-Ruiz III, Mosley-Forrest I and, most recently, Vassiliy Jirov against James Toney. At various times, he has been named Referee of the Year by *Ring Sports, Boxing Scene* and *Flash* magazines. In 1995, he placed second to Mills Lane in a poll conducted by *Boxing Illustrated* to designate the world's "best referee."

But Smoger's legal difficulties have cast a cloud over his boxing future. He is currently licensed to referee fights in Pennsylvania and Connecticut, and at Foxwoods (which is run by the Mashantucket Pequot tribe). However, at least one of these jurisdictions intends to review his status in light of recent court rulings. Last year, the New York State Athletic Commission requested that Smoger voluntarily relinquish his license (which he did rather than face suspension). And when his license to referee fights in his home state of New Jersey expired on July 1, 2002, his request for renewal was denied. He will be eligible to reapply on July 1, 2003.

Meanwhile, outside the ring, Atlantic City mayor Lorenzo Langford has appointed Smoger to the position of city solicitor (lead attorney) for Atlantic City. In that role, he supervises a staff of eight attorneys and nine support personnel.

So to repeat the question: "How should boxing deal with Steve Smoger?" Given his recent judicial record, if he were applying for a referee's license for the first time today, the application would be denied. But it's hard to overlook Smoger's history of sustained excellence in the ring. For two decades, he has been a superb referee. His skills and instincts are excellent.

There was one moment when Smoger's performance did raise a few eye-brows. On March 6, 1999, Lou Savarese fought Lance Whitaker in Atlantic City. Savarese hit the canvas twice. The second time, discretion being the better part of valour, he showed little inclination to rise. Smoger gave him a bit more time and a bit more encouragement than some onlookers thought appropriate. Savarese rose at what seemed to be the count of nine-and-three-quarters and went on to win the fight.

Still, Smoger is widely thought of as fair and unbiased. People in boxing know that certain referees favor the house fighter, but that's not the case with Smoger. Fighters and trainers trust him far more than they trust most referees.

Those who support Smoger continuing as a referee argue that his wrong-doing was unrelated to boxing, except to the extent that he continued to referee fights in violation of an administrative order. They say that the court directive was unreasonable in that it was based on the premise that refereeing "degraded the integrity and impartiality of the bench." They cite Mills Lane, the much-respected former district attorney and judge, who was allowed, indeed urged, to referee fights by the State of Nevada. Moreover, Smoger's defenders say, there is a paucity of world-class referees. As a practical matter, boxing needs Steve Smoger.

But there's a contrary argument that can be made. Those who oppose Smoger returning to the ring state that only in boxing would this be a difficult issue. Smoger might be the best referee in the country right now, they acknowledge. But the fact that he's an excellent referee doesn't excuse his misconduct. Society needs standards and accountability. And where character is concerned, there shouldn't be one set of standards for highly competent officials and another set for officials of average competence.

It's essential that a referee in boxing represent total integrity. Personal integrity must be in place before skill becomes a factor. And the fact that a person has demonstrated a lack of integrity in one area of his professional life can't be isolated from other areas, particularly when each of the areas involves a public trust. A referee is asking the participants in a fight and the public to trust him, just as a judge asks trial participants and the public for their trust.

It's sad, the argument continues, but if a judge acts in such a questionable manner on the bench, can boxing trust him to be completely honest? In a big fight where millions of dollars are at stake? In small club fights where few people are watching? Moreover, disagreements and controversies are inevitable in boxing. In the past, few people have questioned Smoger's integrity in the ring. But now, there's a legitimate concern that any future controversy that involves him as a referee will focus on his prior misconduct. Suppose the boxing world had known of Smoger's judicial problems at the time of Savarese-Whitaker? Allowing Smoger to continue refereeing, the argument closes, will undermine public confidence in boxing and bring the sport into further disrepute.

So what's the proper resolution?

Boxing is a cesspool. Promoters have admitted paying bribes to world sanctioning organizations. Too many state athletic commission officials are corrupt. Conflicts of interest are taken for granted. To single out Steve Smoger for a permanent ban would be unfair and hypocritical. Boxing accepts, and at times extols, much worse conduct.

In the ring, Smoger has carried out his duties with distinction and honor. Still, he has been found guilty of significant wrongdoing. These are not mere technical violations, and they should not be ignored.

Smoger is not now under suspension in any state. Rather, he has relinquished his license in one jurisdiction and it has expired in another. That might not be a bad course of action to follow across the board. Then, after a decent interval, Smoger should be allowed to reapply for a license to referee in each jurisdiction and welcomed back into the fold. ❏

*This article focused on one of the many conflicts of interest that pervade boxing.*

# THE INSURANCE ISSUE

When Vernon Forrest and Shane Mosley fought their rematch on July 20, 2002, the focus was on the fight. But the bout also showcased a troubling side issue. Boxing, more than any other professional sport, is rife with conflicts of interest. Sometimes these conflicts are benign. Other times, they result in horrible exploitation. Thus, it's worth noting that the man who initially agented the insurance policy covering both fighters in Forrest-Mosley II also refereed the fight.

Ultimately, the Black Expo (which was promoting Forrest-Mosley II) got a new insurance agent. In part, that's because the Indiana State Athletic Commission was already under fire for the craven manner in which it had bowed to the WBC in the selection of judges. With Jerry Roth and Tony Castellano having replaced Duane Ford and Fred Jones in the jury box as a consequence of backroom maneuvering, the last thing the Black Expo needed was a referee controversy. But the issue will arise on a regular basis in the future, so let's take a look at what's involved.

As a general rule, boxing promoters purchase several types of insurance. There's signal insurance on big fights in case satellite transmission fails. A promoter who pays a large signing bonus to a fighter might purchase insurance to cover its losses should the fighter be unable to perform. But the most common forms of insurance purchased by promoters are:

(1) General liability insurance: This covers personal injury to individuals other than fighters (for example, fans and media representatives) for all events during a given year. The per-event coverage limitation on these policies for major promoters is generally between $2-million and $5-million. However, for Lewis-Tyson, where fears of a public disturbance ran high, Main Events purchased additional insurance, bringing the coverage ceiling to $15-million.

(2) Non-appearance insurance: This coverage is usually in place for major fights. It reimburses the promoter for expenses should an event be cancelled for reasons other than a breach of contract (for example, an injury to one of the boxers or a hurricane that renders holding the fight impossible).

(3) Boxer insurance: This coverage is designed to pay a fighter's medical expenses for injuries sustained during a bout, or the fighter's estate if a fighter is killed during a bout. It is purchased on a card-by-card basis with policy

limits that are subject to varying state regulation. Most major promoters have policies with a payment ceiling of $50,000 per fighter.

Virtually all of the boxer insurance in the United States is sold through two agents—Joe Gagliardi of San Francisco and Laurence Cole of Texas.

Cole makes his living primarily as an independent insurance agent. Initially, he worked for his father. Then Dickie Cole was named boxing director for the Texas Department of Licensing and Regulation and turned the insurance business over to his son. The company is now called Laurence Cole Insurance Agency.

The bulk of the insurance that Cole sells are typical life, home, and automobile insurance policies. But by his own count, he writes boxer insurance policies for 30 to 40 professional fight cards per month. He also agents policies for wrestling, kick-boxing, tough-man contests, and other martial arts competitions.

Cole has refereed professional fights since 1988. Ironically, on the first card he worked, a novice pro named Jesse James Leija emerged victorious in a preliminary bout. That bit of information bears repeating because, earlier this year, Cole raised eyebrows when he ruled that a cut suffered by Leija in a bout against Micky Ward was caused by a head butt. Thus, when the fight was stopped after five rounds and the decision went to the judges' scorecards, Leija was awarded the victory rather than Ward winning by TKO. Some observers considered Cole's call "blatant hometown officiating."

Cole has refereed 21 world championship bouts; most of them for the WBC and most of them in Texas. Forrest-Mosley II was far and-away his most significant assignment. He did a credible job of officiating although, near the end of round 11, he halted the action in the midst of a Forrest flurry because he mistakenly thought the bell had rung. Also, given the amount of holding by both fighters, Cole should have told them to fight their way out of clinches a few times to see what happened and perhaps change the pace of what Jim Lampley of HBO acknowledged was, "an unsatisfying, inartistic, grappling, holding, struggling, one-punch-at-a-time affair." Still, the end result was a fair one—a unanimous 12-round decision for Forrest.

So what, if anything, is wrong with Laurence Cole selling insurance to promoters for specific bouts and then refereeing those fights?

Arlen "Spider" Bynum (the Texas attorney who acts as counsel for the WBC and has served as on-site supervisor for a number of WBC title bouts) says, "Over the years, we've had horrible problems getting medical and life insurance for the fighters. It's a very difficult type of insurance coverage to find, and Laurence gets promoters what they need for the fighters. He's a fine young man and I have the highest regard for him."

Cole furthers the explanation, noting, "An agent is a mediator between the client and the insurance underwriter, that's all. Obviously, I try to do right by everyone involved, but there's no fiduciary duty to either side. I work with a larger agency in Illinois. We offer 36 different plans for professional boxers with coverage ceilings ranging from $2,500 to $250,000 per injury. That's it. There's nothing wrong."

It's unlikely that a referee who agented an insurance policy would stop a fight too soon out of concern that medical bills might mount. Cole himself makes that point, declaring, "I don't see it. I'm an agent, not the insurance company. If there's a loss, it's not coming out of my pocket."

However, the conflict becomes more real in theory when one considers the fact that promoters often have a rooting interest in the fights they promote, particularly if it's a major fight. For example, it's no secret that Bob Arum will be rooting for Oscar De La Hoya when he steps into the ring against Fernando Vargas. Don King was more than disappointed when Felix Trinidad was knocked out by Bernard Hopkins. Picture then a situation where a promoter says to a referee, "I'll give you my insurance business, but I want you to keep in mind who I'm rooting for."

The money involved in any one fight is so small as to be insignificant. The premium for $50,000 worth of insurance for a given fighter on a given night is about $120. That means, on a seven-bout card, the total premium payment for 14 fighters is roughly $1,680. Cole says that, depending on the policy, his commission ranges from five to 10 percent. If he received a 10 percent commission, he'd be getting $168. That amount is miniscule. Still, over the course of a year, the commissions add up.

Moreover, it's not the amount; it's the principle that's in question. In some ways, a boxing match is like a courtroom proceeding. The ring judges are the equivalent of jurors, and the referee plays the role of a trial judge, directing the flow of the action. Laurence Cole doesn't appear to have done anything illegal or unethical. But most parties to litigation wouldn't want the judge in their case to be the other side's insurance broker.

In short, common sense dictates that referees and judges should not have a financial interest, direct or indirect, in any fight they cover. Obviously, the Indiana State Athletic Commission feels differently about the matter because it had no problem with Cole's dual role. And the Texas Department of Licensing and Regulation, headed by Cole's father, seems equally comfortable with the arrangement because Cole referees in Texas on a regular basis.

Situations like this are one more reason why boxing needs uniform national standards and guidelines and a federal commission to enforce them. ❏

*On Friday, July 18, 2003, three days after this article went online, Bradley Rone collapsed in the ring after the first round of a bout against Billy Zumbrun in Cedar City, Utah, and was pronounced dead at Valley View Medical Center.*

# PROFESSIONAL LOSERS

Kenneth Bentley is a professional fighter. At least, he says he is. And it takes courage to get in a boxing ring, so give him credit for that. But the truth is, based on his record, it's fair to assume that, when Bentley comes to fight, he comes to lose.

Bentley is neither a boxer nor a puncher. He never had a prime. His career record is 8-92-1 with 2 knockouts. In his last 61 fights, he has won once. Still, he's licensed to box by the State of Tennessee, which has hosted 34 of his last 55 fights.

Heavyweight Roy Bedwell has lost 57 of his last 58 bouts. During that stretch, he has been knocked out 33 times. It's more than coincidence that 42 of these 58 fights have been in Tennessee.

Tim Dendy of Tennessee is 0-25-1 in his last 26 fights. Jeff Bowman, another Tennessee hero, has lost 29 of his last 32 bouts. Lester Yarbrough of Tennessee has been on the losing end in his most recent 21 contests.

Boxing in Tennessee is regulated by the Tennessee Board of Boxing and Racing, which is one of seven divisions within the Tennessee Department of Commerce and Insurance. The man responsible for overseeing the sweet science in the Volunteer State is "boxing administrator" Dan Kelly, who recently replaced Tommy Patrick.

Section 68-115-207(c) of the Tennessee Annotated Code provides that a fighter's license may be suspended for "professional incompetence." But Kelly is unmoved. "There's nothing that says a boxer has to win a certain number of fights to keep his license," he said recently. "Watching them in the ring, some of these guys are pretty good. They just get outfought. Who are we to tell a boxer that he can no longer pursue his goals?"

It's no coincidence that Tennessee is the only place in the United States to host a Mike Tyson fight in recent years. But Tennessee is hardly alone in its lack of standards. Virginia, Indiana, Kentucky, Ohio, Missouri, Mississippi, Florida, Georgia, Louisiana, Alabama, and Massachusetts are among the states that allow fighters with egregious records to step into the ring.

Heavyweight Frankie Hines has lost 119 bouts, including one stretch of

55 in a row without a victory. Light-heavyweight Jerome Hill has a 1-49 record. Hines and Hill fight mostly in Tennessee and Virginia.

And speaking of the Old Dominion state, Virginian middleweight Calvin Moody has gone through his last 33 fights without a victory. Cruiserweight Eric Rhinehardt has also found a home in Virginia. Rhinehardt has 50 losses to his credit. In one 16-bout stretch, he was knocked out 15 times.

Indiana middleweight James Rice is winless in his last 28 bouts. Welterweight Nelson Hernandez is also a regular in the Hoosier State. In his last 45 fights, he has suffered 44 losses, 30 of them by knockout. Fighting mostly in Indiana and Kentucky, heavyweight John Jackson has compiled a 4-58-2 record.

Cruiserweight Angelo Simpson, who plies his trade in Georgia, is without a win in his last 28 contests.

Iowa cruiserweight Richie Galvin began his journey through the pros at 1-1-1. Since then, he has gone 1-27-1.

Florida junior-middleweight John Valentin is 1-23-1 in his last 25 fights. Florida cruiserweight Ralph Monday has lost 15 in a row, including 12 by knockout.

Cruiserweight Robert Terrell has lost his last 17 fights, all of them in Louisiana and Mississippi.

Fighting mostly in Massachusetts, cruiserweight Jose Torres has been victorious in two of his last 43 outings. Massachusetts super middleweight Richard Zola started his career at 2-1-1. Since then, he has gone 1-22-1 and lost his last 14 outings.

Then there are the vagabonds, who move from state to state.

Let's start with the heavyweights. Danny Wofford has 97 losses and has been on the winning end in just two of his last 74 fights. Gerald Moore has a career mark of 0-18, with all of his losses coming by knockout in the first two rounds. Caseny Truesdale has won two of his last 44 encounters. Bradley Rone has lost his last 25 bouts in a row. Eric Davis has been on the losing end in 16 of his last 17 fights. Heavyweight Willie Driver has lost 18 of his last 19 contests.

Moving to cruiserweight, Don Ray Pendleton has lost 145 times. Tyrone Mack has lost 16 in a row.

Light-heavyweight Reuben Ruiz has won one of his last 25 bouts. Super-middleweight Larry Kenney has been defeated 16 times in succession.

At middleweight, Jerry Smith has lost 54 fights, including his last 27 in a row. Anthony Ivory has lost 63 times and failed to win in 23 of his last 24 contests. Hector Ramirez has won once in his last 25 outings.

Welterweight Randy Reedy has won twice in his last 40 fights, while light-weight Rick Dinkins is 0-21-1 in his last 22 bouts.

And special notice should be taken of super-middleweight Reggie Strickland, who has 248 career losses.

Invariably, when these men enter the ring, they're billed as "Savvy veteran . . . Experienced pro . . . Been in with top opposition . . ." But most of them have crossed over the line that separates credible opponents who give a good honest effort from pedestrians in a danger zone.

From time to time, the Association of Boxing Commissions talks about the problem, but it never does anything to remedy the situation. "We wish we had the power to suspend some of these fighters," says ABC president Tim Leuckenhoff. "But under federal law, we don't. Unfortunately, a fighter can only be suspended by a state in which he has a license. Sometimes that happens. But a month or two later when the suspension expires, they're back in the ring again. And most of these guys are smart enough to steer clear of states like Nevada, which would put them on a permanent suspension list."

Meanwhile, speaking of Nevada . . . On June 14, 2003, heavyweight Danell Nicholson (who had 41 wins against only four losses) was allowed to fight Ken Murphy, who had lost 10 fights in a row. Nicholson won on a second-round knockout.

Add professional losers to the list of reasons why boxing needs a federal commission.

These fighters are different from perennial losers in other sports. We're not talking about a high school basketball team that loses forty games in a row. Athletes "play" sports like baseball, football, tennis, and golf. No one plays boxing. These men are getting punched in the head, hard. They're prime candidates for brain damage. And when they enter the ring, the spectators aren't paying to watch a competitive fight. They're paying to see someone get beaten up. There's a difference. ❏

# ROUND 4

# CURIOSITIES

*Some of the most entertaining action in boxing takes place away from the ring.*

# THE ALWAYS-EXCITING, PERPETUALLY-SCINTILLATING, KICK-OFF BOXING PRESS CONFERENCE

Boxing's kick-off press conferences have one purpose: to get media coverage. In many respects, they're analogous to Hollywood's annual Academy Awards show, which offers four hours of mediocrity followed by everything interesting being crammed into the final 20 minutes. Kick-off press conferences give the media 90 minutes of self-important corporate executives followed by the main-event fighters talking for two minutes each. But in boxing, instead of Whoopi Goldberg and Billy Crystal moving things along, we get Don King and Murad Muhammad.

In the old days, newspaper reporters and photographers watched dutifully at press conferences as fighters signed contracts to do battle. Then Joe Louis, Rocky Marciano, or whoever would lean over, shake hands with his opponent, and say, "I'm looking forward to a good fight. May the best man win."

Then Muhammad Ali arrived on the scene and turned what was basically a non-event into an occasion of considerable magnitude. Ali dubbed George Foreman "The Mummy" and Leon Spinks "The Vampire" at kick-off press conferences. At the start of publicity for Ali-Holmes, Ali appeared with a mustache and told the media, "You're looking at Dark Gable." Holmes was unimpressed and responded, "His ass is grass, and I'm the lawnmower."

There were times when Ali press conferences had an ugly edge. His "what's my name" torture of Ernie Terrell had its origins in an inadvertent comment by Terrell on the day their bout was announced. And bad feelings still exist from Ali pummeling a black rubber gorilla at the kick-off for Ali-Frazier III and telling the world, "It will be a chilla and a thrilla when I get The Gorilla in Manila." Still, when all was said and done, Ali presided over the glory years for kick-off press conferences. Or as longtime boxing scribe Ed Schuyler notes, "They should have gotten rid of them when Ali retired."

The main problem with contemporary kick-off press conferences is that, although carefully scripted, they're rarely entertaining or clever. "Maybe they're amusing the first time," says Teddy Atlas. "But once you've been through it two or three times, you realize it's the same old BS. First the promoter gets up and talks about how wonderful it is to work with the great

athletic commission of whatever state the fight is in. Then they introduce the
fight sponsors and a representative of whatever casino the fight is at. After
that, you have a bunch of people who hang around the fighters. These are
people who've never accomplished anything on their own in their entire life,
and now they have a platform so they talk forever. It's insulting to the fighters
to make them sit there and listen to that garbage."

Don King has been known to hold press conferences replete with midgets,
clowns, and jugglers. Last year at a Chinese restaurant in New York, King
entered the room carrying a traditional incense offering to the gods while a
troupe of lion dancers followed behind him, banging drums and clanging
cymbals; all this to promote King's soon-to-be-cancelled heavyweight
extravaganza in Beijing. The promoter, Evander Holyfield, John Ruiz and
Hasim Rahman then posed for a photo op, holding what looked like makeshift
fishing poles with heads of wilted lettuce attached. The high point came when
Ruiz's lawyer, Tony Cardinale, told the media, "When the dust settles, everyone will agree that John Ruiz is one of the greatest fighters who ever lived." A
lot of dust will have to settle before people agree on that one.

King's press conferences also seem endless. The over-under line on most of
them is in excess of two hours. Indeed, at the kick-off press conference for
Felix Trinidad versus Mamadiou Thiam, King invoked the names of
47 clergymen and politicians. Thus, the tale of a six-year-old boy who attended
a Don King press conference. When the boy returned home, his mother asked,
"What did Don King talk about?" And the boy answered, "He talked about
four hours."

"Don talks too long," concedes Eric Gelfand (Madison Square Garden's vice
president of public relations for sports properties). "But he always gets you
your TV sound-bite."

By contrast, Murad Muhammad's press conferences are as long as King's,
but with less entertainment value. Lou DiBella once opined, "Murad
Muhammad is Don King without brains." He might have added, without a
sense of humor either.

Bob Arum is a control freak. His press conferences are orderly and to the
point, but aren't particularly well thought of by members of the media since
they're also notoriously short on food. "Every now and then," observes
Michael Katz, "Arum will splurge on a pitcher of ice water."

New York is the favored location for kick-off press conferences because of
the media concentration in The Big Apple. Traditional sites include Madison
Square Garden and the now-defunct All-Star Cafe, but venues have run the
gamut from the Plaza Hotel and Waldorf-Astoria to the battleship
USS Intrepid. Michael Blutrich used to hold kick-off press conferences at a
mob-controlled adult club called Scores, and Tony Paige (then President of the
Boxing Writers Association of America) regularly boycotted Blutrich's
sessions. It's unknown whether Blutrich was offended by Paige's absence, and

it's now impossible to ask him since Michael has vanished into the federal witness protection program.

Memorable moments are few and far between at kick-off press conferences. Most of the gimmicks are pretty corny, such as George Foreman having a platter of hamburgers delivered to him at the kick off for Holyfield-Foreman. Sometimes the unexpected enlivens the scene. Mike Tyson showed up at a press conference to announce a fight on HBO wearing an ABC Wide World of Sports T-shirt. On the advice of Steve Lott, he turned the shirt inside out before the festivities began. However, that was nothing compared to Iron Mike's performance at the September 14, 2000, kick off for Tyson-Golota.

"I don't care about living or dying," Tyson told the assembled media. "I'm a dysfunctional motherfucker . . . Bring on Golota; bring on Lewis. They can keep their titles. I don't want to strip them of their titles, I want to strip them of their fucking health . . . I'm in pain, so I want them to be in pain. I want their kids to see pain. Fuck 'em . . . You don't know me; you can't define me. I'm a convicted rapist, a hell-raiser, a father, a semi-good husband. I raise hell. I know it's going to get me in trouble or killed one day, but that's just who I am. I can't help it . . . Listen, I'm a nigger. No, really, really, listen to me. I'm a street person. I don't even want to be a street person; I don't like typical street people. But, your grandchildren will know about me. They'll be like, 'Wow, wasn't that a bizarre individual?' "

Then the subject of Zoloft was raised, and Tyson responded, "I'm on it to keep from killing you all. I don't want to be on it. I'm jacked up. My sex life is jacked up. My dick don't work."

In January of this year, Iron Mike outdid himself when he bit Lennox Lewis on the thigh at the kick-off press conference for what was to have been, and may still become, the largest-grossing fight in boxing history. Once order was restored, Tyson moved to the front of the stage, grabbed his crotch, simulated masturbation (one hopes it was simulated), and screamed obscenities at the media.

In other words, the script isn't always followed. At the kick off for Sugar Ray Leonard versus Marvelous Marvin Hagler, promoter Arum told the media that Leonard would not answer questions regarding the detached retina he'd suffered several years earlier. Leonard himself put an exclamation point on Arum's words with the declaration, "The eyes are no longer an issue." Whereupon Pat Putnam of *Sports Illustrated* shouted out, "How many fingers am I holding up?"

Lou DiBella, then of HBO, also departed from the script at his employer's press conference to publicize Lennox Lewis versus Oliver McCall II. "This fight shouldn't happen," DiBella told the media. "McCall is unstable. He's on drugs. He's been throwing Christmas trees around hotel lobbies." And of course, McCall suffered a breakdown in the ring against Lewis in one of boxing's more embarrassing moments.

Lennox Lewis and Roy Jones, Jr. are virtually always late for press conferences. Hector Camacho once went to the wrong hotel by mistake, decided he was hungry, and stayed for lunch, thereby blowing off the entire event.

As of late, kick-off press conferences have become more elaborate than in the past. Madison Square Garden spent $30,000 to announce the first Holyfield-Lewis fight and the same amount for Lewis versus Michael Grant. In each instance, there were flashing lights, smoke, mirrors, and sound effects. The kick-off for Holyfield-Lewis I was particularly interesting because Garden officials neglected to seat representatives of the WBC, WBA, and IBF at the dais, which prompted King to throw a tantrum of Shakespearean proportions.

In early 2001, King returned to Madison Square Garden to kick off his middleweight championship series, which was being televised by HBO. The spotlight was supposed to shine that morning on Felix Trinidad, Bernard Hopkins, Keith Holmes, and William Joppy. But instead, King spent the first 20 minutes talking about John Ruiz, who had just won the WBA heavyweight championship on Showtime. Then the promoter posed Ruiz and Trinidad together for a five-minute photo op, while the HBO executives in attendance burned.

Still, when all is said and done, it's clear that boxing's kick-off press conferences are here to stay. So let's give Eric Gelfand the final word as he defends them with the explanation, "Kick-off press conferences are an opportunity to create a feel for the fight. And it makes my day to go home and see a clip from one of our press conferences on ESPN or CNN, or pick up a newspaper the next morning and see a story with a photo of the fighters beside it. A good press conference sets the tone for the entire promotion of a fight."

Thus, prior to Mike Tyson and Lennox Lewis meeting in the ring, don't be surprised if Showtime and HBO televise excerpts from their first encounter with the commercial tag-line, "That was only the press conference. Wait until the fight." ❏

*In 2001, I speculated on what might happen if 16 of boxing's finest got together for a remake of television's "Survivor" series. In 2002, I had them playing golf.*

# THE REAL MASTERS

Earlier this summer, the attention of golf fans around the world was riveted on Tiger Woods and his quest to win all four "majors" in a single calendar year. But away from the spotlight, an equally compelling drama occurred. Buoyed by the success of their joint venture in televising Lennox Lewis versus Mike Tyson, Showtime and HBO decided to jointly promote an 18-hole golf tournament at the hallowed Augusta National Golf Club in Augusta, Georgia.

The format was simple. Sixteen personalities from the world of boxing were entered in the tournament. Announcing duties were split between Bob Costas of HBO and Jim Gray of Showtime. The tournament was taped and will air simultaneously on both cable networks opposite the first game of the World Series. Everyone involved agreed that there would be a news embargo regarding the tournament until after it was shown on television. But—and this is a shocker—not everyone in boxing keeps their word. Thus, yours truly was able to learn the results. And to reward readers who visit this website, those results are recounted herewith.

The golfers were paired in twosomes. Play proceeded as follows:

### Mike Tyson and Lennox Lewis

Tyson showed up at the first tee with Shelly Finkel as his caddy and his own personal gallery that included Stephen Fitch (a/k/a "Crocodile"), Stacy McKinley, and three topless dancers from a local strip club. In an exclusive interview, Finkel told Jim Gray, "Mike is drawn to golf because of the dignity and quiet of the sport."

A problem arose immediately when event organizers succumbed to concerns that Tyson would attack Lewis instead of attacking the golf course. Thus, it was decided that Mike would tee off on his own and Lennox would follow.

Tyson forged ahead with less than satisfactory results. After a sextuplet-bogie on the 13th hole, he ripped an azalea out of the ground and threw it into Rae's Creek. When asked to comment on Mike's conduct, Finkel responded, "I was looking in the other direction when it happened. But Mike tells me he didn't throw an azalea, and I believe him." Asked if he wanted to see the incident on videotape, Finkel replied, "No. Mike tells me he didn't do it, and Mike's word is good enough for me."

Tyson carded an 18-hole score of 187. As he and his entourage left the course, Finkel told reporters, "About the azalea; Mike was angry because the Augusta National Golf Club has no women members, and Mike feels that's a sign of disrespect toward women."

Lewis shot a 98.

### Bernard Hopkins and Felix Trinidad

On the first tee, Hopkins stripped off his shirt to reveal "GoldenPalace.com" written in charcoal on his back. Sadly, the tournament was difficult for Bernard. After his third triple-bogey in a row, he ripped the flag from the pin and threw it to the ground. This upset Felix, who warned Bernard not to throw another flag on the ground. Hopkins then became so engrossed with throwing flags that he lost his concentration and shot 154. Trinidad carded a 107.

### Oscar De La Hoya and Michael Katz

Oscar was accompanied around the course by a horde of shrieking teenage girls known as "Oscar's Army." This displeased Katz, who periodically demanded, "Will you shut them up!" After nine holes, Katz walked off the course in disgust. Oscar shot a 137 and complained to Jim Gray afterward, "The poor score wasn't my fault. Someone put trees, sand, and water all over the golf course."

### Shane Mosley and Vernon Forrest

Initially, Roy Jones was paired with Forrest. But Roy was late for his tee time and was disqualified. Then Mosley was brought in as a last minute substitute and paired with Vernon.

"I know I can beat him," Mosley told Bob Costas. Alas, Forrest is from Augusta. And Vernon has Shane's number.

Final scores: Forrest 98; Mosley 106.

### Don King and Bob Arum

This was a closely watched twosome. Jose Sulaiman caddied for King, and Gilberto Mendoza caddied for Arum. After the round, King told Bob Costas, "I love Augusta; the beautiful azaleas, the splendiferous magnolias, and Amen Corner where a religious man such as myself can commune with The Almighty."

Both King and Arum were disqualified for turning in false scorecards.

### Max Kellerman and Teddy Atlas

On the first four holes, Max lectured Teddy on the proper stance (first hole), proper grip of the golf club (second hole), proper swing (third hole), and proper mindset (fourth hole). As the two men approached the fifth tee, Max began a discourse on proper club selection. At this point, Teddy summoned a rules official and inquired, "Under Georgia law, how many years in prison will I get if I strangle Max?"

Atlas carded a 126; Kellerman, 140.

### Micky Ward and Arturo Gatti

This was a round where the caddies were considered particularly important. Al Gavin attended Ward, and Joe Souza was there for Gatti. Both men went for the green with every shot on every hole. Gatti was cut by a stiff breeze midway through the round, but finished on his feet.

Ward 140; Gatti 147.

### Evander Holyfield and John Ruiz

There was no gallery for this twosome, because no one wanted to see Evander and John compete against one another for a fourth time. However, there was some drama on the sixth hole, when Ruiz fell to the ground moaning and complained that Evander had whacked him in the crown jewels with a golf club. At the end of the round, Evander viewed a tape of the incident and acknowledged, "From that angle, it does look as though John got in the way of my backswing."

Meanwhile, Norman Stone (Ruiz's manager) endeared himself to golf fans around the world with the pronouncement, "If John wins this tournament, he'll be just as much the real Masters champion as Tiger Woods. Besides, John is a better golfer than Tiger Woods is a fighter."

Fox Network immediately offered Woods $5 million to fight Ruiz on *Celebrity Boxing*. Woods accepted, and Las Vegas oddmakers made the fight 6-to-5 pick 'em.

Holyfield and Ruiz both shot 114.

When the results were tabulated, there was a tie for first place between Vernon Forrest and Lennox Lewis. A sudden-death playoff followed. However, in deference to the television networks, I've decided not to reveal who won the playoff. To find out, you'll have to watch the telecast in October. ❏

*This article was part of the build-up to Lennox Lewis versus Mike Tyson.*

# A CONVERSATION WITH ELVIS

Telephone Operator: I have a collect call from heaven for Mr. Thomas Hauser. Will you accept the charges?

TH: Heaven?

Telephone Operator: Yes, sir. It's from a Mr. Elvis Presley.

TH: Is this a nut call?

Telephone Operator: Sir, I've loved Elvis Presley since I was a little girl. Don't you dare call him a nut.

TH: Okay, put him on.

*Click . . . Buzz . . .*

TH: Hello?

Elvis: Howdy, this is Elvis.

TH: Are you for real?

Elvis: Yes, sir. I may be old and I may be fat, but I'm still Elvis Presley.

TH: Why are you calling?

Elvis: I wanted to talk about the fight.

TH: The fight?

Elvis: Yes, sir, Lewis-Tyson. They're holding it in Memphis, Tennessee, right by Graceland. Showtime and HBO have been publicizing it so much that it's all folks are talking about here in heaven. But we don't get many boxing people up here. Most of them are in the other place. So I thought I'd call down to Earth to chat a bit.

TH: This is fantastic! I'm talking with Elvis Presley. What's up, Elvis?

Elvis: Well, to tell the truth; heaven is hard. Right now, I'm horribly obese and strung out on prescription drugs.

TH: Grow a beard and you'll resemble some of our finest boxing writers.

Elvis: Don't be cruel.

TH: Sorry about that. Anyway, what is it about Lewis-Tyson that interests you?

Elvis: Mostly Tyson. I identify with his struggle.

TH: Say what?

Elvis: It's hard being a legend. One day, I was the King of Rock and Roll. And then, all of a sudden, people were saying things like, "Look at fat Elvis. Elvis is pitiful." That's what's happening now with Tyson.

TH: But Elvis, people thought you were sweet. Tyson is the opposite.

Elvis: I know. But you have to understand; it's hard when the whole world knows you're nuts. I remember when people started talking about me frolicking on the bed with underage girls in white panties and shooting out TV screens with a gun. That sort of thing is embarrassing when folks know about it.

TH: Then don't do it.

Elvis: I couldn't stop. It's a compulsion. Like when Tyson grabbed a certain part of his anatomy at his last press conference. Jim Morrison got arrested for doing that on stage when he was with The Doors, but I don't think either one of them could control it. You see, there's a line between what's sexually right and sexually wrong and sometimes that line gets blurred by society. When I was on the Ed Sullivan Show, the TV cameras would only show me from the waist up.

TH: Elvis, what's your point?

Elvis: Sorry, I lost the thought. The prescription drugs are kicking in. Do you think they'd let me sing the national anthem on a closed-circuit hook-up from heaven before the fight?

TH: Try to focus. What is it that causes you to identify with Mike Tyson?

Elvis: Well, both of us were big in Las Vegas, although they let me stay and they kicked him out. Both of us had problems with prescription drugs. The Beatles came over from England and wiped me out. Now Lennox Lewis is threatening to come over from England to wipe out Tyson. Shelly Finkel reminds me of my old manager, Tom Parker. In fact, before Shelly started hanging around fighters, he was a rock-concert promoter. And Tyson and I both have a core constituency that loves us no matter what we do. My constituency is slightly overweight women from the trailer parks of America. Tyson has a different following.

TH: What will —

Elvis: Excuse me; I have to go. The doorbell just rang. They're delivering my pizza.

TH: One last question, Elvis. Who do you think will win Lewis-Tyson? Elvis: I don't know. They say that, when a great performer gets old, he still has one great performance left in him. I remember a night in Las Vegas toward the end. It was pitiful. For forty minutes, I lumbered around the stage. My stomach was bulging. I was groggy from drugs. But there was one moment. The orchestra was playing a slow love song, and I nailed it. For that one song, I was great again.

TH: And?

Elvis: Mike Tyson may be old and Mike Tyson may be fat, but he's still Mike Tyson. He's smarter inside the ring than he is out of it. And the mother can punch . . . Gotta go now. I don't want my pizza to get cold. ❏

*This "color" piece fleshed out my coverage of Lewis-Tyson for the Showtime Boxing website.*

# LEWIS-TYSON, MEMPHIS, AND ELVIS

The lobby of the Peabody Hotel in Memphis has high-ceilings with wood beams and an elegant decor. Each day for six hours, five ducks paddle around an ornate fountain at room center. These are "the world-famous Peabody ducks." Shortly before 11:00 a.m. and then again just before 5:00 p.m., a red carpet is unfurled from a nearby elevator to the fountain. Tourists surround the carpet and fountain as if they were standing along the fairway leading to the 18th green at the Augusta National Golf Course on the final day of the Masters. They are waiting for "the march of the ducks."

Thus it was that, at precisely 5:00 p.m. five days before Lennox Lewis fought Mike Tyson, a hotel attendant carrying a broomstick approached the fountain and waved his stick in the direction of the ducks.

Nothing happened, so the man splashed a bit of water.

Still nothing. The ducks didn't move.

The man tapped the fountain wall.

No response.

*Crack!*

The man whacked the side of the fountain with his stick as hard as he could. And the ducks started moving. This was not a line of proud little ducks marching. This was terror. A man was waving a stick at them, and the man was angry. The ducks wanted to get as far away from him as possible. If the carpet hadn't been lined by hundreds of people, the ducks would have scattered all over the lobby. But things being what they were, the carpet was their only avenue of escape so they waddled down it into the elevator.

(Actually, the ducks didn't know it was an elevator. Most ducks don't know stuff like that. All they knew was that a man with a stick was angry at them.)

Anyway, cameras flashed. And after that, most of the onlookers rushed to the gift shop to buy postcards of ducks, soap shaped like ducks, stuffed ducks, and the like.

Welcome to Memphis, which for one week earlier this month was the Mecca of boxing.

Memphis is home to one-million people and is the eighteenth-largest city in America. It's best known for Beale Street, rhythm and blues, rock and roll, and the Mississippi River, and fancies itself as the pork barbecue capitol of the world. It's also the primary air hub for Federal Express, which gives it the most active cargo airport on the planet.

In 1945, Paul Francis Webster and Hoagy Carmichael memorialized the city in a song entitled "Memphis In June" that spoke of shady verandas and sweet oleander blowing perfume in the air. Chuck Berry had a slightly different take on the metropolis when he recorded "Memphis, Tennessee" in 1959. Regardless, the city's greatest imprint on the national consciousness has come from two untimely deaths. In 1968, Martin Luther King, Jr. was assassinated at the Lorraine Motel in Memphis. Nine years later, Elvis Presley died at Graceland (his Memphis home).

Prior to Lewis-Tyson, Tennessee's biggest moment in boxing had been the 1996 arrest of Oliver McCall for throwing a Christmas tree in the lobby of a Nashville hotel. Six weeks later, McCall suffered a nervous breakdown in the ring in Las Vegas during his second bout against Lennox Lewis. This lack of experience engendered considerable skepticism within the boxing community as to whether or not Memphis would be able to pull the fight off. Jay Larkin of Showtime spoke for many of his brethren when he was asked if Las Vegas would have been a preferable site.

"Oh, yeah," Larkin answered. "For every reason in the world. I don't want to sound like I'm coming down on Memphis, but Las Vegas does it better than everybody. Memphis has been very supportive. But in Vegas, you have 50,000 hotel rooms; you have dozens of world-class restaurants; you have organizations like the MGM Grand that can do this in their sleep. We're very happy this is going to Memphis. For that week, Memphis is going to be the center of our universe. But in retrospect, we all wish it could be in Las Vegas."

Meanwhile, after Tyson's profane outburst at a press gathering in Maui (the only time he spoke openly with the media before the fight), not everyone in Memphis was happy that the fight would be there either. But Mayor Willie Herenton did his best to put a positive spin on things, saying, "If you are asking me, do I or the citizens of Memphis condone the type of statements attributed to Mike Tyson, the answer is no. If you are asking me if Memphis is having any second thoughts about hosting the event, the answer is also no. Listen, we knew from the outset that there were some elements of risk in hosting this event. I regret that those statements were made. In Memphis, we respect women and children. We don't condone inappropriate behavior or language. However, we are still looking forward to hosting this great event."

However, just to be on the safe side, Memphis police director Walter Crews asked a local faith-based group called the Memphis Ten-Point Coalition to preach the gospel of Jesus Christ outside of clubs and the Pyramid Arena prior to the fight.

"The police will take care of the physical, and we will take care of Satan and his boys," explained coalition president, the Reverend Andrew Sullivan. "We will fight a spiritual warfare."

"They (fight fans) are coming to be entertained and are looking to fill a void," added coalition vice president, the Reverend Randolph Chappell. "We will show them it can be filled by the Father, God, through His Son, Jesus Christ."

Thus, it came to pass that, on the night of June 8, the streets of Memphis bore witness to volunteers wearing lime-green T-shirts that proclaimed, "Jesus Christ is the undisputed heavyweight champion of the world."

Meanwhile, the spirit of Elvis hovered above it all. Elvis moved with his parents from Tupelo, Mississippi, to Memphis just before his 14th birthday and graduated from Humes High School in 1953. Four years later, Graceland became his home.

Elvis is remembered as a lover, not a fighter. But from time to time, his life intersected with the sweet science. Elvis tried out for his high school boxing team, but quit the first day after suffering a bloody nose. Later, in the 1962 movie *Kid Galahad*, he played a sparring partner who turned pro.

During fight week, it was noted that Tyson sightings are now as varied as Elvis sightings and just as bizarre. But Elvis idolators bristled at the comparison and dismissed similarities between the two men with observations like, "Elvis was an icon; Tyson is an ex-con," and "Elvis was nuts, but he wasn't nasty."

Others saw a parallel between Elvis and Muhammad Ali. The King and The Greatest shared a genuine fondness for one another and met several times in the 1970s. "All my life, I admired Elvis," Ali later remembered. "When I was in Las Vegas, I heard him sing and it was a thrill to meet him."

Prior to Ali's 1973 bout against Joe Bugner, Presley gave him a bejeweled robe with the words "People's Champion" emblazoned on the back. Muhammad wore it for two fights. "Then I got my jaw broke," he recalled, "and I stopped wearing it. But I felt sorry for Elvis. He didn't enjoy life the way he should. He stayed indoors all the time. I told him he should go out and see people. He said he couldn't because, everywhere he went, they mobbed him. He didn't understand. No one wanted to hurt him. All they wanted was to be friendly and tell him how much they loved him."

But if Ali was sweet, Tyson is sour. And the fear in Memphis was that Lewis-Tyson would turn ugly.

Make that "uglier," because things were ugly from the start. Throughout fight week, there were references to "Disgraceland" and low blows that might cause "great balls of fire." One Memphian posited, "You know things are bad when the prostitutes and the lawyers descend on the town."

By Friday night, the Peabody Hotel was under seige. The lobby was mobbed. The street doors leading to its shops were locked. Pimps, pickpockets, and other hustlers roamed the sidewalks, mingling with the merely curious. A room key or media credential were required for entry into the hotel.

"We're all Johns in a whorehouse," said one writer in town for the fight.
"No we're not," said another. "We're working the joint."

But that was the name of the game. Nevada, New York, California, Texas, and myriad other states had said that Lewis-Tyson would be illegal within their borders. That's why the bout wound up in Tennessee.

Then came the fight. KO 8. It was a memorable night. June 8, 2002, will forever be an important part of boxing lore.

Now Lewis and Tyson have moved on, and Memphis belongs once again to Elvis. "Death Week" is coming up. August 16 will be the 25th anniversary of The King's passing. It should be big. ❏

*A telephone call from a man named Stephen Singer who was seeking leads in fulfilling a personal quest led to this article.*

# IN SEARCH OF JIM ROBINSON

The most valuable signature of any heavyweight champion is that of Marvin Hart, who won the vacant title by defeating 171-pound Jack Root in 1905 and lost in his first defense to Tommy Burns. That' s because there are very few Marvin Hart signatures around.

Similarly, to at least one collector, the most valuable signature of any Muhammad Ali opponent isn't Sonny Liston, Joe Frazier, or George Foreman. It's Jim Robinson.

Robinson was born in Kansas City in 1941 and turned pro at the age of 18. All but two of his fights took place in Florida. He was knocked out in each of his first six bouts. Then he turned things around, winning five of six, before losing 16 fights in a row. All totalled, Robinson's ring record was 5 wins and 23 losses. He scored one knockout and was KO'd 17 times.

Robinson's historical significance lies in the fact that, in his second pro fight, he was a last-minute replacement for Willie Galut in a bout that was held at Convention Hall in Miami Beach. The date was February 7, 1961. Robinson's opponent was Cassius Marcellus Clay, Jr.

"I'd read about Clay," Robinson reminisced years later. "My manager asked me if I wanted to fight him. I said I couldn't 'cause I only weighed 158 pounds. He said, 'We'll work something out.' Then, at the weigh in, he took my finger and pressed down until the scale said 178."

It was Clay's fourth professional fight. Cassius wasn't a big puncher. In fact, despite his greatness, he would score only two first-round knockouts in his entire career. One of those came in his curious rematch against Sonny Liston. The other was against Robinson.

Enter Stephen Singer, 55 years old, heavyset with shoulder-length hair. Singer was raised in New Hampshire. He went to high school and college at Yeshiva in New York. Then he returned home to work at a small used-car business owned by his father in Manchester. The business is still family-owned; run by Singer, four of his brothers, and their brother-in law. But it's no longer small. Merchants Automotive Group leases, rents, services, and sells automobiles and has gross revenues in excess of $150-million a year.

Singer has been an avid sports fan all his life. As a kid, he collected baseball cards and autographs. Next, he turned to New England sports memorabilia.

Then he was bitten by the Ali bug. One of the pieces in Singer's collection is an X-ray of Ali's jaw taken after it was broken by Ken Norton. That bit of history, signed by both fighters, rests in a shadow-box on display at Merchants Automotive Group not far from a life-size sculpture of Ali that stands in a 10-by-10-foot boxing ring.

In 1999, while reading *Sports Collectors Digest*, Singer saw a collage honoring the famed 1927 New York Yankees replete with cut signatures of each player. Properly inspired, he decided to collect a documented signature of every boxer that Ali fought during his professional career.

Ali fought 61 fights against 50 different opponents. Singer began his quest with the help of a sports memorabilia dealer. Once the dealer had gone as far as he could go, 37 of the requisite fifty signatures were in hand. Since then, Singer has garnered a dozen more on his own. "Every autograph has a story," he says. "And the stories are as neat as getting the autographs."

Singer tracked down the daughter of Ali's third pro victim, Tony Esperti, shortly after Esperti's death. She sold him a notarized stock transfer document signed by Esperti after his own wife had died. Zora Folley's widow was located in Arizona and parted with the signature page from her husband's passport.

Ultimately, Singer was left with his own personal "Final Four"—Rudi Lubbers, Alfredo Evangelista, Alejandro Lavorante, and Robinson.

Lubbers was the first to fall. As Singer explains, "I made contact with a boxing enthusiast in Holland who loved Little Richard. I sent him some CDs and a Rocky Marciano postage stamp that he wanted. Then he sent me a postcard that Lubbers had signed years ago. I offered to pay for it, but he told me, no, it was a gift from one collector to another."

Evangelista was next. In Singer's words, "I tracked him down in Madrid and spoke with him on the phone through a translator, but it was very frustrating. Months passed, and nothing got done. Finally, I found a Lubavitch rabbi in Madrid who sent one of his students with a photograph to a restaurant that Evangelista's brother owned. Alfredo came in and signed the photo. The student photographed him signing it so there wouldn't be a problem with authentication. Alfredo wouldn't take any money for signing, so I sent the rabbi a $500 donation."

Lavorante was Singer's most recent acquisition. That presented particular problems since Lavorante was knocked out by Ali in 1962 and died in Argentina two years later as a result of head trauma suffered in his next fight.

Singer hired a researcher who directed him to Lavorante's brother in Mendoza, Argentina. Then, once again, he retained a translator. "Eventually," Singer continues, "I was put in contact with Lavorante's sister, who also lived in Mendoza. She found Alejandro's passport and, after several months of negotiating, we agreed on a price of $2,500. But consummating the deal was complicated because we didn't know each other so we couldn't fully trust each other. Finally, I located a rabbi in Cordoba, Argentina, who flew to Mendoza and completed the transaction."

Singer estimates that he has spent about $35,000 on his "Ali opponents" project. Robinson's signature is the Holy Grail.

"I've spent a huge amount of time and money trying to locate Jim Robinson," Singer explains with a mix of frustration and enthusiasm in his voice. "Robinson fought mostly in Miami and Miami Beach, so I've been in touch with people like Angelo Dundee and Edwin Pope of the *Miami Herald*. I contacted the Florida State Athletic Commission, but all of their records prior to 1980 have been destroyed. I've talked with collectors like Craig Hamilton and historians like Hank Kaplan. I've had librarians and police departments try to track him down. But I've been unable to find Jim Robinson, a Jim Robinson signature, or any family member to help me out. There was a time when I thought I'd found him in Philadelphia. I even sent someone with a check for $350 and a photo to sign. But this Jim Robinson said, 'I'm Jim Robinson; I was a boxer; but I never fought Cassius Clay.'"

Singer doesn't know if the Jim Robinson he's seeking is dead or alive. Anyone with a legitimate lead is urged to call him toll-free at 1-800-288-6999.

Meanwhile, Singer says in closing, "Whatever you do, whether it's selling cars or collecting autographs, you have to do it with passion to have fun. But I'll be honest with you. I didn't realize the scope of this project when I started." ❏

*Most fight fans remember the first fight they went to. So do most boxing insiders.*

# THE FIRST PROFESSIONAL FIGHT THEY SAW

The first professional fight I ever went to was Floyd Patterson versus George Chuvalo at Madison Square Garden on February 1, 1965.

My uncle took me. I was an avid sports fan, 18 years old. I'd been to countless baseball games and seen my share of basketball, football, and hockey. But I'd never been to a fight.

Patterson had been devasted twice by Sonny Liston and come back with victories over Sante Amonte, Eddie Machen, and Charlie Powell. Meanwhile, Liston had lost to Cassius Clay (who then changed his name to Muhammad Ali), and the world was awaiting their rematch. If Ali and Patterson both won, Floyd would get another shot at the crown.

I don't remember much about the undercard, but that's par for the course. The Garden crowd was overwhelmingly pro-Patterson. It chanted his name from time to time, and Floyd responded by winning a unanimous 12-round decision.

Recently, with those memories in mind, I asked some of boxing's finest about the first fight they ever saw. The first professional bout that Don King attended was Sugar Ray Robinson against Artie Levine in Cleveland on November 6, 1946. Robinson won on a 10th-round knockout, but there was considerable controversy surrounding the outcome. Early in the fight, Levine knocked Robinson down. Ray himself later acknowledged that it was the hardest he was ever hit. But after walking Levine to a neutral corner, the referee returned to Sugar Ray and picked up the count at "one"—a quintessential "long count." Other than the Joey Maxim fight, it was the closest Robinson ever came to being knocked out.

King's thoughts regarding that night and the recollections of some of his brethren follow.

### Don King

My first memories of boxing were of listening to Joe Louis on the radio. We all listened to every fight Joe had. It didn't matter who the opponent was. But that night with Robinson was the first fight I was at. What a piece of work Robinson was. He's the greatest fighter who ever lived. I would have loved to promote Sugar Ray Robinson. He was supreme in every way. He'd glide in the ring like a ballet dancer. He could knock you out with either hand, going forward or backward. What a fighter! And the fights were almost incidental to who he was. Sugar Ray Robinson was the classic theatrical production. If I had Sugar Ray Robinson today, he'd be the first billionaire fighter.

### Larry Merchant

It was in the 1940s. I was 10 years old, maybe younger. My uncle had been an amateur fighter, and he took me to see two lightweights named Bobby Ruffin and Johnny Greco fight at Madison Square Garden. This was the old Garden, the one on Eighth Avenue between 49th and 50th Streets. It was my first trip to the Garden. And I think Greco won, but I'm not sure. I will say, though, that the night had a profound effect on me. The next morning, I read in Dan Parker's column in the *New York Daily Mirror* that Ruffin had thrown up in his corner. The way Parker phrased it was, "He gave up his fish dinner." I had missed that. I hadn't seen it happen. And I decided right then and there that, whatever I did in life, I wanted to get closer to ringside so I could see all the action.

### Michael Buffer

My first boxing memory is of my dad keeping me up late one night to watch the rematch between Rocky Marciano and Jersey Joe Walcott on one of those old RCA Victor television sets with the 12-inch screens and big mahogany doors. And I went to a Muhammad Ali exhibition at the Cherry Hills Arena in New Jersey when Ali was in exile. But the first real fight I went to in person was at the Spectrum in Philadelphia in the early 1970s. I was a car salesman at the time; everything from Cadillacs to Volkswagens. I got fired everywhere because I was a lousy salesman, so I just moved from one dealer to another. I went to the Spectrum alone that night. I just wanted to see a fight. A light-heavyweight named Richie Kates fought someone in the main event, got knocked down, and came back to win. I don't remember who the opponent was. At the time, making a living from boxing was the furthest thing from my mind.

### Arthur Mercante

I have a family history in boxing. My uncle, Joe Monte, was a pretty good heavyweight. He fought Max Schmeling at Madison Square Garden in Schmeling's American debut and was ahead on the scorecards when he got stopped by a punch to the solar plexus in the eighth round. He also fought James Braddock three times before Braddock became heavyweight champion. Each fight went the distance. My uncle won one, Braddock won one, and there was one draw. But I never saw my uncle fight. The first professional fight I actually went to was Sugar Ray Robinson against Joey Maxim for the light-heavyweight championship at Yankee Stadium [on June 25, 1952]. I'd started refereeing in the amateurs when I got out of the Navy in 1946, but I didn't get involved with the pros until 1954. Robinson-Maxim was a fight I wanted to see, and I went to the Stadium alone. Sugar Ray fought his heart out. Maxim didn't do much except survive, but that was enough. It was brutally hot and humid. Ruby Goldstein, who was the referee, collapsed from the heat after the 10th round and was replaced by Ray Miller. Then Robinson succumbed to the heat and was unable to come out for the 14th round.

### Lou Duva

It was outdoors at the Market Street Arena in Patterson, New Jersey. I was 10 or 11 years old. My brother Carl fought a guy named Benny Gualano. I carried my brother's bag that night and went into the dressing room with him. My brother won a decision. After that, I started hanging around gyms a lot, and eventually boxing became my life. My brother was a good fighter. I'm talking about an era when guys fought every other week. There were club fighters who had 200 fights. Almost everyone had a day job, driving a truck or working in a factory, and they trained at night. My brother worked in a dye house. He had about 85 pro fights and won most of them. His manager was Bill Daley, who managed a lot of champions. I miss those days. That was the era, baby. That was boxing.

### Marc Ratner

It was Joe Brown against Carlos Ortiz [on April 21, 1962]. Brown was the lightweight champion. He'd held the title for a long time. And this was an era when you didn't have the proliferation of belts that you have today, so being a champion really meant something. I was a fan. Fights weren't nearly as common in Las Vegas as they are now, and I'd just gotten my driver's license, so I went to the Las Vegas Convention Center with some friends. Ortiz won a 15-round decision. It was a big upset. And the boxing bug bit me. A year later, Sonny Liston and Floyd Patterson fought their rematch at the Las Vegas Convention Center, and I was the first person on line to buy tickets for the fight. By the way, I still have the ticket stub from Brown versus Ortiz.

### Cedric Kushner

The first professional fight I went to was the second Ali-Frazier contest at Madison Square Garden [on January 28, 1974]. I was working as messenger for the Australian Consulate with thoughts of someday becoming a rock promoter and no thought at all about ever becoming involved with boxing. I purchased a ticket at the box office in advance and went alone. And it was a thrilling night. I consider myself fortunate to have been there. Afterward, I got Ted Kennedy's signature on my fight program. I remember being surprised that he was at the fight. I had always perceived of him as a liberal. And for a brief period in my life, I didn't think that liberals attended fights because of the violence. But Ted Kennedy was there, and he signed my program for me.

### Don Elbaum

My uncle, his name was Danny Greenstein, was an amateur boxer. Great fighter. Forty-two wins and no losses as an amateur with 41 knockouts. He was also a legendary street-fighter in New Bedford and Fall River [towns in Massachusetts]. Al Weil, who managed Rocky Marciano, begged my uncle to turn pro, but he refused. He fought for fun. [Author's Note: Don Elbaum is a wonderful guy, but he has been known to exaggerate. It's possible that his uncle's record would be remembered differently by others.] Anyway, Uncle Danny was my hero and he took me to my first fight. Willie Pep against Paulie Jackson at Sargeant Field in New Bedford [on July 15, 1947]. It was outdoors, a great summer night. Pep was featherweight champion of the world and he'd beaten Jackson twice before. He won this one too. He boxed Jackson's ears off. He was incredible, a virtuoso artist in total control. At one point, Jackson got him in a corner, threw 20 punches, and missed with every one of them. Each judge gave Willie all 10 rounds. I was eight years old, and I was totally mesmerized, in awe. I went home that night and told my mother that I wanted to be a fighter. Everybody laughed at me, but I was hooked. That night either made my life or it destroyed my life. It depends on how you look at it.

### Seth Abraham

I was a special assistant to Bowie Kuhn [the commissioner of Major League Baseball], and my wife Lynn was a legal librarian at Simpson Thatcher & Bartlett [a Wall Street law firm]. Simpson Thatcher represented Gulf & Western, and Gulf & Western owned Madison Square Garden. Two associates from the firm and their wives were going to see Wilfred Benitez fight Harold Weston [on February 2, 1977], and asked Lynn if we'd like to join them. Benitez won. There was nothing remarkable about the fight, but I found it thrilling. I'd seen countless fights before on television but, sitting at this one, I was struck by the realization that every other sport has some type of time frame; either a clock or a given number of innings or whatever. And a fight can end at any moment. I suppose that's obvious, but it was an epiphany for me, and the excitement of that night stayed with me. A year later, I went to HBO believing that boxing had all the elements of great drama and great television.

### Angelo Dundee

I was born in Philly, which was a hotbed of boxing, and my brother Chris was managing fighters. He's the one who took me to my first pro fight. It was in the 1930s; I think at Philadelphia Arena. I was a school-kid, maybe 13 years old. Tommy Cross fought Norman Quarles. Cross was one of the toughest guys in Philly. He figured to destroy Quarles. But they bumped heads; Tommy got all busted up. And in those days, if you couldn't continue because of a head-butt, you lost, so Quarles won on a technical knockout. God, that was a long time ago.

### Jim Lampley

Cassius Clay versus Sonny Liston on February 25, 1964. We lived in a tract house in Miami. I was 14 years old and a huge Cassius Clay fan. Most of our racist neighbors were offended by the Negro braggart, but he had me totally enthralled. Anyway, I saved up all of my lawn-mowing money and all of my car-washing money and bought what memory tells me was a $100 or $150 ticket. My mom dropped me off at the Convention Center before the fight and picked me up at a designated spot afterward. And when we got home, I was so excited that I climbed onto the roof of our house and started yelling, "I am the greatest! I shook up the world." And that was it. I didn't go to another fight until my audition call for ABC Sports in January of 1986 when Bert Cooper fought Reggie Gross. ABC hired me, and my third fight was my first as a blow-by-blow commentator, Mike Tyson against Jesse Ferguson later that year.

### Emanuel Steward

The first professional fight I went to was Gene Gresham against Leroy Jeffery in Detroit [on November 11, 1957]. I was 14 years old, already boxing as an amateur. Gresham had moved in across the street from where I lived, so he was a hero of mine. Gresham and Jeffery were both undefeated. Gresham won a 10-round decision. And what impressed me most about the night was the difference between professional and amateur boxing, that and the excitement of it all. A year later, I sparred with Gresham. That was special to me.

### Larry Holmes

My trainer, Ernie Butler, took me to a pro-am night at Sunnyside Gardens in Queens when I was 19 or 20 years old. I fought an amateur exhibition that night and don't remember anything about who else was on the card. The first all-professional fights I went to were at Madison Square Garden [on June 26, 1972] when Roberto Duran knocked out Ken Buchanan to win the world lightweight title. I never classify greatness. "Greatness" is a big word. But watching Duran that night, I knew I was looking at a guy who could fight his ass off. Ernie Butler took me to that one too. He told me that night, "If you make it to the big time, this is where you'll be someday." And the next time I went to a pro fight, it was my own. Larry Holmes against Rodell Dupree in Scranton, Pennsylvania [on March 21, 1973]. I'd never gone four rounds before and I was worried about the distance, but I did it. The record book says so—"Larry Holmes, W4." ❑

*As I've noted many times, Don King and Bernard Hopkins are prolific quote making machines.*

# THE QUOTABLE MR. KING AND THE QUOTABLE MR. HOPKINS

Now that Don King is promoting Bernard Hopkins, they constitute boxing's most quotable couple. Neither of them has ever lost a press conference. Give either one a microphone, and a luncheon turns into a dinner. Herewith, a sampling of their thoughts:

Bernard Hopkins: I always had leadership qualities. Fifth grade, sixth grade; if someone was messing with another kid, he'd come to me for protection. It wasn't free. Maybe it was just a peanut butter sandwich with bananas, which was my favorite sandwich, but I always charged something.

Don King [on his first career as a numbers czar in Cleveland]: In the numbers business, you don't have the luxury of an office with file clerks and telephone answerers. You have to do most of it out of your head, always be on the run, and still come out with a profit. I had to establish liaisons, same as I do now in boxing. I started in numbers when I was 19 years old and I went to the top. They called me Kingpin and The Czar and Donald "The Kid" King. I was good.

Bernard Hopkins [on being sentenced to a term of up to 18 years in prison at age 17]: I don't blame the judge. I'm not blaming anyone but Bernard Hopkins for putting myself and my family in that situation. Maybe society put the traps there for me to fall into. But if you fall into them, it's your own fault. I'd been in court 30 times in two years. What else was the judge supposed to do?

Don King [on his time in prison]: Jail was my school. I had one of the most delightful times under desperate conditions. I read Aristotle and Homer. I got into Sigmund Freud. When I dealt with William Shakespeare, I got to know him very well as a man. I love Bill Shakespeare. He was some bad dude. Intellectually, I went into jail with a pea-shooter and came out armed with a nuclear bomb.

Bernard Hopkins [on being in prison]: Boxing was my best therapy. It saved my sanity. They said I was punch-drunk. They said I was crazy. I used to run the prison yard like a gerbil on a wheel, around and around, around and around, saying over and over to myself, "Someday, I'm gonna get out of here. Someday, I'm gonna be a champion."

Don King: White America didn't exactly open up its arms to me. I had to work harder than most people for what I got. I wasn't invited to any board meetings. I had to kick down the doors.

Bernard Hopkins: Every time a fighter steps into the ring, he's risking his life for other people's entertainment. If you don't believe me when I say that, go ask Gerald McClellan.

Don King: There's something I learned a long time ago. You don't get what you deserve in life. You get what you negotiate.

Bernard Hopkins [on the downside of being a professional fighter]: You do get hit.

Don King: "Setback" is in my vocabulary now and then. But "failure" never.

Bernard Hopkins: In the ring, I'm a dangerous guy. I destroy careers. I ruin other people's dreams. In the ring, all fights are grudge matches.

Don King [when asked about Mike Tyson's multi-million-dollar lawsuit against him]: I don't comment on Mike Tyson. Don't have to. Even Ray Charles can see what's happening.

Bernard Hopkins: Boxing is war. Boxing is serious. It ain't no joke; it ain't no show. You have to think violent. Don't cry and complain to the referee, "Bernard is hurting me." We're not in church; we're fighting. If you want to not get a bruise, then go play golf.

Don King: I never met a man I couldn't work with.

Bernard Hopkins [on the WBA declaring him a "super champion" and designating William Joppy as its "world champion," thereby enabling it to collect two sanctioning fees in the middleweight division]: I don't have a college degree, but I know that's double-dipping.

Don King: I ain't asking people to love me; just respect me.

Bernard Hopkins: The business of boxing makes you want to take a shower every time you deal with it.

Don King: You have to understand, bullshit helps flowers grow.

Bernard Hopkins: Losing is part of life. Sometimes you have to lose to get educated. But that should never become an excuse for not doing your best.

Don King: [explaining why he won't tell Evander Holyfield to retire]: The last guy I told to retire was Roberto Duran. I felt about Duran the same way some people feel about Evander today. Duran lost in Detroit to a club fighter named Kirkland Laing. So I invited Roberto to my apartment in New York and told him I loved him and that he had to retire. And what Roberto did then was, he went over to my archrival Bob Arum and beat Davey Moore to win the WBA title and he beat Iran Barkley and he almost beat Marvin Hagler. And then George Foreman comes back at age 46 and wins the heavyweight title. So I learned my lesson about telling fighters when they should retire.

Bernard Hopkins: The reason Roy Jones, Jr. doesn't want to fight me is because I remind him too much of his father when his father used to kick his ass and throw him into the pool and make him swim. And he's also having flashbacks to when his dog got shot by his father when it bit his sister. I've come to the decision now that Roy Jones, Jr. is scared of Bernard Hopkins.

Don King: [on the ubiquitous "black boxes" that are cutting into pay-per-view sales]: No matter how good you are at securing and protecting your signal, there will always be people who steal it. It's like with a bank. No matter how strong your vault is, there will always be people who break in. And you have to admire the rogues. But I will say, the black boxes are a problem, a big problem.

Bernard Hopkins [with more on Roy Jones, Jr.]: Where did a guy that feeds pigs and raises chickens try to become a city hip-hopper with his hat backwards looking like a babbling idiot? What's wrong with the guy? I mean, be proud you're from Pensacola, Florida. If you ain't from New York, don't act like a New Yorker. Now, he's this rough-ryder-hip-hop-DMX Roy Jones Jr. rap-artist gangster. You know what it is? The man wants to be me. Roy's got a complex where he wants to be me.

Don King [on his jewelry]: If you've got it, flaunt it. The baubles get attention. You see, the system puts diamonds at the top. If I wear diamonds, I get the ear of those within the system who are less fortunate than I am and who want to get to the top like I did. It's like the bait going on the hook for the fish. Young pugilists see the glitter and sparkle, and it draws them to me like a moth to a flame. Then, once I do my job properly, the job supercedes the baubles.

Bernard Hopkins: I respect Roy Jones, even if Roy hasn't given proper respect to me. But I don't know about Roy. Roy plays basketball; Roy feeds his chickens. That's a sign of being punchy, when you follow animals around like a big flood is coming.

Don King: If I could go back in time and have dinner with one person; let me think. There's Plato, Socrates, Cicero, Caesar, Frederick Douglas, George Washington Carver, Winston Churchill. I think that Frederick Douglas would be my first choice.

Bernard Hopkins: I've got one of the best chins in boxing. I don't want to prove that to you, but it's true.

Don King: I talk with bravado, but I'm really a henpecked guy. My wonderful wife Henrietta controls all the money in the family and tells me what to do completely.

Bernard Hopkins: If I don't have my spirit, what good is money?

Don King: I love what I do. I love the life I live, and I live the life I love.

Bernard Hopkins: I don't mind Don King or Bob Arum or Cedric Kushner making money. But I'd like to see them with a twisted nose too. ❏

*Marilyn Cole Lownes and I collaborated on this article about black-tie boxing in New York.*

# TOMMY GALLAGHER AND CIPRIANI

It's an odd pairing; boxing trainer Tommy Gallagher and black tie society.

Gallagher's world is club fights. He's an old-school Runyanesque boxing guy, who knows the sweet science from the gutter up. He won the New York City Golden Gloves welterweight crown in 1959 and, two years later while in the military, was a member of the All-Army Boxing team. From 1967 through 1974, he trained amateurs in a YMCA boxing program in Queens. Then, in 1974, he opened "Gallagher's Gym of Champions". The fighters he has worked with over the years include Vito Antuofermo, Mark Breland, Doug DeWit, Eddie Mustapha, Mike McCallum, Michael Dokes, and Donny LaLonde. "What I do best," says Gallagher, "is scout fighters."

Gallagher also is the driving force behind Thomas Gallagher Promotions. Tommy's wife Maureen is the president of TGP. Last year, they promoted four shows, all at Aqueduct Racetrack.

Meanwhile, the Cipriani name is synonymous with elegance. The Cipriani empire began with Harry's Bar in Venice, where a concoction of prosecco and fresh peach juice known as a "Bellini" was first served. Cipriani properties in New York include the Rainbow Room, Harry's Bar and Restaurant at the Sherry Netherland Hotel, Downtown (a smaller bar and restaurant), The Mews (a private catering hall), Cipriani Dolci (a restaurant in Grand Central Station), Cipriani La Specialita (a gourmet deli), and Cipriani 42nd Street.

The latter is particularly imposing. Built in 1921 as headquarters for the Bowery Bank, it has a landmark interior, marble floors, and majestic columns leading to a 65-foot ceiling. Cipriani took the space over in 1999 to service corporate functions and other private parties at $400 a plate. In recent months, the site has hosted such affairs as Puff Daddy's fashion show, the Vogue-VH1 Music Awards, and various New York society charity events.

On March 15, 2002, the worlds of Tommy Gallagher and Cipriani converged when TGP promoted a night of "black tie boxing" at Cipriani 42nd Street. Tickets were priced at $200 and $150. At the start of the evening, an army of white-jacketed waiters circulated through the crowd serving delicate canapes worthy of their surroundings. That was followed by a gourmet sit-down dinner of lobster salad, risotto, lamb, tiramisu, and petits fours. The sounds of swing-era music reverberated throughout the hall.

"They really did this on an uppity scale," one fight fan noted.

Glamour had returned to boxing.

There was a lot of flesh, in and out the ring. Sensuous elegantly dressed women, some of them brought and some of them bought, were much in evidence. Ladies from The VIP Club (a local adult establishment) were seeded throughout the crowd. The sexual energy was palpable as gladitorial combat unfolded amidst grandeur reminiscent of an earlier era. There was a buzz.

At times, the ring action seemed like a cabaret show; so much else was going on. But the battles were real. Yuri Foreman and Brian Viloria showed promised in stopping their opponents. Golden Johnson KO'd Chantel Stanciel in 11. And Tukonbo Olijade moved closer to stardom with a devastating one-punch knockout of Trevor Brown.

Afterward, Foreman, who immigrated to Israel from Russia at age 11 and to the United States in 1999, observed, "In Russia, I was a Jew. In Israel, I was a Russian. Here, I'm a New Yorker, and I love it." Meanwhile, Olajide asked rhetorically, "What better place to look good than this place here?"

Gallagher hopes to promote "black tie" shows monthly and plans to expand to other "in" sites like the Hamptons in tandem with Cipriani. "We're trying to get boxing back in New York on a regular basis," he said at night's end. "To do that, we're aiming for upscale clientele. That's the idea behind the venue and the black-tie bit. I want to make a splash and recapture some of what boxing was like in the 1920s."

He's off to a good start. March 15 at Cipriani 42nd Street was a happening, Everyone who was there got their money's worth. And while Cipriani is known for elegance throughout the world, it needed a Tommy Gallagher to make the night happen. ❏

*Marilyn Cole Lownes and I collaborated again when we journeyed to Atlantic City for the second fight between Micky Ward and Arturo Gatti.*

# THE REFUGE

The hopes of gamblers run high in Atlantic City. And boxing is a sport where glory is always tantalizingly within reach. Add in the Boardwalk, sprinkle the Miss America Pageant, a few roundcard girls, and Boardwalk Hall into the mix. And presto! Boxing and Atlantic City are a match.

The Boardwalk in Atlantic City conjures up images of a journeyman fighter with more of a past than a future. The day before Ward Gatti II, panhandlers and down-and-out loiterers were much in evidence on the streets with Monopoly-board names. The ocean breezes of summer had given way to a chill fog. Huge seagulls flew overhead, landing when and where they chose. After a while, kitsch became seedy as fight fans wandered past a proliferation of outlets offering junk food, shoddy merchandise, two-dollar arcades, psychic readers, and 99-cent wares.

The casinos towered above it all. At Bally's, Caesars, and the Taj Mahal, the assault on the senses was the same. Jangling coins, electronically simulated chimes and bells, an unceasing cacophony of sound. Action, movement, garish colors; a LeRoy Neiman painting come to life.

Most of the people funneling coins into the slot machines that lined the casino floors were destined to lose. To believe otherwise would be to pretend. But in a boxing ring, there is no pretend. In the ring, there's honesty in the winning and losing. The ring is a refuge from phoniness and glitz. And in the ring, on any given night, half of all dreams come true. ❏

*2002 was a glorious year for Lennox Lewis. 2003 was a bit tarnished.*

# LEWIS-KLITSCHKO AND OTHER HAPPENINGS

Lennox Lewis almost gave away the heavyweight championship of the world last Saturday night [June 21, 2003].

It was an exciting dramatic fight. But no matter what Lewis says, he was out of shape and overweight for his bout against Vitali Klitschko. His timing was off. He was sucking air after three rounds. Lennox had thought he could win by simply showing up. He looked like anything but the master boxer he takes pride in being.

As the bout progressed, there was more brawling than boxing and the match-up came to resemble a toughman contest. Lewis' advancing age might also have been a factor.

Klitschko had an edge in the first round and wobbled Lewis with a straight right a minute into the second stanza. After that round, trainer Emanuel Steward told his charge, "He's winning the fight. You've got to take it to him." Lewis did just that, opening up a gaping cut on Klitschko's left eyelid with a glancing right hand early in round three. But by round four, Lennox was exhausted. From that point on, the bout was reminiscent of his 1996 fight against Ray Mercer when, in the late rounds, he had to stand and fight because there was nothing else he could do.

But fortunately for Lewis, Klitschko's eyelid had been ripped open. It was a horrible cut. After six rounds, Dr. Paul Wallace stopped the fight. Klitschko was ahead 58-56 on all three scorecards at the time of the stoppage.

Anybody who draws a parallel between this fight and the Gatti-Ward trilogy is missing the point. Gatti and Ward were in shape to go the distance each time. Lewis wasn't. He rarely threw his jab with authority and fought like the bully in a schoolyard brawl who loses all semblance of technique and simply slugs away.

Meanwhile, no matter how bitterly disappointing the outcome was for Klitschko, the wisdom of the stoppage was confirmed in his dressing room after the fight. Klitschko lay on a table on his back. His wife was holding one of his hands. His brother Wladimir held the other. The doctor who was about to suture the ugly gash was trying unsuccessfully to find a spot on Klitschko's eyelid to put the anesthesia. Wherever he inserted the needle, the skin shredded away. There was both a vertical and a horizontal flap. Cuts of that nature increase the chances of damage to a person's optic nerves and muscles.

Anyone with questions on that point should ask David Reid.

In retrospect, Lewis-Klitschko offers an opportunity to evaluate the California practice of stopping the clock while a ring doctor examines a cut between rounds. The rationale for this practice is that it's important for the doctor to probe closely and his examination shouldn't take away from the 60 seconds allotted to the cutman to do his job. Opponents of the practice argue that a good ring doctor can assess damage by watching the cutman in action and that granting an extra 30 seconds between rounds changes the dynamic of a fight.

Three times on Saturday night, the ring doctor ordered the clock stopped while he examined Klitschko's eye. The beneficiary appeared to be Lewis, who looked as though he needed the extra time to recover more than Klitschko. Further discussion on this issue leading to a national standard would be desirable.

Meanwhile, it's hard to ignore HBO's curious use of Bob Costas, who opened the telecast while Jim Lampley and Larry Merchant were kept off-camera for the first 15 minutes. Costas is a superb play-by-play baseball announcer. He's as good as anyone in the business when it comes to basketball. He's an intelligent, articulate interviewer. But Costas is not a boxing expert.

Lampley and Merchant are the best announcing team in the history of the sweet science. They don't need help. It's an insult to boxing, and also to Lampley and Merchant, to begin a telecast with Bob Costas reading from a teleprompter.

Also, it should be noted that HBO's audience didn't see the actual stoppage of the fight. That's because, at the time, Lampley was, as instructed, reading a full-screen promo for *Real Sports* and *On The Record*. One expects the *New York Post* to dispatch seven reporters to the scene to cover Mike Tyson's release from police custody after a five-o'clock-in-the-morning brawl. But one would hope that HBO, which is the standard-bearer for boxing in today's entertainment-driven world, would have a better sense of priorities.

Then again, one never knows what makes for a big story in boxing. Take, for example, "The Samantha Shoe Caper." Tim Smith broke the story on June 11 in the *New York Daily News*.

"An hour after Arturo Gatti and Mickey Ward went toe-to-toe at Boardwalk Hall in Atlantic City on Saturday night," Smith wrote, "Samantha Davis, the wife of HBO Sports boxing czar, Kery Davis, went toe-to-heel with the Atlantic City boardwalk. The heel of Mrs. Davis' expensive Gucci shoe got stuck in a crack in the boardwalk. She refused to let anyone else dislodge the shoe. After about three rounds of pulling and tugging, 'Shoeless Sam' KO'd the boardwalk. The shoe, heel intact, was saved."

Thereafter, the story spread like wildfire. On June 15, George Kimball of the *Boston Herald* published his own eye-witness account. Never mind that, the same week, Lewis and Klitschko signed to fight on short notice; the Nevada State Athletic Commission enacted a rule requiring MRI testing for all fighters; Joe DeGuardia won an arbitration against Antonio Tarver that will reshape the light-heavyweight division; and Marco Antonio Barrera sued to free himself contractually from his manager and promoter. The Samantha Shoe Caper is a saga teeming with glitz and drama. Gucci footwear is favored by the fashion elite, wildly expensive, and the height of glamour. Moreover, Gucci shoes are known for their "killer heels." This refers to the damage that can be inflicted by a swift kick and also the fact that the heels are murder on one's feet.

Thus, given HBO's penchant for human interest stories, and keeping in mind that Smith and Kimball are among the best role models that the boxing writers fraternity has to offer, I'd like to report (tongue in cheek) the following postscript to Lewis-Klitschko:

Harold Lederman was devastated when he went to the pressroom after the weigh-in and found that the sandwiches and chocolate chip cookies were all gone. "This is horrible," wailed Lederman. "I've been looking forward to those cookies for an entire week." Fortunately, a crisis was averted when someone from the California State Athletic Commission gave Lederman a Three Musketeers candy bar.

Shortly before Lewis and Klitschko entered the ring, Michael Buffer was seen in a panic, frantically running down a Los Angeles street, looking for hairspray. When Buffer finally found a drug store, he ran into Oscar De La Hoya, who was buying hair gel.

Lou DiBella was at home eating spare-ribs just before the fight and got a sliver of pork stuck between his teeth. "Thank God I had some dental floss in the medicine cabinet," DiBella revealed afterward. "But even then, it took forever to floss it out."

Cedric Kushner lost his cell phone. "You can't imagine the wave of panic that swept over me," Kushner later acknowledged. "But I'm quite resourceful, so I dialed my own cell phone number. An attendant in a washroom at the Staples Center, where I had inadvertently left the phone, answered. And I was able to retrieve the phone with a minimum of inconvenience."

And last but not least . . .

Madison Square Garden president Seth Abraham suffered a momentary crisis while dining at La Grenouille on the night of the fight when he noticed a mealy bug on the rose in his button hole. But Abraham, who earned a reputation as one of boxing's great minds while at HBO, didn't panic. He simply discarded the rose and replaced it with one from the floral arrangement on the table in front of him. ❏

*On occasion, I like to bundle some miscellaneous thoughts on boxing.*

# SOME THOUGHTS ON BOXING

The difference between a champion and an also-ran is that an also-ran does things almost right and a champion does them exactly right.

Boxing isn't staged. Things don't happen on cue. That's one of the reasons great fights are so special.

In the toughest of fights, a champion hangs on when a lesser fighter would let go.

It takes great pride to be a great fighter.

A boxing ring is one of the few places where violence is an acceptable means to an end.

One punch can kill a fighter.

Great fighters know who the great fighters are.

Fighters enter into a simple transaction—blood and sweat for gold and glory.

Think about what it takes for a fighter to get up off the canvas. He's being beaten up. He's hurt. He's groggy. His ribs ache. He's getting punched in the face. And he's asking for more.

Boxing is a tough business. It gets tougher when a fighter makes stupid choices.

No matter how good a fighter is, most likely in the end, he'll break your heart.

A loss does more to derail a career in boxing than in any other sport.

In boxing, longevity is a destroyer.

There's no "when" in boxing; only "if."

Success is never final in boxing.

The beatings a fighter endures add up. A fighter has only so many tough fights in his body and mind.

Boxing is a metaphor for life. One moment of violence can change everything.

Boxing has more interesting people per capita than any other business in the world.

Oscar De La Hoya knows how to win rounds, but sometimes he's unwilling to pay the price.

No one can ever bet with certainty against Mike Tyson.

There are times when Roy Jones, Jr. makes putting together a fight deal seem like root canal work. But it's even more unpleasant to fight him.

John Ruiz looks like an affable department store security guard.

Boxing brings out weakness of character, both in and out of the ring, more quickly than any other endeavor.

A boxing promoter is a man who lends you his umbrella when the sun is shining and wants it back when it starts to rain.

Why are bad decisions called "Las Vegas decisions" when the promoter is Bob Arum and "Don King decisions" when the promoter is King?

In boxing, it's easier to fight for one's principles than it is to live up to them.

The world sanctioning organizations are like arthritis. After a while, you get used to the pain. But every now and then, one of them flares up in a particularly troublesome manner.

The logo for HBO Pay-Per-View looks like the logo for a fast-food hamburger chain.

If a ring judge lacks the courage of his convictions, he'll score close rounds for whichever fighter is favored going into a bout. A ring judge who's mentally weak is as unsuited for his job as a fighter who's mentally weak.

Contrary to what people think, James Toney is in shape. Round is a shape.

If they ever make a movie about Lou DiBella, the title role should be played by James Gandolfini.

Having Will Smith play Muhammad Ali is like having Anna Nicole Smith play Anita Ekberg. It doesn't work.

Separated at birth: Harold Lederman and Ed Koch.

Separated at birth: Dr. Margaret Goodman and Jessica Rabbit.

True or false: Don King is playing the role of Captain Hook in a Broadway revival of Peter Pan.

True or false? Pierce Brosnan's contract has been terminated. The next James Bond will be Michael Buffer.

Believe It Or Not: Lou DiBella and Bernard Hopkins got married on the same day, August 28, 1993.

Believe It Or Not: Don King and Seth Abraham were both born on August 20, King in 1930 and Abraham in 1947.

Lou DiBella is finding out that it hurts to be on the cutting edge in boxing.

Boxing is such a chaotic mess that it belongs on the Internet.

Boxing is going to be boxing. No one will ever change it.

There's a school of thought that all is fair in love, war, and boxing.

The business of boxing is like a chess game that goes on and on and on. ❏

*Robson Books has done a great deal for boxing, so it seemed appropriate to write about them.*

# ROBSON BOOKS

The most prolific publisher of boxing books in the world is Robson Books. Jeremy Robson, who founded the company with his wife Carole, was born in North Wales and raised in London. At the start of his career, he worked as a magazine sub-editor, edited several anthologies of contemporary poetry, and served as poetry critic for a weekly newspaper called *Tribune*. In addition, he wrote his own poetry, later published in two volumes by Allison & Busby and Sidjwick & Jackson (which also published Rupert Brooke).

"Then, one day, "Robson recalls," I got a telephone call from the literary editor at *Tribune*, who said that Aldus Books was looking for an editor. Aldus published lavish illustrated books. I got the job, and became the editor of *The World of Marc Chagall*. After that, I edited a book with David Ben Gurion, *The Jews in Their Land*. In fact, Carole and I spent our honeymoon in Israel with Ben Gurion."

Robson was at Aldus for seven years, organizing poetry readings and jazz concerts on the side. Then he moved to Vallentine Mitchell, which merged with an academic publisher that wanted to develop a general trade list. "I brought them a book called *The Goon Show* that sold hundreds of thousands of copies and went to number one on the bestseller list," Robson remembers. "Then, one night at a dinner party, an old school friend who had become a real estate tycoon asked me, 'Why are you doing this for other people? How much money would it take for me to set you up in your own business?'"

Robson Books is now 30 years old. The company was acquired recently by Chrysalis (a British media conglomerate), but Jeremy still oversees its day-to-day operations.

Regarding his tilt toward the sweet science, Robson explains, "My father was always interested in boxing. He was a doctor and on occasion worked at amateur ring contests. Also, having been brought up in an era of anti-Semitism, he was keen on my learning how to box. I was never a boxer, really. But I boxed in school and, at age 14, was school champion in my weight class."

The first boxing book Robson published was *In This Corner*. "Ted 'Kid' Lewis called to complain afterward," Robson remembers. "He was very angry that he'd been described in the book as a dirty fighter. So we talked for a while and wound up publishing his autobiography."

Three dozen more boxing titles followed.

"The prevailing wisdom is that boxing books don't sell," Robson acknowledges. "And to a degree, that's true. But we've had two boxing books on the bestseller list and hope springs eternal for more in the future."

At this point, I should note that four of my own books—*The Black Lights, Mark Twain Remembers, Brutal Artistry,* and *Muhammad Ali: His Life and Times*—have been published by Robson Books. The Ali book is Robson's biggest boxing bestseller to date. But it's just as memorable for the bizarre promotional tour that accompanied its launch in England.

In September 1991, Howard Bingham (Muhammad's longtime friend) and I journeyed to London. Ali was supposed to meet us there. The problem was, he didn't. A week earlier, Herbert Muhammad (Ali's former manager) had taken him to Abu Dhabi in an effort to raise funds for a proposed Chicago mosque that was to be built with Herbert's involvement. Herbert had promised to have Ali in London for the start of our publicity tour. But Herbert didn't like the way I'd portrayed him in the book. And once he had Ali in Abu Dhabi, things changed. The result was a two-week publicity campaign replete with elaborate dinners, book-signings, and interviews that devolved into chaos.

The London media had a grand time with it. "Ali Held In Abu Dhabi," screamed one headline above the subtitle, "Advisors Have Poisoned His Mind." *The Express* ran a page-one photo of Ali sitting with four men in Abu Dhabi above the legend, "Revealed: The Mystery Men Behind Absent Ali." Nor was the story confined to London. "Ali Mystery As Wife Pleads For Safe Return," cried the *Manchester Post*. The *Times of London, Guardian, Independent, Observer, Evening Standard,* and *News of the World*, all weighed in. The British Press Association issued repeated bulletins on the matter including quotes from someone named Rashaad Mousoui, who described himself as a spokesperson for Ali and declared, "Muhammad Ali will not come to London. He does not support the book anymore."

Of greater concern was the fact that Ali had gone to Abu Dhabi with a limited supply of the medication he takes to control the symptoms of Parkinson's Syndrome. Howard Bingham had brought more of the medication to London, but there was no way to get it to Ali. He was cut off from the rest of the world in Abu Dhabi. His own wife Lonnie was unable to speak with him by telephone.

The following spring, I returned to England. This time, Ali was with us and the promotional tour went as planned. There were book-signings in London, Leeds, Nottingham, and Oxford. Interviews and dinners that had been rescheduled went off without a hitch. *Muhammad Ali: His Life and Times* reappeared on the bestseller list, where it had resided briefly the previous autumn. But one moment in particular stands out in my mind.

A book signing had been scheduled for Harrods, and we were told that Mohamed al-Fayed would be at the main entrance to greet us. This was no small occurrence. The owner of Harrods rarely welcomed visitors in person.

In the car on the way to Harrods, Lonnie Ali and I engaged in a bit of fantasy. At most previous book signings, Muhammad and I had been given gifts. Pens were the most frequent offering.

"Wouldn't it be nice," Lonnie said, "if Mr. al-Fayed brought me upstairs to woman's fashions and suggested that I pick out a silk dress." Never having owned a Rolex watch, I thought that one would look nice around my wrist. And if I recall the conversation correctly, Muhammad was too busy eating brownies to take part.

When our car arrived at Harrods, Mohamed al-Fayed was at the door to greet us. A half-dozen bagpipers led us in procession to the room where the book-signing was to take place. During the course of the afternoon, 1,200 people lined up to meet Muhammad. He kissed, hugged, shook hands, posed for photos, and did just about everything else that anyone requested. I should add that Harrods made a handsome profit on the sale of 1,200 books.

When the signing was over, the Harrods representative supervising the event brought us into a back room where some sandwiches and bottles of mineral water were set out on a table. "Is there anything else I can do for you?" she queried.

"Yes," I said. "The other day, I was in your food hall, and you had the best lemon bars I've ever tasted."

"Would you like some to take back to the hotel?"

"That would be great."

An aide was dispatched with appropriate instructions. Ten minutes later, the Harrods representative placed a nicely wrapped box of lemon bars on the table in front of me.

"That will be nine pounds 20 pence," she said.

They didn't give us pens either. ❏

*Over the ages, boxing's practitioners have been a never-ending source of wisdom and humor.*

# WORDS OF WISDOM

Jack Dempsey [on his decision to marry 35-year-old Maxine Cates when he was 20 years old]: I knew about girls. I didn't know about women.

Jack Dempsey [on a drunk who was challenging him to a fight]: Tell him he can have my title, but I want it back in the morning.

James J. Braddock: Here's the situation as far as having the championship and then losing it. You always got to figure there might be somebody better. That's the way boxing is. The champion don't always stand up. There's always somebody coming up to take him.

Tommy Farr [who lost a 15-round decision to Joe Louis]: Every time I hear the name Joe Louis, my nose starts to bleed.

Buddy Baer [after losing to Joe Louis in 1941]: Joe's a great fighter and a credit to his race, but he hit me after the bell.

Joe Louis [after being knocked out by Rocky Marciano]: What's the use of crying. The better man won. I'm too old, I guess.

Billy Conn: Bob Pastor was a nice fellow. I hit him in the balls and knocked his ass through the ropes in the thirteenth round. You're supposed to do anything you can to win. Hit 'em on the break, backhand 'em, do all the rotten stuff to 'em. You're not an altar boy in there. What are they going to do; shoot you for it?

Rocky Graziano: You can take a look at my face, at Jake LaMotta's face, at everybody else's face in the fight game, and you'll know that it's a tough business.

Archie Moore: The ring is a place where a man can project what's in his mind legally.

Rocky Marciano: What could be better than walking down any street in any city and knowing you're the heavyweight champion of the world?

Ezzard Charles: Fight night is a man going to work. It's just a job.

Sugar Ray Robinson [when asked if he still owned a flashy Cadillac]: No more. The car I drive now is a little red Pinto. But I've been there.

Willie Pep: I've got it made. I've got a wife and a TV set, and both of them work.

Sonny Liston [prior to fighting Floyd Patterson for the heavyweight championship]: Colored people say they don't want their children to look up to me. But I wouldn't be no bad example if I was up there. I could tell a lot of those children what they need to know because I passed that way. I could make them listen.

Chuck Wepner [after being knocked down by Sonny Liston and then asked by the referee how many fingers he was holding up]: How many guesses do I get?

Alexis Arguello: To throw a punch through the air, to make it land where you want it to. That is an art, a beautiful art.

Earnie Shavers [on the scene in his dressing room after he was knocked out in the first round by Jerry Quarry]: I was all alone. Even my shadow was hiding.

Earnie Shavers: When you marry your mistress, you create a vacancy.

Jean Pierre Coopman [on fighting Muhammad Ali]: Surviving the fight was more important than the result. It was never a question of winning or losing; just surviving. Yes, I lost the fight; but most of them did against Ali.

George Foreman: The moment the referee holds your hand up in the air and says you're the new heavyweight champion of the world, everything changes.

George Foreman: To work hard for a fight and fight your heart out and take the punches and know you won and everybody else knows you won; and then three judges who never put on boxing gloves in their life take it away from you; that's wrong.

Sugar Ray Leonard: They say that boxing is brutal and violent. But look at football. They don't try to get to the quarterback to shake his hand.

Larry Holmes: All fighters are prostitutes, and all promoters are pimps.

Larry Holmes: To me, I'm better than Ali ever was. I'm better than Joe Louis ever was. In my opinion; my opinion. And I have the right to say that about myself.

Larry Holmes [on members of the media who have criticized his performances in recent years]: Let all the critics who know so much get in the ring with a professional fighter, any fighter, and we'll see how they do.

Randall "Tex" Cobb [on fighting Larry Holmes]: I stuck to my fight plan; stumbling forward and getting hit in the face.

Larry Holmes: None of us is promised tomorrow. If I go 25 more years, that's a blessing. But if I don't, I've done my thing.

Hasim Rahman: In boxing, people take shots at you when you lose. When you lose, everybody has something to say. And when you win, everybody loves you. But I don't take it personally. I'm a diehard Baltimore Orioles fan. I'm like that too.

Lennox Lewis: People can say what they want to about my chin. I know what I can take.

Lennox Lewis: TV has a way of making you seem greater than you are.

Journeyman fighter Michael Murray: Promoters and managers are the farmers, and we are the cattle.

Former fighter Vince Shomo: Boxers get such a raw deal; sometimes I get mad that I was ever a boxer. ❏

*Boxing's non-combatants also have a way with words.*

# MORE WORDS OF WISDOM

Budd Schulberg: I know a good thing when I see it. Fistfighting is a good thing. Every great fight is a rare nugget. If our civilization is indeed declining and if it finally falls, it will not be because Joe Louis clobbered Max Schmeling or took the measure of Billy Conn.

John Schulian: Boxers not only lead more interesting lives than other athletes; they are more willing to talk about them too. Once you get past the boasts, the honesty comes bubbling out. I have listened to fighters recount shootouts and stickups, murder and mayhem. They are allowed no secrets in the ring, and they keep few outside it.

Ralph Wiley: Boxing is an unforgiving sport. In baseball, if you boot a ground ball, it isn't likely to blacken your eye, shatter your cheekbone, or deviate your septum. It could happen, but it's not likely.

Joe Sayatovich [one-time manager of Terry Norris]: It's boxing matches in the amateurs. In the pros, it's fights.

Goody Petronelli [trainer and co-manager of Marvin Hagler]: A trainer can teach a guy how to fight. But a trainer cannot give a fighter a jaw. You either have a good jaw or you don't. They say God created us all equal, but He didn't. He gave some of us an iron jaw, and He created some of us with a tinkle in the chin. Some guys get hit. Bang! They're out like a light. I've had real good fighters who would have been champion if they didn't have that tinkle in the chin. But because of that tinkle, I told them to get a job.

Paddy Flood [trying to inspire Chuck Wepner between rounds of his 1975 fight against Muhammad Ali]: Listen, Chuck; I know you're a big man in Bayonne, and you don't need this fight, and you don't need the heavyweight championship. You got your whiskey route and your bar, and you're a big man with all the ladies. But Chuck, me and Al [Wepner's manager], we've been poor bums all our lives. We got nothing but boxing. You understand? So will you do me and Al a favor, Chuck? Will you win it for us?

Angelo Dundee: I never get involved in my fighters' marital situations. For a trainer, it's a no-no. Whenever a guy comes to me and starts talking about his wife or girlfriend, I say, "Look, do me a favor. Go hit the heavy bag."

J.C. Davis: The defining factor that makes or breaks a fighter is what happens when he gets hit. Pain is the thing. A fighter has to be able to take it physically and mentally. And, believe me, no other athlete feels pain like a fighter. Someone in football might get hit, but the pain is different.

Donald Turner: Nowadays, when a fighter loses a fight, he changes his trainer. But that's not a solution to the problem. Joe Louis was knocked out by Max Schmeling, and he didn't get rid of Jack Blackburn.

Tommy Brooks: All great fighters gamble, but they take calculated risks.

Bouie Fisher: In boxing, there's always people saying bad things about other people. So I say, "Protect yourself at all times and mind your own business."

Ray Arcel: Jack Dempsey was a saloon fighter. With Dempsey, every part of your body was a legal target.

Eddie Futch: I don't know anybody who disliked Joe Louis.

Al Weill [Rocky Marciano's manager]: Rocky was great when he had to be great.

Jim Murray: Rocky Marciano lived life as if it were the 15th round and he was behind on points.

Lou Duva [during heated negotiations with Mike Trainer, who was serving as the attorney for Sugar Ray Leonard]: Let me tell you something, Mike. You don't know which is the right hand and which is the left. You're lucky you came up with one of the greatest fighters in the era. I'd like to see you manage Livingstone Bramble. Then we'd see how smart you are.

Jeanne Ashe [the widow of Arthur Ashe, regarding the tattoo of her late husband on Mike Tyson's arm]: If I could sue a body part, I would.

Cedric Kushner: Ike Ibeabuche telephoned me at three o'clock one morning to tell me that he was seeing demons. I understand why Ike was seeing demons. What I don't understand is why he called me.

Ferdie Pacheco: Let's be honest. Apart from everything else, at its core, boxing is about hurting people.

Jimmy Cannon: When you're a fighter, you're the guy taking the punches. You share everything but the punches. You have no partners in pain. They never give you a contract which entitles them to a percentage of the blows. You don't have to hire an attorney to guarantee you the right to take a beating all by yourself.

Bob Arum: I remember what people do to me; not for me.

John Schulian: Boxing's beautiful people are not a pretty sight.

Cedric Kushner: I love Lou DiBella because he's a dear friend of mine; and I hate Lou DiBella because he's an active competitor of mine. That's boxing.

Chris Mead: Few sights in sports are more brutal than a knockout.

Budd Schulberg: Very few fighters get the consideration of racehorses, which are put out to pasture to grow old with dignity and comfort when they haven't got it anymore.

John Schulian: It isn't just writers who become infatuated with fighters. Guys who are supposed to have brains do, too. ❏

*Most readers responded favorably to the following article, although a few were offended by the fact that I presumed boxing fans might be interested in something other than hardcore boxing. One reader sent an email that said, "Mr. Hauser, you've fallen into the* Sports Illustrated *syndrome. When I pick up a weekly sports magazine, I don't want to see photographs of half-naked women in bathing suits. And when I go to a boxing website, I don't want to read about politics."*

# DON KING AND GEORGE W. BUSH

In January 2001, I reported on how Don King counseled George W. Bush in the art of trickeration, thereby helping him capture Florida's 25 electoral votes and the presidency of the United States. Now, beset by mounting problems, Bush has again turned to King for help. I've received a tape of a recent telephone conversation between the two men. As a service to the boxing community and to the world at large, a transcript of that tape follows:

Don King: Hey!!! How's my main man?

George Bush: Not so good. Things have been difficult lately because of all the corporate scandals we're having. I'm facing an image problem.

Don King: That, my glorious -and-noble leader, is why you have spin-masters. You see, politics is like boxing. No matter how good you are, there will always be people who try to tarnish your reputation. And no matter how bad you are, there will always be people who give you awards and bestow honors upon you. I understand the art of image-making completely.

George Bush: But the problems now are threatening to get out of hand. I thought it would be a good idea to cut taxes for rich people. Then, all of a sudden, the stock market tanked and I've got all these middle-class voters whining about how their retirement funds have vanished.

Don King: There's a simple solution, my fiscally-prudent-MBA-president. You must resurrect the economy. Explain to me, how and when your economic problems started.

George Bush: I think Enron had something to do with it. My friend Kenneth Lay used to run it. At the end of 2001, it was the fifth-ranked company on the Fortune 500.

Don King: Which is like being ranked number five by the World Boxing

Association.

George Bush: Anyway, Enron filed for bankruptcy. I still don't understand what happened.

Don King: What happened was, Enron signed contracts to supply energy to customers for the next 30 years. But Kenny Boy and his cohorts deliberately underestimated future costs and reported their phony projected profits as current income.

George Bush: Then there was Dynegy.

Don King: Once ranked number 30 on the Fortune 500. Its stock has dropped by 96 percent.

George Bush: What happened there?

Don King: Dynegy told investors that the natural gas industry would be profitable in the future and that it had entered into big contracts with other major industry players. But the contracts were phony because the other so-called major players were illusory, and Dynegy knew it.

George Bush: Hey, you're really up on this stuff. I suppose you know about Adelphia Communications too.

Don King: I do indeed. Adelphia is now bankrupt and has stiffed most of its creditors. In fact, Adelphia owes my dear friends at HBO and Showtime millions of dollars that it collected from subscribers for the Lewis-Tyson fight. That's what happens when you file phony financial reports with the Securities and Exchange Commission listing an inflated number of home subscribers.

George Bush: And Worldcom?

Don King: Number 42 on this year's Fortune 500; also now bankrupt. Another global communications company that cooked its books by treating billions of dollars in ordinary costs as capital expenditures.

George Bush: How many millions?

Don King: I said billions. Between six and seven to be precise.

George Bush: That's amazing. It makes the $263-million dollars that Harken Energy lost as a result of conflicts of interest while I was on the board of directors seem like peanuts.

Don King: Not to mention the even smaller $848,000 that you got from the questionable sale of Harken stock.

George Bush: Don't go there, Don. You're giving me a headache.

Don King: I know how you feel. I once trusted Martha Stewart. She was like a sister to me. There was a time when I read Martha's magazine the way Evander Holyfield reads the Bible. And now . . . Forgive me if I weep. I've been betrayed.

*[At this point, there was a gap of 20 seconds in the conversation during which sobbing was heard.]*

George Bush: Don, are you all right?

Don King: Yes, my magnanimous-and-compassionate ruler. Thank you for caring about me.

George Bush: I care about all my campaign contributors.

Don King: That's good to hear, sir, because you aren't the only one with problems. The entire boxing industry is in shambles. Bob Arum is the only promoter who's making money. License fees are down. HBO's budget is flat and spending at Showtime has dropped. I've had to release some of my office staff and let several fighters out of their contracts.

George Bush: Don, I'm shocked. Here we are, on the verge of war with Iraq, and you're worrying about selfish personal economic interests.

Don King: Forgive me, sir; but I thought your administration was supposed to help rich people.

George Bush: Rich isn't good enough anymore. We're here for the super-rich.

Don King: How does it help the super-rich when a white-collar-crime lobby takes over the securities industry?

George Bush: Don, what are you talking about?

Don King: The stock market is in shambles. The lawyers at most major corporations function primarily as defense counsel for senior management. Your first chairman of the Securities and Exchange Commission was Harvey Pitt, who looks like Michael Katz without a neck brace and withheld information about accounting fraud from his own commissioners.

George Bush: Whoah! Hold on there! The inside corporate culture has made America great, and I'm not going to let a bunch of spineless liberals tear that culture down. Besides, it's not fair to hold the chairman of the Securities and Exchange Commission to the same standard of honesty and integrity that the law demands of a proxy statement.

Don King: Sir, folks are complaining and I'm one of them. Something's not right. Forty percent of your last tax cut went to the richest one percent of the American population. And now you're proposing a new set of tax cuts that's even more skewed in favor of the wealthy.

George Bush: Don, I'm very disappointed that you're repeating that sort of un-American class-warfare liberal nonsense. The truth is, if you look at the whole picture, 100 percent of my tax cuts are spread out among 100 percent of the American people.

Don King: That's sophistry, Mr. President. Two plus two does not equal 22.

George Bush: Stop whining. A lot of the techniques I'm using now, I learned from you.

Don King: Allow me, sir, to quote, if I may, from Franklin Delano Roosevelt's second inaugural address: "We have always known that heedless self-interest was bad morals. Now we know that it is bad economics."

George Bush: Who am I talking with?

Don King: Pardon?

George Bush: "Heedless self-interest; bad morals." Don, that's not really you, is it?

Don King: It is now; ever since those motherfuckers at my brokerage house advised me to buy tech stocks for my own account at the same time they were selling theirs. And another thing, Mr. President. Why is it that I'm audited every year by the IRS when your administration hasn't bothered to prosecute 65,000 Americans who have been identified as using offshore accounts to evade taxes totaling billions of dollars annually?

George Bush: Don, it goes back to the campaign contribution thing. You're talking about loyal Americans who are helping to keep me in power so I can pursue policies that are good for America.

Don King: Are you sure they're good?

George Bush: The American people think they are. They voted for my guys in November.

Don King: And the judges in Shannon Briggs versus George Foreman voted for Briggs. That doesn't make it right.

George Bush: Don, you have to understand; we're fighting for the right of Americans to own assault rifles and teach creationism in our public schools. And last month, some Commie liberals criticized me for wanting to put a nativity scene on the White House lawn.

Don King: I guess they thought it was unrealistic to think that there are three wise men and a virgin in Washington DC.

George Bush: You might have a point there. But now that we control both house of Congress, you'll see a lot more wisdom emanating from Capitol Hill.

Don King: Maybe.

George Bush: You can't possibly have doubts.

Don King: I'm trying to be a team player, sir. But I can't help wondering—if con is the opposite of pro, is this Congress the opposite of progress?

George Bush: Don, I'm not sure you understand politics.

Don King: But I understand cons, Mr. President.

George Bush: And I think you'd better change your attitude, fast. I know the difference between back-slapping and back-stabbing.

Don King: Is that a threat, Mr. President?

George Bush: Of course not. Think of it as a promise. And remember, Don, only in America. ❏

*As time passed, I continued to have my say on political issues.*

# ONCE AGAIN, DON KING AND GEORGE W. BUSH

On several occasions, I've posted transcripts of telephone conversations between Don King and George W. Bush. Now, the tape of another conversation has become available and is transcribed herewith. To readers who object, I request that you phrase your e-mails to me in coherent fashion. Try to express yourself without using obscenities. And keep in mind that I'm not impressed by correspondents who invoke Rush Limbaugh as the sole authority in political dialogue. Some of the responses that I received in opposition my previous King-Bush columns were intelligent and well reasoned, but others read as though they were written by a four-year-old on drugs.

Don King: Hello, Mr. President. It's me again.

George Bush: Don, I've love to chat but I'm a bit busy at the moment. I'm the commander-in-chief in a war that's going on in Iraq.

Don King: I know, Mr. President. I've been supporting you publicly and I have great respect for our soldiers overseas. But I'm very concerned.

George Bush: Not to worry. You're a loyal campaign contributor, and I've got your best interests in mind. I even held off on the invasion until after Roy Jones fought John Ruiz so the war wouldn't hurt pay-per-view sales of your fight.

Don King: Thank you, Mr. President. But I have to be honest and tell you that this fixation with Iraq bothers me.

George Bush: Had to do it. That guy over there, Saddam Hussein, is unbelievably bellicose. He's more difficult to deal with than any person I've ever met.

Don King: Obviously, you've never met Bernard Hopkins.

George Bush: It doesn't matter. The American people are behind me on this one.

Don King: That might be true. But, as Will Rogers once said, if you're riding ahead of the herd, it's a good idea to look back over your shoulder now and then to make sure that the cattle are still following.

George Bush: You sound skeptical.

Don King: I am. Before the invasion, I was more worried about North Korea building a nuclear arsenal than I was about Iraq.

George Bush: Hey, that little fat guy who runs North Korea—I can't remember his name—he's nothing. The only reason he got his job is that his father was the dictator before him.

Don King: Remind you of anyone?

George Bush: Look; I know the situation is complicated. I ask myself every day, "Which country would Jesus bomb?"

Don King: I'm not sure Jesus would bomb anyone. And a lot of people I know have similar doubts. It seems like these days everything with your administration is slick packaging and salesmanship.

George Bush: I learned that from you. "The War at the Shore" . . . "The Brawl for it All." You're great at selling fights.

Don King: Thank you, Mr. President. But I deliver on my sales pitches.

George Bush: So do I. We're winning in Iraq.

Don King: You keep saying we are. But our soldiers have already suffered more deaths in this conflict than we did in the entire 1991 Gulf War. And from what I hear, things outside of Baghdad aren't going so well.

George Bush: That was last week. I'm on top of the situation now. Besides, can you think of a better idea than invading Iraq?

Don King: You could have invaded Florida.

George Bush: That's ridiculous. Florida is a state. My brother is governor of Florida.

Don King: That's the beauty of it. Invading Florida will enable you to tell the American people that you're putting the good of the nation ahead of personal interest. I can see it now. You can go on television from the Oval Office and explain that you love the governor of Florida like a brother, but what's right is right and this invasion is necessary to safeguard the American way of life.

George Bush: I'm not sure the American people will buy that.

Don King: Of course, they will. Look at the last presidential election and the chaos in Florida. You can say you're invading to restore democracy.

George Bush: Won't the people of Florida resent being invaded?

Don King: Perhaps. But the truth is, I'm more concerned with changing things here at home than I am with spending hundreds of billions of dollars fighting wars overseas. You tell everyone, "Leave no child behind." But where I come from, millions of children are being left behind. You say "clean air." We get dirty air. You say "clean water." We get dirty water.

George Bush: Not to worry. I've got the same fine minds handling domestic affairs that are working on our foreign policy.

Don King: You have no idea how reassuring that is.

George Bush: Are you being sarcastic with me? I don't like sarcasm, Don.

Don King: I apologize, Mr. President. It's just that certain domestic issues trouble me greatly.

George Bush: Such as?

Don King: The budget deficit.

George Bush: Look, the Democrats ran up big deficits too. They put the entire nation in debt with their liberal social programs.

Don King: But the annual budget deficit went down to zero under Bill Clinton. When he left office, the 10-year budget projection showed a surplus of $6-trillion. You've given us an annual budget deficit of $450-billion dollars, and a large part of that is because of tax cuts for rich people.

George Bush: Don, you don't understand. We can cut taxes for rich people like you and me if we reduce the cost of spending on giveaways like Medicare and Medicaid and rely on the kindness of corporations to care for the American people.

Don King: I've got an idea, Mr. President. Since you're so big on cutting spending for health care, from now on why don't you and every member of your administration get your own medical care exclusively from public health clinics.

George Bush: What!

Don King: You heard me. That way, you'll see how the working-class American people you love so much live. The next time Dick Cheney has chest pains, he can go to the emergency room at a public health clinic.

George Bush: Don, you're giving me a hard time, and I don't like it.

Don King: I'm just telling you the way it is. In the neighborhood I come from, people can get a pizza delivered faster than they can get an ambulance if someone has a heart attack.

George Bush: If your people ate less pizza, they'd have fewer heart attacks. And, by the way, I was talking with some folks over at the Republican National Committee the other day. One of them mentioned something about your giving Hasim Rahman a duffel bag filled with cash to get him to sign with you when he was promoted by Cedric Kushner. How come you haven't sent any of those duffel bags over to the RNC?

Don King: Why should I?

George Bush: Because my administration is working hard on your behalf. Just the other day, I told John Ashcroft that we had to do something to get rid of all those black boxers that are costing you money.

Don King: Not black boxers, Mr. President. Black boxes.

George Bush: Oops! Guess I goofed on that one. Too bad. I thought I could pick up some Hispanic votes.

Don King: Let's put that aside, Mr. President, and go on to something else. You keep saying that America was forced to invade Iraq because Saddam Hussein was building weapons of mass destruction. Now it appears as though that claim was false.

George Bush: But look how clever we were. First, we got Iraq to disarm and allow the inspection of potential weapons sites. Then, once we knew how their military capability was deployed, we invaded. That's the sort of thing you'd think of.

Don King: Maybe, although it will be a long time before another country allows inspectors in to survey its military sites. And just because we can win a war doesn't make it right.

George Bush: But it makes for great photo ops and TV sound bites. Hey! Did you see me on television last month, flying out to that aircraft carrier, doing my imitation of Tom Cruise in *Top Gun*.

Don King: Unfortunately.

George Bush: That's another thing I learned from you, Don; wrapping myself in the American flag.

Don King: But returning to the matter at hand, Mr. President, could you explain to me why 15 of the September 11 hijackers were from Saudi Arabia and none were from Iraq; the money to finance 9/11 came from Saudi Arabia, not Iraq; and we invaded Iraq, not Saudi Arabia.

George Bush: Well, Don, to be honest, a lot of it also has to do with oil. We need access to Iraqi oil in case something goes wrong with the flow from Saudi Arabia. And of course, oil companies like Halliburton will make a nice profit.

Don King: Then from now on, let the oil companies send their own troops. I've been hearing a lot of complaints lately about how your administration is baptized in oil.

George Bush: You're missing the point. In this world, the strong and well-connected take what they can. Besides, I'm not worried. I've got professionals like Dick Cheney and Don Rumsfeld directing my foreign policy.

Don King: Just remember, Mr. President. Noah's ark was built by amateurs. Professionals built the Titanic.

George Bush: You don't understand. This is about freedom; Iraqi freedom.

Don King: Which in this case reminds me of the song lyrics, "Freedom's just another word for nothin' left to lose."

George Bush: I love that song. Janis Joplin was a Texas girl. Did you know that?

Don King: Yes, I did, Mr. President.

George Bush: Those were the days; sittin' around, drinkin', doin' a little coke.

Don King: Mr. President, let me ask you a question. How many more wars do you plan on fighting?

George Bush: As many as I want. Our foreign policy is about justice.

Don King: But the invasion of Iraq looked like just us.

George Bush: Not true. The French were against us, but they're nothing. You can't even get decent Mexican food in Paris. Besides, I'm building a coalition.

Don King: You certainly are, Mr. President. At the moment, you seem to have united one billion Muslims with the rest of the third world and most of Europe against us.

George Bush: The British are with us. And God is on our side.

Don King: Mr. President, God does not bless only America. I'm a patriotic American, and I love this country. But I'm worried. We can't just blow the whole planet up and start over. ❏

*This was an article that I particularly looked forward to writing.*

# BOXING AND THE GOLDEN AGE OF ROCK AND ROLL

A bit of history.

For a long time, major radio stations in the United States wouldn't play rock and roll songs recorded by black artists. Nat King Cole and Johnny Mathis were given airtime, but "race music" was forbidden. That, in turn, gave rise to a phenomenon in the music industry known as the "white cover" version. A black artist like Little Richard would write and record a song that received limited exposure and sold thousands of copies. Then Pat Boone or another white crooner would release a socially acceptable rendition that sold millions. For younger generations who don't understand the implications of Pat Boone trying to sing *Tutti Frutti*, it was the artistic equivalent of Jimmy Lennon, Jr. intoning gansta rap.

In the mid-1950s, a white disk jockey named Alan Freed began playing black music. The time was right. The culture of segregation was changing. In February 1959, for the first time ever, a rock and roll song by a black recording artist became the best-selling "pop 45" in the nation. The singer was Lloyd Price, and his ticket to history was *Stagger Lee.*

Price had been appearing in small clubs since 1952, when he wrote and recorded *Lawdy Miss Clawdy* at age 19. *Stagger Lee* brought him to new heights. As it was climbing to the top of the charts, he was booked for a show at the Top Hat Lounge in Louisville. When he arrived at the club, a tall good-looking 16-year-old was waiting outside for him.

"This crazy kid rushed over," Price remembers. "He was saying, 'Mr. Price, I'm Cassius Marcellus Clay, Jr.; I'm the Golden Gloves champion of Louisville, Kentucky; someday I'm gonna be heavyweight champion of the world; I love your music; and I'm gonna be famous like you.' "

Price's response was simple and blunt: "Kid, you're dreaming."

"But we got along," the singer reminisces. "You couldn't help but like him. The Top Hat Lounge was a popular place and, each time I played there, I saw him. After a while, I started looking for him and bringing him in with me. He had all sorts of questions about music and traveling, but mostly he wanted to know about girls. There were a lot of things he didn't know, and he asked me how to make out with girls. I told him, 'Just be yourself, and the girls will like you.' Although as part of the lesson, I gave him a couple of dollars and said, 'Always have some money. That's the beginning of hanging out with the foxes.'"

Thus began a life-long friendship between the two men. Price had a string of hits with songs like *Personality* and *I'm Gonna Get Married*. Meanwhile, Cassius Clay had a pretty good run of his own. There was one time though, when harsh words were exchanged between them. It came in 1980, when Ali was planning to fight Larry Holmes.

"Don't do it," Price told him. "It's over. Father Time is calling. You've got to hear the bell."

"You don't know nothing about boxing and getting old," Ali retorted. "You're a singer, not a fighter."

Then Price told Ali a story about going out on a national tour in 1963. As a favor to a friend who was trying to break into the music business, he agreed to let one of the friend's groups open for him. The arrangement lasted until Price realized that his warm-up act was getting more applause than he was. Then, being a showman, he sent them packing with the request that his friend send him a different opening group.

"Who did you get rid of?" Ali queried.

"Some guys I'd never heard of before," Price answered. "Smokey Robinson and the Miracles. And the next opening act made me look even worse. The first night they were on, when they finished their set, there was such pandemonium that I told the band to take a 10-minute break before I went out so the audience could calm down and I wouldn't look bad by comparison."

"Who were they?"

"Three black chicks called the Supremes."

At that point, Price called his friend (Berry Gordy, who was in the process of founding Motown records) and told him to stuff his groups where the sun didn't shine. "Just send me one guy to open," he instructed.

Whereupon Berry Gordy sent him Marvin Gaye.

"And that was it," Price told Ali. "I said to myself, 'I don't know what these folks have, but whatever it is, I don't have it.' So I took myself off the road, bought a club in New York, and signed a 15-year contract to be the exclusive promoter for Motown concerts in Manhattan. I heard the bell."

Ali didn't listen. He fought Holmes anyway. But that bit of Americana remains the best story I've ever heard about knowing when it's time to leave center stage. Rock and roll, like boxing, is for the young. And it's no surprise that the great names of boxing, like the rest of us, cherish the music they loved when they were young. Here's a sampling:

Don King: There were so many stars when you reflect on them. Jackie Wilson, Lloyd Price, Sam Cooke, the Moonglows, the Cadillacs, Brook Benton, Sarah Vaughan, Ed Townsend, the Shirelles, the Platters, the Drifters, all the doo-wop groups. And you can't leave out Fats Domino, Chuck Berry, Little Richard. God, that brings back a lot of memories. It was a wonderful era; the golden age of rock and roll.

Larry Holmes: I was just a little-bitty boy [Holmes was born in 1949] during what you old people call the golden age of rock and roll. I didn't get into music until the middle of the '60s. But what I'll say is, music is about feelings. People sing about what's happening in their lives. And the feelings can be happy or sad or angry or life-is-okay, but the music doesn't have to be ugly. And today, the singing is all about putting other people down and motherfucker this and motherfucker that. The oldtime groups came out on stage wearing good-looking matching suits and danced and moved around. The guys today walk out wearing baggy pants looking like shit. And they got no talent. Little Richard was a great entertainer, not just a singer. He could dance. He played the piano. He did his own thing with his own style, and people didn't care about his sexual side. Little Richard was a show all by himself. Fats Domino was more laid-back than Little Richard. He wasn't the kind to dance and jump around, which was probably good that he didn't 'cause he might have had a heart attack. But besides singing, Fats Domino played great piano. Chuck Berry, Lloyd Price, Brook Benton; all those guys had style and talent. And, please, don't make me out to be an old man when you write your story.

Don King: Then Motown came in and revolutionized the music industry all over again. Smokey Robinson, Martha and the Vandellas, the Temptations, the Four Tops. I sang on stage with the Four Tops once at the Hilton Hotel in Las Vegas. They invited me up there with them and whatever they sang, I just sang along. I was the Fifth Top. You've got to mention the Supremes. And there was Stevie Wonder, Wilson Pickett, Otis Redding, Marvin Gaye, Aretha Franklin. Don't forget James Brown. And the disk jockeys, Alan Freed, Freddie Crocker, Gary Dee, Dick Clark.

Earnie Shavers: I live in England now in a small town near Liverpool, which was where the Beatles started. But I was more into the old rock and roll. The beat was great. That's what did it. And the music came from the heart. Little Richard dressed nice. He was a little strange, still is. But he was good. The Platters were wonderful. *The Great Pretender* was my favorite of the songs they did. I remember the day my older brother brought home a couple of Elvis Presley records. I said, 'Elvis Presley? Who's that?' And my brother told me, 'Listen, this boy has the same beat as most of the black guys.' Elvis was Elvis. What more can I say? There was Jackie Wilson, the Drifters. Everybody loved Sam Cooke. I loved that music. Still do. Just last week, I was listening to Fats Domino.

Don King: I never got into the Beatles, but I love Mick Jagger. Mick Jagger is a terrific talent, a real cool cat. He goes on and on and on. And Elvis was fantastic. They used to jump on him because he was wiggling and all that, acting like a black man. But Elvis was a tremendous wonderful great performer, and Colonel Parker [his promoter] did a good job with him. I've been to Graceland. Seeing where Elvis lived, his airplane, the music room; I've done that a couple of times.

Muhammad Ali: If you wanted fast music, Little Richard was the king. But Little Richard didn't do love songs, so if you wanted slow music, you had to listen to someone else. Sam Cooke, Lloyd Price, Ben E. King, Fats Domino; I liked all of them. I don't want to name too many names because I'll leave someone out and hurt their feelings. And Elvis could sing. Don't matter what color he was. The music will never be as great as it was then.

Don King: I got tapes; I got CDs. I still have some of the old 45s and LPs. Tutti-frutti allerooti . . . A-wop-bop-a-looba . . . A-wop-bam-boom! ❏

*For dramatic purposes, boxing and organized crime are a perfect fit.*

# TONY SOPRANO DOES BOXING

The whole world is waiting for season number five of *The Sopranos* on HBO. And yours truly has a copy of the finished tapes. Plot summaries for each of the 13 episodes follow.

### Episode No. 1

Still reeling from the break-up of his marriage, Tony grows increasingly depressed. In quick succession, he has one-night stands with a receptionist from Sotheby's, two dancers from the Bada-Bing Club, and a mud-wrestler from the Bronx. Then Christopher Moltisano tells him about a fighter named Joey Delafemaratta who shared a room with him in drug rehab. Joey is a heavyweight, white, and he can punch. Tony decides to manage the fighter.

### Episode No. 2

With great fanfare, Tony holds a press conference at Artie Bucco's restaurant to announce the signing of Joey Dee to a long-term contract. Major journalists are absent, but it costs a fortune to feed all the freeloading dot.com writers who show up. Meanwhile, Tony's depression over the loss of Carmela continues and he calls Dr. Melfi, telling her, "I'd like to see you. Not in your office. For lunch. Now that I'm not your patient anymore, you can see me outside the office; right?"

Dr. Melfi responds, "Anthony, I know where your mind is going with this, and it's entirely inappropriate. You're a former patient and you're a married man."

"I'm a separated married man. Carmela left me. And besides; I didn't hear in your objection that you're a married woman, which tells me something."

Dr. Melfi is firm in her refusal, so Tony makes an appointment to see her at her office. "I need help," he admits. "I'm asking for help."

### Episode No. 3

Tony shows up for his session with Dr. Melfi and talks mostly about missing Carmela. He also gets a trainer for Joey Dee and puts Christopher in camp as an assistant trainer to keep an eye on things. Knockout victories over Vinnie Maddelone and Richie Melito follow. Meanwhile, Uncle Junior's retrial on racketeering charges begins.

*Episode No. 4*

Tony meets with representatives of several world sanctioning organizations in an effort to get Joey Dee ranked. To his astonishment, he learns that this will cost big bucks. "I have to pay to get my fighter ranked," he complains to Paulie Walnuts. "This boxing business is more corrupt than waste management." Twenty thousand dollars in cash comes out of the duck feeder. One week later, Joey Dee is the 10th-ranked heavyweight in the world. Meanwhile, Carmela retains Jimmy Binns as a divorce lawyer, and Tony goes one up on her by hiring Judd Burstein.

*Episode No. 5*

Joey Dee is now ready for a big fight. Tony's first two choices for an opponent are John Ruiz and Chris Byrd. He considers them beatable, and each holds a world title. But when Tony sits down to negotiate the bout with Don King, he finds that DK wants six options on Joey's services and other consideration. It's frustrating, but then a golden opportunity arises. Joey Dee signs to fight Mike Tyson. While the Tyson-Dee negotiations are going on, Carmela plans a trip to Italy with Meadow.

*Episode No. 6*

Tony is still depressed, so Dr. Melfi puts him on Zoloft. Thereafter, his mood brightens but there's a new problem. Because of the Zoloft, Tony can no longer get an erection. A press conference is held to announce Mike Tyson versus Joey Dee. The bout will take place at Boardwalk Hall in Atlantic City, the site of Tyson's greatest glory. At the press conference, Tony and Mike confide in one another regarding the effect that Zoloft has had on them. "They call me Iron Mike," Tyson says ruefully. "But it's not like iron anymore."

Later that day, Carmela and Meadow depart for Italy.

*Episode No. 7*

Paulie Walnuts starts hanging around the Tyson camp, trying to ingratiate himself with Crocodile and Panama Lewis. "You're my kind of guys," he tells them.

Meanwhile, Carmela and Meadow arrive in Italy. In Rome, Carmela stands at the edge of the Trevi Fountain and fantasizes about Furio. In Florence, Carmela gazes at Michelangelo's statue of David and fantasizes about Furio. In Venice, Carmela rides in a gondola on the Grand Canal and fantasizes about Furio. In Naples, Carmela is sitting with Meadow in a small cafe when she sees Furio at a table across the room. Their eyes meet. Furio rises from his chair and they rush to embrace one another. Meadow returns to the hotel alone, and Carmela accompanies Furio to his apartment. They disrobe. They look lovingly at one another. And Furio is impotent.

Carmela returns to her hotel and Meadow inquires, "How was it?"

"Not the way I thought it would be," Carmela answers. "At least your father could get it up."

### Episode No. 8

Christopher's girlfriend, Adriana, visits him at Joey Dee's training camp as Joey continues to train for the big fight. Adriana and Christopher are kissing on Christopher's bed, and he tells her that they can't have sex.

"Why not?"

"It a team sort of thing," Christopher answers, his face radiating deceit. "Fighters aren't supposed to have sex when they're training for a fight. And we don't want Joey to feel deprived, so the rest of us are also abstaining."

Then Adriana sees a used condom on the floor by Christopher's bed, storms out in a huff, and goes home to compile a list of things to tell the FBI. That same day, Carmela returns home from Italy.

### Episode No. 9

Tony is concerned about the referee and judges for the Tyson-Dee fight. And in truth, he'd like an edge, so he asks Assemblyman Ron Zellman to set up a meeting with Larry Hazzard (chairman of the New Jersey State Athletic Board of Control). "All I want is a fair shake and to protect my fighter," Tony tells Hazzard. "You know, maybe disqualify Tyson if he looks like he might do something wrong. How about that referee who worked Tyson's fight against Lennox Lewis in Memphis?"

Meanwhile, Uncle Junior is worried about his trial, but Tony tells him that there's no cause for concern. Bobby Baccilieri has had a talk with a juror. Another hung jury is planned. That leads Uncle Junior to complain, "Goddamn it! Each trial, the goddamn lawyers are costing me a fortune."

### Episode No. 10

Ginny Sack asks Shelly Finkel if she and some of her friends can have lunch with Mike Tyson. Shelly laughs and tells her, "That wouldn't be possible." That leads Johnny Sack to believe that Shelly has insulted his wife, and he wants to whack him.

"Leave Finkel alone," Tony orders. "If you want to whack someone, whack Max Kellerman. The little shit went on national television last Friday night and called Joey Dee a bad joke."

At the close of the episode, Carmela, Tony, and their respective lawyers meet to discuss a financial settlement, and Uncle Junior dies of a heart attack.

### Episode No. 11

It's fight week Atlantic City. At the final pre-fight press conference, Michael Katz calls Tony "mob scum." Tony's sister, Janice, makes eyes at Donald Trump, and Trump orders one of his bodyguards to "get that pig away from me." Janice is upset and asks Tony to defend her honor, but all he says is "Jesus, Janice, give me a break." So Janice goes to Bobby Baccilieri for help.

"When Karen died, I helped you through your crisis. Now it's your turn to help me."

"I don't know," Bobby answers. "I mean, Trump's got guys around him all the time. It's not like you just go up to Donald Trump and punch him out."

"I want him whacked," responds Janice. "Dead. You'd have done it for Karen."

### Episode No. 12

Janice gets whacked. Bobby Baccilieri tells Sylvio, "I had to do it. She was driving me crazy. I couldn't stand it anymore."

Bobby and Silvio dismember Janice's body and put it in several Hefty bags. They're carrying the bags through the lobby of the Taj Mahal when they come face-to-face with Tony.

"What's in the bag?" Tony inquires. Not waiting for an answer, he takes one of the bags from Silvio. "Jesus! That's as heavy as Janice."

Silvio and Bobby exchange worried looks and a knowing smile crosses Tony's face.

"Let me help you carry those things," Tony says.

At the weigh-in, Tony sees Michael Buffer and rushes over to him with his son.

"Do me a favor, Mr. Buffer. This is my son, AJ. He loves you. Could you say 'let's get ready to rumble' for him."

"For $5,000," Buffer answers.

### Episode No. 13

It's fight night in Atlantic City. Meanwhile, Furio calls Carmela. He's in New York with a pocketful of Viagra and pleads to see her. They meet at the Rainbow Room for a romantic dinner. Then Furio brings Carmela to his hotel room and is impotent again.

On the fistic front, Tyson KOs Joey Dee in 16 seconds. After the fight, Tony returns to his suite at the Taj Mahal, alone and forlorn. There's a knock on the door. Tony is so depressed that he doesn't even think in terms of danger. Life doesn't matter to him anymore. He simply opens the door. Carmela is standing there.

"Hello, Anthony. Do you have plans for the night?"

Tears well up in Tony's eyes. He and Carmela embrace. Then Tony remembers that he's still on Zoloft. "There might be a problem in bed," he tells her. ❏

# GEORGE FOREMAN ON CHARACTER

*Each Christmas for the past few years, this column has been devoted to some thoughts from George Foreman. Earlier this year, I talked with George about character and self-respect. His words make a pretty good holiday message.*

Character doesn't just evolve on its own. It has to be acted upon every day of our lives. But now, we've got a whole generation of young people, and another generation that's not so young anymore, who haven't found anything in their lives to promote character. And that's sad. Life is so brief. You have to do more than just try to have a good time. You have to ask yourself, "What am I giving to other people? What will I leave behind?"

Part of the problem is that writers today don't hold people to the same standards they used to. The written word is very powerful. You can go back and look at ancient civilizations. Their cities are gone; their palaces have been destroyed. But some of the things that were written back then have been preserved to this day. So many people, especially young people, think that everything now is about digital and television, but nothing will ever surpass the written word. Character has to be written about. Writers used to give us character. But now, too many writers have abandoned character. Almost anything is acceptable as long as it makes a good story. But you don't just teach character through words. You teach it by example. For a lot of young people, character comes from who they imitate. I don't like the phrase "role model." It sounds too commercial to me. I'd rather talk about being an example.

When I was young, I saw very few good examples. I saw a lot of sports heroes. When I look back on myself in my teens, I was like an empty bottle. Each day, I saw another person I wanted to be like, walk like, talk like. Sonny Liston, Jim Brown; you know the names. If they're not nice, don't be nice. They buy fleets of cars; so when you make it, you should buy fleets of cars. Some of those guys were good people. But when I grew older and got to know them, a lot of them were downright nasty or stuck-up clowns.

I remember once when I was 19 years old, I was walking with Sonny Liston and some of his people. We passed a woman who was kind of top heavy and very good-looking. She was out with her husband. Sonny stopped and stared, very obvious like. Then he looked at the woman's husband and said, "Yeah! I'm lookin'. Yeah! Yeah! What are you gonna do about it!" And when Sonny said that, his people laughed. So there I am, 19 years old, and I thought that's the way a man is supposed to be.

It all changed for me at the end of my first career in boxing. I was heavy-weight champion of the world at age 25. Then I lost to Muhammad Ali; came back and won five fights in a row. But I still wasn't happy with who I was. In 1977, I went down to Puerto Rico and lost a fight to Jimmy Young. And in the locker room afterward, I died. I truly believe that. In the locker room after the fight, I was dead for a moment and came back to life. And I'll tell you some-thing. In that split second when you're about to die, you don't think about fame, you don't think about money. You think about people. That experience tore up everything I believed in. Before that, I wasn't an atheist, but I didn't really believe in God. God, to me, was something people told you stories about when you did something wrong to scare you and make you act better. But in that moment, I realized that treating people right was more important than anything else in the world.

That's when I left boxing for the first time. For a while, it was hard. When you're a famous athlete, everyone is always giving things to you and doing things for you. I didn't know how to do anything for myself. In those 10 years, I learned how to do things the hard way; things other people think of as simple. How to clean up after myself. How to stand in line and buy something in a store when I didn't have much money and not be embarrassed. I became a preacher. I gained a lot of weight. I'd go around the country preaching, not always dressed the best, and no one knew who I was. I wasn't flying first class anymore. I was in the cheapest economy seat I could buy. One time, I remember, I was on a plane, and the stewardess came over to me and said, "Hey, big guy. That seat is kind of tight. After we take off, I'll bring you up to first class. I can't give you a meal there, but you'll be more comfortable." And that meant a lot to me. I said to myself, "Hey, people are good. People are nice."

And something else very important happened to me when I left boxing the first time. I found out who I am, and I became happy with who I am. That might sound easy, but it's hard for a lot of people. I know, it was very hard for me, but I finally learned that you have to cast off everybody else you're trying to imitate and be yourself. Forget about trying to be like sports heroes. Forget about trying to be like this person or that person. Just be the best person you can be. You need self-respect before you can respect other people properly.

You know, I was at an open house at school for one of my children after I fought Michael Moorer and won back the heavyweight championship. The teachers and parents were all saying, "Look, there's George; there's George." And I said, "No, no, no! This is open house. It's about the children. Every one of them is as important as me."

And now that I have the money to do things I might not have been able to do before, I say to myself, "I like my life the way it is. Why change it?" I'm the best dishwasher in the house. I make the best egg-white omelet in the house. I mop the floor better than anyone else in the family. Why should I let someone take that away from me? I possess my life now. I'm happy. I'm me and only me. ❑